INSIGHT
GUIDES

EGYPT

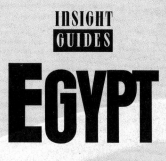

Directed by Hans Johannes Hoefer
Edited by Hisham Youssef and John Rodenbeck
Photographs by Albano Guatti

A P A
PUBLICATIONS

EGYPT

Second Edition
© 1989 APA PUBLICATIONS (HK) LTD
All Rights Reserved
Printed in Singapore by Höfer Press Pte Ltd

ABOUT THIS BOOK

In your hands is the culmination of two years of work, research and fun. **Hans Hoefer** is the founding father of the *Insight Guides* series. Trained in Germany as a graphice artist, he settled in Singapore after years of wanderlust. During his travels he hit upon a novel guidebook formula and in 1970 he published his first title, *Insight Guide: Bali*, which became the seminal work for this widely acclaimed series.

Harvard graduate **Hisham Youssef**, project editor of *Insight Guide: Egypt*, is a native Egyptian who has traveled all over the country. His many credits include serving as photographic editor for the *Harvard Crimson* and as photographer for a *Lampoon* parody of *Newsweek* magazine. Yousseff was also a contributing photographer to *Insight Guide: New England*.

John Rodenbeck coordinated and edited the work of all the writing staff in Cairo. A Harvard graduate who has lived in Cairo since 1964, he brings to the book a lengthy and close acquaintance with Egyptian society. In 1978 he founded SPARE (The Society for the Preservation of the Architectural Resources of Egypt) and for two years he served on the executive committee under Mrs Sadat in the Egyptian Society of Amateurs of Archaeology (ESAA). Rodenbeck's other activities include acting in three Egyptian feature films, writing, editing, and publishing. He is the co-founder of the Hoopoe Press, a small publishing house based in Cairo and Washington D.C., and is professor in the Department of English and Comparative Literature at the American University in Cairo.

The principal photographer for this book is **Albano Guatti.** A native Italian, Guatti is based in New York City where he does a lot of travel and commercial photography. The wealth of his work shown throughout the pages of this book possesses a unique vision of Egypt—the land and its people. His photographs have been published in many other travel books, calendars, and magazines and he is co-founder of a publishing house in New York City.

Ayman Taher, whose photography is among the best in the book, is a native Cairene who has lived in Egypt all his life. His main hobby, which has grown into a professional interest is scuba diving. He has an international reputation as one of the best underwater photographers in the world.

Some of the best images in this volume are due to **Richard Nowitz**, who has lived and worked in Jerusalem for 10 years. He has traveled many times in the Sinai peninsula and elsewhere in Egypt. Nowitz is also a regular contributor to Apa's travel guides.

Many writers brought their own personal flavor to this book to provide it with an unusually exciting look into Egypt's rich culture and contemporary society.

Jill Kamil, a contributor to the history section, is an Egyptologist and author of many popular books including the best-selling Longman series of guidebooks to the ancient sites: *Sakkara and Memphis*, *Upper Egypt*, which covers places visited on a Nile cruise, and *Luxor*. Her *Coptic Egypt* has been published by the American University in Cairo Press. Born in Kenya, and educated in South Africa, Kamil has spent most of her life in Egypt.

Another contributing writer, **Elizabeth Maynard** writes, "if it hadn't been for the fact that my Viriginian grandmother fell off a donkey in front of the old Shepheard's hotel in 1897, she might never have met my Eng-

Hisham Youssef   *John Rodenbeck*   *Jill Kamill*   *Elizabeth Maynard*

lish grandfather who happened to be smoking on the terrace at the time. He rescued the lady and proceeded to fall in love with her. Several months later, braving the scowls of her haughty father, he married her in the parlor of the plantation house on the James River. Most of their married life was spent plying back and forth between India, England and America. My father, who appeared on the scene in 1900, remembered going through the Suez Canal in a P&O Liner sometime before World War I. Many intervening happenings and coincidences in England and Virginia finally brought me back to Cairo, where I have spent more than 15 eventful years."

William Lyster, who wrote the section on Medieval Egypt, was born in Texas. While living in London, he began traveling through the Middle East during holidays, making his first visit to Egypt in 1968. He later moved to Cairo, where he began the serious study of Islamic art and history at The American University. He is currently engaged in lecturing on the Islamic art of Egypt and lives in Heliopolis, a suburb of Cairo.

Max Rodenbeck, born in Virginia, U.S.A., is a free-lance journalist who has lived in Cairo most of his life. He not only speaks fluent Arabic—his conversational skills were perfected in the coffeehouses he describes in these pages—but also reads and writes it. His knowledge of the city has brought him commissions to lead tours and oversee cartographical projects, but he has also traveled extensively and intensively throughout Egypt and the rest of the Middle East. His colorful coverage of Arab politics is esteemed among specialists; and his contributions to this guide are a good sample of the style and sensitivity that have made him well known.

Carina Campobasso has a B.A. from Harvard in Middle Eastern and Arabic history, and lived in Egypt for two years.

Alice Brinton, who writes about Alexandria, belongs to an American family that has been identified with the city for three generations. Alice herself lived mainly in Beirut as a child, but returned to Egypt in 1975 to work for several years as a journalist, becoming Cairo correspondent for ABC, the American network. Though she now lives and writes in Paris, she continues to spend a few weeks in Egypt every year.

Cassandra Vivian, responsible for much of the Travel Tips section, is a very versatile lady. Among her credits are a photo exhibition at the Carnegie Museum of Natural History, a video on Egypt entitled *The Monuments of Ancient Egypt* and a photo book, *Egypt: Touching the Land*. Born in Monessen, Pennsylvania, a small steel-town south of Pittsburgh, Vivian moved to Cairo in 1976.

Among the other photographers who contributed to *Insight Guide: Egypt* are: **Joseph Hunwick, Lyle Lawson, John Barthwick, Jo Yogerst, Barbara Gundle** and **Gregory Lawler**—all of them frequent contributors to Apa's *Insight Guide* series.

People who contributed in other ways include: Fouad Sultan, Egyptian Minister of Tourism; Muhammad Nessim, Director of the Egyptian Agency for the Promotion of Tourism; Adel Taher, former Minister of Tourism; Ahmad al-Saeed of *al-Ahram* Newspaper and his archives staff, and Gloria Karuouk, Curator of the Creswell Collection at the CAS Library of the American University in Cairo.

Apa Publications

William Lyster   *Max Rodenbeck*   *Cassandra Vivian*

CONTENTS

HISTORY & PEOPLE

PLACES & FEATURES

TRAVEL TIPS

WELCOME

It isn't only archaeologists, peering into tombs or poring over potsherds, who have been intrigued by Egypt. The history of Western culture shows that the Land of the Nile has often exercised a potent spell over quite ordinary people, sometimes because of the appeal of "mystery" in its Pharaonic past and sometimes because it answers to pipedreams of Oriental luxury, licence, and splendor. With such a variety of allurements, in fact, Egypt — or someone's idea thereof — has inspired styles in everything from decorative iron casings for heavy 19th-Century German machines to paper packaging for 20th-Century American condoms and cigarettes. It's no exaggeration to say that Egypt has even influenced Western fashion in matters of life and death, often grotesquely so.

Mummies, Egyptian and Otherwise: Western interest in mummified flesh, for example, arose when word spread, in medieval times, about the therapeutic value of powdered *mumia* in the treatment of a wide variety of ailments. The matter taken out of skulls and stomachs was believed to be especially effective; and by the 16th Century mummies so fascinated Westerners that an active trade began. Ancient burial grounds were dug up, mummies were stripped of their coverings and sent piecemeal to the apothecaries of Europe. When word of this highly-prized medication reached Francis I, king of France, he made haste to acquire a small quantity, mixed with powdered rhubarb, which he reputedly carried in a little packet everywhere he went.

Although embalming in the ancient Egyptian manner never became a fashion, two rich and influential men, Louis XIV (1638-1715) and Alexander Douglas, 10th Duke of Hamilton (1767-1852), ordered their bodies to be mummified. The body of King Louis survived for only about 15 years, but the Duke of Hamilton's may have lasted a little longer. It was embalmed in 1852 in a ceremony carried out after the Egyptian fashion, with T.J. Pettigrew, First Professor of Anatomy at Charing Cross Hospital and author of a *History of Egyptian Mummies*, as 'embalmer and chief ritualist.' The Duke's body was laid to rest in a genuine Egyptian sarcophagus housed in an enormous mausoleum.

Bonaparte's Inspiration: Descriptive accounts and sketches made by travelers during the 18th Century joined with a trickle of small objects — scarabs, amulets, *shabtis* and a multitude of fakes — to excite interest in Egypt as a source of the "primitive," a search for which was one of the century's cultural preoccupations. An "Egyptian" fashion thus followed hard upon an "Etruscan" fashion, which had grown in turn directly out of the classical heritage from Greece and Rome. Napoleon's expedition to Egypt, with 69 assorted *savants*, took place largely in response to this new fashion.

Buildings and Furniture: Meanwhile, during the late-18th and early-19th Centuries, buildings began to be constructed to resemble ancient temples, with a series of pylons or with facades like shrines. Interior decorations included chimney-places with Egyptian deities carved in bold relief.

Between 1790 and 1830, and again between 1860 and 1880, furniture was also frequently Egyptian-inspired: wooden chairs were carved with the hind legs of a lion or an ox, cabinets had such decorative motifs as the lotus and papyrus plants; and book-ends, ink-stands, vases and wine-coolers were decorated with Egyptian motifs, symbols, or texts.

Grave-Robbers Galore: An event that captured popular English interest in 1812 was the opening of The Egyptian Hall in Piccadilly as a museum of "natural curiosities." Later used as a theater, the building itself was designed as an amalgam of Egyptian motifs. Over the central lintel the wings of the hawk-headed Horus held a sun disk and two lions, representing Today and Tomorrow, were seated back to back. In 1821 the Egyptian Hall displayed the latest finds, casts and sketches by the British-naturalized Italian strongman-turned-excavator, Giovanni Belzoni, who had cleared the Temple of Abu Simbel and shipped tons of treasures back to England.

There was at that time no restriction on grave-robbing and ancient burial grounds were pillaged, not just for priceless jewelry and funerary equipment, but for anything movable.

Fascination with ancient Egypt was naturally enhanced by literature. Handsome, well-illustrated books, many of which have become collectors' items, were published. Yet, human nature being what it is, there was always an eager market for the esoteric and a publisher to fulfill the demand: the so-called *Book of Fate*, for example, went through 22 editions between 1822, when Champollion deciphered the Rosetta Stone, and 1835. Supposed to have been translated into English from German, it was allegedly based on an original hieroglyphic text, which was said to have been ''in the possession of Napoleon, late Emperor of France.''

With a new era of scholars and explorers in the later 19th Century, Egyptian inspiration in architecture and furniture design subsided and the great collections were built up in the museums of the world, where the general public could now enjoy the material remains of ancient Egypt without traveling to the Nile Valley. Obelisks in public places had already been fashionable at the end of the 16th Century, when Pope Sixtus V had re-erected four of Rome's 13 ancient souvenirs. Now they became interesting once again. The Paris obelisk was erected in the Place de la Concorde as early as 1833. In 1878 London put its obelisk, acquired as booty in 1801, in place on the Thames embankment; and the obelisk in Central Park, New York, was erected in 1881.

The United States had first been offered an obelisk by the Khedive Ismail on the occasion of the opening of the Suez Canal in 1869, another landmark in the history of fashion. Ismail's celebrations extended archaeological knowledge to the sphere of theatrical entertainment anticipating cinematographic spectacles such as *Cleopatra* and *Raiders of the Lost Ark*. There had been other ''Pharaonic'' spectacles before — *The Magic Flute*, for example, and there are more than 70 operas based on the story of Antony and Cleopatra — but this time the French scholar Mariette was commissioned to do the libretto for an opera aimed specifically at evoking the splendor of ancient Egypt. Verdi's *Aida* was not commissioned for the opening performance — *Rigoletto* was given instead — but premiered in Cairo two years later and has remained the most popular of Verdi's operas.

Tut Fever: The event that would capture world attention to a degree unrivaled by anything archaeological before was, of course, the discovery of the Tomb of Tutankhamen in 1922. Its 5,000 dazzling works of art were widely publicized through new techniques of communications, including the first film footage in the history of archaeology. Thousands of sightseers made their way to the Valley of the Kings. They wanted to be in on the discovery; and they also wanted to have a relic from the tomb. Local antique dealers, ready to fulfill the demand, ordered their collections from Cairo to be returned to Thebes and local craftsmen turned out instant *antikas* wholesale, bearing the royal cartouche. Even bottled sand said to have come from the tomb chamber was sold to tourists.

It was Tutankhamen, again, who brought ancient Egypt to a wider Western audience than ever before, during the exhibition of some of the treasures from his tomb in Paris in 1967, London in 1972, four cities in Russia in 1973, and seven in the United States in 1975. This exhibition can be regarded as the latest landmark in the history of ancient Egypt's impact on Western fashion. The sight of the dazzling works of art from the richest discovery in the history of archaeology resulted in a burst of modern imitations.

Today it is not so easy to acquire a genuine antiquity, due to strict measures to curb the plundering of tombs and temples, but replicas of the sacred cat of ancient miniatures of Tutankhamen's mask fashioned in gold, or good imitations of ancient Egyptian jewelry can all be purchased in any big museum shop. So can bath-mats, ashtrays, table linen and countless other household and personal objects featuring anything from the royal visage of Tutankhamen to Horus spearing crocodiles.

Egypt produced one of the earliest and most magnificent civilizations the world has ever witnessed. Five thousand years ago, when Mesopotamia was still the scene of petty squabbling between city states and while Europe, America, and most of western Asia were inhabited by Stone-Age hunters, the ancient Egyptians had learned how to make bread, brew beer and mix paint. They could smelt and cast copper, drill beads, mix mineral compounds for cosmetics, and glaze stone and pottery surfaces. They had invented the hoe, the most ancient of agricultural implements, and had carried out experiments in plant and animal breeding.

Egypt is a land of unusual geographic isolation, with well-defined boundaries. To the east and west are vast deserts. To the north is the Mediterranean Sea. To the south there was, before the construction of the High Dam at Aswan, a formidable barrier of igneous rock, beyond which lay the barren land of Nubia. Within these recognizable boundaries, however, was a land divided; Upper Egypt extended from Aswan to a point just south of modern Cairo and was largely barren, apart from a narrow strip of land flanking the river; the Delta, or Lower Egypt, spread from the point where the Nile fanned into a fertile triangle some 125 miles (200 km) before reaching the Mediterranean Sea. Linking Upper and Lower Egypt was the vital artery, the river Nile.

Before water from the Nile was harnessed by modern technology, the annual flood, a direct result of the monsoon rains on the Ethiopian tableland, spilled into the floodplain every year, depositing a thick layer of alluvial soil. Since rainfall in Egypt is almost nonexistent, the people were entirely dependent on the river for their crops; and it was ultimately on the fertility of the soil that ancient Egyptian civilization was based.

The earliest inhabitants of the Nile Valley were hunters who tracked game across northern Africa and the eastern Sudan, later joined by nomadic tribes of Asiatic origin who filtered into Egypt in sporadic migrations across the Sinai peninsula and the Red Sea. Late Paleolithic settlements (c. 12000 B.C.– 8000 B.C.) reveal that both these newcomers

Preceding pages: arabesque patterns; obelisk and statue; pyramid; desert life; festival tent; Egypt; minaret; old postcard; Great Temple. Left, gesticulations.

and the indigenous inhabitants had a hunting and food-gathering economy. At first they remained isolated from one another. Gradually, however, their lives became bound to the ebb and flow of the annual flood.

As the water rose each year, in July, they were obliged to draw back from the banks. By August, when the river waters swept across the lowlands, they took to the highland plateau and pursued hunting activities, tracking antelope, hartebeest, wild ass and gazelle with lances, bows and arrows. During the first half of October the river attained its highest level, and thereafter began to subside, leaving lagoons and streams which became natural reservoirs for fish.

A variety of plants grew from the fertile, uniform deposit of silt. During this season of plenty, hunting was at a minimum. From January to March seasonal pools dried out and fishing was limited, but in the swampy areas near the river there were turtles, rodents and Nile clams. At low Nile, during April, May and June, game scattered, food became scarce, and hunting was actively pursued once more.

Despite their diverse origins, therefore, there was a natural tendency for the people to group together during the 'season of abundance' and to split up into smaller groups during the low-flood season or during periods of drought.

Religion and Agriculture: As a certain rhythm formed in their lives, they observed that the gifts of their naturally irrigated valley depended on a dual force: the sun and the river, both of which had creative and destructive powers. The life-giving rays of the sun that caused a crop to grow could also cause it to shrivel and die. And the river that invigorated the soil with its mineral-rich deposits could destroy whatever lay in its path or, if it failed to rise sufficiently, bring famine.

These two phenomena, moreover, shared in the pattern of death and rebirth that left a profound impression on the people: the sun that 'died' on the western horizon each evening was 'reborn' in the eastern sky the following morning; and the river was directly and unfailingly responsible for the germination or 'rebirth' of the crop after the 'death' of the land each year. This natural sequence of rebirth after death undoubtedly lay at the root of the ancient Egyptian belief in the afterlife. As inevitably as the sun rose each morning and the flood arrived each year, man, it was believed, would rise and live again. Rebirth was a deeply-rooted concept because it arose from awareness of nature's changeless cycles.

It is believed that agriculture was introduced into the Nile Valley about 5000 B.C. Once grain (a variety of domesticated barley from Asia) could be cultivated and stored, the people could be assured of a regular food supply, an important factor in the movement away from primitive society towards civilization. Agriculture made possible a surplus of time and economic resources, which resulted in population increase and craft specialization. Polished stone axes, well-made knives, and fine-quality pottery vessels were produced, as well as ivory combs and slate palettes, on which paint for body decoration was prepared.

Slowly, assimilation took place. Some vil-

many cultures of the Nile Valley had formed into two distinctive political entities, Upper and Lower Egypt.

Beginnings of History: The Old Kingdom: Unification of the two lands has been ascribed to Narmer (Menes), 3100 B.C., who set up his capital at Memphis, at the apex of the Delta. He was the first king to be portrayed wearing both the White Crown of Upper Egypt and the Red Crown of Lower Egypt. He stands at the beginning of Egypt's ancient history, which was divided by an Egyptian historian called Manetho — who lived c. 280 B.C. — into 30 royal dynasties from Menes to Alexander the Great. The dynasties were subsequently combined and grouped into three main periods: the Old Kingdom or Pyramid Age, the Middle Kingdom, and the New Kingdom. Although

lages may have merged as their boundaries expanded; or small groups of people may have gravitated towards larger ones and started to trade and barter with them. As they became more dependent on one another, there was a natural fusion into larger social units. The affairs of the various communities became tied to major settlements, which undoubtedly represented the richest and most powerful of them. This tendency towards political unity occurred in both Upper and Lower Egypt. In Upper Egypt, the chief settlement was Nekhen, where the leader wore a conical White Crown and took the sedge plant as his emblem. In the Delta, the capital was Buto, and the leader wore the characteristic Red Crown and adopted the bee as his symbol. The

further divided by modern historians, these periods remain the basis of ancient Egyptian chronology.

The Old Kingdom, from the third to sixth Dynasties, (2686 B.C.–2181 B.C.), is considered by many historians as the high-water mark of achievement. A series of vigorous and able monarchs established a highly organised, centralized government. The great pyramids of Giza, on the western bank of the Nile southwest of Cairo, have secured undying fame for Khufu (Cheops), Khafre (Chephren) and Menkaure (Mycerinus). They ruled during a period of great refinement, an aristocratic era, which saw rising productivity in all fields. Cattle and raw materials, including gold and copper, were transported in donkey caravans from the Sudan and Nubia. Sinai was exploited for mineral wealth and a fleet of ships sailed to Byblos (on the coast of Lebanon) to import cedar wood. The "Great House," *peraha*, from which the word *pharaoh* is derived, controlled all trade routes throughout the land, as well as all the markets.

Most of the buildings of ancient Egypt, including the royal palaces, were built of perishable materials such as brick, wood and bundles of reeds, while tombs were built of stone, to last for eternity. This distinction gives the erroneous impression that the ancient Egyptians were preoccupied with thoughts of death. Evidence to the contrary is abundant. Wishing to ensure bounty in the afterlife similar to that enjoyed on earth, they decorated their tombs with a wide variety of farming scenes, manu-

legs carved in the form of the powerful hind-limbs of an ox or lion; the handle of a spoon was fashioned to resemble a lotus blossom, and the calyx sometimes formed the bowl of a wine glass. Chests and boxes were richly inlaid with ivory.

The End of the Old Kingdom: In the Old Kingdom the power of the pharaoh was supreme and he took an active part in all affairs of state, ranging from determining the height of the Nile during the annual inundation to recruiting a labor force from the various provinces or to lead mining and exploratory expeditions. The king also participated in public ceremonies and supervised the planning and construction of shrines or temples.

Naturally, such responsibility was too much for a single pair of hands and he therefore

facturing processes and leisure activities, as well as scenes from their personal lives.

The Old Kingdom tombs at Saqqarah, south of Giza, are adorned with painted relics of the deceased, his wife and children, overseers of his estates, supervisors of his factories, scribes, artisans and peasants. The graphic portrayals of everyday life are clear evidence that the ancient Egyptians took pride in beautiful possessions: chairs and beds (which often had leather or rope-weave seats or mattresses fastened to the frame with leather thongs) had

Left, temple of Hatshepsut, Deir al Bahari, Luxor. Above, the Ramesseum, Luxor.

delegated power to the provincial lords, who were often members of the royal family. The provincial nobility became increasingly more wealthy, began to exert power, and the result was an inevitable weakening of centralized authority. At the end of the Sixth Dynasty some of the provinces managed to shake themselves free from the central government and establish independence. The monarchy collapsed. The Old Kingdom came to an end.

The period known as the First Intermediate Period, between the seventh and the early 11th Dynasties, saw anarchy, bloodshed and a restructuring of society. The provincial lords who had gained power and prestige under the great monarchs began to reflect on the traditional beliefs of the their forefathers. It was a time of

23

soul-searching; and great contempt was voiced for the law and order of the past. Some magnificent literature has been passed down from this age of lost values: songs, on the one hand, expressing sorrow and disillusionment at the desecrating of the monuments of ancestors, and on the other, voicing skepticism as to whether man's elaborate preparation for the afterlife was worth the trouble.

A powerful family of provincial lords from Herakleopolis Magna (near Beni Suef in Middle Egypt) achieved prominence in the ninth and 10th Dynasties and restored some degree of order. In Upper Egypt, meanwhile, in the Theban area (near Luxor), a confederation had gathered around a strong family, the Intef and Mentuhotep family, who slowly extended their authority northwards until there was a

Labyrinth'' and declared by Herodotus to be more wonderful than the pyramids of Giza. Goldsmiths, jewelers and sculptors perfected their skills, as Eyptian political and cultural influence extended to Nubia and Kush in the south, around the Eastern Mediterranean to Libya, Palestine, Syria and even to Crete, the Aegean Islands, and the mainland of Greece.

In the Middle Kingdom an increasingly wealthy middle class led the ordinary man to aspire to have what only members of the aristocracy had had before: elaborate funerary equipment to ensure a comfortable afterlife. To pay homage to their legendary ancestor, Osiris, at the holy city of Abydos, thousands of pilgrims from all walks of life made their way there each year, leaving so many offerings in pottery vessels that the site acquired the

clash with the family from Herakleopolis. A civil war resulted in triumph for the Thebans.

The Middle Kingdom: The Middle Kingdom covers the 11th and 12th Dynasties (c. 2133 B.C. – 1786 B.C.). Amenemhet I, whose rule heralded a revival in architecture and the plastic arts, as well as a breakthrough in literature, established the 12th Dynasty, one of the most peaceful and prosperous eras known to Egypt. Political stability was soon reflected in material prosperity. Building operations were undertaken throughout the country; and there is hardly a town in Egypt without some physical trace of the Middle Kingdom. Amenemhet III constructed his tomb at Hawarah (Fayyum) with a funerary monument later described by classical writers as ''The

name of Umim al-Gaab, which means ''Mother of Potsherds.''

According to legend, Osiris was a just and much-loved ruler who taught his people the arts of making agricultural implements, rotating crops and controlling the waters of the Nile. He also taught them how to adapt to a wheat diet and how to produce bread, wine and beer. Isis, his devoted wife, was equally loved. She taught the people how to grind wheat and weave linen with a loom.

Osiris had a brother, Seth, who was secretly jealous of his popularity and conspired against him. Seth tricked Osiris into entering a chest, had it sealed, then cast it into the Nile. Brokenhearted, Isis went in search of the body of her husband, eventually found it, and hid it. But

Seth was out boar-hunting and discovered the body. He tore it into 14 pieces, which he scattered all over the land. Isis again went in search of Osiris, this time in the company of her sister Nephthys. They collected the pieces and, according to one version of the myth, bound them together with bandages. The two sisters lamented over the body of Osiris, fanning it with their wings in order to bring life back to it. Isis then descended on her husband in the form of a winged bird, received his seed, and brought forth an heir, Horus, whom she raised in the marshes of the Delta until he was strong enough to avenge his father's death by slaying Seth. Horus took over the throne on earth and the resurrected Osiris became king of the underworld.

Spread of the Osiris Cult: To the Egyptians, the

his power to give life. It was believed that a mummy, like a grain, would revive.

The cult of Osiris thoroughly captured the popular imagination in the Middle Kingdom; and it became desirable to have a stele or tombstone erected at or near Abydos, in order for the spirit of the deceased to join in the annual dramatization of his resurrection enacted by the priests. Later, during the New Kingdom, when Thebes became capital, deceased noblemen were often embalmed, then borne to Abydos and placed temporarily in the precinct of the temple there, before being interred at Thebes. If for some reason they could not make this pilgrimage after death, it was made symbolically: their tombs were decorated with reliefs of boats bearing their mummified bodies to Abydos.

weeping and lamentations of Isis and Nephthys were a classic expression of sorrow. The traditions of the loyalty and devotion of Isis to her husband, of the piety of Horus, who avenged his father's death in a triumph of good over evil, and of the benevolence of Osiris, who was killed, but rose to rule again, survived for centuries. To evoke the resurrected deity, it became common practice to place grain in a mummy-shaped linen container, water it, and let it germinate through the cloth. This so-called "Body of Osiris" exemplified

Left, inscription on a granite sarcophagus from the Valley of the Kings, Luxor. Above, tomb paintings in the Valley of the Kings, Luxor.

The End of the Middle Kingdom: The Hyksos: Measures may have been taken to suppress the power of the provincial rulers. In fact, at the end of the 13th Dynasty they once again rose against the crown. During this period of national instability the Hyksos (a Manethonian term corrupted from *Heka-khasut* meaning 'rulers of foreign countries'), who are believed to have come from the direction of Syria, rose to power, and challenged Egyptian authority. With horses and chariots (hitherto unknown in Egypt), they swept across the northern Sinai, fortified a stronghold at Tel ad-Deba, south of Tanis in the northeastern Delta, moved towards the apex of the Delta, and swept southwards. The damage done to Egypt's great cities can only be guessed at.

Pharaohs of later times inscribed declarations that they "restored what was ruined" and "raised what had gone to pieces," but the almost total absence of contemporary documents during the Hyksos occupation leaves scant evidence of what actually took place.

The humiliation of foreign occupation came to an end when Ahmose, father of the New Kingdom (18th to 20th Dynasties, 1567 B.C.–1320 B.C.) started a war of liberation and finally expelled the hated invaders from the land. This first unhappy exposure to foreign domination left a lasting mark on the Egyptian character. The seemingly inviolable land of Egypt had to be protected and to do so meant not only to rid the land of enemies, but to pursue them into western Asia. Out of the desire for national security was born the spirit

has bequeathed us more numerous or mightier monuments than Thebes. The ancient city stood on both sides of the Nile; and few places in Egypt are so ideally suited to monumental purposes. The ranges of hills to both the east and west curve away from the river's bank, leaving broad plains on either side. The Temple of Luxor was originally built by Amenhotep III, great-grandson of Thutmose III, whose reign was one of the most trouble-free times in Egyptian history. The country was united; the empire made labor cheap and wealth abundant. At Karnak, Amenhotep III built a huge pylon, stone towers on each side of the entrance to the great temple, which was dedicated to Amon, god of Thebes. Between the temples of Luxor and Karnak Amenhotep were beautiful gardens laid out along an

of military expansion characteristic of the New Kingdom.

The New Kingdom: The New Kingdom (1567 B.C.–1080 B.C.) was the empire period. The military conquests of Thutmose III, in no fewer than 17 campaigns, resulted in the establishment of Egyptian power throughout Syria and northern Mesopotamia, as well as in Nubia and Libya. Wealth from conquered nations and vassal states poured into Thebes (Luxor). The caravans were laden with gold, silver; ivory, spices, and rare flora and fauna. The greater part of the wealth was bestowed upon Amon who, with the aid of an influential priesthood, was established as Amon-Ra, "King of Gods."

Perhaps no other city in the ancient world

avenue of sphinxes.

The 18th Dynasty was an age of unparalleled grandeur. It was also a period of transition. Old values were passing and new ones were emerging. The spirit of the age was based on wealth and power. But grave discontent, especially among the upper classes, was apparent in criticism of the national god Amon and the materialism of the priests who promoted his cult.

Akhenaten's Revolution: It was in this atmosphere that Amenhotep IV (Akhenaten) grew up, the pharaoh who would revolt against the priests and order reliefs to be defaced, shrines to be destroyed, and the image of Amon to be hacked away. Akhenaten founded a new city at Tell al-Amarna, in Middle Egypt, and promoted worship of one god, the Aten, the life-giving sun.

Certain innovations had already begun to transform the character of Egyptian art in the early years of Akhenaten's reign. By the move to Tell al-Amama, these had become radical reforms. For centuries portrayals of the pharaoh had been stylized; he was always depicted as strong and powerful, and artists were not empowered to improvise. Now, with the consent, it seems, of Akhenaten, figures in varied movements were sculptured in exquisite low relief. Akhenaten himself wished to exaggerate his physical imperfections in order to emphasize a pharaoh who was a mortal; representations of earlier pharaohs had portrayed them as physically perfect god-kings.

Unfortunately, the ideal needs of a religious

Dynasty. The 5,000-odd objects catalogued from the tomb are now known to represent a unique accumulation of objects that date back not only to the so-called Amarna period, but even to the reign of Thutmose III.

Empire-Builders: Horemheb, the general who seized the throne at the end of the 18th Dynasty, was an excellent administrator who reestablished a strong government and started a program of restoration, which continued into the 19th Dynasty, when the pharaohs channeled their boundless energies into reorganizing the army after its disastrous setbacks during Akhenaten's rule. Seti I, builder of a famous mortuary temple at Abydos, fought battles against the Libyans, Syrians and Hittites; Ramses II, hero of a war against the Hittites, with whom he signed a famous peace

community and the practical requirements of governing an empire were not compatible. After the deaths of Akhenaten and his half-brother Smenkare, Tutankhaten came to the throne and the priests of Amon made a spectacular return to power.

Tutankhaten's name was changed to Tutankhamen and in an elaborate ceremony the young king appeared before the rejoicing public. It is thanks to the discovery of the tomb of this boy-king by Howard Carter in 1922, that we know of the splendor of the 18th

treaty, was also celebrated as a builder of great monuments, including the famous temples at Abu Simbel; and Ramses III not only conquered the Libyans, but successfully protected his country from the 'People of the Sea.'

All these warrior kings of the 19th Dynasty raised magnificent temples in honor of Amon, elaborately embellished and adorned. It was both a duty and privilege to serve the state god, who granted them military success; and successive pharaohs systematically tried to outdo their predecessors in the magnificence of their architectural and artistic endeavors, especially in the great Temple of Amon at Karnak. It

Left, grand Porticoe of the Temple of Philae near Aswan. Above, frieze showing captives, Abu Simbel.

became a temple within a temple, shrine within a shrine, where almost all the pharaohs wished to record their names and deeds for posterity. As new pylons, colonnades and shrines were built, valuable blocks of inscribed stone from earlier periods are often used; and in cases where it had been found necessary to remove a construction completely, it was simply dismantled and buried. The Sun Temples of Akhenaten suffered this fate: thousands of their distinctly uniform, decorated sandstone blocks, known as *talatat*, were buried in various places in Karnak, such as beneath the flagstones of the great Hypostyle Hall.

The Hypostyle Hall at Karnak is the largest single chamber of any temple in the world. Seti I was responsible for the northern half of the hall and Ramses II built the southern portion, but many other 19th-Dynasty pharaohs recorded their names there, honoring Amon.

Ramses III (1182 B.C.–1151 B.C.) was the last of the great pharaohs. His ever-weakening successors fell more and more under the yoke of the priests of Amon who controlled enormous wealth. According to a text known as the Harris Papyrus, written in the reign of Ramses III, Amon possessed over 5,000 divine statues, more than 81,000 slaves, vassals and servants, well over 421,000 head of cattle, 433 gardens and orchards, 691,334 acres of land, 83 ships, 46 building yards and 65 cities and towns. Naturally such a priesthood wielded enormous power. Gradually they came to regard themselves as the ruling power of the state and, at the end of the 20th Dynasty, in 1080 B.C., the high priests of Amon seized the throne and overthrew the dynasty. Theoretically, the country was still united. In fact, the government became synonymous with corruption. Anarchy blighted the land and occupation by successive foreign military powers was the result.

Centuries of Foreign Rule: In 950 B.C., Sheshonk, from a family of Libyan descent, but completely Egyptianized, took over leadership. His Libyan followers were probably descendants of mercenary troops who had earlier been granted land in return for military service. The Libyan monarchs conducted themselves as pharaohs and their rule lasted for two centuries.

In 720 B.C. a military leader, Piankhi, from the region of Kush (northern Sudan), marched northward. Because his people had absorbed Egyptian culture during a long period of Egyptian rule he did not view himself as a conquerer, but as a champion freeing Egypt from the forces of barbarism that he felt had engulfed it. The Egyptians, however, did not regard the Kushites as liberators and it was only after a military clash at Memphis, when the foreigners surged over the ramparts of the ancient city, that the Egyptians surrendered.

Like the Libyans before them, the Kushites established themselves as genuine pharaohs, restored ancient temples, and were sympathetic to local customs and institutions.

The Assyrians, who bear the reputation of being the most ruthless of ancient people, conquered Egypt in 671 B.C., putting an end to Kushite rule. With a well-trained army they moved south from province to province, assuring the local population of a speedy liberation from oppression. After the Egyptians rebelled against the new invaders and drove them north again, the Assyrians staged a counterattack, scaling the walls of the ancient city of Memphis and taking it by force. Realizing that occupation of Upper Egypt was necessary for the complete pacification of the country, they marched southward again, this time desecrating monuments, killing people and looting temples.

After these long centuries of foreign rule Egypt knew but one short respite: a brilliant revival, called the Saite Period, ensuing after an Egyptian name Psamtik liberated the country from Assyrian occupation in 664 B.C. He turned his attention to reuniting Egypt, establishing order and promoting Egyptian tradition. The unflagging efforts of this great leader and the Saite rulers that followed him to restore order and former greatness led them to pattern their government, religion and society on the Old Kingdom, a model already 2,000 years old. Instead of channeling their energies into creating new forms, they fell back on the past. The conservative policy of the Saite rulers helped to earn for Egypt the reputation it has long borne of being a civilization devoid of creativity and individuality.

Egypt's revival came to an end when the Persian King Cambyses occupied the land in 525 B.C. and turned Egypt into a Persian province. The new rulers, like the Libyans and the Kushites before them, showed respect at first for the religion and customs of the country in an effort to gain support. But the Egyptians were not deceived and as soon as an opportunity arose, they routed their invaders. Unfortunately, they were able to maintain independence for only about 60 years before another Persian army reconquered Egypt. This time there was less tolerance of local customs. When Alexander the Great marched on Egypt in 332 B.C., he and his army were welcomed by the Egyptians as liberators.

19th-Century engraving of the Temple of Philae. Unfortunately the color has since faded considerably.

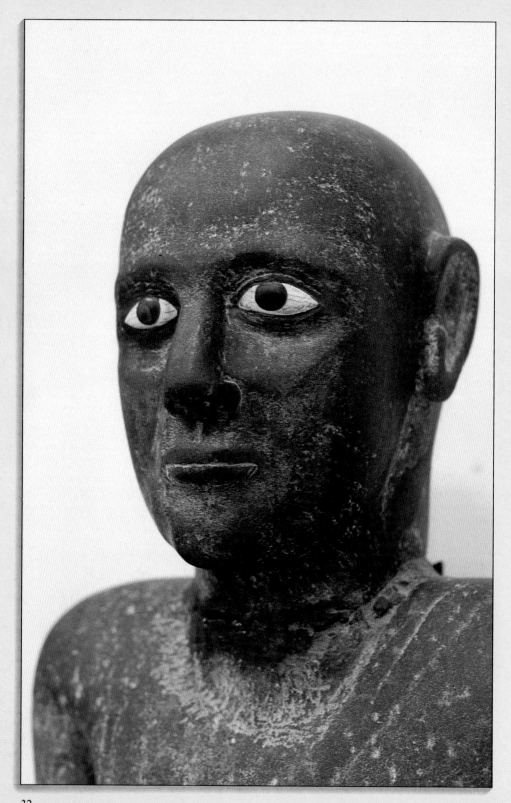

THE PTOLEMAIC PERIOD

Alexander the Great: When Alexander marched on Egypt, the Egyptians had no reason to fear that this would mark the end of their status as an independent nation. He first made his way to thickly-populated Memphis, the ancient capital, where he made an offering at the Temple of Ptah, then lost no time in traveling to Siwah Oasis to consult the famous oracle of Amon-Ra. When he emerged from the sanctuary he announced that the sacred statue had recognized him; and the priests of Amon greeted him as the son of the god.

Before he left Egypt, Alexander laid down the basic plans for its government. In the important provinces (*nomes* in Greek), he appointed local governors from among Egyptian nobles; he made provision for the collection of taxes, leaving to local officials (*nomarchs*) the task they had been trained to do for thousands of years; and he laid out the plans for his great city and seaport, Alexandria, so situated as to facilitate the flow of Egypt's surplus resources to the Archipelago and to intercept all trade with Africa and Asia.

When Alexander died from a fever at Babylon, his conquests fell to lesser heirs. Egypt was held by a general named Ptolemy, who gradually took over leadership first as satrap, then governor and, finally, in 305 B.C., as King Ptolemy I. During the three centuries of Ptolemaic rule that followed, Egypt became the seat of a brilliant empire once more.

The First of the Ptolemies: Ptolemy reputedly transported Alexander's body from Babylon to Egypt, where it was laid in a marble sarcophagus filled with white honey. He did not continue Alexander's practice of founding independent cities. In fact, with the exception of Ptolemais, on the western bank of the Nile in Middle Egypt and the old Greek city of Naucratis in the Delta, only Alexandria represented a traditional Greek city-state. Ptolemy chose instead to settle his mercenary troops (Greeks, Macedonians, Persians and Hellenized Asiatics) among the Egyptian population in towns near the capitals of the provinces into which Egypt was divided. Although these were towns of some considerable size, they had no self-government and were probably regarded by the Greeks as not much more than villages, despite the designation *polis*: Hermo-

polis, 'city of Hermes' (modern Ashmounein), for example, and Herakleopolis, 'the city of Heracles' (modern Ihnasiya), to the south of the Fayyum. In this fertile depression in the western desert, many of Ptolemy's troops were pensioned with large tracts of newly reclaimed land. Many of the settlers married Egyptians and by the second and third generations their children bore both Greek and Egyptian names.

In Alexandria Greeks formed the bulk of the population, followed in number by the Jews. But there was also a large Egyptian population, which lived west of the city, in the old quarter of Rhacotis. Alexandria occupied the strip of sandy soil between Lake Mareotis and the sea, where the island of Pharos stood, surmounted by its famous lighthouse, one of the Seven Wonders of the World. The island was artificially connected with the mainland, which resulted in a spacious harbor being formed on the east; and a few miles farther east was Canopus, which became a popular Greek tourist city.

The Serapis Cult: Ptolemy I introduced a cult designed to provide a line between his subjects, Greek and Egyptian. He observed that the Apis bull was worshipped at Memphis, which was even then a thriving religious center, and assumed, wrongly, that the cult was popular and widespread. The deceased Apis was known as Osiris-Apis or "Oserapis," from which *Serapis* was derived. Ptolemy himself supplied Serapis with anthropomorphic features and declared him to be a national god. To launch the new deity on his career, Ptolemy announced that he had had a dream in which a colossal statue was revealed to him. No sooner did he communicate his revelation to the people than a statue of Serapis was put on view, closely resembling his vision: a man with curly hair, a benign expression and a long beard.

The cult of Serapis was to have some success throughout Greece and Asia Minor, in Sicily, and especially in Rome where, as the patron god of the Ptolemaic empire, its presence enhanced the empire's prestige. In Egypt Serapis was worshipped in every major town, but especially in Alexandria and Memphis, where the Serapeum, the temple of Serapis in the necropolis of Saqqarah, became a famous site. The Ptolemaic rulers adorned a semi-circular space in front of the temple with statues of Greek philosophers, including one of a contemporary, Demetrius of Phalera, who stands leaning on a bust of the new god. Accomplished not only as a poet and philosopher, but also as an orator and statesman, Demetrius had been named governor of Athens when he was only 28, but was forced to flee nine years later when the city was attacked by the one-eyed king of Asia, who was also a rival of Ptolemy. Taking refuge in Alexandria, he may well have advised Ptolemy on the management of the Serapis cult there; and it was perhaps he who suggested the foundation of the Library, which was to be the ancient world's greatest storehouse of knowledge.

Alexandria: Alexandria became capital in place of Memphis and was soon to become the major seat of learning in the Mediterranean world, replacing Athens as the center of culture. Ptolemy II commissioned Egyptians to

most famous textbook ever written, standard until the beginning of this century; and Archimedes, the greatest mathematician and mechanist of antiquity, inventor among other things of the Archimedian Screw. Alexandrian astronomers revised the Egyptian calendar, then, some two centuries later, the Roman one, creating the Julian calendar that was used throughout Europe until the end of the Renaissance. Literary critics and scholars edited classical texts, giving them the forms we now know. Living poets such as Theocritus, Callimachus, and Appollonius Rhodius received generous support.

The Ptolemies regarded Egypt as their land and they played a dual role in it, conducting themselves both as bearers of Greek culture and as guardians of Egyptian culture. The

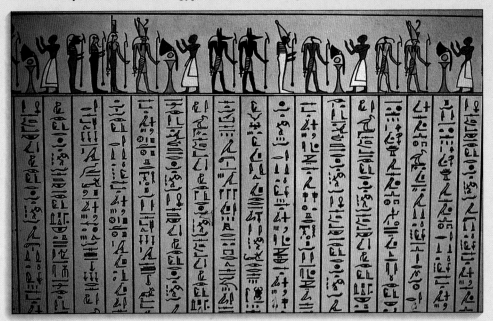

translate their literature into Greek; and a priest called Manetho wrote the history of his country. Ptolemy III issued a decree that all travelers disembarking at Alexandria should have taken from them, in exchange for an official certified copy, any literature in their baggage. Research, especially with practical aims, was also fostered; and distinguished astronomers, mathematicians, geographers, historians, poets and philosophers gravitated to the Mouseion or Museum attached to the Library, which was a research institution. Among the famed scientists who worked in Alexandria were Eratosthenes, the greatest geographer of antiquity, who measured the circumference of the earth to within fifty miles; Euclid, author of the *Elements*, the

roles were separate, yet interrelated. They resided in Alexandria, the great intellectual center; yet as pharaohs they lavished revenues on local priesthoods for the upkeep of temples or at least exempted them from taxes. One aspect of the power of the pharaoh was his capacity to uphold religious order; and the Ptolemies thus continued an ancient tradition. In their conscientious provision for temples, they not only maintained the Egyptian sense of prestige, but also helped ensure the continuation of both ancient rituals and the class of priests, scribes and scholars who understood and carried them out, the sustainers of Egyptian tradition. Architects and artists tackled the task of construction and restoration with vigor. The temples were built on traditional lines, often on the sites of more ancient temples. The walls were adorned with scenes depicting Ptolemaic kings in the manner of the ancient pharaohs, duly equipped with names and titles in hieroglyphics. Like the ancient pharaohs, they fulfilled religious duties and made ceremonial journeys up the Nile, enjoying the public worship of political leadership that was a long-standing feature of life in Egypt.

Influence of the Greek Language: Bilingual Egyptians realized long before the conquest by Alexander that if they transcribed their own language into the Greek alphabet, which was well known among the middle classes and was simpler to read than demotic — the cursive form of hieroglyphics in its latest development — communication would be easier. Scribes started transliterating Egyptian sounds into the

the Roman period. Demotic graffiti have been found, in the Temple of Isis at Philae that date to as late as A.D. 452, when widespread use of script other than Coptic had long died out.

Greek also became the mother-tongue of the Jews in Egypt, who constituted the second largest foreign community. Many had been imported as soldiers, even before the arrival of the Ptolemies. For example, the Persians had established a Jewish garrison as far south as the island of Elephantine, (opposite Aswan), which has left records in Aramaic. When Palestine fell under the control of Ptolemy I in 301 B.C., he brought back Jewish mercenaries, who joined the already-established communities. Unable to speak Hebrew, which had disappeared as a living language, Egyptian Jews soon felt a need to translate their sacred

Greek alphabet, adding seven extra letters from the Egyptian alphabet to accommodate sounds for which there were no Greek letters. The emergence of this new script, now known as Coptic, cannot be dated precisely. The earliest attempt to write the Egyptian language alphabetically in Greek, feeble and faulty but important, appears in an inscription dating to the Kushite Dynasty (750 B.C. — 656 B.C.) at Abydos; and there was a later time when Coptic and demotic were used simultaneously since literature in demotic survived well into

Left, elegant hieroglyphs show the skill of ancient scribes. Above, the Greco-Roman Museum in Alexandria has a superb collection of Ptolemaic artifacts.

books into Greek. According to legend, 72 translators were chosen from among the most learned Jewish scholars and the resulting version of the Old Testament, written in Alexandria, is known as the *Septuagint*.

The striking resemblances in Biblical and Egyptian expression and imagery are not surprising in view of the centuries of contact between Egyptians and Jews in Egypt. For example, an Egyptian sage called Amenemope (c.1320 B.C. — 1080 B.C.), whose works were widely distributed, admonished, "Set thyself in the arms of God," while Moses declaimed. "The eternal God is a dwelling place, and underneath are the everlasting arms." "Yahweh weigheth the hearts" says Proverbs 21:2; and it has not passed unobserved that the only other doctrine in which a god weighs the human heart is the myth of the court of Osiris in the underworld, where it is weighed against the feather of truth. The Biblical description of men being fashioned out of clay by Yahweh is likewise similar to the ancient Egyptian image of men being fashioned on a potter's wheel out of clay from the river Nile by the god Khnum. The analogies between the Book of Proverbs and the words of Amenemope are beyond doubt, in fact, and indicate direct borrowing in thought and expression.

Racial and Cultural Conflicts: The Ptolemies encouraged other foreigners to come and live in Egypt. The immigrants included Syrians and Persians, as well as Greeks, who took up residence in the Delta, in certain quarters of Memphis, and the Fayyum, where an enormous settlement grew up. Egypt in Ptolemaic times was inhabited by an extremely diversified foreign population, as well as an already highly stratified Egyptian society. There was a strong anti-Egyptian feeling among the sophisticated Greeks, who did not encourage Egyptians to become citizens of Alexandria and the Greek cities. Further, although they held the Egyptian culture in reverence in many ways, they did not learn the Egyptian language or writing. Even the Greek masses, fascinated by the 'sacred mysteries' and 'divine oracles' of the Land of Wonders, nevertheless held the Egyptians in contempt. Papyruses found in the Greek cities, which provide a wealth of documentary evidence of how such communities lives, clearly reflect disdain for the Egyptians.

There was also an anti-Greek feeling among the Egyptians, who had a strong sense of cultural superiority to anyone who did not speak their language. Herodotus had remarked on this attitude even in Persian times. Although there is evidence that Egyptian priests and officials collaborated with the Ptolemies, there is also evidence that they rebelled frequently, resentful of the fact that they were treated as a conquered race. Prophetic writings were widely circulated among the Egyptians, promising the expulsion of the foreigners. One Upper Egyptian province in particular, the Thebaid (Luxor), remained the most ardently nationalistic.

The Last of the Ptolemies: Towards the end of the second Century B.C. there were economic problems and political unrest in Egypt, along with a decline in foreign trade. Territories outside Egypt were lost, since the last of the Ptolemies were weak leaders, and the prosperity of the kingdom waned. The court, rich in material weath and lax in morals, became the scene of decadence and anarchy.

By the last century of Ptolemaic rule the Egyptians had acquired a position that was somewhat nearer in equality with the Greeks than they had enjoyed under the earlier Ptolemies; in fact Egyptian veterans received allotments of land like the Greeks, which may have been made possible as a result of rival claimants to the throne rallying the native population for popular support. It is important to note the emergence of a landed, wealthy Egyptian segment of the population, who were ardently nationalistic and had little respect for the settlers. It was from their ranks that Coptic Christianity's great spiritual leaders were to arise.

Cleopatra VI, the most famous of the Ptolemies, came to the throne at the age of about 18, as co-regent with her even younger brother Ptolemy XII. They were at that time under the guardianship of the Roman Senate and Romans interfered in the rivalry between them, which led Ptolemy to bandish his 21-year-old sister from Egypt. Cleopatra sought refuge in Syria, with a view to raising an army and recovering the throne by force of arms. When the ageing Julius Caesar came to Alexandria in 47 B.C., he took the side of the banished queen and set her on the throne. In June of 47 B.C. Cleopatra bore his only son, Caesarion.

A little over five years later, she met Mark Antony at Tarsus. Their legendary love brought her three more children, but alienated Antony from supporters in Rome. Antony's purported will, stating his wishes to be buried at Alexandria, angered many Romans, and gave Octavian the excuse he was looking for, to declare war on Antony. Octavian marched against him, defeating him at Actium and capturing Alexandria. Antony committed suicide; and Cleopatra, the last monarch to bear the title Lord of the Two Lands and to wear the crown bearing the sacred uraeus, the snake of Upper Egypt symbolizing kingship, is recorded to have caused her own death by the bite of an asp. Caesarion, who had been co-regent since 43 B.C., was murdered; and Octavianus became sole ruler in 30 B.C. Egypt thenceforth was a province of the Roman empire, subject only to the emperor, who lived in Rome, and to viceroys or prefects nominated by the emperor, who followed the example of the Ptolemies and represented themselves to the Egyptians as successors of the ancient pharaohs.

Right, Roman funeral mask, Graeco-Roman Museum, Alexandria.

21995

THE ROMAN PERIOD AND EARLY CHRISTIANITY

The Roman occupation of Egypt, ostensibly a mere extension of Ptolemaic rule, differed markedly from it. While a mutual hostility towards the Persians and a long history of commercial relations bound Egyptians and Greeks together, no such affinity existed between Egyptians and Romans. Alexander the Great had entered Egypt without striking a blow; Roman troops had pitched battles with Egyptians almost immediately, from Alexandria on the Mediterranean coast to Thebes in Upper Egypt. The Ptolemaic kings had lived in Egypt; the Roman emperors governed from Rome and their prefects took over the position formerly held in the scheme of government by the kings. To the Egyptians the prefect, not the emperor, was therefore the royal personage. And the prefect did not perform the ceremonial functions of divine kingship, which was by tradition highly personal. There was thus a drastic change in the climate of leadership.

Augustus made the mistake of arousing the ire of the Greeks when he abolished the Greek Senate in Alexandria and took administrative powers from Greek officials. Further, in response to an appeal by Herod, king of Judea, he not only agreed to restore to him the land that had been bestowed on Cleopatra during her short refuge in Syria, but also agreed to grant self-government to the Hellenized Jews of Alexandria. This caused great consternation among the Greeks, who had founded the city and had distrusted Roman ambition from the beginning. Their formal request to Augustus to retract the privileges granted the Jews was ignored. Fighting soon broke out, first between Greeks and Jews, then with the Romans' participation when they tried to separate the two. The unrest that marks the beginning of the Christian era in Alexandria had already begun. Ships in the harbor were set on fire, the flames spread and the Mouseion Library was burned. An estimated 490,000 rolls of papyrus perished.

The Romans thenceforth stationed garrisons at Alexandria, which remained the capital; at Babylon (Old Cairo), which was the key to communications with Asia and with Lower Egypt; and at Syene (Aswan), which was Egypt's southern boundary. They controlled Egypt by force, and regarded the land as no more than a granary supplying wheat to Rome. Consequently, an enormous burden of taxation was placed on the people of the Nile Valley. A census was imposed on villages throughout the land and house-to-house registration of the number of residents was made, which might have been considered normal procedure in Rome, but was regarded as an infringement on their privacy by Egyptians. Calculations of the wheat quota were based not on the productivity of the land, but on the number of men in a village.

Egyptians who had enjoyed certain privileges under the later Ptolemies and acquired considerable wealth received no special consideration by the Romans, but had their problems compounded when the Emperor Trajan declared that peasant farmers should be recruited for the Roman army. Hadrian reduced rentals on imperial lands and exempted citizens of Greek cities and Greek settlers in the Fayyum from taxation, but the Egyptian rural population was assessed at a flat rate, without regard for income, age or capacity for work. There is evidence of hardship from the first half of the first Century. There are records of men having "fled leaving no property," 43 in number, then 60, then 100 from a single village. Some took refuge in remote areas of the desert, while others hid in caves and ancient tombs flanking the Nile Valley. When men fled or hid, their families suffered the penalties.

The Romans made an overt show of respect for Egyptian priesthoods by constructing new temples or completing older ones built by the Ptolemies. The temple to the goddess Hathor at Dendera, for example, which was started under the later Ptolemies, was completed some 185 years later under the emperor Tiberius; and temples in the traditional style were completed at Esna, Kom Ombo and Philae. It is worthy of note, however, that the sites for these temples were chosen for their strategic position as well as for the sake of ancient tradition. Esna had been a center for local commerce from earliest times; Kom Ombo, situated on a hill, commanded the trade routes to Nubia in the south; and Philae was situated on Egypt's southern border.

Temple lands elsewhere, however, were annexed and placed under the control of the Roman government. Local priests were allotted only a small part of sacred property and their own material wealth was curbed. The produce of vineyards, palm groves and fig

Preceding pages: St. Antony's Monastery in the Eastern Desert dates from the Fourth Century. Left, chapel in the Monastery of St. Baramus.

41

plantations owned by temples was collected by Roman officials and taxes were levied on sheep, oxen, horses and donkeys. A Roman official held the title of "High Priest of Alexandria and all Egypt" and was the supreme authority over all the temples.

Under Roman rule the wealth of the land was siphoned off for the benefit of Rome. Egypt was treated as a private estate of the emperor and a pleasure-ground for the Roman upper classes, who visited Egypt in vast numbers, coming to see the Pyramids of Giza, the Apis bull at Memphis, the ancient city of Abydos, the Colossus of Memnon, or the healing centers at Deir el Bahri and Philae.

Early Christianity: Such were conditions in Egypt during the first century of the Christian era, when according to tradition the apostle

science, mathematics and the humanities were also taught there. Significantly, the emergence of the school coincides with the first direct attacks by the Romans on the Christians of Alexandria.

Clement (160-215), a convert from paganism who succeeded Pantanaeus, is regarded as an early apostle of Christian liberalism and taught in Alexandria for more than 20 years. He was succeeded by Origen (185-253) the theologian and writer who is regarded as the greatest of the early Christian apologists. Born of Christian parents, Origen joined the Catechetical School at an early age, attended lectures by Pantanaeus and Clement, and later taught there for 28 years. Like Clement, he was highly critical of the Gnostic movement (from the Greek *gnosis* or 'knowledge'.)

Mark preached in Alexandria. Remains from the period of the diffusion of the new faith in Egypt are scant, but New Testament writings found in Bahnasa in Middle Egypt date from around the year 200, and a fragment of the gospel of St. John, written in Coptic and found in Upper Egypt, can be dated even earlier. They testify to the spread of Christianity throughout Egypt within a century of St. Mark's arrival.

The Catechetical School of Alexandria was the first important institution of religious learning in Christian antiquity. It was founded in 190 by Pantanaeus, a Christian scholar who is believed to have come to Alexandria approximately 10 years earlier. Its scope was not limited to theological subjects, because

Gnosticism: The origin of the Gnostic communities is obscure and until recently not much was known about them: the Gnostics were hounded into silence, in the name of orthodox Christianity, from the fourth Century onward and their writings were burned whenever they could be found. Fortunately, a collection of manuscripts was discovered in Nag Hammadi in Upper Egypt in 1945. These texts, which have raised important questions about the development of Christianity in Egypt, are copied from original writings that cannot be dated with certainty, but may date from as early as the second half of the first Century.

The 12 Nag Hammadi codices were collected by Egyptians and translated into Coptic, the Egyptian language of the time. They vary widely in content, presenting a syncretic spectrum of heritages that range from Egyptian folklore, Hermeticism, Greek philosophy and Persian mysticism to the Old and New Testaments. The codices include a "gospel of Thomas," a compilation of sayings attributed to Jesus (in the opening passage of which is the claim that the words were spoken by the post-resurrection Jesus to Thomas Didymus Judas); extracts from Plato's *Republic*; and apocrypha ("secret books") related to Zoroastrianism and Manichaeism. Little wonder that the Gnostics came under violent attack by orthodox Christians. The codices reveal, nevertheless, that the Gnostic movement was not only far more widespread than was previously thought, but of greater historical consequence

plated by reason and allowed the material world only a formal existence. Ascetic disciplines were part of their ethical code, which urged them to ascend from the bonds of matter to the spiritual world, to become ecstatically united with the divine.

The first Neoplatonist, Ammonius Saccas, had been the teacher of Origen and was a lapsed Christian, while his famous successors — Plotinus, Porphyry, Iamblichus, Hypatia, and Proclus — were all pagans. Plotinus, born in Asyut, was the most influential, making many converts at the imperial court in Rome. Porphyry, his student, came to be regarded by the Christian bishops as their greatest enemy — they burned his books in public — and the last important work of the school was Proclus' defense of the pagan philosophical tradition

than hitherto supposed.

Neoplatonism: A more formidable rival to Christianity in the long run came directly from pagan thought: Neoplatonism. Coalescing in Alexandria during the third Century, this philosophical school revived and developed the metaphysical and mystical side of Platonic doctrine, explaining the universe as a hierarchy rising from matter to soul, soul to reason, and reason to God, conceived as pure being without matter or form. Neoplatonists understood reality as the spiritual world contem-

Left, ancient religious manuscript illuminated in Coptic. Above, St. Antony's Monastery amid the surrounding desolation.

against Christianity. More than one Christian was a student of Neoplatonism, nevertheless, and even Porphyry found Christian readers and translators, by whom Neoplatonic ideas were co-opted into the teachings of the early Church.

Major Neoplatonic works survived intact, moreover, and by the end of the Middle Ages a handful of Europeans could read them in the original. As knowledge of Greek began to extend outside the clergy, aristocratic study-groups sprang up, most notably in Florence, and Neoplatonism rapidly became a fashion, then a movement. Within a few years its influence had spread from Northern Italy throughout Western Europe, largely creating that cultural consensus we call the Renaissance.

Thus a common element in the paintings of Botticelli or Titian, the engravings of Dürer, the sculpture of Michelangelo, or the poetry of Shakespeare, which distinguishes them from earlier European art, is their rootedness in Neoplatonic images and ideas. For two centuries or so, while a 1000-year-old Christian orthodoxy came increasingly into question, these images and ideas were to be the conceptual currency of every educated European.

They were also modern man's first key to an understanding of the ancient pagan culture that the early Church, in Egypt and elsewhere, had conscientiously set out to destroy. As with most revolutionary groups, its motive was ideological zeal, which began with a sense of being not only embattled, but persecuted.

Religious Persecution: The Emperor Septimius Severus decreed in 202 that municipal councils should be set up in all the nome capitals. His purpose may have been to upgrade the status of the Egyptians and make them more responsible, but Egyptians saw the measure as restrictive, resisted it, and were severely penalized. Threats and intimidation gave way to a new wave of brutality, especially in areas where Roman presence was strongest.

The first systematic attempt to put an end to Christianity by depriving the church of both its leaders and followers took place under the Emperor Decius (249-251), who ordered Egyptians to participate in pagan worhsip in the presence of Roman officers and to submit certificates of sacrifice. Those who refused were declared to be self-avowed Christians and were tortured. Some Christians sent in false certificates; others managed to escape to the solitude of the desert. Many, however, were willing to die rather than abjure their faith; and their martyrdom further accelerated the Christian movement.

Beginnings of Monasticism: St. Paul the Theban, orphaned as a youth, and St. Antony, who came from a family of landowners with a certain status in society, were two of Egypt's earliest and greatest spiritual leaders. Both lived lives of meditation and prayer at about this time; each, unknown to the other, had chosen a retreat in the Eastern Desert in a range of mountains near the Gulf of Suez. St. Paul, older than St. Antony and with the gift of healing, is believed to have retired to the desert at the age of 16 to escape the persecutions of Decius. St. Antony was born of fairly wealthy parents, but as a result of visionary inspiration, sold his inheritance and gave his money to the poor, then retreated to the cliffs flanking the Nile Valley, later settling beneath a range of mountains known today as the South Qalala (Mount Clysma in Roman times).

The weight of taxation had forced other people to renounce their material possessions, but these two men became regarded as having special powers and a special relationship with the divine, attracting other eremites to draw near them. By this time thousands of ascetics, whose original models may be traced to pre-Christian times in Egypt, were living either alone or in small groups and were looking for guidance from masters, like St. Paul and St. Antony, who would give instruction in an atmosphere of security and spirituality.

As with most great movements that spread beyond the borders of the country in which they first took root, contradictory traditions as to the origins of monasticism have emerged. St. Jerome credits St. Paul the Theban with being the first hermit. In both Coptic and Western tradition, however, St. Antony, whose fame spread as a result of the biography written after his death by Athanasius in 350, holds a more prominent position, and Copts regard him as the prototype of the Egyptian anchorite. He took refuge from those who came to see him in a cave high up in the rugged mountains, while his disciples kept him supplied with provisions. The cave, which can still be seen, is situated at the end of a narrow tunnel approached from a ledge, below which is a small terrace believed to be the place where he used to weave baskets from palm leaves.

In 284 the Roman army elected Diocletian emperor and his reforms mark a turning-point in the history of Christianity. The appalling social and economic conditions throughout the Roman empire led him to reorganize it along military lines. He divided Egypt into three major provinces, separated civic and military powers, then imposed new methods of tax assessment based on units of productivity. Under Diocletian's reforms Egyptians were forced into public service and, to facilitate control, Latin was introduced as the official language, even in provinces where Greek had previously been used for official documents.

Unification of the Roman empire was undoubtedly the reason for these reforms, but Egyptians had had enough. They rebelled so violently that Diocletian decided that if they could not be subjugated, they should be eliminated. They were dismissed from government service, their property was confiscated, and their houses leveled. Searches were made for Christian literature and copies of the scriptures, when found, were burned. Though thousands died during the terrible persecutions

Modern Coptic painting retains Byzantine influence, right.

RING
THE BELL

of Diocletian, unknown numbers escaped to refuge in the deserts, taking their zeal for Christianity with them, to create new converts.

The Christian church celebrates both martyrs and confessors. The latter are those who did not die for their faith but lived to spread it. In a world of want and violence, a religion that preached a message of common support and a blessed life after death was embraced with enthusiasm.

Early Monastic Reform: St. Pachom (Pachomius in Latin, referred to as *Anba Bakhum* in Arabic), born about 285, first saw the benefits of organizing the widespread anchoritic communities and therefore became the founder of a form of cenobitic monasticism that took his name. A native Egyptian who only learned Greek late in life in order to communicate with strangers. Pachom established a community near Akhmin, where the caves in the hills flanking the Nile floodplain were populated with large numbers of ascetics. Pachom drew them together and began to formulate a rule to govern their lives. He introduced a schedule of activities for every hour of the day and night, emphasizing that a healthy body provided a healthy spirit, and stressed that there should be no excesses of any kind, even in spiritual meditation.

Pachom's aim was to establish a pious, enlightened and self-sufficient community that would set an example to others. An applicant for admission did not have to exhibit spectacular feats of mortification of the flesh. Although there are numerous examples of physical self-torture in the lives of the Desert Fathers, a candidate for Pachomian monasticism merely had to undergo a period of probation, after which he was clothed in the habit of a monk and officially joined the community. The monks were grouped into "houses" or "settlements" within the monastery, each according to trade or activity. A supervisor was responsible for each house. The head of the monastery and spiritual leader of the whole community was an abbot, who ensured that the rules laid down by Pachom were strictly adhered to.

Leading disciplined lives, the monks brought productivity to the soil, revived crafts and, more importantly, were in communication with non-Christian neighboring communities. There is abundant evidence in the surviving records of various monasteries that the monks aided the people economically by providing them with their crop surpluses, as well as products from craft industries. Moreover, although the monks were looked upon as mortals to whom God had given the power of healing, they nevertheless supplied medication to those who came for a cure. They even played a role as mediators in popular grievances, whether between members of a single family, or, as was frequent, in disputes over land or water rights between neighbors. Pachomian monasteries were not isolated in remote stretches of the desert, but in many cases were within easy reach of valley settlements, where the rural community looked to them for guidance.

Pachom's first monastery was so successful that he moved on to found a second similar institution and yet another, until he had founded no fewer than 11 monasteries in Upper Egypt, including two convents for women. Not all the ascetic communities adopted St. Pachom's Rule. Those that had grown up around spiritual leaders like St. Antony or St. Makarius, the son of a village priest, seem, on the basis of archaeological considerations, to have continued a semi-cenobitic form of monasticism: the monks only met once a week for mass and a communal meal, followed by a meeting at which work was allocated for the forthcoming week. St. Pegol, founder of the White Monastery in Middle Egypt modified Pachom's rules and introduced a few more.

All Christian monasticism stems, either directly or indirectly, from Pachomian monasticism: St. Basil, organizer of the monastic movement in Asia Minor, whose rule is followed by the Eastern churches, visited Egypt around 357; St. Jerome, translator of the Bible into Latin, made it known to the West; and St. Benedict who founded monasteries in the West in the sixth Century, used the model of St. Pachom, but in a stricter form.

Conversion and Controversy: The famous revelation of the Emperor Constantine in 312, which resulted in his conversion to Christianity, was followed by the Edict of Milan, according to which Christianity became the favored religion throughout the Roman empire. It was at last safe to admit to being a Christian in Egypt. Unfortunately, the theological disputes that had plagued the early Christian movement became even fiercer in the fourth and following centuries.

The controversies centered on the attempt to define the Incarnation: If Jesus was both God and Man, had He two natures? If so, what was their relationship? Defining the nature of Jesus of crucial importance to a new religion that attracted people from many backgrounds, with different traditions, concepts of godliness, and styles of worship, was extremely

Left, sign on monastery entrance shows that visitors are now welcome.

difficult. It concerned such definitions as "Father," "Son," "begotten," and "unbegotten."

The chief antagonists were the Arians, so called after Arius, an elderly Alexandrian presbyter, and the Monophysites, led by Alexander, bishop of Alexandria. The former held that "a time there was when He was not," in other words, that Jesus did not have the same nature as God the Father. The Monophysites regarded this doctrine as recognition of two gods and a reversion to polytheism. They believed that Father and Son were of one nature, that Jesus was both divine and human.

The dispute was discussed in a highly charged atmosphere and reached such an impasse that Constantine felt impelled to define officially a dogma to unify Christian belief.

great deal for his eloquence, reasoning and persistence that the Nicene Creed, to the effect that Father and Son are of the same nature, was sanctioned and remains part of the Christian liturgy.

Constantine formally received the decision of the bishops and issued a decree of banishment against those who refused to subscribe to it. Arius was denounced as a heretic and his books were burned. Bishop Alexander and Athanasius returned to Egypt triumphant. The former had emerged from the Arian controversy as the Orthodox Patriarch of Alexandria and a universally accepted doctor of the Christian Church. The monastic orders, moreover, were stamped with ecclestical approval.

The Decline of Alexandria: Soon after the Coun-

The Council of Nicea, convened in Asia Minor in 325 for this purpose, was the earliest and most important church council, the first meeting between the Church and the State. It was attended by the Emperor Constantine and 318 bishops, with their delegations, from Egypt, Syria, Assyria, Asia Minor, Greece and the West. The Syrian and Assyrian delegations included bishops from Antioch, Jerusalem and Armenia; Goths and Romans represented the West; and the Alexandrian delegation included the bishop Alexander, Athanasius his deacon, Arius his antagonist, and a large body of monks and hermits.

Although Alexander officially led Egypt's delegation, it was his deacon, Athanasius, who was his chief spokesman. And it says a

cil of Nicea, Constantine moved his capital to the ancient Greek town of Byzantium, which became Constantinople or "Constantine's city", and was to gain much of the importance and prestige that had once belonged to Alexandria. The new metropolis was embellished with great monuments from many ancient cities, including an obelisk over 33 yards high shipped from Egypt. Known as "New Rome," Constantinople became a storehouse of Christian and pagan art and science and rapidly usurped the reputation Alexandria had held as a seat of learning since Ptolemaic times.

The see of Alexandria had already faced another setback when the Arian leaders were recalled from banishment at the entreaty of

Princess Constantia. Constantine's successor, Constantius, favored the Arians, deposed Athanasius, drove out his followers at sword point and placed his own bishop, Georgius, on the throne of the see of Alexandria.

Thus began an era when ecclesiastical dignitaries excommunicated one another in Egypt and mobs sacked churches of opposing factions. Athanasius was driven into exile five times and sought shelter with hermits in their isolated caves, living with St. Antony near the Red Sea or in a monastery in Kharga Oasis. During his exiles, Athanasius successfully reconciled the differences between monks and hermits, some of whom did not want to join a monastic order.

Under Theodosius I Christianity was formally declared the religion of the empire and

Egypt. Tombs were ravaged, walls of ancient monuments scraped, and statues toppled. In Alexandria the famous statue of Serapis was burned and the Serapeum destroyed, along with its library, which had replaced the Mouseion as a center of learning. It was a folly of fanaticism in the name of orthodoxy not, ironically, so different from that which had earlier oppressed Christianity. In 415 under Theodosius II, Patriarch Cyril expelled the Jews of Alexandria from the city; and Hypatia, the learned and beautiful Neoplatonist, was cruelly murdered.

In the fourth and fifth Centuries many ancient temples were converted into monastic centers — Dayr (monastery) al-Medinah and Dayr al-Bahri, both in the Theban necropolis, are two well-known examples — or churches,

the Arians were again declared heretics. The Monophysite bishops of Alexandria were reinstated, but as a result of the partition of the empire between the Emperor Honorius of Rome and the Emperor Arcadius of Constantinople, their power was limited. Egypt fell under the jurisdiction of the latter and the so-called Byzantine rule of Egypt began.

Byzantine Period: Theophilus was made Patriarch of Alexandria and displayed tremendous zeal in destroying heathen temples. A wave of destruction swept over the land of

Left, drawbridge leading to the keep at the Monastery of St. Baramus, Wadi Natrun. Above, monastery of St. Paul in the Eastern Desert.

as in the second court of the mortuary temple of Ramses III at Medinat Habu and the Court of Amenhotep III in Luxor Temple. One of the earliest Christian buildings in Egypt was constructed between the Birth House and the Coronation House of the Temple of Hathor at Dendera, using some of the blocks from the Birth House. It is possible that this church was the famous Christian center somewhere in the neighborhood of Dendera that St. Jerome alludes to as sheltering an assembly of 50,000 monks to celebrate Easter.

Pilgrims came from all over the Christian world to visit the monasteries in Egypt. The bishop of Bahnasa estimated the number of monks in Middle Egypt at 10,000 and nuns at 20,000, living in 40 monasteries and convents. Archaeology has revealed a huge monastic settlement in Kharga Oasis, in the Western Desert, dating from the fourth Century, with a necropolis at Bagawat containing over 200 chapels. Wadi Natrun, recently revived as an important monastic center, once had 50 monasteries and over 5,000 monks. East of Wadi Natrun, at Kelya (from the Latin for "cell"), a site described by such Christian writers as Palladius and Rufinus, there are more than 750 abandoned hermitages dating from around the fifth Century. In the biography of St. Macrufus, who lived in the sixth Century, the village of Ishnin an-Nasarah is reported to have had "as many churches as there were days in the year."

Despite the growth of the Christian movement, factional disputes continued, especially

when the see of Alexandria officially lost precedence to the see of Constantinople at the Council of Constantinople in 381. There had been riots so violent that the Catechetical School, a central force in the intellectual life of Alexandria for nearly two centuries, had been destroyed. Egypt's opposition to the Melkites, or "Emperor's men," representing Constantinople, became the latest episode in a long struggle for independence that was political as well as religious.

Foundation of the Coptic Orthodox Church: Convened in 451, the Council of Chalcedon signalized Byzantine determination to exert authority in Egypt. A new statement of dogma declared that Christ had two Natures "concurring" in One Person. When the Egyptians refused to endorse this revisionist doctrine, their Patriarch was formally excommunicated, but the Melkite appointed to fill his place could only be installed in Alexandria after a massacre of Monophysite leaders and a regular pillage of the city, carried out by imperial troops.

From this time onward, Egypt generally had two Patriarchs, one representing the orthodoxy of Constantinople, the other upholding the Monophysite beliefs of the majority of Egyptian Christians, embodied in the Coptic Orthodox Church, the national Church of Egypt, which emerged as a separate entity. The English word *Copt*, meaning "Egyptian Christian," is derived from the Arabic *qibt*, which is derived in turn from *Kyptaios*, the Coptic form of the Greek word *Aigyptios* meaning simply "Egyptian." In modern usage it also designates not only the last stages of the ancient Egyptian language and script, but also the distinctive art and architecture that developed everywhere in Egypt except Alexandria — which remained attached to cosmopolitan forms — during the country's Christian era. It is used, finally, to refer to most of modern Egypt's Christian minority, who officially constitute about nine per cent of the population and who continue to be identified with the same intense patriotism that distinguished their forebears.

The Emperor Zeno's attempt in 482 to heal the breach between Churches was unsuccessful, but after strengthening his garrison and deporting the more outspoken Copts to Constantinople, he let matters rest. There were no more significant disturbances until the reign of Justinian (528-565).

The End of Byzantine Rule: Under Justinian, the Copts were only saved from persecution, so enthusiastically inflicted during his reign upon all heretics, pagans, and Jews, by the interest of the Empress Theodora, his wife, who was Monophysite in sympathy and even more wilful than he was. After Theodora's death, however, Justinian sent Alexandria a patriarch-prefect determinedly armed with both civil and religious powers. Greeted by a mob, which stoned him when he attempted to speak in church, the new bishop retaliated by ordering the troops under his command to carry out a general slaughter. This act quelled immediate resistance, but completed the alienation of the Copts, who henceforward simply ignored any ecclesiastical representatives from Constantinople.

Left, Coptic icon showing Virgin and child. Right, cowled monk crossing drawbridge, Wadi Natrun.

50

EGYPT UNDER ISLAM

The Arab Conquest: In the early seventh Century, while the great rival Byzantine and Sasanian empires were exhausting themselves in a futile and costly struggle for supremacy, the Arabs were being spiritually and politically united by the Prophet Muhammad. His call for the creation of a Muslim community (the *Umma*) obedient to the commands of God, as revealed in the Holy Quran, cut across tribal conflicts and forged the Arabs into a single nation. Under the leadership of his successors, the Caliphs, the energy of the Arabs was directed outward against the contending empires of the north, who were too weak to resist an unexpected invasion from the heart of the Arabian Peninsula. Inspired by both the duty of waging *jihad* (Holy War) against non-believers and the promise of rich booty, the Muslim armies conquered all of Persia and half of the Byzantine empire between 636 and 649.

The Byzantine province of Egypt was invaded in 639 by 'Amr ibn al-' As, one of the ablest of the early Muslim generals, who had visited Alexandria in his youth and had never forgotten the Egyptian capital's public buildings, populous streets or obvious wealth. Acting on his own initiative, without the sanction of the Caliph in Madinah, 'Amr justified his actions by saying that the people of Egypt were sheep, that its land was gold, and that it belonged to whoever was strong enough to take it. Masters of hit-and-run tactics, his horsemen easily defeated a Byzantine army near the ancient ruins of Heliopolis in 640, then set about besieging both the fortress of Babylon, at the head of the Delta, and Alexandria itself. Paralyzed by internal problems and foreign wars, the Byzantines were unable to reinforce their army in Egypt. Babylon fell in 641 and the rest of the country was formally surrendered soon after.

The Arabs were aided in their conquest by the indifference of the native Egyptians, the Copts, whose political and religious disputes with Constantinople, never resolved, had made them deeply hostile to Byzantine rule. Not yet interested in converting subject peoples to Islam, which they still viewed as a purely Arab religion, the Muslim conquerors favored the Coptic Church over the Byzan-

Preceding pages: detail of marblework from the Mosque of Aqsunqur, 14th Century, Cairo. Left, the prayer niche at the Mosque of Sultan Hassan.

tine establishment and allowed it autonomy, using it to assist them in collecting the poll-tax levied on all non-Muslims.

During the siege of Babylon, the Muslims had camped to the north of the fortress and it was here that 'Amr founded Fustat, a garrison city for the internal control of the Nile Valley.

Gradually Fustat was transformed from a military base into the administrative and commercial capital of the Arab province of Egypt. Arabic began to replace Greek as the language of government, culture and commerce in the city and in time filtered down to the rural population, causing the local Coptic language to be all but forgotten.

The 'Abbasid Caliphs: The rapid growth of the new Islamic empire brought in its wake a host of problems. Tribal differences among the Arabs began to reassert themselves as various factions fought over the spoils of conquest and the leadership of the Umma. These conflicts, usually expressed in religious terms, deeply divided the Arabs and resulted in over a hundred years of rebellions and civil wars. A semblance of Muslim unity was reestablished in 750 when the 'Abbasid family seized control of the empire. Brought to power by a coalition of Arab and Iranian forces, they established a more international state, centered in Baghdad, that drew upon the services of all Muslims, irrespective of racial origin.

In Egypt, as a symbol of the new regime, a new administrative capital was built to the north of Fustat. Known as Al-'Askar or "the Cantonments," this military suburb became the official residence of the provincial governor, his army and bureaucracy. Never much more than an extension of Fustat, it was in time absorbed by the earlier town's own northern expansion.

During the first 200 years of Muslim rule Egypt was a pawn rather than a true participant in the wider political issues that dominated the affairs of the Islamic empire. Controlled by a series of military governors appointed by the Caliphs in the East, most of the country's great agricultural wealth was channelled into the coffers of the central treasury. The power of these governors was severely curtailed by short terms of office and by restrictions placed upon their internal authority to prevent the establishment of an independent state in Egypt. This imperial policy, while successful in delaying the break-up of the Muslim empire, ensured that the men directly ruling Egypt had little real commitment to the country.

The result was oppressive taxation and widespread official corruption, which brought Egypt to the verge of economic collapse in the early ninth Century. This state of affairs also reflected the progressive decline of 'Abbasid authority throughout the empire, which was simply too large to be effectively ruled by one man.

In order to hold their state together the Caliphs in Baghdad began to employ Turkish slave armies to act as a counterbalance to their turbulent Arab and Iranian subjects. Far from being slaves in the Western sense of the word, these Turks were groomed as a ruling caste, loyal only to the 'Abbasids. The

court and was posted to Egypt in 868 at the age of 33. Taking advantage of rivalry amongst the 'Abbasid family and their Turkish armies, Ibn Tulun was able to gain total control of the provincial government, establishing the first autonomous Muslim state in Egypt. By drastically reducing the imperial tribute to Iraq and by reinvesting the country's wealth in his new domain, Ibn Tulun brought about a period of prosperity for ruler and ruled alike. One of his first actions as independent sovereign was the creation of a strong army made up of Turkish, Greek and Sudanese slaves, with which he conquered all of Syria in 878.

To celebrate his independence Ibn Tulun built a new royal city to the north of Al-'Askar called *Al-Qatai'* or "the Wards" after

power of the Turkish generals became so great and the upkeep of their armies so costly that the Caliphs were compelled to distribute whole provinces to them in lieu of pay. In this manner Egypt became in 832 a private fief of the new Muslim military elite. Unwilling to leave the political nerve center of Iraq, which might result in a loss of influence, the generals appointed their own governors to Egypt, who acted as their own rather than the Caliph's agents.

Independence under Ahmad Ibn Tulun: The most famous Turkish governor and the man responsible for the inauguration of Egypt's medieval era of greatness was Ahmad Ibn Tulun. The son of a Turkish slave, he had been raised and educated in the 'Abbasid

its division into separate districts, each housing a different contingent of his multiracial army. At its center was the great mosque of Ibn Tulun, completed in 879, the finest surviving example of Muslim architecture from the High 'Abbasid period in the world.

Ibu Tulun died in 884 and was succeeded by his 20-year-old son Khumarawayh. With his father's army he extended the borders of the Tulunid state to the Euphrates, forcing the 'Abbasids to recognize his sovereignty.

In 896 Khumarawayh was murdered by slaves from his harem and was succeeded by his two sons and a brother, noteworthy only for the extravagance of their life-style and incompetence of their rule. After exhausting the state treasury and alienating the army, they were deposed and murdered, one after the other, leaving Egypt too weak to resist the reestablishment of direct 'Abbasid rule in 905. As an example to future rebels against 'Abbasid authority, the city of *Al-Qatai'* was razed to the ground, only the mosque of Ibn Tulun being spared, while the surviving male members of the Tulunid family were taken in chains to Baghdad.

For the next 30 years Egypt was again ruled by a series of oppressive and ineffectual provincial governors, appointed from Iraq. The growing threat of the Shi'i Fatimid dynasty, centered in Tunisia, who twice invaded Egypt during this period, however, demanded a more effective form of government in the Nile Valley. The 'Abbasids were therefore

collapsed in the face of the Fatimid invasion of 969.

The Origins of the Fatimids: The Fatimids were a radical Shi'i sect that believed their Imams (leaders) were the only rightful rulers of the Muslim world. Basing their claim on their direct descent from the Prophet Muhammad through his daughter Fatima, they viewed the 'Abbasids as usurpers, and dreamed of uniting all of Islam under the banner of Shi'ism.

The origins of this rivalry date back to the first years of the Islamic era, when the early Muslims were divided over who was to succeed Muhammad on his death in 632. The majority of his followers, who were to become the Sunnis, favored the election of one of their members as Caliph, while a minority,

compelled to allow the establishment in 935 of a new semi-autonomous state in Egypt, founded by Muhammad Ibn Tuglij, known as "the Ikhshid," an ancient Central Asian royal title. His main task was the creation of a strong Egyptian buffer state to prevent further Fatimid eastern expansion.

On his death in 946, he was nominally succeeded by his young sons, but the real power was in the hands of their regent, the Nubian eunuch Kafur. Kafur's strong rule held the Ikhshid state together, but on his death it

Left, engraving of the Mosque of Ibn Tulun from the *Description de l'Egypts*. Above, vaulted *Iwan* in the 14th-Century mosque of Sultan Hassan.

who became known as the Shi'a, supported a hereditary principle, which would preserve the Caliphate within the Prophet's family.

Among the most extreme of the various Shi'i sects that grew out of this conflict were the Isma'ilis, of whom the Fatimids were the most successful members. They attributed a semi-divine status to their Imams, the Fatimid Caliphs, believing that they possessed a special esoteric knowledge which made them infallible and thus the only men capable of leading the Umma to perfection. The Imams controlled a vast secret organization, the Da'wa, which would send highly trained agents throughout the Muslim world, winning converts and preparing the way for the eventual takeover of the Isma'ili Caliphs. Their message, combining a simple messianic promise of justice for all with a complex religio-philosophic doctrine, based on neo-Platonic thought, appealed to illiterate and intellectual alike, causing deep concern among the Sunni 'Abbasids, now in marked decline.

The conversion of the Kutama Berbers of Algeria by an Isma'ili agent in the early 10th Century supplied the Fatimids with an army and a North African kingdom, but their dreams were set on Egypt. The death of Kafur supplied the Fatimid Caliph al Mu'izz with the chance he had been waiting for.

The Founding of Al-Qahirah: In 1969 Egypt fell to his general Jawhar, a military slave of European origin, whose first action was the construction of a new royal enclosure to house the victorious Al-Mu'izz and his Shi'i government. The new Fatimid capital was named *Al-Qahira,* "The Subduer", which was later corrupted by Italian merchants into *Cairo.*

Separated from the predominantly Sunni population of Fustat by a mile of wasteland, Al-Qahirah's high walls could only be penetrated by the Isma'ili elite. Within were two great palaces, the home of the Imam and his court bureaucracy. Its religious and intellectual center was the mosque of Al-Azhar, the headquarters of the Da'wa and the main congregational mosque of the city. The rest of Al-Qahirah's 300 acres were filled with gardens, hippodromes and military barracks housing the Imam's army.

The initial military success of the Fatimids was short-lived. After gaining control of Palestine and the holy cities of Mecca and Medina, they encountered stiff Byzantine resistance in Northern Syria. Attempts to strengthen their army with Turkish slave soldiers only succeeded in fostering a dangerous rivalry between their original Berber supporters and the new Eastern recruits. To offset their military failure the Fatimids turned to the realm of trade, creating a commercial empire with links stretching from China in the east to the Italian city states in the west. Fustat became a major trade emporium, as well as one of the principal centers of artistic production in the Muslim world. Aided by a strong navy and the growth of a prosperous middle class, Fatimid Egypt became fabulously wealthy.

Secluded in the luxury of their fortress city, the Fatimid Imams underwent a dramatic change. Plans for the conquest of the 'Abbasid empire were postponed indefinitely and the more radical aspects of their esoteric teachings were toned down. Little effort was made to convert the predominantly Christian and Sunni Muslim native population to Shi'ism, while the external activities of the Da'wa were largely occupied with establishing trade connections with sympathetic foreign powers. As a minority Muslim sect in Egypt, unconcerned with proselytizing, the Fatimids were extremely tolerant, employing Sunnis, Christians and Jews equally in the runing of their state. Ibn Killis, an islamicized Jew, was Grand Wazir under al-Mu'izz and his son Al-Aziz, and was largely responsible for creating the Fatimid administrative and financial systems. Al-Aziz's powerful and influential Christian wife ensured that her co-religionists filled the bureaucracy of her husband's government, causing some discontent among the Sunni Muslim population of Egypt.

The Mad Caliph: The shift from a revolutionary millenniumistic theocracy to a conservative and materialistic state deeply conconcerned the third Fatimid Caliph Al-Hakim (996-1021). Universally described as insane by medieval Arab historians, Al-Hakim was preoccupied with revitalizing the spiritual mission of the Isma'ili movement and with the maintenance of his personal power in the face of Fatimid governmental opposition. His measures were usually extreme, brutal and unpredictable, but not without purpose. His persecution of Christians and Jews was an attempt at breaking their governmental influence and a means of winning popular Muslim support. Decrees aimed against women, forbidding them from leaving their houses or possessing independent wealth, besides being a concession to public morality, were probably directed against his sister, Sitt al-Mulk, an influential opponent of his policies. When he allowed a group of extremist Iranian Isma'ilis to proclaim his divinity in 1017, he was only carrying the spiritual pretensions of his family to their ultimate limits. In this, however, Al-Hakim had gone too far. Riots of protest broke out in Fustat and his radical devotees were forced to flee to Lebanon where they founded the Druze religion, which still believes Al-Hakim to be the incarnation of God.

The Fatimid hierarchy, feeling threatened by Al-Hakim's eccentric behaviour, decided the unstable Imam had to go. While he was riding his donkey alone in the Muqattam Hills at night, as was his custom, Al-Hakim mysteriously disappeared, almost certainly murdered on the orders of his sister and the

Right, moving van with the 16th-Century mosque of Qanibay in the background. Near Citadel, Cairo.

58

Fatimid elite, who now took charge of the government.

Fatimid Hey-day: During the long reign of Al-Mustansir (1036-1094) Fustat reached the peak of its prosperity. With a population of almost half a million living in five-storey buildings, complete with running water and sophisticated sewer systems, it was one of the great cities of its age. Despite Egypt's wealth the Fatimid state rapidly began to decline. The Turkish troops, who had largely replaced their Berber rivals, were unruly and a constant threat to internal security. As a countermeasure Al-Mustansir's mother, Umm Ma'add, a former Sudanese slave, who now ruled in her son's name, began employing Sudanese troops to check the powers of the Turks. A civil war ensued, leaving the Caliph a puppet of successive military cliques, constantly fighting amongst themselves.

A sequence of seven low Niles between 1066 and 1072 plunged the country into further chaos. Famine and plague spread throughout the Nile Valley, reducing the people of Fustat to cannibalism. The Turkish soldiers looted the Fatimid palaces on the pretext of arrears of pay, emptying the Caliph's treasury and dispersing his great library of 100,000 books. Al-Mustansir secretly called in Badr al-Jamali, the Fatimid's Armenian governor at Acre in Palestine, to restore order. A surprise attack on Al-Qahirah in 1072 crushed all opposition and won Badr al-Jamali full dictatorial powers. He now had to face an impending invasion by the Seljuk Turks, masters of an empire stretching from Central Asia to Egypt's eastern border. The walls of Al-Qahirah, with massive new gates, were rebuilt to withstand the expected siege. A segment of these walls still survives in excellent condition on the northern side of the royal city.

The sudden break-up of the Seljuk empire after 1092 saved the Fatimids from certain defeat, but left the Middle East crowded with petty Muslim states. Their lack of unity facilitated the victories of the first Crusade of 1099, launched in response to the Seljuk conquest of Jerusalem a few years earlier. The Crusaders were themselves divided into four, often hostile, principalities, more concerned with their individual short-term needs than with the establishment of a single strong Christian kingdom.

Left, traditional festive sugar dolls, called "brides".

The rise of the Zangids of Mosul, who began absorbing their Muslim neighbors and preaching *Jihad* against the Crusaders in the first half of the 12th Century, meant that it was just a matter of time before the Christians were encircled and picked off one by one. Both sides realized that Egypt weakened by dynastic and military rivalries, yet incredibly wealthy, was the key to victory. Whoever controlled her vast resources could dominate the whole region.

Salah ad-Din Takes Power: The Fatimids tried to play one side against the other, but in 1169 were compelled to submit to the Zangid general Salah ad-Din, who abolished the Fatimid Caliphate in 1171, reestablishing Sunni Islam in Egypt. The Fatimids were the last Arab dynasty to rule Egypt. From this point on the country would be under the control of Turks and related peoples from the eastern Islamic world, a situation that would continue until the 1952 revolution.

In theory Egypt was now a part of the Zangid empire, ruled by Nur ad-Din, a man dedicated to *jihad* against the crusaders; in reality it was firmly in the hands of his Kurdish general Salah ad-Din. Refusing to leave Egypt until it was secure from crusader attack and Fatimid resurgence, Salah ad-Din fell out with his master, who wanted Egypt's resources for his own war effort. Sending only apologies and excuses, Salah ad-Din set about building a power base. His enlarged army was stationed in the newly constructed Citadel, situated on an outcrop of the Muqattam hills, about halfway between Al-Qahirah and Fustat. The two urban centers were linked to the new fortress by a series of walls, to facilitate the defense of the Egyptian capital, setting the stage for the future development of one unified city.

In order to uproot the memory of Fatimid rule, Al-Qahirah was deprived of its royal status by being opened to the common people. A huge northward population shift followed, resulting in the decline of Fustat as the major center of trade and production in Egypt. A new educational system, based upon the *madrasah,* a state supported institution for the teaching of Islamic law, was introduced from the east to ensure the establishment of an orthodox Sunni bureaucracy. Only *madrasah* graduates, well grounded in Sunni legal practice, would be employed in the new government of Salah ad-Din, eliminating all Shi'i sympathizers from positions of power in the state.

Resisting the Crusades: The death of Nur ad-Din in 1174 and the subsequent break-up of his empire left Salah ad-Din undisputed master of Egypt. He spent the next 13 years conquering the divided Zangid principalities of Syria and placing them under the control of his family, the Ayyubids. With Egypt and Syria once again united, Salah ad-Din turned on the Crusaders, who were decisively defeated in 1187 and confined to a few coastal towns.

The capture of Jerusalem and Palestine established Salah ad-Din as a champion of Islam, but also triggered off the Third Crusade in 1189. Led by Richard the Lion-Heart of England and Philip II of France, the Christians retook Acre, but were unable to advance further. The peace settlement of 1192 recognized Salah ad-Din's gains, leaving the Crusaders in possession of a small coastal strip of Palestine. Having

Ayyubid neighbors than of an external enemy. The sultans, as a result, were hesitant about engaging in serious warfare, preferring to use diplomacy to achieve their aims. In particular, military conflicts with the Christians of the Palestinian coast were avoided as a matter of policy, out of fear of sparking off a new Crusade.

This threat remained very real, as the crusading zeal of Western Europe, motivated now more by the promise of material gain than by spiritual objectives, was increasingly directed against Egypt rather than Palestine.

The Sultan Al-Kamil (1218-1238) was able to defeat a Christian invasion of the Nile Delta in 1221, but to avoid a repetition of the experience came to a peaceful agreement, with the Holy Roman Emperor Fre-

reestablished Muslim unity in the region and broken the power of the Christians, Salah ad-Din died the following year a satisfied man.

The Ayyubid empire created by Salah ad-Din was a federation of sovereign city states, loosely held together by family solidarity. The rulers of Egypt, the wealthiest and most centralized of the provinces, exercised a vague suzerainty over their kinsmen, which they used to limit the endless intrigues and power struggles that dominated Ayyubid internal politics. As the head of the family, the sultans of Egypt had the right to demand military aid from their brothers and cousins in Syria, but this was often reluctantly given, the minor princes being more afraid of their

derick II in 1229, whereby Jerusalem was declared an open city, accessible to Muslims and Christians alike. This solution to the crusading problem proved unpopular with religious fanatics on both sides and hostilities were soon resumed.

The last major Ayyubid sultan, As-Salih (1240-1249), whose ruthless rise to power had made enemies of most of his relatives, could no longer rely on the support of his Syrian kinsmen. Faced with the growing threat of a Mongol invasion from the east, led by the sons of Chingiz Khan, who had already devastated Iran and eastern Europe, Al-Salih began building a Turkish slave army, loyal only to him, to defend the Ayyubid state.

The fighting abilities of As-Salih's new military slaves or Mamluks, who were known as the Bahris after their original barracks next to the Nile River (Bahr al Nil), were put to the test in 1249, when the Sixth Crusade of St. Louis IX of France invaded Egypt. During the course of the hostilities As-Salih died, but news of his death was concealed by his wife, Shagar ad-Durr (Tree of Pearls) and the Mamluk amirs, to allow his son, Turan Shah, to reach Egypt and claim the Ayyubid Sultanate. Turan Shah arrived in time to witness the defeat of the French king by the Mamluks in 1250. Alarmed by the power of the Bahris, the new Sultan began to replace them with his own men. Fresh from a major victory and confident of their strength, the Mamluks were not to be ousted so easily. Instead, they murdered Turan Shah and seized control of Egypt.

The Bahri Mamluks: To legitimize their *coup d'etat*, the Mamluks proclaimed Shagar Ad-Durr Sultan on the strength of her marriage to As-Salih. The Ayyubid princes of Syria, refusing to accept the loss of the richest province of their empire to a woman, prepared for war. Needing a man to lead her army, Shagar ad-Durr married the Mamluk commander, Aybek, who now ruled as sultan with his new wife. The Ayyubids were defeated in 1251 and Aybek, encouraged by his victory, conquered Palestine. The 'Abbasid Caliph, afraid of the approaching Mongol army, formalized a peace settlement in 1253 between the two sides, in the name of Muslim unity.

To strengthen his position, Aybek in 1257 began negotiating a second marriage with a princess of Mosul. Unwilling to share her power with another woman, Shagar ad-Durr had her husband murdered in his bath. Aybek's Mamluks, enraged by the death of their master, seized his queen and handed her over to the former wife of Aybek, whom he had been compelled to divorce by Shagar Ad-Durr upon becoming sultan. Egypt's only woman sultan was then beaten to death with wooden bathclogs, in the presence of her rival.

The Mamluks had proved their military prowess against the Crusaders and the Ayyubids, but were now called upon to face a far greater threat, the heathen Mongols, who in 1257 swept through Iraq into Syria, brutually crushing all Muslim resistance. Undefeated in battle and with the resources of an empire stretching from China to the

borders of Egypt, the Central Asian hordes seemed on the verge of extinguishing Muslim civilization in the Middle East. Only the Mamluks remained to stop them and at the battle of 'Ayn Jalut in 1260 they did, becoming the saviors of Islam.

Under their first great sultans, Baybars al-Bunduqdari (1260-1277) and Qalawun (1280-1290), the Mamluks emerged as the foremost military power of their age. Kept in top fighting shape by the constant threat of the Mongols, now centered in Iran, the Mamluks recaptured Syria and expelled the last of the Crusaders from the Palestinian coast.

The Mamluk System: The political system created by Baybars was based on a military slave oligarchy. Young Qipchaq Turks would be brought to Egypt as slaves, converted to Islam and given a thorough military training. On completion of their education they would be freed and enrolled in the private army of one of the great Mamluk amirs, who collectively controlled all of Egypt's resources and governmental positions. The most powerful amir would be chosen as Sultan. Although the position possessed certain military advantages, the Sultan was rarely strong enough to dispense with the services of the men who had brought him to power.

The foundation of the system was the intense loyalty the individual Mamluk felt for his military house (*bayt*). His political fortunes were linked to those of his amir, whose rise or fall in the state hierarchy would determine his own advancement. If his *bayt* was successful, the common Mamluk could expect to be promoted to the rank of amir and in time even to the Sultanate. Success required great solidarity however, coupled with extreme ruthlessness in the struggle with the rival houses. The Mamluk political environment was therefore dominated by intrigue and the striving for power amongst the *bayts*. The Sultan tried to manipulate these conflicts to maintain his position, but if he was unsuccessful, he would be destroyed by the ambitions of his amirs.

Position within the Mamluk hierarchy was dependent upon slave origins. The children of Mamluks were prevented from following their fathers' military career and as a result the army required a steady flow of new Turkish slaves to replenish its ranks.

The Reign of An-Nasir Muhammad: The one exception to this rule was that the son of a sultan often succeeded his father as a stop-gap ruler without power, allowing the Amirs time to determine who was the strongest without resorting to civil war. Once this issue had been decided the son was deposed and re-

Left, Rosetta is famed for its brick architecture and lattice-work windows.

placed by a sultan with real authority. In this manner Qalawun's son An-Nasir Muhammad was made nominal sultan by his father's amirs in 1294, at the age of nine. After ruling for a year he was deposed, but then reinstated in 1299, when the amirs fell out amongst themselves. Throughout his second reign An-Nasir was under the strict tutelage of the Amirs Salar and Baybars al-Jashankir, the real powers behind the throne. To prevent him from establishing his independence, the young sultan was kept in a state of penury, a humiliation An-Nasir never forgot. Finding his situation unbearable, An Nasir abdicated in 1309 and retired to a distant Syrian fortress, where he began to organize a loyal army. Taking advantage of the power struggle that followed his retirement, An-Nasir regained the Sultanate in 1310, beginning his third reign, which was to last for 31 years.

Having been raised in an atmosphere of intrigue and double-dealing An-Nasir emerged at the age of 25 as a ruthless, suspicious and absolutely despotic sultan. Resolving to rule alone, after the miseries of his youth, he murdered the amirs of his father one by one, replacing them with his own men. Unwilling to trust even the amirs of his own *bayt,* An-Nasir inaugurated an era of peace to prevent arming a potential rival with the command of an army. A period of flourishing trade and great prosperity ensued that witnessed the apex of Muslim civilization in Egypt.

An-Nasir was a great builder and patron of the arts; and it was under his rule that Cairo grew into a single unified city, filled with great palaces and splendid mosques. The mosque of Al-Maridani, completed in 1341, survives as a testimony to this golden age of Mamluk architecture.

An-Nasir's success in mastering the Mamluk system brought about the beginning of its decline. So firmly did he hold the reins of power that on his death in 1341 no amir was strong enough to replace him. Instead he was succeeded by a series of weak sons and grandsons, manipulated from behind by shifting coalitions of An-Nasir's amirs.

His policy of peace, while filling the state treasury, caused the Mamluks to neglect their military training. A whole generation grew up without ever having fought a major war, a serious deficiency for a state founded on martial superiority. Instead the Mamluks devoted themselves to competing with each other for political and cultural preeminence. Their lust for power was matched only by their love of luxury and of grand buildings, with which they continued to beautify Cairo.

The reign of Sultan Hasan (1347-1361) saw the outbreak of the Black Death, which rocked the economic foundations of Egypt by decimating its population. Whole districts of Cairo were wiped out, indirectly benefiting the sultan, who inherited the property and valuables of the plague's victims. With this unexpected windfall Hasan financed his great mosque, completed in 1362, the grandest of all Mamluk buildings.

The Circassian Mamluks: For 41 years after the death of An-Nasir, 12 of his direct descendants ruled Egypt as nominal sultans. In 1382, however, the Amir Barquq (1382-1399) seized control and began distributing all positions of power to his fellow Circassians. This second Mamluk dynasty maintained the same political system as the Qipchaq predecessors. An important difference, however, was that the Circassians were brought to Egypt not as boys, but as young men. Instead of being molded by the rigors of a Mamluk education, they arrived in Cairo with clear ideas of how to manipulate the system to their own benefit. Ambitious, unruly and deficient in their military training, they were a terror to the inhabitants of Egypt, but poor soldiers.

Unable to defeat the invading Tamerlane in 1400, the Circassians watched helplessly as the new Central Asian conqueror devastated their Syrian province. Repeated outbreaks of plague throughout the 15th Century decimated the ranks of the unacclimatized Mamluks, whose replacement was both costly and difficult. The external threat of strong neighbors and the chronic outbreak of factional fighting at home further drained the treasury, forcing the sultans to adopt the short-sighted economic policies of excessive taxation, debasement of the currency and the introduction of state-owned monopolies.

Despite the decline in their military and economic position, the Circassian Mamluks continued to live and build in the grand Bahri manner. The Sultan Qaitbay (1468-1495), a master politician, managed to maintain the prestige of the Mamluk state, while devoting himself to his true love, architecture. His tomb complex in the Northern Cemetery is the most refined and elegant of his many great works.

The chief failing of the Circassians, however, was their refusal to adopt modern military methods. Bred to be a cavalry elite they despised gunpowder as unmanly. Their major rivals in the early 16th Century, the Ottoman Turks, had no such snobbish qualms. When the two forces finally clashed at the battle of Marj Dabiq in 1516, the Mamluks were literally blown off the field by superior cannon fire. Following this victory, the Ottoman Sultan Selim the Grim conquered the Mamluk Sultanate and Cairo became provincial capital of a new Muslim empire centered in Istanbul.

Egypt as an Ottoman Province: The Ottomans, engaged in continual warfare with the Safavid dynasty of Iran and the Christian West, could not afford to spare the necessary men to uproot the Mamluks from Egypt completely. Instead they were incorporated into the Ottoman ruling elite and held in check by a provincial governor and a garrison of crack Ottoman troops, the Janissaries. The Mamluks were therefore allowed to maintain their *bayt* system, continuing to import new Circassian slaves, albeit on a drastically reduced scale.

Cairo, although no longer a major political center, remained an important commercial Spanish silver from the New World, upset the balance of power in Egypt. The office of governor was now sold to the highest bidder, and then re-sold at the first opportunity, to supply the central treasury with a steady flow of cash. The governors, rarely ruling for more than three years, could never therefore establish effective control over Egypt. The Janissaries, forced into local trade by the steady devaluation of their fixed salaries, became little more than armed shopkeepers and artisans.

The rise of 'Ali Bey al Kabir (1760-1772) saw the remergence of the Mamluks as an international power. By destroying the rival *bayts,* the governor, and the Janissaries, 'Ali Bey became master of Egypt with the title "Shaykh al-Balad." Expanding into Arabia

emporium, despite the loss of much of its international trade to Europe. The Europeans had been forced by the high prices caused by the Mamluk monopolies to search for new routes to the East that bypassed Egypt. The discoveries of Columbus and da Gama gradually transformed Ottoman Cairo into an economic backwater, sustained largely by a newly-developed trade in coffee.

In the 17th Century, military defeats brought decline to the Ottoman empire; and rampant inflation, caused by the flood of

Above, painting on the wall of a house in Luxor.

and Syria, he was on the verge of reestablishing the Mamluk empire when he was betrayed by his lieutenant Abu'l-Dhahab, secretly in the pay of the Ottomans. Abu'l-Dhahab was rewarded for his treachery by being murdered, in 1775, by an Ottoman agent.

Deprived of its strong leadership, the Mamluk *bayt* of 'Ali Bey fragmented and Egypt was plunged into a devastating civil war, which lasted until 1791. Although order was restored by the victory of Murad Bey and Ibrahim Bey, the economy of the country was in ruins. In this unsettled state, Egypt was invaded in 1798 by the French under Napoleon Bonaparte.

The French Expedition: On the morning of

July 21, 1798, not quite under the impassive gaze of the Sphinx, the combined musketry and artillery of 29,000 French troops smashed a headlong onslaught of Mamluk cavalry. Like Alexander the Great's conquests 21 centuries earlier, which led to a millennium of European dominance in the Mediterranean, the Battle of the Pyramids marked a turning of the tide against the East. It also roused Egypt from the slumber of 300 years as an Ottoman province.

The conquest of Egypt was ostensibly carried out on the orders of Bonaparte's superiors in Paris, whose overt objective was to threaten Britain's lucrative Indian trade from a Middle Eastern stronghold. In fact, however, the French expedition was largely inspired by irrational factors, of which by no means the least was Bonaparte's own romantic pursuit of glory, his notion of the inevitable triumph of will: like Alexander's Greeks and Macedonians, the new European invaders were led by a charismatic young fanatic who habitually confused his own lust for power with the destiny of his people.

A scientific mission comprised of 60 *savants* accompanied the expedition. Their task was to compile a complete dossier on Egypt's antiquities, people, topography, flora and fauna. The introduction to their massive 24-volume *Description de l'Égypte* hints that it was above all a militant sense of national grandeur that had drawn the French to Egypt.

Bonaparte's expedition was doomed from the start. Within a week of the raising of the *tricolore* over Salah ad-Din's Citadel, the British had summarily sunk the French fleet off Abu Qir and the Mamluks under Murad Bey had fallen back to Upper Egypt, from which they continued to conduct a successful guerilla war.

In Cairo, Egyptians meanwhile looked upon Bonaparte's attempts to clothe the ideals of *liberté, egalité,* and *fraternité* in the veil of Islam and to pose as the liberator of the country from the wicked Mamluks with equal scorn. While he strutted about in oriental garb, hobnobbing with the sheikhs of Al-Azhar, his officers, constrained by the loss of their gold with the sunken fleet, imposed extortionate taxes on the populace. Resistance was met with the burning of villages and daily beheadings at the city gates. Three hundred houses were requisitioned in Cairo for French use; and republican troops, ignoring instructions to feign Islam, caroused drunkenly in the streets, creating further enmity. An uprising in October was only crushed by blasting away at the center of the city with grapeshot and heavy cannon fire.

Hoping to regain momentum and impress his constituency in France, Bonaparte decided to embark on a campaign in Palestine. Again, superior French artillery brought quick victories. Gaza fell within a few days, then Jaffa, where he had two thousand Turkish prisoners herded down to the beach and shot in cold blood. These efforts to terrorize opponents into submission failed, however, and at the fortress of Acre in northern Palestine the French were brought to a halt. Reinforced from the sea by a British fleet, the Turkish garrison held out for two months, while Bonaparte's army was decimated by malaria and dysentery. By the time he saw reason and opted for retreat, his force had dwindled to 15,000.

Despite the propaganda churned out in Arabic by his printing press — the first in modern Egypt — his attempt to portray the Palestine *débâcle* as a victory was not greeted with enthusiasm in Cairo at all. At last, with communications to Paris cut by the marauding British, his own troops disillusioned, and the natives growing still more restless daily, he wisely concluded that his personal ambitions were unlikely to be served by further lingering. Fourteen months after his arrival, Bonaparte packed his bags and slipped home in such apparent haste that General Kléber, Bonaparte's second-in-command, received the first news of his appointment as the new General-in-Chief of the Army of the Orient scrawled on an abandoned scrap of notepaper.

Although the French remained in Egypt two more years, defeating two Turkish attempts to dislodge them, the hopelessness of their mission finally forced them to succumb. Kléber was assassinated at Azbakiyyah in June of 1800 and the task of negotiating with an Anglo-Ottoman force that landed in the Delta in the autumn of 1801 was left to his successor. Mercifully, the French, now numbering only 7,000, were allowed to return to France. In three years of occupation, they had failed to meet any of their strategic objectives. Britain still dominated the seas, the Ottomans had reinforced their hold on the Levant, and the Egyptians, though impressed by the power of European science, technology and military organization, had rejected what little they saw of the infidel's civilization. The noise and the shock had been great, but in Egypt the grand Expedition had done little more than drop the ominous calling card of imperialism.

Turco-Syrian tiles at the Mosque of Aqsunqur, Cairo, right.

67

MUHAMMAD ALI AND MODERN EGYPT

Founder of Modern Egypt: Muhammad Ali Pasha, who held autocratic sway over its people for nearly the entire first half of the 19th Century, is credited with having laid the foundations of modern Egypt. In addition to building an empire, he carried out reforms aimed at modernizing Egypt itself and founded the dynasty that was to rule it for almost 150 years, until the revolution of 1952.

Muhammad Ali was born in 1769 in Kavalla, Macedonia, in what is now part of modern Greece, but then belonged to the Ottoman Empire. Early in his career he served as a tax collector, then obtained a commission in the imperial army, entering Egypt as second in command of an Albanian contingent when the sultan sent Ottoman troops to join the British in expelling the French, who had occupied the country since 1798. After the French and British troops left Egypt, the Ottoman troops stayed on to reassert the sultan's authority. During the four ensuing years, however, Egypt was reduced to anarchy, with Mamluk beys fighting among one another and against the Ottomans, who were divided along ethnic lines and fought among themselves. In 1805, having had enough of chaos, the people of Cairo finally turned to Muhammad Ali to restore order; and in May of that year, on behalf of the populace, the Rector of Al-Azhar declared the deposition of the Ottoman appointee, naming Muhammad Ali the new viceroy. Such an appointment was the prerogative of the sultan in Constantinople, but the sultan himself, presented with the *fait accompli*, confirmed the Cairenes' choice a few weeks later.

Despite the sultan's acceptance of Muhammad Ali as viceroy, his position was tenuous. Defeating a British force at Rosetta in 1807 consolidated his power, but bold steps were still required. Boldest and bloodiest was his extirpation of the rebellious Mamluk beys. On the first of March, 1811, he invited 470 adherents of the leading *bayt* to a ceremony in the Citadel. Assembled to take their leave, the departing Mamluks had to pass downward through a narrow passageway to a locked gate, where the Pasha had arranged for their massacre by his Albanians. This incident left no opposition and for the next 37 years his authority was absolute in Egypt.

Preceding pages: interior of the mosque of Muhammad Ali at the Citadel, Cairo. Left, a contemporary engraving of Muhammad Ali Pasha with his *shibuk*.

A New Empire: Among Muhammad Ali's best known undertakings are his military conquests. In 1811, at the request of the Turkish Sultan Mahmud II, he sent troops into the Arabian province of the Hijaz to combat the Wahhabi movement, a fundamentalist sect of Islam that threatened the sultan's authority. In 1816 Egyptian troops entered the Nejd, the Wahhabi's homeland, and by 1818 all of western and central Arabia was under Egyptian control.

After the Arabian campaigns, Muhammad Ali sent an expedition under one of his sons up the Nile to gain control of the Sudan's mineral resources and its active slave trade, which he saw as a possible source of manpower for the army. Next came campaigns in Greece. At the request of the sultan, an army commanded by his son Ibrahim was sent to Crete in 1822 to quell an uprising against Ottoman control. In 1824 a second expedition, again commanded by Ibrahim, sailed from Alexandria for the Morea, now known as the Peloponessus. The Peloponessus was subjugated, then Missolonghi was taken, but this reassertion of Ottoman power provoked the major European states, Britain, France and Russia. An allied fleet sent to mediate ended by sinking the entire Egyptian fleet at Navarino in 1827.

Muhammad Ali's last successful expansionist venture was his Syrian expedition of 1831. Using a quarrel with a governor as a pretext, he sent in Ibrahim with an army of peasant conscripts. At the end of 10 months all of Syria had acknowledged him as overlord. In 1832 Ibrahim pushed on into Anatolia, defeating the Ottomans at Konya. Before he could occupy Constantinople, however, Russian intervention again brought European interests into play; and in 1833 an agreement was signed between the sultan and his unruly vassal, by which Egypt was formally accorded rule over Crete and Syria in return for an annual tribute.

With the Sudan, the Hijaz, and these new acquisitions, the Egyptian empire rivaled the Ottoman in size, although Egypt itself was still nominally a part of the Ottoman empire and Muhammad Ali still only a Pasha, the sultan's viceroy. In 1839 the sultan attempted to regain Syria by force. Ibrahim's own crushing victory over an Ottoman army at Nezib was followed by the desertion of the Ottoman navy to Alexandria and these two events led to a European crisis. Britain, Russia and Austria, desperate to maintain the Sick Man of Europe, sided with the sultan, while France supported Muhammad Ali. British and Ottoman troops invaded Syria, a British fleet anchored off Alexandria, a British squadron occupied Aden, and France mobilized for a European war. This catastrophe was averted when Muhammad Ali signed an agreement by which his rule was to be made hereditary, but which also confirmed the sultan's suzerainty.

The terms of this suzerainty were agreed upon under European pressure in 1841: the Egyptian navy, forbidden to build new ships, was virtually abolished; the Egyptian army was reduced to 18,000, who were to wear Ottoman uniforms and be commanded by Ottoman senior officers; all of Ibrahim's conquests were to become Ottoman provinces administered directly from Constantinople;

principal export. By 1840 he had planted more than 16 million trees and built roads and bridges where none had ever existed. Before Muhammad Ali, in fact, Egypt was a country where wheeled vehicles had long since passed out of use: the 30-odd carriages he imported for his government and household are thus the direct ancestors not only of the cars and trucks in modern Egypt, but also of all the "traditional" carts.

Land tenure and tax systems he reformed by nationalizing all property and making himself titular owner of all land. Under this *étatiste* system, government monopolies marketed almost all important goods and agricultural produce, paying the peasants fixed wages calculated to encourage production. The new scheme eliminated the iniquitous tax farming

and the viceregal succession would devolve upon the eldest male of the Muhammad Ali line.

Modernizing On All Fronts: Shorn of his acquisitions abroad, the Pasha turned his remaining energies back to the task of modernizing Egypt. The ultimate aim of these endeavors may have been his family's aggrandizement, but the benefits to his country were enormous. They include, for example, the massive upgrading and extension of Egypt's irrigation system and the introduction of a multitude of exotic plants, many of them now naturalized in Egypt. Rice, indigo and sugarcane were massively encouraged, as well as the cultivation of long-staple ("Egyptian") cotton, which would later become the country's

system that had prevailed earlier; and it is generally agreed that the lot of peasants was somewhat improved, especially after 1841, when they could go back to tilling the soil. They still remained liable to the *corvée*, however, an obligation to provide labor for such public works as cleaning canals, which would become increasingly resented. The population nearly doubled during Muhammad Ali's reign, approaching 5 million in 1848.

Muhammad Ali also created modern industries in Egypt, initially to supply only his army and navy, but later to supply the country as a whole. Beginning with an industrial complex at Bulaq, the Nile port of Cairo, where the famous Bulaq Press was set up, he built shipyards, foundries and armament factories. Tex-

72

tile mills, the basis of the European Industrial Revolution, soon followed. Since a primary aim was to avoid dependence upon Europe, the infant textile industry was protected by embargoes and subsidies, but this step toward economic independence was foiled, like his foreign policy, by European interests: the provisions of 1841 made Egypt subject to the tariffs that prevailed throughout the Ottoman empire, which allowed cheaper imports, mainly from Britain, to flood into Egypt.

In other respects his efforts were more successful. The Bulaq Press was to become the most distinguished publisher in the Arab world. Its production of printed books was an essential element in the creation of a new intellectual élite, which would gradually replace the European experts recruited during his early

Egyptian educational system.

The one subject on which Muhammad Ali is known to have been fanatical was public health. Swamps were drained, cemeteries were moved, hospitals, infirmaries and asylums were built, a school for midwives was established, and French-trained physicians were appointed as public health officers in all provinces to see that measures were carried out. In Cairo accumulated rubbish was cleared and seasonal ponds, like the famous one at Azbakiyyah, were filled, while the beginnings were made of a new street system that would allow the use of wheeled vehicles. The city's dancing prostitutes, who appear to have fascinated European visitors of the period, were banished to Upper Egypt.

In Alexandria Muhammad Ali established a

years in power. To form this élite, new secular educational institutions were created, the first in Egypt since the Ptolemies, and from 1813 onward the brightest young men were sent off for further studies to Europe. The rewards of this system and the policy behind it would first be visible a generation or so later under Muhammad Ali's grandson Ismail. Subsequently suppressed by the British for 25 years, the system had already produced future leaders, who would not rest until it was revived, to become the core of the present

Left, Muhammad Ali Square, Alexandria. Above left, Ibrahim Pasha, right, Khedive Ismail, a spendthrift but visionary ruler.

Quarantine Commission, thus identifying the city once again as the country's main port of entry after 1000 years during which Rosetta, Damietta and even Qusayr had been more important. Shipyards, military bases and a new palace for the Pasha himself were made practicable by digging a new canal to link the city once again with the Nile. Entire new quarters would be laid out in the European style, as it became not only the country's summer capital, but also the home of its largest foreign enclave, enriched by the cotton trade. It was here that the Pasha died in 1849, 80 years old, but predeceased by his son, the gallant Ibrahim, to whom he had given the viceregal throne less than 11 months before.

Muhammad Ali's Successors: It was unfortunate that. Ibrahim ruled as viceroy only five weeks, since he had shown himself to be a good leader. His nephew, Abbas, the only son of Muhammad Ali's second son, Tussun, became viceroy and immediately rejected all his policies. While Muhammad Ali had been eager for Western agricultural and technical ideas, particularly those of the French, Abbas was xenophobic, disliking the French in particular and favoring the British, to whom he granted a railway concession, only as the lesser of two evils. A reactionary traditionalist, he summarily expelled all the French advisors upon whom his grandfather had depended, closed all secular or European schools, and turned for support to religious leaders, including the sultan as the Caliph of Islam. He was as autocratic as his grandfather, but earned the

agriculture and education. The railway opened in 1855 and Said's private train can be seen in Cairo's Railway Museum. Said also instituted new policies that were less autocratic than those of his father, abolishing certain government monopolies and restoring private ownership of land.

Open to European influences, Said is perhaps best known for his friendship with Ferdinand de Lesseps, to whom he granted a concession for the Suez Canal. As originally granted in 1854 this concession was one of the great swindles of all time, with terms extremely disadvantageous to Egypt. It was rumored, in fact, that Said did not even bother to read the concession before signing it. Recognizing later the enormity of his error, he managed to have it renegotiated and got somewhat more

Le Caire
Ataba-el-Kadra

gratitude of the peasants by his negligence, which left them in comparative peace, even though he milked them by restoring the old tax-farming system. The economy was of no interest to him except as a source of revenue. Apart from the British railway completed after his death, the sole positive relic of his six-year rule was that he left full coffers and no foreign debt, an accomplishment that his two successors were unable to repeat.

When Abbas was murdered in 1854 by two of his personal bodyguards, his uncle Said, nine years younger, but the eldest of Muhammad Ali's surviving sons, succeeded him. Said again reversed the direction of the government, favoring a return to his father's programs and to abandoned projects in irrigation,

favorable terms, but only at the cost of an indemnity of more than three million Egyptian pounds. To pay this sum he was forced to take Egypt's first foreign loan, thus not only setting a dangerous precedent, but planting a time-bomb under his successor Ismail, the third of Ibrahim's four sons, who became viceroy on Said's death in 1863.

Ismail the Magnificent (1863-79): Acceding at the age of 33, Ismail was older than any of Muhammad Ali's other male descendants, but younger than any of his predecessors. Under his rule the modernization begun by Muhammad Ali moved forward with new dynasism. Reviving his grandfather's policy of independence from the sultan, Ismail sought to transform Egypt into a country that Europe would respect in European terms. Rapid development was the order of the day, but since these terms had also come to include imperialism, an early gesture was to send a Sudanese batallion to the aid of the French during their brief occupation of Mexico, 1863-67. Later expeditions were not to prove so successful; and in the end Ismail himself would fall a victim to European imperialism.

In 1866, by payments to the sultan and an increase in tribute, he secured a change in the hereditary principle from seniority to primogeniture, thus guaranteeing the throne to his own line, and permission to maintain a standing army of 30,000. The same year he summoned the first Chamber of Deputies, a move that pleased European critics as representing a step towards constitutionality. The

Mubarak, whose talents approached genius in several fields and who would later serve Ismail as Minister of Education, Director General of the State Railways, Minister of Endowments and Minister of Public Works. Ismail and Mubarak had thus known Paris as it was before the Second Empire: an essentially medieval city, largely slums and only partially touched by modernization under Bonaparte, dirty, ill-drained and picturesque, where noisy alleys overhung with washing wound among decayed palaces and townhouses, which now served the poorer part of the population as tenements. When Ismail saw the transformation wrought by Haussmann — the new city, with its broad boulevards and parks — he was dazzled: and on his return to Egypt he sent Mubarak likewise to have a look, appointing

The Suez Canal

following year he obtained the Persian title of Khedive (‘‘Sovereign’’), borne by his heirs down to 1914, as well as the right to create institutions, issue regulations, and conclude administrative agreements with foreign powers without consulting Constantinople. His new independence was signalized in June 1867 by Egypt's autonomous participation in the Exposition Universelle in Paris.

Ismail had been sent as a student to Paris by Muhammad Ali in 1844, one of a delegation of 70 that also included a young man named Ali

Left, Ataba Square, Cairo, circa 1910. Above, before the advent of air travel, the Suez Canal was the main link between Europe and Asia.

him Minister of Public Works in the meantime. The result was the transformation of Cairo, which received from Ismail and Ali Mubarak the essential configuration it was to retain for a hundred years, in spite of the fact that Mubarak's master plan was never fully realized.

The changes made in the city during the few months just before the opening of the Suez Canal, in November 1869, were the capstone of five years of feverish modernization throughout the country. Two other major canals, the Ismailia, connecting Cairo with the Great Bitter Lake, and the Sweetwater, joining it to supply the length of the Canal zone, had already been completed. Municipal water and gas companies had been set up in 1865 and

Cairo's main railway station had been inaugurated in 1867, completing a system now hundreds of miles long that included the new cities of Port Said and Ismailia. Telegraph linked all parts of the country, which was so transformed that even skeptics were forced to acknowledge that Egypt under Ismail was becoming a modern power.

Foreign Debts Come Home: The sultan's response to the festivities, however, was to send Ismail a decree forbidding him to undertake foreign loans without approval, a reminder of his position as a vassal. A massive bribe secured confirmation in 1873 of all the rights obtained earlier, as well as permission to raise a large army, for which Ismail had hired American officers, Northern and Southern veterans of the Civil War. The American war had already brought wealth to Egypt by raising the price of cotton, enriching the new class of landowners that Said and Ismail had created. Since the Khedive and his family still owned one fifth of Egypt's cultivable land and managed it along the most up-to-date lines, much of the new wealth came Ismail's way. Not enough, however, even coupled with Egypt's tax revenues, to keep pace with his ambitions, his largesse or his financial carelessness. In the confusion of public and private exchequers, colossal debts had been run up, amounting to less than chickenfeed by today's standards, but sufficient to allow professions of alarm in Paris and London, where Ismail's independence was already being regarded as a threat to the *status quo*. Meanwhile his country itself looked increasingly tempting, not only as a strategic base or a source of raw materials, but as an expanding market for European manufactured goods.

Most of the debt was the result of little less than swindle, perpetrated by European adventurers who had flocked to Alexandria from the beginning of the reign, the largest swindle, like the first of the debts, being an inheritance from Said: the Suez Canal, built using the *corvée*, at Egyptian expense. In 1875, after swinging another huge loan of which he actually received only a third in cash, Ismail was forced to sell his shares in the Canal Company to Britain, which then sent out experts to look into his debts. An Anglo-French Dual Control set up to oversee his finances began creaming off three quarters of the annual revenues of Egypt to pay European creditors. Ismail was forced to liquidate his personal estates, which included several factories, and to accept British and French ministers in his cabinet. Adroitly playing the few cards left to him, he evaded a complete takeover of his government until finally the Europeans lost patience. Putting pressure on the sultan, they

had Ismail deposed, the acting British and French Consuls-General delivering the sultan's telegram to him in person.

Intervention and Occupation: His son Tawfiq, whom Ismail himself later described as having "neither head nor heart nor courage," was no match for adversaries who had defeated his father and thus broken the mainspring of Khedivial power. The Chamber of Deputies had shown unexpected resistance to foreign interference, but the only real force in the country was the army, where an administrative struggle between Turco-Circassian officers and native Egyptians had ended with the latter in control. Their chief spokesman, a senior officer named Ahmad 'Urabi, was appointed Minister of War and thus found himself at the forefront of Egyptian resistance to further European intrusion. This cause had nothing to do with Ismail's forgotten dream of an independent Egypt, but it temporarily united nearly all social classes, from Turco-Circassians, intellectuals and landowners to peasants, and made 'Urabi the only permanent figure throughout a series of changing governments.

Presented abroad first as a military dictatorship, then as an anarchy dangerous not only to European interests, but also to the sultan's, this situation provided the final excuse for intervention. Over the sultan's protests, British warships bombarded Alexandria on July 11, 1882. Hoping to regain status after repeated humiliations through the instrument of these invaders, Tawfiq abandoned his own government and put himself under their protection. Support for a provisional government also melted away. Near the end of August, 20,000 redcoats were landed on the supposedly sacrosanct banks of the new Suez Canal and two weeks later the Egyptian army under 'Urabi was crushingly defeated at Tell al-Kabir. British justice thwarted Tawfiq's revenge at 'Urabi's subsequent trial and he was sent with other members of the provisional government into exile in Ceylon.

Thus ended 19th-Century Egypt's double experiment at modernization, twice balked by European displays of power, though the cultural, social and even physical marks left on the country by Muhammad Ali and Ismail have so far proven indelible.

British Rule: Lord Cromer (1882-1907): Evelyn Baring, who became Lord Cromer in 1891, first came to Egypt in 1879 as the British financial controller during the Dual Control of France and Britain. He stayed only briefly in that capacity, but returned in 1882 to become the Consul–General.

In 1882, the British government promised an early evacuation of its troops, but they lingered on and more and more British subjects arrived in Egypt to form a civil service corps. Since the British refused to formalize their presence, the British Consul-General, although officially vested only with the same powers as other consuls-general, became the *de facto* ruler of Egypt, with absolute authority in both its internal and foreign affairs.

Despite his high-handed manner, Cromer is generally credited with having believed that he acted with the best interests of the rural masses at heart. Declaring himself ''a friend of the peasants,'' for example, he abolished the hated *corvée*. And as the country became financially solvent and even prosperous during the relative stability of the Pax Britannica, taxes were rationalized and eventually lowered, thereby further improving their lot. To

By this time, cotton had become the mainstay of the Egyptian economy, accounting for 90 percent of foreign earnings in the period from 1900 to 1910. Other food crops, the most important of which was corn, continued to be grown and Egypt was still able to feed its growing population without depending on imports, though its consumer goods otherwise came from abroad. Its role within the British Empire was essentially to supply raw materials and a market for manufactured items, like any other colony or possession. Cromer therefore discouraged both industrialization and higher education, putting an end to the kind of autonomous development that before the Occupation had made Egypt, with Japan, unique among countries of the non-Western

pendence on the annual flood.

General view of the Nile Barrage.
Vue générale du Barrage.

Vignion & Zachos, Cairo & Luxor. No. 1107.

other Egyptians, however, he was less friendly and sympathetic.

The most important achievements during this period were the completion of the Delta Barrage in 1890 and the building of the first Aswan Dam in 1902. Begun under Muhammad Ali, the Delta Barrage made double and triple cropping possible in the Delta and thus greatly increased agricultural output, while the Aswan Dam, coupled with barrages at Asyut (1903) and Esna (1906), extended the same system to Upper Egypt, reducing de-

Above, the Delta Barrage, completed in 1890.

world. It is therefore not surprising that the years of the British occupation helped to solidify nationalist awareness in Egypt.

Abbas II Hilmi (1892-1914): This awareness received added stimulus after 1892, when Abbas Hilmi, Tawfiq's 18-year-old son, succeeded as Khedive. Educated at a Swiss school and at the celebrated Theresianum in Vienna, Abbas II was typical of the new Egyptian elite that had been created by Muhammad Ali's and Ismail's educational designs. In Egypt under Cromer, however, there was no real role for this elite or even for Abbas himself to play, as the Consul-General made humiliatingly clear to the young Khedive at the earliest opportunity. Abbas' response was to seek out the young nationalist leaders, who like himself had been educated in European secularist ideals, and provide them with financial support.

Al-Azhar, the great religious university founded by the Fatimids, which could claim to have served as the center of Egyptian patriotism at many times in the past, was strangely quiescent during this period, though Cromer did not hesitate to raise the specter of "Muslim fanaticism" with the politicians in London whenever it suited his purpose. Cromer appears to have succeeded, in fact, where Bonaparte failed, effectually co-opting the religious establishment into the system of control exercised by the Occupation.

Egypt in the Gilded Age: Secular nationalism drew growing strength between 1890 and 1906 from the country's enormous prosperity,

as much as 50 percent of Cairo's population growth could thus be attributed to European immigration; and by 1914, more than 90 percent of the paid-up capital of all companies registered in Egypt would be in European hands. Under the impact of such numbers, old native habits changed with increasing rapidity. Cairo and Alexandria were irrevocably transformed by the real estate boom of 1896-1907 into European-looking cities, as Muhammad Ali and Ismail had intended, while European dress, already customary at the courts of Muhammad Ali's successors, became the middle-class norm, as it is today.

Europeans of another kind also flocked to Egypt during this period, but for briefer stays usually lasting only a single winter season: the aristocracy, for whom it became, as Ismail had

derived almost exclusively from cotton. Doubling production offset an initial fall in prices, which then nearly trebled. Despite the lack of an industrial base, real per capita income during the first decade of this period was to remain unsurpassed until the influx of petrodollars in the 1970s. The land-owning class created by Said and Ismail grew even richer, merging with the old and new elites, and thousands of Europeans immigrated to Egypt to share their wealth: Greeks and Italians chiefly, but also Britons, Frenchmen, Swiss, Germans and Belgians, all of whom received special privileges under the Ottoman Capitulations, which granted them immunity to Egyptian laws and taxes.

In the last years of Cromer's proconsulship,

foreseen, the first of many playgrounds. Improved schedules and faster service had revolutionized steam travel well before the end of the century, making it possible then to get from London or Paris to Alexandria or Cairo with far more speed and ease by rail and ship than one can by the same means now. Shepheard's was already famous, but other celebrated hotels — the Savoy, the Continental, the Mena House, the Semiramis, the Heliopolis Palace — were all built between 1896 and 1910 to accommodate the luxurious tastes of a rich and titled clientele that would vanish into the holocaust of 1914 and never really reappear.

The Dinshwai Incident: As Cromer approached retirement from Egyptian service in 1906, he was contemplating changes to allow for more self-government, but his autocratic rule had left him few friends in the country. And in that year the Dinshwai Incident occurred. Casually shooting domestic pigeons that belonged to peasants in the Delta village of Dinshwai, who tried to stop them, a group of British officers wounded a woman and four men. Outraged villagers surrounded them, beat them, then held them to await the arrival of the police. One of the officers escaped and ran through the noon-day heat to a nearby British army camp, but collapsed and died of sunstroke just outside the camp entrance. A peasant who had tried to help him was beaten to death on the spot by British Tommies. This murder was subsequently forgotten. To consider charges of premeditated murder against the villagers of Dinshwai, however, a special Tribunal was set up, under a recent law that suspended normal operation of the Egyptian Criminal Code specifically in cases involving "crimes of violence against officers and men of the army of Occupation." The Tribunal was empowered by this law to inflict extraordinary punishments, including the death sentence, without appeal.

Composed of two Egyptians and three Englishmen, the Tribunal met in Dinshwai for 30 minutes then, out of 52 accused, sentenced eight villagers to 50 lashes, 11 to periods of penal servitude ranging from a year to life, and four — including a 17-year-old boy and a 60-year-old man — to hanging. Though public executions had been outlawed two years earlier in one of Cromer's reforms, the villagers of Dinshwai were then mustered and forced to witness the carrying out of these sentences.

No one connected with this incident — to which Egyptians at the time could only respond with helpless grief — was ever forgiven.

Cromer's successor as Consul-General, Sir Eldon Gorst, spoke Arabic, having lived many years in Egypt, and was ready to effect change in British policy. He cultivated a friendship with the Khedive, whom he permitted to wield more power, and undertook several reforms. Egypt's first secular university was allowed to open in 1908 and provincial councils were encouraged towards more autonomy. Unfortunately Gorst's arrival coincided with a worldwide slump. Blamed for the ensuing crash, his policies were resented by British civil servants in Egypt and misinterpreted as signs of weakness by Egyptians. In 1910, rec-

ognizing their failure, he resigned and in 1911 Lord Kitchener succeeded.

Kitchener had served as Commander-in-Chief of the Egyptian army and knew Egypt well, but his ideas of how to govern it were very different from Gorst's. He introduced new regulations for censorship, school discipline and the suppression of conspiracy. Once again the Khedive came under the Consul-General's strict authority. In 1913, however, he introduced what seemed to be a liberal reform: a new constitution that provided for a Legislative Assembly. It met only once before World War I broke out.

The Protectorate (1914-22): The outbreak of the war was the catalyst for a series of important events. Severing the 400-year old Ottoman connection, Britain declared Egypt a protectorate, thereby finally formalizing the authority it had had for the past 32 years. Martial law was imposed and Kitchener left to assume supreme command of the British forces while Sir Henry McMahon replaced him with the new title of High Commissioner. Abbas Hilmi, who had been in Constantinople when the war started, was forbidden to return, then declared a traitor and deposed. His two young sons being excluded from succession, his uncle, 60-year-old Husayn Kamel, was made ruler, with the title of Sultan, by the British. There was little enthusiasm in Egypt for either side in the war, but much resentment of the arrogance of British power.

At the end of the war, the nationalist movement was stronger than ever and a dynamic new leader had emerged to direct its efforts. Saad Zaghlul was an Azhar-educated lawyer of pure Egyptian peasant ancestry. His mentor had been a Muslim modernist and nationalist intellectual of an earlier generation, Muhammad Abduh. Imprisoned briefly for his participation in the resistance of 1882, Zaghlul later practiced law for several years, becoming legal advisor to Princess Nazli, who kept an important salon, then a judge. During this period he married the daughter of a pro-British Prime Minister, and was shown favor by Cromer, who appointed him Minister of Education. It was not until the Protectorate was declared in 1914 that, angry at Kitchener's treachery to the constitution he had supported in 1913, Zaghlul joined the nationalist ranks.

Emergence of the Wafd: The Egyptians served the British cause in the war without treachery, if not wholeheartedly, and when it ended, they expected to be compensated for this cooperation. As soon as the armistice was signed, Zaghlul requested the British government, through Sir Reginald Wingate, who had replaced McMahon as High Commissioner in

1917, to be allowed to go to London to present Egypt's case for independence. Although Wingate, recommended that Zaghlul's request be granted, London refused. This uncompromising position only hardened nationalist sentiment; and by early 1919, they were demanding no less than complete independence, with representation at the Peace Conference in Paris. Following demonstrations in Cairo, Zaghlul and three other nationalists were exiled to Malta. This move and continuing British obstinacy provoked the successful uprising that Egyptians refer to as the Revolution of 1919. Violence was accompanied by a general strike that engaged Christians and Jews, as well as Muslims, of both sexes and all social classes. A Field-Marshal, Lord Allenby, was sent to replace Wingate, recalled because of his support of the Egyptians' demands. After appraising the situation, however, Allenby promptly brought Zaghlul home from exile, and gave him permission to go to Paris. With other members of the *Wafd*, as his followers had come to be called (*wafd* means "delegation" in Arabic), Zaghlul attended the conference, but failed to secure his major objective. On the same day the Treaty of Versailles was signed, in fact, Allenby issued a proclamation reaffirming the Protectorate.

The Wafd, headed by Zaghlul, came to speak for the whole country during this period. It was extremely popular among the masses, but its anti-imperialist stance also appealed to the Turco-Circassian elite and it was by no means a party of the people. In fact, its ranks consisted mostly of Egyptian professionals, businessmen and landowners, whose interests the Wafd represented right up until the time all political parties were outlawed under Nasser.

In November 1919, the British government decided to send a mission to Egypt to study and make recommendations on the form of a constitution for the Protectorate. Acknowledging that "nationalism had established complete domination over every social and articulate element," however, the mission's report recommended that although Britain should maintain military forces in Egypt and retain control over foreign relations, the protection of foreign interests, and the Sudan, Egypt should be declared an independent country. But the report was not published until the end of 1921, and meanwhile Zaghlul was arrested and exiled again, this time to the Seychelles.

For his part, confronted with the political realities of Egypt, Allenby had privately made conclusions similar to those of the mission though he did not hesitate to assert British authority by liberally using British troops to quell unrest. In February 1922, upon his return

from a visit to England, he bore a proclamation unilaterally ending the Protectorate, but reserving four areas of British control. Three weeks later Egypt's sovereign independence was officially declared; and Sultan Fuad, chosen by the British from among several candidates to succeed his brother, Husayn Kamel, upon the latter's death in 1917, became King Fuad. A constitution based on Belgium's was adopted in 1923.

Fuad as King (1922-36): The Wafdists at first rejected this declaration of independence, with its four "reserved points." When Zaghlul was finally allowed to return from the Seychelles, however, they sought to participate actively in the upcoming elections, which they won by an overwhelming majority. Zaghlul became Prime Minister in early 1924.

As Prime Minister, Zaghlul gave up none of his demands connected with completing independence, which included the evacuation of all British troops and Egyptian sovereignty over the Sudan. His hopes for the fulfillment of these demands were raised as he took office in January, when a Labor government came to power in England. In November, however, less than a year after the Wafd's landslide victory, the assassination of Sir Lee Stack, the British Commander-in-Chief (Sirdar) of the Egyptian army and Governor-General of the Sudan, put an end to optimism. Allenby delivered an ultimatum to the Egyptian government, though it had clearly not been responsible, making punitive demands. Badly shocked, Zaghlul accepted most of them, but refused to agree to the withdrawal of Egyptian troops from the Sudan, the right of Britain to protect foreign interests in Egypt, or the suppression of political demonstrations. Defiance seemed impossible, however, and he could only resign, leaving it to a successor to accept all the British conditions.

During this crisis, in December 1924, King Fuad took the opportunity to dissolve the Wafdist Parliament and rule by decree. When elections were held in March 1925 and the Wafd again won by an overwhelming margin, the King again dissolved Parliament. A third set of elections in May 1926 also gave the Wafd a majority, but the British vetoed Zaghlul's reinstatement as Prime Minister. His health already shattered by the Stack murder, which had betrayed him, Zaghlul died a few months later.

Royal Dictatorship: Mustafa An-Nahhas succeeded Zaghlul as the leader of the Wafd and

Right, by the turn of the century, European-style dress was the norm for middle class Egyptians.

80

21-7-1914

during the following four years, the struggle between the Wafd and King Fuad took the same pattern, with the Wafd winning general elections and the King dissolving the Parliament to appoint his own ministers. In 1930, Fuad appointed Ismail Sidqi Pasha as Prime Minister and replaced the 1923 constitution with his own royally-decreed one. Sidqi's three-year dictatorship was outwardly a period of relative calm and stability in Egypt. Two successors managed to maintain Fuad's constitution until 1935, when nationalist, popular and British pressure combined to force him to restore the constitution of 1923.

Negotiations for an Anglo-Egyptian treaty concerning the status of Britain in Egypt and the Sudan had been underway, but had broken down. In the end it was an alarming external the League of Nations, of which it became a member in 1937.

Faruq (1936-1952): After 1936, political leadership and the internal political situation both deteriorated. King Fuad died in April 1936 and his son, Faruq, still a minor, succeeded him. The Wafd split, and a new party — the Saad Wafd — was formed. Extremist organizations also emerged, such as Misr Al-Fatat, an ultra-nationalist pro-royalist group that combined elements of religious fanaticism, militarism and a deep admiration for Nazi Germany and Fascist Italy. Its para-military wing, called the Green Shirts, was modelled after Mussolini's Fascist youth movement, and battled in the streets with the Blue Shirts, a para-military wing of the Wafd. In 1928, Hassan Al-Banna had founded the Muslim Brother-

event, Italy's invasion of Libya and Abyssinia, that finally brought Egypt and Britain together. An Egyptian delegation headed by Prime Minister An-Nahhas, fearing Italian more than British imperialism, reached a quick agreement in an Anglo-Egyptian treaty that was signed in August 1936.

This treaty became the basis of the two countries' relations for the next 18 years. Among other things, Britain agreed to withdraw its troops from everywhere except the Suez Canal Zone, to support Egypt's desire to end the Capitulations (the old agreements, dating from the days of the Ottoman Empire, that gave foreigners special privileges in Egypt, including exemption from Egyptian law), and to back Egypt's application for admission to hood, the stated aim of which was to purify and revitalize Islam. But the Brotherhood had political aspirations as well and began to take an active part in politics in the late 1930s. It has since been a force with which every Egyptian government has had to contend.

During the inter-war period, agriculture remained the backbone of the Egyptian economy but the native Egyptian middle-class began to invest in factories and the process of industrialization began again, albeit in a modest way. This process was greatly stepped up after World War II and again after the military came to power in 1952. Along with industrialization inevitably came urbanization. Population pressure in rural areas encouraged migration from the country to the city by the rural poor in search of jobs. Beginning in the inter-war period, this shift has since helped to make Cairo one of the most densely packed cities in the world. But two-thirds of Cairo's population growth has been indigenous, reflecting the same processes that are rapidly urbanizing the rural countryside itself.

World War II and its Aftermath: When World War II broke out, Britain took control, in accordance with the terms of the Treaty of 1936, of all Egyptian military facilities, although Egypt itself remained officially neutral for most of the war. The government necessarily supported the British, but many Egyptians did not, while clandestine army groups and Al-Banna's Muslim Brotherhood not only rejected the idea of cooperation but secretly plotted the government's overthrow.

terrorist arm during the war to undertake violent action against the government and the British, and even communist elements were gaining strength. In addition a new political force had appeared, the Free Officer movement in the army, led by Gamal Abdel Nasser. Fiercely nationalistic, completely disillusioned with the government, it denounced what it saw as Britain's humiliating occupation of Egyptian soil. The leaders of the Free Officers were in contact with the Muslim Brotherhood and although some of the two groups' aims coincided, the Free Officers refused Al-Banna's offer to join forces. So the two organizations plotted rebellion independently and clandestinely, waiting for the right moment for action to arrive, while the king and the politicians, wrapped up in internal

Wishing you a Happy Christmas and a Bright New Year.

In February 1942, with tanks drawn up in front of Abdin Palace, the British installed their own candidate as Prime Minister at gun-point, the Wafdist An-Nahhas, thus not only poisoning Anglo-Egyptian relations for more than a decade, but also discrediting the Wafd itself.

At the end of the war, Egypt was in a precarious situation. Prime ministers and cabinets changed often; the Wafd, the Saadist party and the king (whose wanton behavior now alienated the Egyptian people) were mutually hostile. The Muslim Brotherhood had created a

Left, a 1933 ad for Cook's tours. Above, British servicemen had these cards printed to give their correspondence an Egyptian flavor.

conflicts, remained largely oblivious of them.

The disastrous defeat of the Arabs — the Egyptian army at their forefront — in Palestine in 1948-1949 fed fuel to the Muslim Brotherhood, whose volunteers had fought bravely, and its membership rapidly increased. The defeat also increased the disaffection of the army with both the palace and the government, which it accused of complicity in a scandal involving defective arms. Both the Muslim Brotherhood and the Free Officers plotted to take power; and to this end the Brotherhood carried out a series of terrorist operations, including the assassination of the Prime Minister, Noqrashy Pasha, in December 1948. By now aware of the danger that the Brotherhood represented, the government retaliated with massive arrests of its members and Al-Banna himself was assassinated in February 1949.

Black Saturday: In 1950, riddled with corruption and bad leadership, the Wafd was again elected to power. It instituted disastrous economic policies, but sought to hold onto popularity by releasing many members of the Brotherhood, abrogating the 1936 treaty, and calling for the evacuation of British troops from the Canal Zone. Resistance to British troops in the Canal area took the form of guerilla action with the tacit approval of the government. In January 1952, a second Dinshwai occurred when the British beseiged and overran a post manned by Egyptian auxiliary police, who fought to the last man. Rioting broke out in Cairo, which the authorities either

General Mohammed Neguib, had seized power. Disillusioned by both their corrupt and impotent government and their dissolute king, the Egyptian people greeted the news with joy.

The Nasser Era (1952-70): Lacking a specific program other than to wipe out government corruption and instability and affirm Egypt's independence from foreign domination, the young officers moved quickly to consolidate their power. On July 26, King Faruq was forced to abdicate in favor of his son, only six months old, and the same day he left with his family for exile in Italy on the royal yacht. The constitution was repealed and all political parties were suspended. In June 1953, the monarchy was formally ended and a republic declared.

General Neguib, brought into the Free

would not or could not control. On January 26, the day known as Black Saturday, foreign shops, bars and nightclubs were burned and British landmarks such as Shepheard's Hotel and the Turf Club disappeared forever.

During the next six months the situation deteriorated rapidly. The king dismissed the Wafdist cabinet and a succession of prime ministers followed as the weakened government tried to counter the clandestine army movement, of which it had finally become aware. The climax came in the night of July 22, when the Free Officers took over key positions in a bloodless *coup d'état* engineered by Nasser and other members of his organization. In the morning of July 23, the Egyptians were informed that the army, commanded by

Officers' plans late to serve as a figurehead, an older and respected officer to command the confidence of the people, was declared President and Prime Minister of the new republic. Other Free Officers were installed as his ministers, Nasser becoming Deputy Prime Minister and Minister of the Interior. Neguib tried to assert the authority he only nominally held, but by May 1954 Nasser was Prime Minister and virtual dictator of the country.

Nasser's first important public act as Prime Minister was the amicable negotiation of a new Anglo-Egyptian treaty that provided for the gradual evacuation of British troops from the Canal Zone. The agreement was signed in October 1954 after six months of negotiations. Although his opponents grumbled that it was not favorable enough to Egypt, since it provided that the British could use the Canal base in times of war, Nasser was generally hailed as the leader who finally ended foreign occupation in Egypt.

In the period following Neguib's ouster, Nasser made a further series of moves that increased his popularity at home, but also brought him the attention of political leaders and journalists abroad. In April 1955, he attended the Bandung Conference of Afro-Asian states, announcing soon after Egypt's commitment to positive neutrality or non-alignment and its refusal to join the Baghdad Pact, a military alliance including Iraq and Turkey, which the United States and Britain hoped to establish in the Middle East as a way of maintaining Western influence. With

ended by the intervention of the United States and the Soviet Union, forcing the three aggressors to withdraw. Nasser had won an important victory with very little effort and became the symbol of the defiance of imperialist domination. His popularity, not only in Egypt, but the entire Third World, was assured.

This popularity persisted despite increasing repression in Egypt after the Suez War. Arresting thousands of communists, socialists, "feudalists," Muslim Brethren, and other alleged opponents of the regime, the state's intelligence apparatus became the most important center of power next to Nasser himself. Many of its detainees would not be released until several years after Nasser's death.

On the economic front, one of Nasser's first important policies had been the institution of

Nehru and Tito, Nasser became one of the leaders of the Non-Aligned Movement.

The turning point in political orientation away from the West came in June 1956, after the United States withdrew its financing for the High Dam at Aswan. Nasser nationalized the Suez Canal and announced that he would use the revenues from it to build the dam. His charismatic declaration provoked the fury of France and Britain, whose nationals owned the Canal; and with Israel they launched a tripartite attack on Egypt. The invasion was

Left, King Faruq admiring a bust of his father, Fuad. Above, President Gamal Abdel Nasser.

land reform. Ownership of land was limited to 200 acres per person. Holdings beyond this limit — subsequently reduced many times — were taken over by the government and redistributed among the peasants. Otherwise the new regime remained conservative, encouraging private enterprise during at least the first four years of the Revolution.

Arab Socialism: It was not until July 1961, five years after the Suez War, that Nasser adopted a comprehensive program of rapid industrialization, to be financed in part by nationalization of all manufacturing firms, financial institutions and public utilities. The July Ordinances also limited land holdings to 100 acres per person and put a ceiling on salaries. Meanwhile, private property was confiscated from foreigners, members of the royal family and the rich in general. Bank accounts, land, houses, furniture, clothing, jewelry and even books belonging to 4000 families were seized, in an effort to deprive the old upper classes not only of their capital assets and political influence, but also of the private culture that had set them apart from the masses. Created to further the new program decreed that year, the Arab Socialist Union was to remain the only legal avenue for political activity open to the Egyptian people for more than a decade.

As Nasser built respect for Egypt abroad, he began increasingly to wave the banner of Arab Unity, although early in the Revolution he had shown little interest in the other Arab countries. This new facet of his foreign policy led

sent troops to aid republican forces there in 1962, while Saudi Arabia aided the royalists. The two countries did not withdraw their troops until 1967, when they were forced to come to an agreement in order to face a common enemy, Israel.

The Six-Day War: The Arab-Israeli war of June 1967 was a blow from which Nasser never really recovered. Following growing tension in the area, he demanded in May 1967 that U.N. troops stationed in the Sinai be withdrawn and announced a blockade of the Straits of Tiran. Probably only bluff on Nasser's part, these moves were quickly taken advantage of by Israel. On June 5, it launched a sneak attack simultaneously on Jordan, Syria and Egypt, wiped out the entire Egyptian air force on the ground, and in six days had occupied the

in 1958 to a union between Egypt and Syria, later joined by Yemen, called the United Arab Republic, which it was hoped all the other Arab countries would eventually join. Initially more enthusiastic than the Egyptians, the Syrians were soon disenchanted, first by the Egyptian bureaucracy, then by the July Ordinances, which toppled their government. A new military regime took Syria out of the Union in 1961, after only three-and-a-half years. Egypt nevertheless retained the name of the United Arab Republic until after Nasser's death. The anniversary of the union is still celebrated and Syria still flies the UAR flag.

Nasser's next unfortunate undertaking in the name of Arab unity and socialist progress was his five-year embroilment in Yemen. He

Golan Heights, Gaza, Jerusalem, the West Bank and the Sinai. Israeli troops crossed the Suez Canal and were ready to march on to Cairo. Only a ceasefire quickly worked out by the United States and the Soviet Union prevented further disaster. In the aftermath of the war Nasser resigned, but resumed his post the next day following mass demonstrations calling for his return.

However popular he remained, the old charisma was gone and Nasser himself was a broken man. His announcement of a War of Attrition against Israel in 1969 merely encouraged Israeli attacks on civilian targets. Efforts to salvage a wrecked economy, no longer even agriculturally self-sufficient proved fruitless. His last important act was an attempt to reconcile King Hussein and the Palestinians after the bloody events of Black September 1970, when the king tried to crush the PLO in Jordan. In late September, he helped to negotiate an accord by which Hussein, Arafat and other Arab leaders agreed to end the fighting. He died of a heart attack the day after the signing of the accord and was escorted to his grave by more than three million people.

The Sadat Era: Upon Nassser's death, Anwar Sadat, his vice president, succeeded him to the presidency. No one expected Sadat to last long in this position, but he proved more skillful than his opponents. In May 1971, with what he called a ''corrective movement,'' he consolidated power by dismissing high-ranking government officials who openly or secretly opposed him. Another surprise move the fol-

Arab unity and seek a separate peace with Israel, by which, after much delay, it regained most of its lost territory. The dramatic opening of this process was his visit to Israel in November 1977, during which he addressed the Knesset. It resulted in the Camp David accords, signed under U.S. patronage in March 1979. Furthered by massive and continuing infusions of U.S. aid, the accords were greeted in Egypt with euphoria, but this mood rapidly dissipated as differences between Egyptian and Israeli interpretations of them became clear. Arab countries meanwhile denounced the Camp David accords as treachery to them and to the Palestinian cause, broke off relations, and expelled Egypt from the Arab League, which it had been instrumental in creating in 1947.

lowing year was the expulsion of the Soviet technicians, teachers and advisors who had been in Egypt for more than a decade. After a long period of close relations with the Eastern bloc, Egypt was turning towards the West.

Sadat's boldest initiative was his launching of the fourth Arab-Israeli war in October 1973. The outcome of this war was by no means a total victory, although Sadat proclaimed it one, but it did allow Egypt to regain pride.

It also gave Sadat enough prestige to ignore

Left, desert flowers bloom in the debris of a recent war, Sinai peninsula. Above, mementos of Sadat's dramatic presidency linger.

On the economic front, Sadat announced a liberalizing Open Door policy aimed at revitalizing the Egyptian economy and encouraging foreign investment and private enterprise. This policy included reducing exchange restrictions, reforming banking laws, offering privileged conditions to Arab and other foreign investors, allowing the overt development of a private sector parallel to the public, and encouraging competition between the two as a stimulus to reform in state-owned enterprises. The confiscations carried out under Nasser's regime were meanwhile tested in court at last and declared illegal.

As predicted by many, the Open Door policy led to almost instant riches for a sizable minority, thus creating a mini-boom that attracted a flood of foreign consumer goods and dozens of banks. It also imported massive inflation, however, which widened differences between the new rich and older salaried classes, as well as the working-class poor. The drain of Egyptian brains and brawn to neighboring oil-rich countries meanwhile became a torrent, which would continue more or less unabated even after Camp David, when all other links between Egypt and the rest of the Arab world would be broken. Remittances from abroad, long the mainstay of the Syrian, Lebanese and Jordanian economies, began to emerge as the single most important factor in the Egyptian economy. Real estate prices soared as returning Egyptians sought to invest income earned in Libya, Iraq, or the Arabian Penin-

sula in something safe back home.

Remittances and Revivalism: The significance of remittances, however, continued to be ignored by both Egyptian and foreign experts until as late as 1980. Their conventional *étatiste* models assigned the task of development solely to the government and had no room to record any revenues except those of the public sector. These models remained the basis of planning, and suggested that the state had no intention of surrendering any real degree of control. An *étatise* experiment in January 1977 — withdrawal of long-standing subsidies on basic commodities, unaccompanied by any promise of higher wages or lower taxes — led to two-day riots among the salaried and unsalaried

poor and had to be cancelled. Reminiscent of Black Saturday, the violence was clearly directed at newly acquired wealth and demonstrated widespread alienation.

The Arab Socialist Union was abolished and the beginnings of new political parties were formed.

The repression of Nasser's regime had been relaxed and many of its victims had recovered property and were even compensated. Its shadow, however, remained and contributed to this popular alienation, which was later compounded by Sadat's ambiguous peace with Israel, his consequent isolation from the rest of the Arab world, and the increasingly high-handed style of his government, which assumed monarchical trappings in an atmosphere of corruption and crony capitalism. Overt opposition began to gather round the new political parties, including a revived Wafd, while less public opposition crystallized in Islamic revivalism. Thanks to Sadat's lifting of systematic repression and to his encouragement of religion as an anodyne, the Muslim Brotherhood had regained most of its freedom of action, but there were other more radical groupings, one of which carried out his assassination on October 6, 1981, during a ceremony commemorating the crossing of the Suez Canal.

The Mubarak Years: After nearly three decades of authoritarian rule, Vice President Hosni Mubarak ascended to the Presidency. While honoring commitments made under the Open Door policy and at Camp David, Mubarak's regime has since curtailed crony capitalism, fulfilled promises of more democratic government, and sought to reestablish ties with other Arab states, especially those upon which Egypt is now economically dependent.

Egyptian society has become very complex. The population is now mostly urban rather than rural, eats and sleeps surrounded by walls of concrete rather than mudbrick, and works in industry, commerce, services, or the governmental bureaucracy rather than in agriculture. Authoritarian structures, frequently bolstered in the past by middle-class fears of the masses, have come to be seen as not only contrary to the dynamics of recent Egyptian history, but as wasteful and inefficient. Increasing democratization is therefore expected to bear both political and economic fruit and has become the center of Egyptian hopes.

Above, Anwar al Sadat, Egypt's second president. Right, Presidents Sadat and Hosni Mubarak pictured on posters.

ENDANGERED MONUMENTS

Until 1965, when the Aswan High Dam held back its first flood, very few of the millions of structures built by Egyptians throughout their history were ever intended to last more than a few months or at most a few years. Imhotep's architectural revolution at Saqqarah made the permanence of building in stone possible as early as the third millennium B.C., but for most of the ensuing centuries the idea of permanence was extended only to religious structures. Even the pharaohs' palaces, for example, which must have been delightful, were built of perishable materials, essentially no different from those that went into the making of any typical villager's house before 1965. Ancient dwellings have therefore disappeared, while ancient religious structures, the pharaonic tombs and temples, remain, their survival an anomaly. They are the most tangible link between modern Egypt and its ancient past, a link that may often look massive, but is in reality all the more precious for being tenuous and very vulnerable.

Apart from the obvious motives provided by the necessity for maintaining Egypt's cultural heritage, the question of conserving pharaonic monuments involves two major considerations: archaeology and tourism. Once a building has been thoroughly documented, its archaeological purpose has been fulfilled; and as far as archaeologists are concerned it can then be filed away for future reference. When the Secretary-General of the Egyptian Antiquities Organization officially requested a distinguished Belgian expert in 1946 to outline the best method for conserving a pharaonic tomb or temple, the answer was that a well-sealed door should be installed and that the whole monument should be reburied beneath the sand. And this method has actually been used, not only between digging seasons, but as a long-range tactic. In 1969, for example, the French Archaeological Institute, working in collaboration with the Antiquities Organization, excavated and cleared an extraordinary sixth-Century monastic complex near Esna, secured the necessary data, then reburied it, publishing a complete report three years later. The site has thus been saved for future generations.

Putting the Sphinx on Show: The Sphinx,

which has become an endangered monument, might have been preserved by this tactic. Though cleared many times in its earlier history, it had been allowed to rest safely under sand until 1925, when it was cleared again and repaired. Since its stone is very soft, however, it is subject, once exposed, to massive erosion by the sand-blast of Giza's incessant winds. Wear was observed and the most up-to-date steps were taken. Chemical injections, intended to harden and consolidate the stone, were made, though the long-term effects of such treatment were still unknown. Unfortu-

nately, it resulted in weakening the Sphinx rather than strengthening it; and subsequent erosion has proceeded at such a rate that there are now fears that its head may topple off.

The Sphinx, like the Solar Boat and many of the painted tombs at Luxor, is thus rapidly being sacrificed to tourism, which is not only an important industry in general for Egypt, but also specifically supports the Antiquities Organization and all its multifarious activities, including excavation, restoration and conservation. Egyptian archaeologists therefore face a dilemma. So do many foreign archaeologists, as well, for unless they are supported by their government (like the Germans, the Poles, the Egyptians and the French) or by an endowment (like the Swiss),

Left, paw and head of sphinx. Above, Cleopatra, detail from the Temple of Dendera.

they are dependent (like the British and the Americans) upon private donations, which are often linked with tourism.

The problem of the Sphinx underlines some of the other ironies surrounding reconstruction of pharaonic monuments, more and more of which is being undertaken primarily for the sake of tourism, rather than for purely archaeological reasons. Reconstruction may be archaeologically desirable and even necessary at certain sites, such as Saqqarah or the great temple-sites of Upper Egypt, where much of what the contemporary sees is the result of painstaking reconstruction by archaeological experts, who cleared away sand and reassembled jumbled heaps of stones in their search for knowledge. Once documentation has been completed, however, most

exercise a special claim to ''preservation,'' as representing a vital part of an international cultural inheritance. But motives for moving the rock-cut Abu Simbel temples, unknown until 1813, are best understood as a mixture of the aesthetic, the commercial, and the purely sentimental. There were eccentrics among the archaeologists, indeed, who argued that the best way to preserve both Philae and the Abu Simbel monuments within the cultural heritage was to let them drown, as Philae had annually since completion of the first Aswan dam in 1902: their fabric would thus have been saved not only from the dangers of dismantling and reconstruction, but from the far worse ravages of tourism.

It was precisely for the benefits of tourism, however, that both Philae and the Abu Simbel

archaeologists can bring themselves to accept even a building's complete destruction with a certain equanimity, as they have had to do at Kelya, the great Christian site in the Western Delta, or at Fustat on the edge of Cairo, which is being covered with new public housing.

Philae and Abu Simbel: The archaeological outcry over the Nubian antiquities doomed by the construction of the High Dam at Aswan thus had less to do with the wish to preserve what had already been recorded, for example, than with the loss or destruction of vast amounts of physical data that had not yet been archaeologically surveyed.

Philae was famous throughout the Mediterranean world in antiquity and could therefore, like Mont St. Michel or Patmos,

temples were moved to their present positions. Though Egyptologists are even more thrilled than other people by these two sites, neither of them represents the cutting edge of modern archaeological research; and the sums finally expended on these two projects — nearly US$30 million for moving Philae and more than US$40 million for Abu Simbel — probably amounted to far more than the total that has been spent on archaeology itself since the beginnings of Egyptology as an international discipline a century ago.

Urban Conservation: Generally standing on rural or desert sites in isolation from present-day communities, pharaonic tombs and temples have little significance for local people unless they can be exploited for immediate material gain. Living and working near these sites long before the emergence of such modern abstractions as "the cultural heritage," Egyptian villagers have therefore traditionally used them only for their own evolving purposes, ignoring them otherwise, as photographs and drawings from the 19th Century plentifully demonstrate. Local indifference allowed them to tumble or be buried under sand, but also created an absence of environmental complication that has since made many of them relatively easy to excavate, clear, reconstruct, record, restore and eventually conserve.

This situation contrasts totally with that of Egypt's medieval and modern monuments, nearly all of which stand in the urban setting of Cairo. The ancestors of Cairo, moreover,

lows political, economic, or cultural irrelevance — these materials have insured that Cairene buildings dating from the seventh Century onward still remain more or less intact.

Secular buildings frequently fell victim throughout the middle ages to new architectural schemes, but street patterns were maintained and religious buildings were often restored by succeeding generations, embedding them so firmly in the urban environment that they largely define it. Conservation of Islamic streets and individual monuments thus involves not only questions of cultural heritage, archaeology and tourism, but also a host of other considerations, including all the usual concerns of the city-planner, ranging from sociologial issues to problems of rehabilita-

were not only the mudbrick towns of the Old and New Kingdoms, but also the cities of the Hellenistic world, typified by Ptolemaic Alexandria, where the notion of architectural permanence had been extended for the first time in Egypt to secular buildings, making it a "city of marble." Burnt brick and stone thus became the materials of the new metropolis. Coupled with a remarkable history — Cairo has known earthquakes, plagues and fires, but (uniquely among Middle Eastern cities) has never undergone the utter devastation that fol-

Left, scene at Karnak Temple, Luxor. Above, the Temple of Abu Simbel on Lake Nasser.

tion, water-supply, electrification and sewerage.

Egypt's first conservation organization, the Khedivial government's Committee for the Conservation of Monuments of Arab Art, was set up in 1881 specifically to protect medieval Islamic buildings, which had not only fallen into dilapidation, but were additionally threatened by new development. Many had in fact already been sacrificed to Ali Mubarak's master plan under the Khedive Ismail (see the historical section), while work on reconstructing pharaonic monuments, by contrast, had hardly begun. The committee's criteria and techniques were identical with those of similar European organizations and are now quite outdated, but during the 70 years of its existence it completed some remarkable tasks, beginning with an index of 800 buildings.

In 1952 it was absorbed into the Antiquities Organization, which carried out almost no urban or medieval restoration or conservation for nearly 30 years, largely because it had no access to its own revenues. The result, by 1980, was near-disaster. Apart from the conditions caused by modern traffic, industrialization, declining cultural and economic levels, and increasing population density, the city's water delivery and sewerage systems had collapsed, raising the water-table in some places almost to the surface, well above the impermeable footings so cleverly installed by medieval builders. Walls soaked up water or drew it up by capillary action and began to disintegrate chemically, while badly restored

or unrepaired roofs began to collapse.

Great changes have taken place since 1981. There is no program for urban rehabilitation, a normal component in any large-scale restoration scheme, but the Antiquities Organization has at least tackled the problem of the medieval monuments themselves. Gaining access to its own revenues, it has spent millions of pounds from 1982 onward and has been largely successful in carrying out not only restoration but urgently needed repairs. There is still a great deal to be done and the basic conditions of life in the medieval areas of the city, which make them look like slums, have hardly been touched.

But Cairo's special flavor comes from its combination of the medieval and the modern:

its 19th- and early 20th-Century buildings are as important to its character as its great Mamluk monuments, to which they are often directly related. Many of these buildings, like Ismail's elegant streets, parks and squares, have already fallen victim to tasteless and shoddy development. Awareness of their value to the city as a whole, however, has spread recently even into the public sector. A stiff new law passed in 1983 brought previous regulations up-to-date, covering all historic buildings and their environs with new protection, but excluding those less than 100 years old from registration on the Index except by specific decrees of the prime minister. The fate of Cairo's later neo-Islamic, Beaux-Arts, Art Nouveau, and Art Deco buildings thus still hangs in the balance. Moratoria on building permits, arising directly out of public dismay at what seemed to be the city's wholesale destruction, have slowed the pace of their disappearance dramatically, however, and a campaign mounted since 1985 has already succeeded in indexing a handful of the most important.

Egypt has thus brought itself back in line with the theories and practices currently employed in Europe and in Turkey, where conservation is a national concern. Techniques are gaining in finesse and legislation has been appropriately readjusted. The conservation of entire areas, now the norm in European or American practice, has not yet been tried in Cairo except in limited zones — such as the Citadel or the enclosure of Babylon at Misr al-Qadimah (Old Cairo) — where the Antiquities Organization is in complete control. No other agency seems willing or able to assume any part of the necessary planning or decision-making burden, thus leaving the organization to effect what it can within its own mandate.

Beyond all these concerns, of course, is the question of caring for the environment throughout Egypt as a whole. Today's tourist, Western or Arab, is less likely to be a monument-hunter than to be searching for a pleasant spot to recharge and recuperate. He is attracted by precisely the same qualities that will make the country likewise attractive to future Egyptians themselves. To squander natural and cultural resources now is therefore to make the country not only less liveable in the future, but also less viable as a place anyone would want to visit. That fact is beginning to be thoroughly understood.

Above, Al Azhar, the world's oldest university, undergoing restoration. Right, the mosque of Al-Hakim.

PEOPLE

When God created the nations, so Arab wisdom has it, he endowed each with two counterbalanced qualities: to the intelligence of the Syrians he thus added factiousness; to Iraq he gave pride, but tempered it with hypocrisy, while for the desert Arabs he compensated hardship with good health. And Egypt he blessed with abundance at the cost of humility.

It does not require a deep understanding of the past to feel that as far as Egypt is concerned God has withdrawn the first half of his covenant — or that, at any rate, He's made a new deal with the desert dwellers. As any Egyptian will explain, it is not many generations since Egyptian donations fed the poor of the holy cities of Mecca and Medina, in what is now Saudi Arabia. To the desert Arabs, however, God has recently given abundance, in the form of oil, while Egypt, formerly the land of plenty, has received unaccustomed hardship, in the form of war and overpopulation. Once the breadbasket of the Roman Empire, Egypt now follows only Japan and the Soviet Union as an importer of food and only India in the league of aid recipients.

Grace Under Pressure: Yet poverty is a relative thing and, perhaps because of their humility, Egyptians bear it with considerable grace. In the poorest hinterland of the south, a foreign traveler recently overheard a conversation between two venerable farmers: "These poor Europeans," said one, "They will do anything to escape their horrible climate. I saw one the other day who'd come all the way here on a bicycle." "Yes," replied the other, "their land is covered with ice all year round. Look at us. We've got sunshine, water, everything." "It is indeed terrible," concluded the first. "The *khawaga* I saw didn't even have money to buy proper trousers — he was riding about in his underwear!"

Egyptian humility takes many forms. One is a tragic sense of life, arising from a tragic view of history. While the West embraces the idea of progress as a solution to all man's ills, the Egyptians, who have a great deal more experience to draw on, have an impulse to turn towards a utopian past, perhaps to a time when Muhammad's successors, the four Rightly-Guided Caliphs, brought justice, prosperity, and true belief to the land. Centuries of transitory regimes have sapped their confidence in the merely temporal. Belief in man-made institutions is not firm.

The defeat suffered by Egypt in the 1967 war, one of the most humiliating in modern times, would have brought on a revolution in almost any other country. Yet when Nasser, in an emotionally charged speech, offered to resign, the response was dramatic: millions of Egyptians poured into the streets demanding that he stay. His willingness to share their humiliation brought forth instant sympathy from the Egyptian masses, who saw it as more important that his intentions had been morally right than that he had failed to realize them in actuality. His tragedy was, after all, theirs — the tragedy of decline that is repeatedly embodied in their history.

Islam and Popular Piety: Any visitor to Egypt will be struck by the piety of its people. Humility is inherent in the very word *Islam*, the religion of nine-tenths of Egyptians. Islam (from the Arabic root *salima*, to be safe; *aslama*, to surrender *salaam*, peace) means "submission," whether it be to God, to fate, or to the social system framed by the Qur'an.

Most Westerners find the continuing dominance of Islam in what purports to be an age of reason perplexing. The important thing to recognize is that the Qur'an — literally, a "recitation" — is the word of God in Arabic as directly transmitted by Muhammad. The power of the World thus has a strength in Islam unmatched by the literature of any other "revealed" religion; and the beauty of the Qur'an, by definition "inimitable," is cited as a miracle in its own right. It is not extraordinary that many modern Egyptian tastes, habits, and preferences are referred directly back to the Qur'an.

While there are many atheists and agnostics in Egypt, the vast majority stick tenaciously to belief in a supreme deity and the imminence of the Day of Judgement. The month-long, dawn-to-dusk fast of Ramadan, still officially observed by the entire country, bears witness to Islam's pervasiveness, but even the Coptic minority, conscious of being members of one of the earliest Christian sects, maintains a degree of devoutness that is often bewildering to Western Christians. Re-

Preceding pages: group of *Saidis* or Upper Egyptians, Sohag; Wissa Wassef Art School in Giza. Left, an unusual moment of seriousness.

ligious expressions of a kind that have almost vanished from European speech proliferate in everyday language. "God willing," "By God's permission," "Praise God," "Our Lord prevails," — all are as common as the word "Goodbye" is in English. But *Goodbye* long ago lost its original religious meaning while in Egypt such meanings have not been forgotten. The proper response to the typical greeting "*Salam aleikum*" (Peace be upon you) is thus "*Aleikum as-salam wa rahmat Allah wa barakatu*" (Upon you be peace and the mercy of God and his blessings).

Apart from piety, however, this exchange also reflects a point of Arab etiquette — any greeting must be followed by a response that outdoes the first speaker in punctilio — and religiosity, though abundant, is not always

Jest, Gibes and Practical Jokes: Egyptian piety is also balanced by a deep love of mischief. If anything can compete in public esteem with holiness, it is wit; and Egyptian humor holds nothing sacred. Political jokes are particularly sharp and irreverent, but Egyptians make use of the smallest incident to provoke laughter. The fullest laugh is a delight in itself, starting off low and gutteral and ending in a shriek of pleasure. In a cafe or bar, wisecracks are fired back and forth with increasing hilarity until the whole company falls off their chairs.

Sages have often remarked that while the condition that formulates much of Western behavior is the sense of guilt, arising from an individual "conscience," in the East in general it is shame, arising from a sense of

heartfelt. The 19th-Century chronicler Edward Lane observed that "it is considered the highest honor among Muslims to be considered religious; but the desire to appear so leads many into hypocrisy and pharisaical ostentation."

For many, particularly among the poor, belief in the supernatural extends beyond orthodoxy to a world of genies and spirits of the dead. Fertility rites are still held in Upper Egyptian temples; and magicians, witches and priests do a brisk trade in spells and potions. Although much of this activity — and particularly the *Zar*, a folk rite of exorcism by trance — is frowned upon by the official religious establishment, it enjoys continuing popularity.

public disapproval or contempt. Egyptian children, raised with the idea that whatever you can get away with socially is morally permissible, must rank among the world's most naughty. This trait sometimes persists into adulthood, where it is reinforced by a cultural backlog of wise-guy folk-heroes such as the legendary Goha, whose countless exploits are marked by both asinine failure and impudent success. More locally and historically Egyptian mischievousness has its roots in the legacy of centuries of repressive government. Numerous are the stories that celebrate the victory, through cunning and trickery, of the poor *fellah* over wicked pashas or foreigners.

This love of trickery has its drawbacks, as

the 15th-Century Egyptian historian Al-Maqrizi noted in an unflattering portrayal of his countrymen: "That which dominates in the character of the Egyptians is the love of pleasure . . . They are extremely inclined to cunning and deceit: from their birth they excel in it and are very skilful in using it, because there is in their character a basis of flattery and adulation which makes them masters in it more than all the peoples that have lived before them or will live after them."

Maqrizi notes, among other things, that the Egyptians of his time showed a distinct disdain for study. This indifference to study, it must be said, is very pronounced to this day, in a tendency to attempt to achieve goals by means other than hard labor and careful the bounds of morality. This attitude explains, more than political exigencies, the heavy presence of police throughout the country. Belief in the need for coercion and forced restraint is strengthened by religious attitudes. It is commonly presumed that without the just guidance of Islam, society would fall apart. Yet many Egyptians rightly contrast the violence of American society and the high levels of suicide in other countries with the peace and security of Egyptian life. Where else in the world can two people let themselves go in argument and attack each other in the street, knowing that any passerby who is a good Muslim is duty bound to intervene? For this reason few arguments turn more than gently physical, no matter how bloodcurdling the threats shouted may sound.

planning, a habit of mind that even President Mubarak castigates in his fellow citizens. Although much of it can be attributed to overcrowding and a faulty educational system, the degree of cheating in Egyptian schools and universities is scandalous.

Coercion and Conformity: Shame has other manifestations. Unjustly, Egyptians are generally not trustful of one another, believing that it is only by overt pressure that people can be prevented from overstepping

Left, village girl. Above, Bedouin gathering firewood.

Attitudes to sex are also framed by the same phenomenon. Women are constantly pestered in the streets, largely because it is believed that really masculine men cannot resist the temptations of sex. The same is held to be true of women — perhaps even more so. Thus foreigners often find the Egyptian atmosphere highly charged sexually, which explains the Victorian view of Egypt as a land of licentiousness, a view that is still part of the Western mythology of the Orient in general. Until the Western sexual revolution of the 1960s, Egyptian views of the issue were certainly far more healthy and uncomplexed than those prevailing in the West. Sex in all its aspects is openly discussed by both men and women, but also lurks at the edges

103

of even ordinary conversation. Since the Arabic language itself is full of sexual innuendoes, its richness lends a wonderful bawdiness to Egyptian talk and especially to humor.

The Mazes of Matrimony: Marriage, however, is deemed an absolute prerequisite for sex, as well as for full adulthood and respectability. Particularly among women, whose freedom is still very much limited by rigid social norms, finding and keeping the right husband is thus the major focus of life. Since the 1920s, when the veil was finally discarded, substantial progress towards equality of the sexes has been made, but it is still the rule for a girl to remain in the care of her father until the day she is passed into the care of her husband.

Respect for parents and elders is so strongly ingrained that it is likewise uncommon for even a male child to leave home before marriage; and these days few urban Egyptians can afford to marry before the age of twenty-five. Despite Islam's flexibility on the subject — easy divorce and polygamy are both sanctioned — marriage is regarded as a binding agreement, made more absolute by economics. For this reason, young couples are expected to work out every detail of their future life — housing, furniture, a dowry for the wife as a form of divorce insurance — before signing the contract.

Extravagant weddings testify to the importance of the institution. Wealthy families will blow thousands of pounds on a binge in one of the five-star hotels, complete with a fanfare of trumpets, lurking video crews, famous belly dancers, singers and other entertainers. The weddings of poor families are equally extravagant — they too are expected to flaunt their pride and generosity — and much more fun. Whole streets are closed off and the affair takes place in the open air. Street musicians, acrobats, boy dancers, and slick masters of ceremonies keep things lively as the male guests tuck into the free beer, hashish, and opium. Eventually the bride and groom, the latter by now somewhat over-relaxed, climb into a flashy car draped in ribbons, to be borne through the streets with a triumphant blaring of claxons.

"Money and children," the Qur'an says, "are the embellishments of life." Egyptians adore children, and large families are the norm. In many ways, the family is more important than the individual as a social unit, extending not only over several generations but also to distant cousins. The fierce vendettas which still rage in Upper Egypt, often claiming dozens of lives over many decades, illustrate this point. Family honor and prestige are serious matters, particularly in the countryside. The crime columns regularly tell of adultery-related murders: "A woman's honor, according to a well-known saying, "is like a matchstick: it can only be used once."

In the cities, political and business alliances are often reinforced through marriage. Because numerous children enlarge the family's potential for wealth and influence, and also because it is believed that it is healthier for children to grow up with lots of brothers and sisters, family planners have had a hard time bringing down the birth rates.

Egyptian mothers are notoriously soft on their children. Centuries of high infant mortality, sexual roles that give house-bound wives complete responsibility for children, and lingering belief in the power of the evil eye mean that mothers are inclined to cater to their child's every whim for fear that some harm may befall him or her. This is particularly true in the case of favored boys. It is not uncommon, in fact, for a woman's strongest emotional tie to be with her eldest son rather than her husband. As infants, children are wrapped in swaddling and thoroughly doted upon. By the time they are old enough to walk, however, they are usually left to spend their time as they wish. This combination of coddling and freedom is often cited as a reason for the strength, self-confidence and even obstinacy of the Egyptian character. It has also been said that belief in the evil eye has a psychological benefit: it reinforces personality by giving people the feeling that they possess powers both to inflict harm and to attract the envy of others.

Life-Support Systems: Beyond the family, Egyptians have a strong attachment to their immediate community. Village solidarity — when not torn apart by blood feuds — is extremely strong. In the big towns the *hara* or alley is the main unit of social bonding. Partly because crowding in the poorer districts limits privacy, people help each other out in innumerable ways, lending money, sharing videos, and even testifying against strangers to the police.

The main function of *hara* solidarity is to defend the interest of the community. Gangs of local toughs, whose mandate varied from protection of neighborhood women against strangers to simple extortion rackets, formed part of the urban landscape until quite recently. One of the toughest gangs in Cairo ruled

Right, portrait of a man in full traditional garb.

the neighborhood around Bab Zuwayla and was run by a lady famed for her frequent exercise of knocking men out with a head butt. Such drama is rare nowadays, but it is nonetheless true that strangers are carefully watched. Foreigners are deemed unworthy of this kind of attention, since they are presumed to be unaware of the more difficult aspects of Egyptian life, but young unmarried Cairene males seldom venture into a strange neighbourhood alone.

Peculiarities of Places: Regional loyalties persist strongly as well. Each major town and province has its acknowledged characteristics, from Alexandria in the north to Aswan in the south. Like the inhabitants of other port cities, Alexandrians are known chiefly for their toughness and willingness to fight, but

right miserable away from city streets, Cairenes on vacation are apt to pine for the bustle and crowds of the metropolis.

The Saidis are the Polacks of Egypt, with the difference that the traits attributed to them — simple-mindedness, credulity, and impulsiveness — have a remarkable ring of truth. Saidis joke even about themselves, being too open-hearted to pass the buck. A sample joke: an Alexandrian, a Cairene and a Saidi are dying of thirst in the desert, when a genie appears and allows each a single wish. The Alexandrian says, "I wish I were on the beach at Montaza surrounded by girls," and vanishes. The Cairene says, "I wish I were praying in the mosque of Hussein in Cairo," and vanishes. The Saidi, looking dismayed, turns to the genie and

also for their cosmopolitan outlook and business acumen. The peasants of Lower Egypt and the Delta are regarded as hardworking, thrifty, and serious-minded. Rashidis, from Rosetta, are supposed to be kindhearted, while Dumyatis, from the town of Damietta at the Nile's eastern mouth, are reckoned to be untrustworthy. Menufis, from their province in the heart of the Delta, the homeland of Presidents Mubarak and Sadat, are renowned for their cunning.

Cairenes, like New Yorkers or Cockneys, are seen as slick, fast-talking and immoral. Simply being from the capital allows them to sneer at less sophisticated compatriots, a Cairene habit that their country cousins do not find endearing. Uneasy and often down-

says, "I'm so lonely. Couldn't you please bring my friends back?" On the positive side, Saidis are noted for their generosity, courage, virility and sense of honor.

The dark-skinned Nubians of the far south, an ancient people with their own languages, are considered to be the most gentle and peaceful of Egyptians. Long isolated by the cataracts that made the Nile above Aswan impassable, Nubian life, relaxed and carefree, had a unique charm. Nubian villages are spotlessly clean, the spacious mudbrick houses always freshly painted, and both men and women are apt to be more enterprising than their Egyptian neighbors.

The desert Bedouin, of which there are numerous tribes, have not given up their ancient occupation of smuggling, despite increasing sedentarization, and fierce tribal loyalty is still maintained. The Bedouin are feared, scorned, and envied for the wild aristocratic wilfullness of their ways. The old rivalry between these freewheeling bandits of the desert and the hardworking peasants of the valley has all but died out — largely through intermarriage — but their pure Arab blood and the beauty of their women still inspire admiration.

Pride and Prejudice: But this catalog of accepted regional differences obscures an essential homogeneity of attitudes and feelings. Despite differences and despite the bitter legacy of imperialism — of defeat, occupation and dependence — pride in Egypt and "the Egyptian way" is fervent. An old

cooperation by expelling Soviet advisors in 1972.

It is characteristic of the Egyptians — with the exception, naturally, of the Saidis — that they prefer compromise to conflict. By inclination, habit, and training, Egyptians are tactful and diplomatic, even to the point of obsequiousness. The proverb "Eat what appeals to you, but wear what appeals to others" embodies a cardinal rule. This rule governs not only what Egyptians wear — all but the poorest of the poor take care never to appear in public unless clean and neatly dressed — but also all but the most intimate of conversations: speech with a stranger should thus adhere to the formulas of flattery and light-heartedness. It likewise governs the Egyptians' attitude to any agent of the powers

Arab adage: "I and my brothers against my cousins, I and my cousins against my tribe, and I and my tribe against the world" serves to illustrate this point. The purpose of all allegiances, it is felt, from the family to the neighborhood to the region to the nation and even beyond, is to prevent being pushed around. For this reason, few Egyptians were surprised when Sadat, to the astonishment of the rest of the world, reversed a decade of

Left, three generations of a Cairo family. Above, man, beast and water-wheel.

that be, whether it be the boss, a wealthy foreigner, or the President of the Republic.

Forms of address in Egypt are complex and varied, as befits a highly stratified society. A taxi driver may be addressed, for example, as "O Chief Engineer" or "O Foreman." (Note that, when sitting in a taxi, one is a temporary guest and not merely a fare: it is therefore insulting for a lone male passenger to sit in the back seat by himself.) A person of high social standing should be addressed as "Your Presence," while a person of respectable but indeterminate standing is "O President" or "O Professor." An older person is "O Teacher" or "O Pilgrim," the latter referring of course to someone who has made the pilgrimage to Mecca. Even Turkish titles —

107

bey, pasha, hanem — survive, though they have no legal standing, and are used for courtesy's sake or humorous effect.

This diversity, while lending a great deal of charm to the simplest exchanges, in fact underlines the cohesiveness of the society rather than its disparateness: the Egyptian world-view sees all men as equals, but allots to each a specific status and with it a role. It is often remarked how Egyptians act out these roles with a sense of the dramatic. Nowhere are bureaucrats so bureaucratic from head to toe, rich men so fat, criminals so comically sinister, movie stars so glitzy, intellectuals so full of *Angst* or mothers so haplessly maternal. In the West, people seek individuality in the clothes they wear and in the mannerisms, speech and opinions they adopt. Egyptians

tom of the social pile, but their very existence testifies to general poverty. It would take the average worker a year to earn the price of a Cairo-New York round-trip ticket. As in Dickens' London, the vast majority are poor — and conscious not only of their poverty, but also of their majority.

Display of wealth in Egypt is often, to Western eyes, vulgar. But the flaunting of riches only confirms that, in a society forced to count pennies, money carries a special prestige. As a rich merchant, whose life-style is otherwise modest, commented, "Yes, I would rather have spent my money on something other than a Mercedes. But you wouldn't believe how much it saves me. I don't have to waste time — or money — proving myself. I get instant respect."

prefer to look like what they are.

Making Do: As in many other Third World countries, sharp disparities of wealth exist. There are some 50,000 millionaires, and for a time in the late 1970s, poverty-stricken Egypt was importing more Mercedes cars than any other country in the world. On Cairo's streets the contrast between the elegance of imported luxury and the rolling slum of a packed bus or the pathetic heap of a trash-collector's donkey cart is often shocking.

Trash collectors, known as *zabbalin* or "garbage people," live in conditions of appalling squalor, their homes nestled among putrid mounds of refuse, which they bring from the city, sort through and sell for recycling. The *zabbalin* represent the absolute bot-

Open Doors, Closed Options: Materialist ostentation has been particularly rife since the mid-1970s, when President Sadat reversed 20 years of socialist legislation with the announcement of his *Infitah*, or Open Door policy. Before him, Nasser had worked to redistribute the country's wealth, parceling out the great feudal estates, seizing the property of the richest families and reinvesting it in new state industries. Nasser's policies brought dignity to the majority at the expense of the few, but also frightened off private initiative. Not many landlords bothered even to paint their houses, for fear of attracting the tax man, while the state absorbed the burden of having to feed, clothe, house and employ its people. With *Infitah*, the lid was abruptly removed; and luxury imports boomed as money came out of Swiss banks or from under the floorboards. Fortunes were made overnight and a new class of fat cats replaced both the Nasser-era technocratic elite and the pre-Revolutionary landed gentry.

Allowing Egyptians underpaid at home to work profitably abroad, *Infitah* has brought improved living standards generally in the form of more TVs, more cars, better clothing, and a richer diet, but it has also inflated expectations and undermined social cohesiveness. Neither the poor nor the old elites approve of the *nouveau-riche* of today; and now that the quick money has been made, a new generation must face the prospect of a life of toil unrelieved by dreams of socialist utopia or the simplicity of the good old days.

looms still more menacingly on the horizon. Schools in Cairo already operate three shifts and a new school must be built every day.

Four wars in 30 years, after three of which the army had to re-equip from bootstraps to fighter aircraft, imposed an immense sacrifice on the Egyptian people. Shortage of cash meant that no more than temporary relief could be found from the burdens imposed on an already inadequate infrastructure by a burgeoning population. Only when the flow of foreign aid began to pick up in the late 1970s could the government begin to tackle such basic and long-term problems as sewage, electricity, telephones, drainage, traffic and drinking water. Cairo's air pollution and Alexandria's sewage remain monumental health problems, while neglect of education

A country without dreams can be a depressing place. The primary condition of Egypt — too many people — doesn't help. In 1968, when Israel was reveling in its conquest of the Sinai peninsula and half a million inhabitants of the cities along the Suez Canal had been made homeless, a journalist asked President Nasser what his major worry was. Without hesitation, he replied, "The thousand new Egyptians born every day." A generation later, the population pyramid

Left, funeral in the Fayum. Above, native scene of a wedding. Tapestries are woven by children.

has led to a frightening plunge in the already low literacy rate.

Products of a school system that stifles curiosity and promotes learning by rote, more and more young Egyptians feel a sense of frustration regarding the future. Among men, those who do not go on to university or manage to obtain an exemption must face three years of military service, often under conditions of extreme hardship. In the bigger cities, many younger women find jobs before marriage, but the majority stay at home and hope for the best. Better prospects await the one in ten young Egyptians of both sexes who attend university, but the country's dozen institutions of higher learning are appallingly overcrowded, understaffed and disorganized.

109

Despite rigid examinations, many graduates emerge barely qualified for the professions they hope to enter.

Until recently, the government nevertheless followed a policy of providing employment for every university graduate. The result has been that the Egyptian bureaucracy and public-sector industry, which together employ half of the non-agricultural workforce, is catastrophically overstaffed. Various studies have shown that the average government employee actually works for between six and 30 minutes a day. Low salaries and lenient employment policies have encouraged apathy and abuses at every level — obstruction and obfuscation, absenteeism, corruption, or simply intolerable rudeness to the ordinary taxpayer, who foots the bills.

New Anxieties: Low pay and a general loathing for the bureaucracy has meant that government jobs have lost must of their prestige. Increasingly one finds university graduates working as taxi-drivers, plumbers, mechanics and the like. The money is better and tradesmen stand a likelier chance of saving in order to get married, though with inflation and the limited availability of decent apartments, many are obliged to scrimp for years before they can establish a household. In the past decade over three million Egyptians — a people famed for their love of home — have gone abroad, most of them with the sole purpose of saving enough money to get married. Since typical salaries in Egypt range from 75 to 150 pounds a month, emigrants can often earn as much in a couple of years in the oil-rich Gulf as they would in a lifetime at home. Remittances from expatriates have become the key foreign currency earner for Egypt and the relative wealth of returning emigrés has been a major factor in pushing up prices.

Universally aspired to in Egypt, marriage provides no passport to a life of ease. The typical lifespan is not long — perhaps 55 years — and many Egyptians appear to die of worry or grief before they reach the stage when they require medical care, which is frequently inadequate anyway. Money, in particular, causes endless anxieties: feeding, educating and underwriting the marriages of numerous children is not cheap, especially when respectability must be maintained at all costs. While families and neighborhoods provide a degree of support unimaginable in the West, they also eliminate privacy; and the smallest problems quickly become everybody's business. The housing shortage means that too many people are often cooped up in the same house; and there are districts of Cairo where the average density is three to a room. In such conditions, already living under constant emotional and physical strain, many Egyptians additionally face the sort of calamities that in other countries have been relegated to sensationalist fiction: collapsing buildings, bursting sewers, bizarre accidents caused by murderous traffic or industrial hazards, Kafkaesque lawsuits or bureaucratic tangles.

Compensations: An atmosphere of melancholy pervades life, but strangely enough, the salient characteristic of the Egyptians is their cheerfulness. They are past masters at coping. Life's perpetual torment is approached with a sense of drama. All problems and situations are so endlessly discussed and analyzed that they end by becoming mere topics of amusement. The tales of intrigue, frustrated love, good fortune or catastrophe that even the simplest people relate in connection with their own personal lives retain a quality of wonder reminiscent of *The Thousand and One Nights*. Everyone has a story.

One of the reasons Egyptians therefore love crowds is that — far more, somehow, than in other countries — each face has a distinct expression, an emotional vitality reflecting depths of personal experience, much of it unhappy. The protective structure of society, based on the strength of family ties, allows Egyptian men and women to give free rein to their emotions. Families, neighbors and countrymen at large can all be relied on for compassion, commiseration or help. This solidarity makes Egypt one of the safest countries in the world. When someone shouts "Thief!" on the street, every shop empties as all and sundry help to chase the culprit, who is almost invariably caught and hauled off to the nearest police station by a gesticulating mob. Throughout Egypt, fewer murders are committed in a year than take place annually in any typical large city in America — a comparison reflecting the fact that Egyptian society allows fewer people to be marginalized. Every person has his recognized place, his special niche in the scheme of things.

Among the few who are pushed to the margin are the intellectuals, those who take the facts of life or the issues of politics too seriously. Burdening oneself with principles runs contrary to Egypt's propensity for en-

while dervishes dance to exhaustion to the rhythms of the *dhikr* (chanting in remembrance of God), local kids try out the swings, shooting galleries and assorted tests of strength, as their elders look on benignly. For a whole week the town or neighborhood around the tomb of the saint will resound with an ebullience of excitement and good will.

But even fun is not what it used to be. Respectable middle-class folk scorn the dowdy and unorthodox *mawalid*. Video tapes or television, with their fare of tinny, overdramatic soap operas, trashy foreign serials and official sloganizing, now provide the entertainment of the majority. These appurtenances of modern life have a powerful effect in a largely traditional society. Glorifying the bourgeois and "liberal" attitudes of the city,

joying the moment. Laughter heals all wounds; and if Egyptian wounds are more than most other people's, so likewise are there few other people who laugh so easily.

Time Out: Egypt's true carnivals, in the form of *mawalid* or saint's days, offer a glimpse of this street energy in concentrated form. Push-carts hawking everything from plastic machine guns to chick peas sprout overnight, vying for space with the tents and sleeping bodies of country pilgrims. On the Big Night,

homogenizing Egyptian life, television has also deprived it of much of its vitality.

It will be a long time yet, though, before the Egyptian people lose their appeal. Sensitivity and kindness still abound. Solicitous for the welfare of their fellows, Egyptians are invariably helpful, hospitable and friendly — indeed, almost to a fault: asking directions needs care, for example, since the response may be generated by a sense of social duty rather than by actual knowledge. Generosity is taken so much for granted that it is considered unseemly to offer thanks too profusely for a gift for fear of being insulting.

The warmth of human relations brings Egypt a *douceur*, a soft sweetness, that has always been the best part of its charm.

Left, an *erqsusi*, a vendor of licorice drink. Above, pottery kiln.

EGYPTIAN COFFEEHOUSES

In crowded Egypt, Allah can be counted on for two great mercies: endless sunshine and abundant free time. Small wonder that the street café, where much of these two great resources is spent, is so ubiquitous an institution. Few men — for the café, like much else in Egyptian society, is a solidly male preserve — permit a day to pass without killing a few minutes in a café exchanging jokes that turn the trial of life into a spectator sport.

When Edward Lane wrote his sociological classic *Manners and Customs of the Modern Egyptians* in the 1830s, he judged the number of cafés in Cairo at over 1,000. Then, as now, the café was the centerpiece of street life, the axis of commerce and the vortex of opinion. Given a similar ratio of one café per 400 people, the megalopolis of today would contain over 30,000 such establishments.

Atmospherics: The *qahwa* — Arabic for both "coffee" and "café" — is defined loosely. It can be anything from a bench, a patch of charcoal, a tin pot and three glasses to a cavernous saloon reverberating with the clack of dominoes, the slap of cards and the crackling of dice. In Cairo, a café may serve as the headquarters of a street gang, the meeting place for homesick provincials, or the rendezvous of intellectuals. There are cafés for musicians, black marketeers, leftists, Muslim extremists, homosexuals, retired generals, pimps, and wholesalers. There is even a café for the deaf and dumb, where absolute silence belies the animated conversation conducted by gesture alone and where the waiter balances a tray in one hand and takes orders with the other. In short, there are cafés for members of any class, profession, or persuasion.

The ideal café adjoins a small square in the back streets of a popular quarter. The simple decor of its exterior, replete with calligraphy and patterned tiles, will reveal the sense of style its patronage demands. The few outdoor tables will be shaded by a tree or vine, while the ground will have been sprinkled with water to keep down the dust. A pungent sweetness emanates from the interior, where sawdust covers the floor. An elaborate brass *sarabantina*, a cross between a steam locomotive and a samovar, occupies pride of place on the counter at the back of the room, behind which

Left, veteran smoker of the *sheesha* or water pipe. Right, Délices, a classically Alexandrine establishment.

striped glass jugs for water pipes line the walls. Just returned from the neighborhood barber, the patron puffs judiciously as he takes in the crime column of the morning paper. The *qahwagi* or waiter keeps up a continuous banter between forceful shouts to the tea boy, meanwhile dodging the shoeshine man as he shuffles by, tapping his box suggestively with a brush. The noise leaves the customers unfazed, absorbed as they are in their own affairs and in the passing life of the street.

Liquid Incidentals: Atmosphere is only the most visible of the pleasures the classier

café offers. To begin with, of course, there is the pleasure of indulging in a hot drink. Tea, introduced in the 19th Century, has replaced coffee as the staple. The powerful Egyptian version of the brew takes some getting used to. Since cheap tea dust is the preferred variety, it is no use anticipating delicate flavor. Tea is drunk as a fix, as strong and sweet as possible. It is best to make no compromises with local taste: sugarless, Egyptian tea is unpalatable. Some connoisseurs go as far as to say that the truly classic glass of tea should be only faintly translucent, with a mild aroma of kerosene from extended boiling on a Primus stove. In this form, tea is the perfect antidote to the hottest, dustiest, and most pestiferous of days.

Long used by the Arabian Bedouins, coffee

was introduced to Cairo by Sufi mystics in the 16th Century. The dervishes' adoption of the stimulant to prolong their ecstatic trances brought the wrath of the orthodox clergy down upon the bean. As with tobacco, controversy raged for decades before the weight of popular taste concluded the debate. Commerce played a crucial role, since Cairo quickly became the hub of the coffee trade. Grown in the mountains of Yemen and shipped from the Red Sea port of Al-Mukha (hence our term *Mocha*), the beans changed hands at Cairo to be forwarded to Istanbul and, with the westward advance of caffeine addiction, to the capitals of Europe.

Arabic coffee is still prepared and served in centuries-old style, without the fancy gadgetry of European invention. Sugar, then powdered coffee are added to hot water and brought to

mended for coughs, *erfa* (cinnamon) and *yansun* (aniseed) for the throat to *helba* (fenugreek) for stomach complaints. *Karkadé*, the scarlet tea of a hibiscus flower, is a specialty of Aswan. Packed with vitamin C, it is delicious hot or cold. *Sahleb*, a steaming cream, concocted from dried orchids and topped off with chopped nuts, is a winter favorite. In summer, cafés serve cooler drinks, ranging from lemonade, *tamarhindi* (tamarind), *erqsus* (licorice), and *farawla* (strawberry) to the ever more pervasive *Kukula*, *Bibs* and *Shwibs*, the commercially bottled soft drinks that have run old local brands off the market.

A Smoker's Paradise: The Egyptian café is a paradise for the serious smoker and has perfected the ultimate tobacco tool. The *sheesha* or water pipe cools, sweetens and lightens the

boil in a brass *kanaka*. The *qahwagi* brings the *kanaka* and cup on a tin tray and pours the liquid with solicitude, preserving the *wish* — the "face" — the thick mud which sits on the surface before settling. In the better cafés, a dark blend spiced with cardamon is used. In all establishments, the customer must specify how he wants his coffee — *saada*, or sugarless, *'arriha*, with a dash of sugar, *mazbut*, medium, or *ziyada*, with extra sugar. In some "European cafés," qahwa Faransawi or French coffee is served.

Of far more ancient origin — and of more interest to the inquisitive traveler — are the hot medicinal infusions which can still be found in many cafés. The bases of these potations range from ginger, *ganzabeel,* which is recom-

taste of burning leaves, makes a soothing gurgle and provides a pleasant distraction for idle hands. It is an instrument of meditation to be indulged in diligently and serenely, like an act of love.

Two kinds of tobacco are used. The most popular is *ma'assil*, a sticky blend of chopped leaf fermented with molasses. There are dozens of national brands of *ma'assil* and even more local varieties. It is pressed in small clay bowls which are fitted into the *sheesha* and lit with charcoal. *Tumbak*, the other variety, is loose dry tobacco wrapped into a cone with a whole leaf. While *ma'assil* is easy to smoke, a cone of *tumbak* may take an hour to exhaust, by which time the smoker may be ready for the cancer ward.

Until recently, hashish smoking was not uncommon in public places, especially at night. The *ghoraz*, or hash dens, of Cairo were famed throughout the Arab world. Official crackdowns however, have relegated this once-popular entertainment to seedy back alleys and private homes.

Some of Cairo and Alexandria's grander cafés offer intoxication in the form of liquor, but with the post-Revolutionary departure of the large Greek and Italian communities, these café-bars have lost much of their former glory. Brandy on ice is the most popular of a bewildering array of potions, none of which exactly inspires confidence. Their consumption appears to induce a thunderous, rippling and infectious form of laughter unique to Egypt, a mood of good cheer which makes such low-

draw the regular crowds. Despite the mass media and the telephone, average citizens still find that the best source of news — not to mention gossip, rumor, slander and fantasy — is among cronies at the local café. Formerly, any political candidate worth his salt began his campaign by making the round of cafés, ordering drinks on the house for any and all.

With the penchant for nostalgia and complaint that characterizes their country, afficionados will affirm that cafés are not what they used to be. Like the introduction of radio in the 1930s, which signalled the decline of traditional storytellers and poets, the more recent plague of television has led to a marked decline in the public entertainment. Luckily, most café owners leave their sets off except during major football matches. At such times,

life bars unforgettable.

Live Entertainment: Every café offers more innocent diversion in the form of cards (*kutshina*), backgammon (*tawla*) and dominoes. These games are not meant to be challenging to the intellect, but are played rather as an excuse for exchanging the insults and hyperbole for which the Arabic language is an unparalleled medium.

It is good conversation and companionship — sports in which the sociable Egyptians notably surpass everyone else in the world — that

Left, café patrons. Above, a café in Luxor.

when the two great teams of Ahli and Zamalek clash, the cafés are thronged with supporters. When a goal is scored, roars of applause echo across the whole country. Many cafés now have videos and offer a nightly dose of Indian romance, Egyptian humor, or American violence.

The time for dropping in on a café is the late afternoon, when the sun's dying rays turn duncolored buildings to gold. The Umm Kulthoum program on the radio begins at five. The same song issues from every doorway as, like smoke lazily breathed from a *sheesha*, the great Egyptian diva's voice sweetens the melancholy air. At such times, a hush falls over the country, until the evening *adhan* rouses the faithful to prayer.

PLACES

Egypt occupies 385,000 square miles (1 million square km) of Africa's driest and most barren corner, where the Mediterranean to the north nearly touches the Red Sea to the east. They are divided from each other and bridged only by the Sinai peninsula, which is geologically African, but geographically belongs to Asia. South and west, beyond wide barriers of desert, stretches the great body of the rest of Africa, to which Egypt is umbilically connected, in addition, by the slender nourishing lifeline of the Nile.

As it crosses the Sudanese border into Egypt, the Nile has already traveled 3,000 miles (5,000 km). Leaving mountain lakes, it has roared down cascades, steamed through swamps, and finally carved a serpentine path through a thousand miles of rock and sand. The temple of Abu Simbel, its four seated guardians regally awaiting the dawn, has witnessed the Nile's passage from Egypt's southern frontier for more than three millennia. Although the temple now backs into an artificial mountain above an artificial lake, it has lost none of its power to awe.

The artificial lake, the world's largest, is Lake Nasser, stored up behind the High Dam, just south of Aswan, a 20th-Century achievement that has changed the face and pace of Egypt forever. It is only below the High Dam that the rich Nile Valley blossoms into life.

An ancient frontier town, where the colors and smells of Africa blend with those of the East, Aswan itself marks the southern limit of navigation from the Mediterranean. Graceful lateen-rigged *feluccas* swish around the rock islands of the First Cataract, on one of which the famous temple of Philae stands. Cruise ships stop here and return from here northward, passing village after village, pharaonic temple after temple: Kom Ombo, Edfu, Esna, Luxor, Dendera and Abydos. At Luxor they pause in the center of the largest agglomeration of ancient building the world can offer, anchoring between the East Bank's great temple complexes of Karnak and Luxor and the West Bank's vast funerary cities, sited at the foot of the forbidding ridge that marks the beginning of the Sahara.

Further north, the river meanders timelessly on through fields fringed with date-palms, dotted with ambling water-buffalo. At length, with something of a shock, it swirls beneath the many bridges of Cairo. Fourteen million people inhabit this Arab-Mediterranean-African metropolis, whose vitality, variety, and sheer noisiness make them seem even more numerous. Here the medieval glory of Islam is preserved in domes and minarets, exquisite marble and metalwork. To the west of Cairo the Pyramids of Giza continue to present their mountainous geometry as they have for 200 generations, while the Sphinx erodes impassively at their feet.

At Cairo the Nile exfoliates into the Delta, spreading itself lushly until, much diminished, it finally reaches the Mediterranean Sea. Joined to the Nile by canals is Alexandria, Egypt's most important coastal city. Since its founding by Alexander the Great this celebrated seaport's fortunes have risen, fallen, and risen again in rhythm with those of the Mediterranean itself. From here a flat coastline stretches east and west, its fine white sand touched only recently by development.

The Nile and its Valley are not all there is to Egypt. Deep in the deserts and now accessible to the casual visitor lie miraculous islands of living green: the Oases. More life abounds in the salty depths of the Red Sea — which offers underwater sightseeing second to none, unsurpassed coral and teeming tropical fish — although it, too, is ringed by desert. And there is the Sinai peninsula, linking Asia and Africa at the head of the Red Sea, a landscape of striking beauty. Its ragged red mountains and odd verdant valleys have an other-worldly, almost magical quality. God certainly showed his usual flair in choosing such a place for his rendezvous with Moses. What is harder to understand is why he ever commanded Moses to leave Egypt.

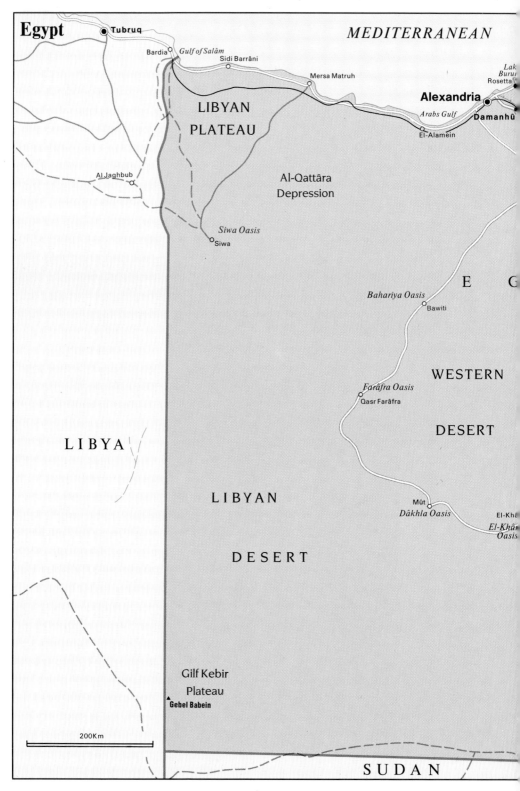

Egypt

Tubruq

MEDITERRANEAN

Bardia

Gulf of Salâm

Sidi Barrâni

Mersa Matruh

LIBYAN

PLATEAU

El-Alamein

Arabs Gulf

Lak Buru
Rosetta

Alexandria

Damanhû

Al Jaghbub

Al-Qattâra
Depression

Siwa Oasis

Siwa

Bahariya Oasis

Bawiti

E   G

WESTERN

Farâfra Oasis

Qasr Farâfra

DESERT

LIBYA

Mût
Dâkhla Oasis

El-Khâ

El-Khâ
Oasis

LIBYAN

DESERT

Gilf Kebir
Plateau
▲
Gebel Babein

200Km

SUDAN

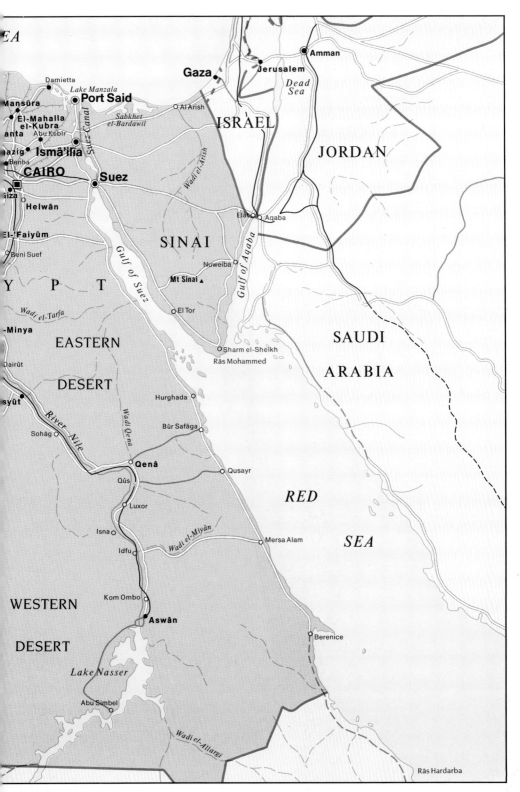

EA

Damietta

Mansûra

El-Mahalla
el-Kubra
Abu Kebîr

anta

azig • Benha

CAIRO

iza

Helwân

El-'Faiyûm

Beni Suef

Y P T

Wadi el-Tarfa

-Minya

EASTERN

Dairût

syût

Sohâg

River Nile

DESERT

Lake Manzala

Port Said

Suez Canal

Sabkhet
el-Bardawil

Ismâ'ilia

Suez

Al 'Arîsh

Gaza

ISRAEL

Jerusalem

Dead
Sea

Amman

JORDAN

Wadi el-Arîsh

SINAI

Elât Aqaba

Nuweiba

Mt Sinai ▲

El Tor

Gulf of Suez

Gulf of Aqaba

SAUDI

ARABIA

Sharm el-Sheikh

Râs Mohammed

Hurghada

Wadi Qena

Bûr Safâga

Qenâ

Qûs

Luxor

Isna

Idfu

Kom Ombo

Aswân

WESTERN

DESERT

Lake Nasser

Abu Simbel

Qusayr

Wadi el-Miyân

Mersa Alam

RED

SEA

Berenice

Wadi el-Allaqi

Râs Hardarba

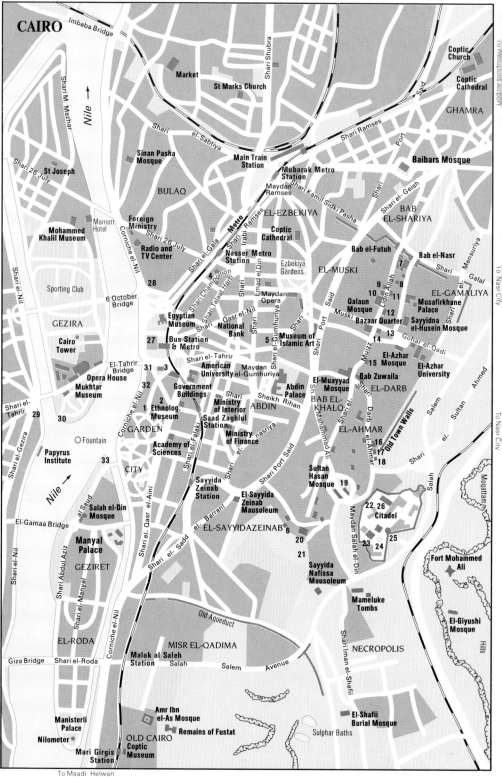

CAIRO

To Alexandria, Nile Delta

Imbaba Bridge

To Heliopolis Airport

Market

St Marks Church

Shari Shubra

Coptic Church

Coptic Cathedral

GHAMRA

Shari el-Sabtiya

Shari el-Sabtiya

Sinan Pasha Mosque

Main Train Station

Shari Ramses

Shari Ramses

Baibars Mosque

BAB EL-SHARIYA

St Joseph

Shari 26 July

Shari M. Mazhar

Nile →

BULAQ

Mubarak Metro Station

Maydan Ramses

Shari Kamil Sidki Pasha

Shari el-Geish

To Nasr City

Mohammed Khalil Museum

Marriott Hotel

Foreign Ministry

Shari 26 July

EL-EZBEKIYA

Coptic Cathedral

Bab el-Futuh

Bab el-Nasr

Shari el-Galal

Mensuriya

Radio and TV Center

Nasser Metro Station

Ezbekiya Gardens

EL-MUSKI

7

EL-GAMALIYA

To Nasr City

Sporting Club

GEZIRA

6 October Bridge

28

4

Maydan Opera

Qalaun Mosque

Bazaar Quarter

8

9

10

11

12

Musafirkhane Palace

Sayyidna el-Husein Mosque

Cairo Tower

Egyptian Museum

National Bank

27

Bus Station & Metro

5

Museum of Islamic Art

13

14

15

El-Azhar Mosque

El-Azhar University

Opera House

Mukhtar Museum

El-Tahrir Bridge

31 3

American University el-Gumhuriya

Maydan el-Gumhuriya

Abdin Palace

El-Muayyad Mosque

Bab Zuwaila

EL-DARB

32

Government Buildings

BAB EL-KHALQ

To Nasr City

2 Ethnolog. Museum

Ministry of Interior

Saad Zaghlul Station

ABDIN

Sheikh Rihan

EL-AHMAR

29

30

GARDEN

Academy of Sciences

Ministry of Finance

16

17

18

Fountain

33

CITY

Sayyida Zeinab Station

Sultan Hasan Mosque

19

22 26

Citadel

Papyrus Institute

El-Sayyida Zeinab Mausoleum

23

24

25

Salah el-Din Mosque

EL-SAYYIDAZEINAB

6

Fort Mohammed Ali

Manyal Palace

GEZIRET

20

21

Sayyida Nafissa Mausoleum

El-Giyushi Mosque

EL-RODA

El-Gamaa Bridge

Giza Bridge

Shari el-Roda

Old Aqueduct

MISR EL-QADIMA

Malak al Saleh Station

Mameluke Tombs

NECROPOLIS

Hills

Manisterli Palace

Nilometer

Amr Ibn el-As Mosque

Remains of Fustat

Sulphar Baths

El-Shafii Burial Mosque

Mari Girgis Station

OLD CAIRO Coptic Museum

To Maadi Helwan

To Pyramids of Giza

CAIRO, MOTHER OF THE WORLD

"I can't believe this city!" a young American visiting **Cairo** for the first time said recently. "If I hadn't come here, I couldn't possibly have imagined anything of what it's really like." His reaction is typical and echoes a 600-year-old remark recorded by Ibn Khaldun, the great medieval Arab historian and social theorist, who reported a traveler telling him in 1384 that "what one can imagine always surpasses what one sees, because of the scope of the imagination, except Cairo, because it surpasses anything one can imagine."

And when Ibn Khaldun finally came and saw the city himself, it certainly lived up to expectations: Cairo, he wrote, is "the metropolis of the universe, the garden of the world, the anthill of the human species, the throne of royalty, a city embellished with castles and palaces, its horizon decorated with monasteries and with schools, and lighted by the moons and stars of erudition."

What Ibn Khaldun was looking at was a city that had been devastated by the Black Death three decades earlier — the same plague that also depopulated the little city of mid-14th Century Europe — and had entered a long twilight of decline. It remained nevertheless the greatest metropolis on earth, still larger in both population and extent than any city west of China. Enriched by the spice trade, by traffic in luxury goods, and by re-distribution of urban and rural properties among the diminished population, its sultans and amirs continued to adorn the city with increasingly extravagant architecture. Pious endowments multiplied, providing a haven for Muslim scholars as they fled from the genocides of the Reconquista in the West or Tamerlane in the East, drawn to Cairo, like Ibn Khaldun himself (who was of Spanish origin), by the reputation for generous support of intellectual activity that the city had already enjoyed for three centuries.

City of 1001 Nights: It was during this period, sometime between 1382 and 1517, that the stories we know as *The Arabian Nights* were given their final form, not in the almost legendary Baghdad of Harun Al Rashid, but in the real Cairo of the Circassian Mamluks, a city of wonders, where miraculous reversals of fortune, as history records, were an everyday occurrence. "He who hath not seen Cairo" says a character in one of these tales, "hath not seen the world. Her soil is gold; her Nile is a marvel; her women are like the black-eyed virgins of Paradise; her houses are palaces; and her air is soft, as sweet-smelling as aloeswood, rejoicing the heart. And how can Cairo be otherwise, when she is Mother of the World?"

The Mother of the World is an old lady now, somewhat long in the tooth. The gold in her soil has ceased to glitter, her Nile has been thoroughly tamed; and though her women still have many admirers, her palatial houses are being rapidly demolished to make way for concrete high-rises, while her sweet-smelling air has achieved the highest pollution index in the world. She has become, in other words, a thoroughly modern metropolis.

The most radical changes have come within the past 10 years. In 1960 fewer than 40 percent of the Egyptian people were city-dwellers and only one out of every eight Egyptians was a Cairene. The city then had a population of less than 3.5 million. Today 80 percent of Egyptians live in an urban setting, one out of every three lives in Cairo, and the city's population has passed the 14-million mark, doubling every 10 years. In terms of population alone Cairo is not merely the largest city in Africa or the Middle East or the Arab World, but the largest within its third of the globe, an area defined by the longitudes of Brazil and India and by the North and South Poles.

Recent growth is clearly related to the population explosion taking place everywhere in the Third World. But the modern city occupies a position at the head of the Nile Delta that has been strategic for five thousand years and that has consequently seen many urban foundations, of which Cairo itself is merely the largest and the latest.

Memphis: The most important of Cairo's predecessors was the city of **Memphis**, founded by Menes, traditionally regarded as the first king of the first Dynasty, on land reclaimed from the Nile in about 3100 B.C. The site lies 15 miles (24 km) by road south of Cairo on the western side of the Nile. It can be reached by driving down the eastern bank and crossing the bridge over the

131

river south of Helwan; or by crossing the river directly into Giza and then driving south either along the main highway that goes from Giza to Upper Egypt or along the far more attractive agricultural road that runs south from near the Giza Pyramids. The ruins of Memphis surround the village of **Mit Rahinah**, which derives its name from a temple of Mithras that was built here under the Romans, long after the days of the city's greatest glory.

There is very little to see at Memphis now except one of Ramses' two colossi (the other may be seen in front of Cairo's central railway station at Ramses Square where it was re-erected in 1955). More has been brought to light in the course of recent excavation and surveying by British, American and Egyptian experts, but the casual visitor is advised to enjoy the serenity of the surrounding groves of date-palms, meditate briefly on the perishability of power, then push on up the road. Ahead, on the desert plateau overlooking the green of Memphis, is a portion of the ancient capital's necropolis, the vast cemetery of **Saqqarah**, with religious and funerary monuments that span a period from the 27th Century

B.C. to the 10th Century A.D., standing in the midst of an even larger pyramid field that stretches for miles to the north and south.

Saqqarah: The ticket office at the entrance to the Saqqarah necropolis stands above the valley temple attached to the **pyramid of Unas**, last king of the Fifth Dynasty (c.2375 B.C.–2345 B.C.), which houses the earliest Pyramid text: the ceremonial causeway linking the two has been excavated and the pyramid, visible at the end of it half a mile away, is one of the easiest for a visitor to enter. Dominating the whole area, however, is the **Step Pyramid** of Zozer (Third Dynasty, 2668 B.C.–2649 B.C.), the earliest of all the pyramids and the first great monument in the world to be built of hewn stone.

The main parking lot for the area is conveniently located just below the Step Pyramid enclosure, magnificently restored under the direction of the French archaeologist J.-P. Lauer, whose work continues. The entire complex within the enclosure, including shrines, courtyards and the Step Pyramid itself, was the conception of a single man, Imhotep, Zozer's chief of works, who was perhaps

The Step Pyramid of Zoser at Saqqarah circa 3,000 B.C.

the first recorded genius in history. An inscription left behind by a New Kingdom tourist venerates him as "he who opened the stone" and he was later identified with magic, astronomy and medicine, finally becoming deified in the sixth Century B.C. Translating motifs from more perishable materials, such as wood or papyrus reeds, into stone, the Zozer complex displays many features that became a permanent part of the Egyptian architectural vocabulary and a few that have apparently remained unique.

The Step Pyramid can be entered only with special permission; the tour takes several hours, and there is no lighting inside. A cross-section, however, would reveal its complexity, arising from the fact that it began as a *mastaba* (from an Arabic word that refers to the usual oblong shape), a one-storey tomb of common type. Even here Imhotep showed his originality, for his *mastaba* was square rather than oblong and built of stone rather than the usual mud-brick. On a clear day, the Step Pyramid is easily visible from Cairo, nine miles (15 km) away as the crow flies.

A conscientious visit to Saqqarah can take all day and the local tradition is to make the occasion an excuse for a picnic, usually eaten in the ruins of the **monastery of St. Jeremiah,** which are quite close to the parking lot below the enclosure on the opposite side of the causeway to the pyramid of Unas. Founded in the sixth Century A.D. and destroyed in the 10th, it is this monastery that has supplied the objects to be found in Rooms 6 and 7 of the Coptic Museum.

Cheerful Realism: Not to be missed, no matter how short a visit, are two Sixth Dynasty *mastabas*, the **tombs of Mereruka and Kagemni,** who were both viziers of King Teti (c.2345 B.C.–2333 B.C.). Nestled next to the pyramid of Teti, northeast of the Zozer complex, these two structures promise nothing to the outside. The interior walls of both, however, are carved with lively scenes of domestic life, probably designed and executed by the same hands, showing the interests and pursuits of the Old Kingdom nobility: hunting, horticulture, husbandry, music and dancing, preparations to ensure that the next world would be as bountiful as this one. The artist's carved workmen exchange hieroglyphic one-liners; and such is the acuteness of

Entrance to the funerary complex of Zoser at Saqqarah

his observations that over 50 different species of fish have been readily identified by modern experts from these stone depictions. Almost as satisfying are the scenes in the sixth-Century *mastaba* **of Ankh-ma-hor**, a few steps away in the same group of tombs, which show similar pursuits, but are particularly famous for their depictions of craftsmen (jewelers, metalworks, sculptors) and physicians.

Directly west of the pyramid of Teti, a kilometer away and connected with it by a dirt road parallel to what was once an avenue of sphinxes, is a rest house serving cold beer and soft drinks. Near the rest house, left of the dirt road, is the double fifth-Dynasty **tomb of Akhte-hotep and (his son) Ptah-hotep**, high officials under the kings preceding Unas. To the right of the road is the **tomb of Ti**, their slightly older contemporary. Here too are remarkable scenes from daily life, including depictions of children's games (Ptah-hotep) and boat-building (Ti).

Bulls and Baboons: Below the rest house is the **Serapeum**, the catacomb of the sacred Apis bull, whose rites were witnessed by Herodotus during his sojourn in Egypt. A circle of statues representing Greek poets and philosophers, set up by Ptolemy I (323 B.C.–282 B.C.), marks the entrance, but except for the size of the bulls' sarcophagi, in which no taurine remains have ever been found, the Serapeum itself offers little to stimulate either logic or the imagination, though it makes a nice temporary retreat on a hot day. Immediately to the north are graveyards for the mummies of other animals: baboons, now extinct in Egypt, though they can still be found in the Sudan; and ibis (three species were known to the ancients, identified by modern experts as Sacred, Bald and Glossy), now very rare, though the name is often given locally to the cattle egret. In the same area are tombs from the First Dynasty (3050 B.C.–2090 B.C.) and the 30th (380 B.C.–342 B.C.), curiously adjoining in space though separated by 17 centuries in time.

Just south of the Zozer complex, beyond the pyramid of Unas, is the recently discovered (1950) unfinished **Step Pyramid of Sekhemhet**, Zozer's successor (2649 B.C.–2643 B.C.), overlooking an area where there has been a great deal of archaeological activ-

A sphinx at Memphis near Saqqarah.

134

ity. Here in 1975, while looking for the tomb of Maya, an official of Tutankhamen, the Egypt Exploration Society discovered a tomb prepared for Horemheb, Tutankhamen's general, who would become a pharoah himself (1321 B.C.–1293 B.C.). Eleven years later, Maya's tomb was finally found, but not before an enormous amount from other burials had been cleared away and examined testifying to the area's incredible richness.

Following further south, accessible on foot, by donkey, horse, or camel (which can be rented at the rest house) or by a vehicle with four-wheel drive, are several more monuments: the **pyramid complex of Pepi I** (2332 B.C.–2283 B.C.), the **pyramid complex of Djedkare Isesi** (2414 B.C.–2375 B.C.) with the pyramid of a queen nearby; the tomb of **Shepseskaf** (2504 B.C.–2500 B.C.); the **pyramid complex of Pepi II** (2278 B.C.–2184 B.C.); and three other pyramids, one of them identified as belonging to Userkare Khendjer (c.1747 B.C.).

In the Saqqarah area alone, in fact, no fewer than 15 royal pyramids have been excavated, creating a zone more than three miles (five km) long. And what has been discovered thus far is only a tiny fraction of what lies still buried under the sands which must cover innumerable unknown tombs, including — somewhere — that of Imhotep, the great architect.

The relationship of all these monuments to Memphis is made clear by the fact that "Memphis" is derived from one of them: the pyramid of Pepi I, which was called *Men-Nefer*, "Established and Beautiful." Replacing the older epithets that had identified the city — "The White Wall," "That which Binds the Two Lands Together" — this term, rendered in a Greek form, has become the name by which we know the ancient capital. But the Saqqarah monuments themselves are only part of the Memphite necropolis as a whole, which extends north along the desert plateau beyond Giza to Abu Rawash and southward to Dahshur and Mazghuna, a total distance of about 20 miles (33 km).

Pyramids of Dahshur: Off-limits to foreigners for years because of a local military base, the peace and quiet beauty of the agricultural countryside around Dahshur have attracted many of Cairo's

professional class, who have built rural retreats here. Failing an invitation from one of them, the most pleasant time of year to visit the seven royal pyramids of Dahshur is mid-winter, when a lake forms within an artificial embankment below the **Black Pyramid**, built of brick but unused by Amenemhet III (1842 B.C.–1797 B.C.), one of Egypt's most colorful kings. Amenemhet's pyramid and temple complex at **Hawarah** on the edge of the Fayyum was visited by Herodotus, who describes it as a wonder greater than the pyramids of Giza; and his building of another smaller pyramid here seems to have been a gesture, not uncommon, towards the old capital's prestige. The dark color that gives it its modern name arises from the fact that it has been systematically stripped of its original white limestone covering. The view of it across the lake is one of the most charming in Egypt, worth the three-mile (five km) drive from Saqqarah. Its inscribed capstone is in the Egyptian Museum.

There are two other 12th-Dynasty pyramids here, another from the 13th-Dynasty, and a third not yet identified. Most striking, however, are two Fourth Dynasty pyramids, built by Snefru (2613 B.C.–2589 B.C.). The southernmost of these two pyramids is the third largest in Egypt and is easily distinguished, standing about 300 yards further into the desert beyond the pyramid of Amenemhet III, not only by its bulk, but by its peculiar shape, which has led it to be called the **Bent Pyramid**: the 54-degree slope of its sides changes halfway up to a shallower angle of 43 degrees, as if the builders either feared for its stability or were in a hurry to finish their work. Visible a mile and a half away almost directly north is its companion, sometimes called the **Red Pyramid**, which uses a 43-degree angle throughout its height, the earliest known to have been completed as a "true" pyramid, built less than 60 years after Imhotep's great discovery. The Bent Pyramid made internal use of cedar trunks imported from Lebanon, still intact, as beams, and is externally the best preserved of all the pyramids, thanks to an ingenious construction method that made stripping its surface difficult. About 650 yards northwest of the Bent Pyramid, between it and the Red Pyramid, are the remains of Snefru's mortuary temple, re-dedicated

The Pyramids of Cheops and Kefren at Giza.

to him during the Middle Kingdom and under the Ptolemies, when many ancient cults were revived.

Snefru was the father and immediate predecessor of Khufu (2589 B.C.–2566 B.C.), better known by the Greek form of his name as Cheops, builder of the **Great Pyramid** at Giza. Khufu's own immediate successor, Djedefre (2566 B.C.–2556 B.C.) built a pyramid at **Abu Rawash**, six miles (10 km) northwest of Giza, which marks the northernmost limit of the Memphite necropolis; and three miles (five km) south of Dahshur, at **Mazghuna**, are two ruined pyramids possibly marking its southernmost limit. Still further south are other royal pyramids associated with other more temporary capitals, while occasional non-royal pyramids can be found even south of Luxor. Six more pyramid sites belonging to the Memphite necropolis — four structures from the Fifth Dynasty, one of them hardly begun, at **Abusir**, and two uncompleted pyramids at Zawayet al-'Aryan — have been discovered between Saqqarah and Giza.

Pyramids of Giza: The **pyramids of Giza** (called *al-Ahram* in Arabic), the only survivors among the Seven Wonders of the World, are not hard to find. Standing at the end of a boulevard (Shari' al-Ahram) on the desert plateau above the western edge of Giza, across the river from Cairo, they can most usefully be seen in combination with a visit either to Saqqarah or to the modern villages of Kirdassah and Harraniyyah.

Kirdassah, situated at the end of an old caravan route to Libya, three miles (five km) north of Shari' al-Ahram, formerly supplied goods for desert traders and has become a center for weaving, textiles and ready-made clothing, including the *gallibiyas* that Westerners know as "kaftans." **Harraniyyah**, three miles (five km) south of Shari' al-Ahram on the road to Saqqarah, houses the famous **Wissa Wassef tapestry workshops** in a group of buildings that have won international acclaim for their architecture. Now managed by the widow of founder Ramsis Wissa Wassef, the workshops export tapestries worldwide, usually made to order, though there is always a good selection on view. Half a mile or so farther down the same road an outstanding collection of modern Egyptian painting and sculpture is visible at the

The Sphinx.

Aida Gallery, which holds special exhibitions throughout the winter season.

At the foot of the pyramids, on the road leading up to them from Shari' al-Ahram, is the **Mena House Oberoi Hotel**, which incorporates the old **Mena House**, one of the most celebrated hotels in the world. Connected by a tramline to Cairo in 1900, shortly after its opening, it soon rivaled the famous **Shepheard's**, entertaining statesmen at three historic international conferences, the latest in 1978. Its lavish neo-Islamic decor has been carefully preserved by its new managers.

The most striking thing about the Giza pyramids is their size. The **Great Pyramid of Khufu** was originally 480 feet (150 meters) high and incorporates 2.3 million stone blocks averaging more than 2.5 tons in weight. Contrary to popular belief, however, it is neither the biggest pyramid in the world — that distinction belongs, according to the *Guinness Book of Records*, to the Quetzalcoatl pyramid at Cholula, south of Mexico City, which covers an area more than three times as extensive — nor was it built by slaves. Teams of skilled laborers on three-month hire were supplemented by a permanent work force of local quarrymen. Other crews cut limestone and granite construction blocks at Tura and Aswan and transported them across or down the Nile to the building site. There was housing for 4,000, suggesting large and permanent administrative and support staffs.

Pyramid Power: Climbing the Great Pyramid is strictly forbidden, which does not prevent local "guides" from offering their services or the foolish from accepting them. Illicit climbs have resulted in one or two fatalities annually for the past several years and are not recommended, though the task may look easy from a distance. Stripped of their smooth white Tura limestone upper casing and extensively quarried lower down for granite from the 11th Century A.D. onward — no major monument built in Cairo between 1087 and 1517 was without a contribution from the pharaohs — its sides slope at an angle of 52 degrees, the normal gradient for all the pyramids built after Snefru's Bent Pyramid and Red Pyramid at Dahshur.

Except for their size, the isolated silhouettes of all the later large pyramids in Egypt would therefore have looked

Open air theater at the Pyramids of Giza.

exactly like the Great Pyramid. Each, however, would also have stood within an enclosed complex, like Zozer's at Saqqarah, and would have been further particularized not only by inscriptions, but also by a cap that was possibly either painted or gilded.

The interior of the Great Pyramid can be visited and includes a grand gallery with a corbelled roof that is itself regarded as one of the most remarkable architectural works of the Old Kingdom. East of the Great Pyramid is the site of Khufu's mortuary temple, identified by the remains of a basalt pavement, north and south of which are two boat pits. Near its base at the south are two more boat pits, one of which was excavated in 1954, when a complete dismantled river barge was found, probably secreted there to serve some magical purpose in connection with the sun cult. Beautifully re-assembled, it can be admired in the **Solar Boat Museum** that has been constructed on the site.

The causeway leading from the Great Pyramid's mortuary temple to its valley temple is largely ruinous and cannot be excavated at its lower end thanks to the encroachment of modern buildings, but

just south of it, close to a group of three subsidiary pyramids, the only undisturbed tomb thus far found of the Old Kingdom was uncovered in 1925. Though the sarcophagus in it was empty, it was identified as the tomb of Queen **Hetepheres**, wife of Snefru and mother of Khufu, and yielded extraordinary objects, including a carrying-chair and a portable boudoir, with its linen curtains as well as its gilt bed and chair, all of which may be seen in the Egyptian Museum.

The Sphinx: The pyramid of **Khafre** (Chephren 2589 B.C.–2566 B.C.), just south of the Great Pyramid and second to it in size, not only preserves a considerable part of its limestone casing at the top, but is also the most complete in relation to its surrounding complex, which includes the **Sphinx**. Intended originally to represent a guardian deity in the shape of a lion, the Sphinx had Khafre's face, disfigured and beardless, it is said, thanks to Mamluk artillery practice. Later associated with the sun god and with Horus of the Horizon, as a Greek drinking song scratched on one of its toes during the Ptolemaic period attests, it was apparently the object of

Tapestry in progress at the Wissa Wassef Art School, Giza.

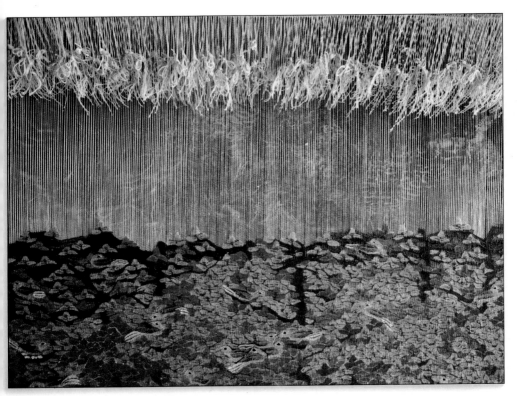

pilgrimages, especially during the 18th Dynasty. In front of it stands a granite stele set up by order of Tuthmosis IV (1423 B.C.–1417 B.C.), who records a dream he had while still a prince: while he was resting under its shade during a hunting expedition, the Sphinx appeared to him and spoke, promising Tuthmosis the kingdom if he would clear away accumulated sand from around its feet. The story is good enough to be re-told and has consequently circulated for centuries since as a folk tale involving later rulers: in one malicious 20th-Century version the hero is Gamal Abdul Nasser and the boon the Sphinx asks for is an exit visa.

And Baby Makes Three: The third of the royal pyramids at Giza was begun by Menkaure (Mycerinus, 2532 B.C.–2504 B.C.), Khafre's successor. By far the smallest, it was apparently left unfinished at Menkaure's death and hurriedly completed by his son, Shepseskaf, whose own tomb at Saqqarah has already been mentioned. There are signs of haste throughout the complex, even in the pyramid itself, which may have been intended originally to be encased entirely in red granite. In the end only 16 courses of granite were laid and some of the blocks were left undressed, the upper portion of the pyramid being encased in the usual limestone. Brick was used to finish off the mortuary temple, causeway and valley temple, though they had been begun in limestone and some of the blocks weigh as much as 200 tons, showing that the failure to complete it in limestone was by no means due to a decline to technical mastery. The ruins of the valley temple, now covered again with sand, were cleared many decades ago and yielded several important sculptures, including the schist pair of King Menkaure and Queen Khamerenebty now in the Boston Museum and the superb graywacke triads of Menkaure embraced by pairs of goddesses, all bearing the features of a lady who may be the same queen, now in the Egyptian Museum.

The City of the Sun: Clustered around the three great pyramids are scores of lesser tombs, some of them small pyramids, originally laid out in orderly rows along the same north-south axis as the tombs of the pharaohs. It seems clear that all the tombs at Giza, including the three great pyramids, were connected not only with Memphis but with the royal cult of Re,

the universal sun god, centered at On, the city the Greeks called **Heliopolis** (City of the Sun). Heliopolis stood 15 miles (25 km) northwest of Giza and thus 20 miles (32 km) almost directly north of Memphis, at the edge of the flood plain on the opposite side of the Nile, at a site that is now not easy to find in the modern district of Al-Matariyyah.

Mentioned in the Bible (Genesis 41:45, "And Pharaoh called Joseph's name Zaphnathpaaneah; and he gave him to wife Asenath the daughter of Potipherah priest of On"), Heliopolis was another of Cairo's ancient predecessors. The primary theological center of Old Kingdom Egypt, it was finally displaced in importance by Thebes, but not before its priests had developed and written down elaborate rituals, liturgies and mythologies that revolve around the sun god Re and a host of lesser deities known as the Great Company. Ramses III (1182 B.C.–1151 B.C.) the last of Egypt's great pharaohs, is recorded as endowing Heliopolis with over 12,000 serfs and more than 100 towns, not to mention buildings, statues, gold, silver, linens, precious stones, birds, incense, cattle and fruit. Many earlier kings had erected obelisks there.

Even in ancient times, Heliopolis had begun to suffer a decline that eventually led to systematic pillaging. Strabo, who visited the site in 24 B.C., recorded its desolation and 14 years later a pair of obelisks erected by Tuthmoses III (1504 B.C.–1450 B.C.) were removed by the Romans to adorn their new Caesarium, the temple of the recently deified Julius Caesar in Alexandria. Some 19 centuries later, during the reign of Khedive Ismail, these two monuments found their way out of Egypt altogether and became the "Cleopatra's Needles" of London and New York, which have nothing at all to do with any of several Cleopatras. Only one obelisk, from a famous pair erected in the reign of Senusert I (1971 B.C.–1928 B.C.), survives on the site, where it has been re-erected by the Egyptian Antiquities Organization. Otherwise there is virtually nothing left of ancient Heliopolis. It is quite unconnected with the modern suburb sometimes called by that name.

"How Many Miles to Babylon?": Modern Cairo began at a point, halfway between Memphis and Heliopolis, where a road crossed the river, using the present island of Rawdah as a stepping stone.

A hazy Cairo seen from the Pyramids of Giza.

Since there were no other roads across the Delta, this road not only connected the Old Kingdom's administrative and religious capitals, but was the main passage into Egypt from the East, giving access to the rest of the country. During the Late Dynastic period a small fortress was built here and after a canal linking the Nile with the Red Sea was completed by the Persian occupiers under Darius I (521 B.C–486 B.C.), the site became even more important. The Greeks called it **Babylon**, a name that should not be confused with Mesopotamian Babylon and that probably derives from some such Egyptian name as *Pi-Hapi-n-On* or *Per-Hapi-n-On*, meaning ''The Nile House of On.'' Under the Emperor Trajan (98 A.D.–117 A.D.), after more than a century of Roman occupation, when Heliopolis had long been moribund, the old canal was reopened and a new fortress was built, one of three to control the whole of Egypt. The Alexandrian astronomer and geographer Claudius Ptolemy recorded a visit he made to Babylon within the following half century, when he found a thriving town already established around the fortress with the canal running through it.

Memphis still remained important, however, one of its New Kingdom suburbs (*Hikuptah* — ''The Temple of the Ka of Ptah'') having supplied the Greeks and their Roman successors with *Aigyptos* as the name of the entire country.

Cairo's Real Name: In the Mediterranean world of the Greeks and Romans, states usually took their names from the cities that were their origin and from which the sovereignty of their rulers ultimately derived. This historical logic could not apply to regions where there were no cities, to tribal or nomadic societies, or to the ancient empires and monarchies of the Middle East, where sovereignty rested in rulers who made and unmade cities. Egyptians themselves thus knew their country by many names, of which the most common during the Roman period was probably *Kemet*, ''The Black Land,'' from which the Arabic word ''alchemy'' is derived. Throughout the rest of the Semitic-speaking Middle East, Egypt was called Misr, the name it still bears in Arabic, which is, of course, the present language of the country.

When the Arabs conquered Misr in 641 A.D. and founded a new capital next to the walls of Babylon, this capital

Tents, sometimes still appliqueed by hand, are used for funeral wakes as well as festivals.

acquired the name of the country as a whole, which became more and more appropriate as new quarters with new names were added and it expanded to become the metropolis not only of Egypt, but of the Arab world, a huge city containing many distinct areas with their own lesser names. The Western name "Cairo" derives from "Al-Qahirah," the name of a single one of these later quarters as understood by medieval Italian merchants, who mistook it for a complete city like their little walled towns. Neither "Cairo" nor "Al-Qahirah" was ever used by Egyptians themselves to designate their capital city until recent decades, when "Al-Qahirah" was adopted, under Western influence, by the mass media. For the Cairene in the street and for most Egyptians Cairo remains "Misr," as it was officially for centuries.

Foretaste of Glory: The remains of Roman and Christian Babylon can be found in the area thus known as **Misr al-Qadimah**, which confusingly translates into "Old Cairo," though it is as distinct from Al-Qahirah as Misr al-Gadidah ("New Cairo") is from ancient Heliopolis, and should not be mistaken for repre-

The mosque and tomb of a local holy man.

senting more than a foretaste of Cairo's medieval glory. Here too are interesting remains from Egypt's Christian era, as well as one monument from the years immediately following the Arab conquest. Largely intact until the British occupation, what is left of the Roman fortress of Babylon can be visited conveniently in conjunction with the **Coptic Museum**, and can be reached by taxi or by metro. The metro stop is **Mari Girgis** (St. George) and stands opposite the modern Greek Orthodox church of the same name, which is actually built on a Roman tower. At this point the metro line itself follows an old course of the Nile, which in Roman times washed a shoreline just beneath Babylon's walls. The grounds of the museum begin immediately south of the tower and are entirely within the fortress walls.

Founded by private benefactors on land belonging to the Coptic Church, the museum was taken over by the Egyptian government in 1931. Though there are hundreds of ancient Christian sites in Egypt, there are none in which the churches themselves have not been abandoned, destroyed, or extensively rebuilt inside and out. It is therefore only the

The mosque and tomb of a local holy man.

Coptic Museum that can now give us some idea of what the interior of a fifth-, sixth- or seventh- Century church was like. Objects excavated in Upper Egypt and in the ruins of the monastery of St. Jeremiah at Saqqarah are of particular interest and experienced travelers can see the relationship between them and remains from Sudan and Ethiopia, where the Coptic Church also represented a national religion. The museum's most prized relics, however, are the "Nag Hammadi Codices," a collection of nearly 1,200 papyrus pages bound together as books — the earliest so far known with leather covers — sometime soon after the middle of the fourth Century. Written in Coptic, the Codices draw syncretically upon Jewish, Christian, Hermetic, Zoroastrian and Platonic sources and have thrown extraordinary light on the background of the New Testament, particularly the Epistles, by revealing that Gnosticism, hitherto supposed to be only a Christian heresy, was in fact a separate religion.

Ancient Churches: Babylon is mentioned in St. Peter's first epistle, most scholars now concede, in connection with St. Mark's Egyptian mission, and local legend claims it as one of the many places in Egypt where the Holy Family rested. The monks and martyrs who elsewhere created the heroic age of the Coptic Church seem to have passed it by, and there are no specific documentary references to any church structure earlier than the Arab conquest. Babylon could not have had much importance as a Christian center until four centuries later, when it had long since been absorbed into Misr. The **Patriarchate of St. Mark**, robbed of the saint's relics by Venetians in 828, was transferred there from a declining Alexandria sometime after 1048.

Not only at Babylon, however, but all over the future site of Misr there were certainly scattered churches and monastic settlements long before the conquest. Many were later destroyed, but some were undoubtedly incorporated in later structures. Atop the two bastions of the southern gate of the Roman fortress, for example, is the **Church of the Virgin**, referred to locally as **Al-Mu'allaqah** ("The Suspended"), a seat of the Patriarchate for centuries, one portion of which is claimed to date to the fourth Century; and within the walls are several

The faithful at prayer in the 14th-Century mosque of Mu'ayyad, Cairo.

others — the **churches of St Sergius and St. Bacchus, St. Barbara, St. Cyril and St. John**; a second church of the Virgin, known as **Qasriyyat al-Rihan** (''Pot of Basir''); and a **convent of St. George** — with an almost equal claim to antiquity. Outside the fortress walls, but still within the neighborhood of Old Cairo, are no fewer than a dozen more churches that were well documented in medieval times, when Muslim historians dated the foundations of some of them back to as early as the eighth Century.

A visit to the churches within the fortress walls is made particularly pleasant by the fact that this enclosed area is entirely controlled by the Egyptian Antiquities Organization, which has undertaken a great deal of cleaning and restoration. The interiors of the churches typically follow a basilican plan and cheerfully mix the ancient with the modern, between which local worshippers make little distinction. The use of pews, for example, is a 20th-Century innovation inspired by Western Protestantism, but the use of cymbals or triangles in services may be traced back to the pharaohs. The oldest, finest and most portable objects have all been removed either to the Coptic Museum or to other collections around the world. One of the sanctuaries of the Suspended Church has the remains of some fine frescoes attributed to the seventh or eighth Century, however, and the buildings of the convent of St. George include an intact reception hall belonging to a Fatimid-period house, with magnificent wooden doors 22 feet (seven meters) high.

These churches are all Coptic Orthodox, of course, but during Lent they become pilgrimage sites for Catholics as well. In the 17th and 18th Centuries the Franciscan Friars had the right to celebrate mass in the sanctuary of the Holy Family at the church of St. Sergius and St. Bacchus, which marks a traditional resting-place of the Holy Family and is thus venerated by both Catholic and Orthodox. The Coptic Church commemorates the Flight into Egypt on the first of June with a celebration of the Divine Liturgy.

Another People of the Book: Also within the walls is the **temple of Ben Ezra**, one of Cairo's 29 synagogues, a reminder of Egypt's role not only in fostering the Saphardic Rabbinical tradition, but also

Newly - finished chairs, Cairo.

in providing a home for Karaite Jews (before the 10th Century) and Ashkenazi Jews (from the 16th Century onward). Originally a church dedicated to St. Michael the Archangel, the building was closed under the Fatimid Caliph Al-Hakim (996-1021), then sold to the Saphardic community. Among other functions it served as a *geniza*, a repository for documents made sacrosanct by being sworn under oath, which could not be casually discarded without sacrilege. Since these documents cover several centuries and include such mundane items as contracts, bills of sale and letters of credit, they constitute an extensive record of medieval Mediterranean trade and commerce, an invaluable prize for foreign scholars. Largely rebuilt in the 19th Century, the building has been restored since 1980.

Beyond Old Cairo, three miles (5 km) to the southeast, reachable by car from the suburb of Maadi, is the **Rabbinical cemetery**, which is considerably older than the synagogue of Ben Ezra. Ya'kub Ibn Killis, the Jewish vizier of the Caliph Aziz (975-996), is buried there, as is Rabbi Hayim Kapusi, whose grave site, like that of Rabbi Ya'kub Abu Hasira in the Delta, continues to draw Saphardic pilgrims from Europe and North Africa. There is also a small Karaite cemetery.

Fustat the First Arab Capital: Immediately to the east of Old Cairo, in an enormous area slowly being covered with new buildings, is the site of **Fustat**, the first Muslim capital at Misr, founded by Amr ibn al-'As in the course of the Arab conquest. Excavations here have uncovered the remains of elaborate water storage and drainage systems, the foundations of private houses and apartment blocks, and thousands of objects made of wood, paper, ivory, glass, metal, or ceramics, ranging in date from the eighth Century to the 14th and in provenance from Spain to China. The most significant of these objects may be seen in the **Islamic Museum**, including a sensational find made in 1980: block-printed papers, which confirmed archaeologically the long-held belief that the art of printing was known in Fatimid Egypt within decades after its invention in China, at least four centuries before its transmission through Central Asia to Europe.

There is little to see at the site now to suggest the importance Fustat still had as a residential, manufacturing and interna-

The 'Adli Street Synagogue built in 1905. Cairo once contained over thirty synagogues

146

tional trading center even after the government had moved to new quarters farther north. One monument of the early period still remains in Old Cairo, however, and another, carefully preserved, stands at the tip of Rawdah Island, just across an intervening channel of the river.

The **mosque of 'Amr ibn al-'As** is 300 yards north of the Roman fortress on the main road parallel to the metro line. Erected in 641 or 642, it was rebuilt in 688, 710, 750 and 791, then doubled to approximately its present size in 827, thus testifying to Fustat's rapid growth. After several subsequent centuries of neglect, it was restored in the 13th Century, rebuilt after the great earthquake of 1303, then partially rebuilt again a century later. Near the end of the 18th Century, just before the French invasion, it again underwent another massive rebuilding, which has been followed by several restorations. The latest work, carried out on a large scale between 1980 and 1983, has sought to recreate its appearance as it might have been in 827. Only an expert could now pinpoint older construction, but the site is important as marking that of the first mosque in Africa and the current neo-Fatimid structure provides some idea of how its ninth-Century version could have inspired the building of Cairo's greatest mosque, the mosque of Ibn Tulun.

The **Nilometer** at the southern tip of Rawdah Island is easy to see from across the river — it is distinguished by a conical cap — but not so easy to find from any point on the island itself; and even 19th-Century travelers, who had no one-way streets to cope with, usually hired a guide. The only north-south street on the island giving access to the Nilometer is the easternmost, which can only be approached from the west. An ideal approach, often used in the 19th Century and recently rediscovered by local yachtsmen, is by water. Boats can be moored at a landing on the southeastern corner of the island near an inlet to one of the conduits feeding the Nilometer. The conical dome is a reconstruction made in 1893 of a 17th-Century Ottoman dome that had been destroyed by the French in 1800; and its interior is covered with fine Turkish tiles. The substructure, however, which is the Nilometer itself, dates essentially from 861, which makes it the oldest intact

Traditional Mashrabia woodwork in a modern apartment, Cairo.

Islamic monument in Cairo and the only survivor from the Abbasid period. Consisting of a calibrated stone column standing upright in a stone-lined pit with a staircase, it is particularly notable for the pointed arches used at its uppermost intake level, three centuries before the appearance of such arches in Europe.

The Mosque of Ibn Tulun: In 872 the Caliph's name was removed from the Nilometer by order of the city's 38-year-old Turkish governor, Ahmad Ibn Tulun, who would not only declare himself independent, but within 10 years would make Misr the center of an empire stretching from southern Turkey to Sudan and from Cyrenaica to the Euphrates. Cramped by the growth of Fustat, the Abbasid caliphs had already built themselves a new military quarter, **Al-'Askar**, to the north; and Ibn Tulun felt the need for something grander. The result was **Al-Qatai'** ("The Wards"), a new town built over an entire square mile, large enough to include a walled hippodrome, a hospital, a menagerie, mews, gardens, markets, baths, residential quarters (classified by occupation or nationality), reception and *harim* ("harem") palaces for Ibn Tulun him-

self, and a large governmental complex, which was attached to a great congregational mosque. When the Abbasids repossessed Misr for the Caliphate in 905, this mosque, one of the architectural glories of the Muslim world, was the only building left standing in Al-Qatai'.

Though it is now approached by the narrow streets that grew up around it, most taxi drivers can find it, since it is situated between two landmarks, the Citadel and the popular modern mosque of Sayyida Zaynab, just west of the Qasabah, the great north-south thoroughfare of Mamluk Misr. Several restorations — the earliest was in 1297, the latest in 1981 — have kept it in order without destroying its authenticity, though one must imagine its inscriptions and decorations as painted or gilded. Built in the imperial style of the Abbasid court at Samarra in Iraq, where Ibn Tulun had lived as a young man, it is constructed of red brick and stucco — original materials, rather than granite, limestone and marble borrowed from other sites, as is often the case in later mosques — and its courtyard covers 6.5 acres (2.5 hectares). The sycamore-wood frieze of Quranic verses surround-

Four Cairene gentlemen.

ing the court is more than a mile and a quarter long.

The Main Street of Misr: Adjoining its northeastern corner is the **Gayer-Anderson Museum** (Bayt al-Kiridlyyah): two houses, one of the 16th Century, the other of the 17th, each comfortable by the standards of its time, have been delightfully joined together to create a single larger dwelling with a *salamlik* (reception suite) and *haramlik* (harem suite), both filled with antique furniture from all over the Middle East. One entrance to the Gayer-Anderson Museum leads from the mosque of Ibn Tulun. Another entrance, opposite, can be used as an exit and gives on to a cross street called Shari' Tulun, which leads eastward (left) after less the 100 yards into the **Qasabah**, medieval Cairo's main street.

Defining itself in the centuries after Ibn Tulun's death, the Qasabah linked all the city's parts on a north-south axis; and at the height of Cairo's medieval prosperity it had become more than eight miles (13 km) long, not only connecting the mosque of Ibn Tulun with older sites to the south, such as Fustat, and newer quarters to the north, such as Al-

Qahirah, but also extending all the way into a suburban zone of villas and pleasure domes that lay beyond Al-Qahirah's northern walls. Changing its name as it moves from quarter to quarter, it can still be followed — on foot, of course — from Ibn Tulun northward for more than three miles (five km) into the heart of modern Cairo's historic zone.

Shari' Salibah: There is so much to see of the rest of medieval Cairo however, that it is best to take the Qasabah piecemeal. The first major cross-street it intersects with, for example, about 300 yards up the Qasabah to the north, is **Shari' Salibah**, a special joy for the architect or city-planner. On the northeast corner of the intersection is a delightful Ottoman-style *sabil-kuttab* ("fountain school") built in 1867 by the mother of Abbas I, the successor of Muhammad Ali, beautifully restored in 1984 by the Egyptian Antiquities Organization. (There are many of these "fountain-schools" in Cairo, which were endowed by the pious for the public dispensation of the "two mercies" commended by the Prophet — water and religious teaching — and were consequently always constructed in two stor-

The courtyard of the Mosque of Ibn Tulun in Cairo, ninth Century.

ies, with a public water-dispensary below and a school for Quranic instruction above, at the city's busiest spots.) And unmistakable just beyond the northeast and southeast corners of the intersection, one on either side of Shari' Salibah, are the massive facades of two "colleges" built by the Amir Shaykhu, commander-in-chief of the Mamluk armies under Sultan Hassan ibn an-Nasir Muhammad ibn Qalawun (1334-1361), who had him murdered in 1357.

Shaykhu's *madrasah* (built in 1349, on the left) and his *khanqah* (built in 1355, on the right) represent two classic Cairene architectural types, both introduced two centuries earlier by Salah-ad-Din. Persian in inspiration, the *madrasah* provided the perfect architecture for religious propaganda: a courtyard mosque made cruciform in plan by building into it four vaulted halls (*liwans*), where instruction could take place simultaneously in the four systems of legal thought regarded as orthodox by Sunni Muslims (Hanafi, Malaki, Shafi'i, Hanbali). A *khanqah* is a Muslim "monastery," a mosque with attached dwelling areas that are designed to serve as a hostel for Sufis (Muslim mystics). Sufis differ from Christian monks chiefly in not being sworn to celibacy and in being held on the whole by somewhat looser external discipline; Shaykhu's *khanqah* thus accommodated 700 Sufis, though it contains only 150 rooms surrounding a central mosque with a courtyard, many of the mystics being expected to lead lives outwardly indistinguishable from those of more ordinary citizens. These two buildings frame Shari' Salibah as one looks in the direction of the Citadel, creating a gorgeously "oriental" vista that is equally impressive seen from the opposite end, looking back towards Umm Abbas's *sabil-kuttab*.

Farther up Shari' Salibah in the direction of the Citadel is the first free-standing *sabil-kuttab* in Cairo, built by Qaitbay in 1479, beyond which the street suddenly emerges into the **Qaramaydan** (Maydan Salah ad-Din). This enormous square was the site of Ibn Tulun's hippodrome and the Mamluks' polo-ground, where their pageants, races, matches, musters and military displays took place under the gaze — and the guns — of the Citadel.

A Masterpiece and its Modern Mate: At the northwestern corner of this square loom

Cluster of mosques seen from the Citadel, Cairo.

two colossal religious buildings, one on either side of the entrance to a street called Shari' Qal'ah (but better known under its old name as Shari' Muhammad Ali) confronting each other gatewise just as the Shaykhu *madrasah* and *khanqah* do in Shari' Salibah, though on a much larger scale: the **madrasah** of **Sultan Hasan**, Shaykhu's teenage master, built between 1356 and 1363; and the **Rifa'i mosque**, built to complement it architecturally, exactly as Shaykhu's *khanqah* does his *madrasah*, between 1869 and 1912.

Visitors sometimes fail to understand that these two buildings were constructed more than five centuries apart, since the modern mosque not only shows perfect respect for its older neighbor across the street in fabric, scale and style, but also collaborates with it in creating a monumental setting to mark the termination of Shari' Muhammad Ali as it enters the Qaramaydan, framing a view of the Citadel in the distance even more dramatically than the view up Shari' Salibah does.

Inside the Rifa'i mosque Mamluk motifs have been reproduced with luxurious fidelity, demonstrating recognition of the Mamluk style as Cairo's distinguishing trademark, an almost "official" style and thus particularly suitable in a mosque identified with the ruling dynasty. Originally endowed by the mother of the Khedive Ismail, it houses her tomb as well as those of the magnificent Khedive himself and four of his sons, including Husayn Kamil (1853-1917) and King Fuad (1868-1936). King Faruq's body rested here temporarily before final burial in the Southern Cemetery; and Muhammad Reza Pahlevi, the last Shah of Iran, whose first wife was Faruq's sister, was buried here in 1980.

A great parade of Sufi orders, with chanting, banners and drums, takes place annually in Cairo on the eve of the Prophet's Birthday. Despite the Revolution, it traditionally begins here at the Rifa'i mosque, marches down Shari' Muhammad Ali, up Shari' Port Said, then down Shari' al-Azhar — wide new European-style streets constructed by the Dynasty between 1873 and 1930 — to end at the popular **mosque of Sayyidna Husayn**, which was built by the Khedive Ismail at the same time the Rifa'i mosque was begun.

27 different kinds of marble were imported for the floors of the Mosque of Sultan Hasan in Cairo.

Sultan Hasan's *madrasah*, across the street, provided a daunting model, since it is probably the greatest of the Bahri architectural monuments, second only to Ibn Tulun's mosque in grandeur of conception among all the buildings in Cairo. The walls are 117 feet high and so solidly built that it was used twice — in 1381 during a Mamluk revolt against Barquq and again in 1517 during the Ottoman invasion — as a fortress. It was originally planned to have four minarets, including two over the entrance portal, but in February 1360, while the building was still under construction, one of these two fell, killing 300 people, and the second was never built. One of the two remaining minarets collapsed in 1659 and was replaced by the present smaller version, an Ottoman construction in the Mamluk style, in 1672, when the dome was also replaced. The architectural daring that caused the difficulties is made clear, however, by the sole original minaret, still standing at the western corner: it is over 265 feet high, taller and more massive than any other in Cairo.

The complex originally included a market, apartments and a well at its northern end, of which little remains.

The original wooden doors at the entrance, covered with bronze and filigree silver in geometric patterns, were removed by Sultan Mu'ayyad Sheikh in 1416 for use in his own mosque near Bab Zuwaylah, where they are still visible; and the original marble floor was stripped by Selim the Grim for shipment to Istanbul after the Ottoman conquest. What is left, however, is stunningly impressive and since 1982 has received continual attention from the Egyptian Antiquities Organization, which has carried out careful restoration.

The Citadel: The **Citadel** was begun by Salah-ad-Din in 1176 as part of a plan to enclose all of Misr, for the first time, within a system of walls, for which it would serve as the major stronghold. By 1182, when he had gone northward again to fight his last series of victorious campaigns against the Crusaders, it was virtually complete; and though it was later modified in detail, particularly under Muhammad Ali, it has never since been without a military garrison.

In 1218 Sultan al-Kamil, Salah ad-Din's nephew, took up residence in it and from that time until the construction of Abdin Palace in the mid-19th Cen-

The Citadel seen from the Sultan Hasan Mosque Cairo.

tury, it was also the home and seat of government of all but one of Egypt's subsequent rulers, even Ottoman viceroys. The Lower Enclosure contains the famous gate-passage where Muhammad Ali conducted a massacre of Mamluks in 1811, which may be approached by an 18th-Century gateway, restored in 1988. It is best seen, however, from the terrace of the Police Museum on the upper level, which contains the Southern and Northern Enclosures, nearly two-thirds of the Citadel's total area. The Citadel is maintained by the Egyptian Antiquities Organization as a prime tourist attraction. A parking lot, landscaping, plenty of historical interest and good public facilities have combined with cleaner air, more open space, less noise, and lower temperatures than anywhere else in Cairo to make this part of the Citadel a popular place for families on Fridays and holidays.

Visible from nearly anywhere in the city below on its site at the highest point of the Southern Enclosure is the **Muhammad Ali** mosque. Built between 1830 and 1848, it was not completed until 1857. Designed by a Greek architect in accord with purely Ottoman models, it owes nothing to Egypt but the materials from which it is made and a few intermingled pharaonic and Mamluk decorative motifs, though it adds a wonderful picture-postcard element to the city's skyline. The clock in the courtyard, a charming touch of the period, was a gift made by Louis-Philippe of France in 1846, a belated exchange for the obelisk of Ramses II from the Luxor temple, now standing in the Place de la Concorde, which Muhammad Ali had given the French in 1831. The Pasha himself is buried here under a marble cenotaph.

The view over the city from the belvedere near the mosque is remarkable on a clear day. Across a little court is the **Gawharah Palace**, built by Muhammad Ali in 1814, gutted by fire during a theft in 1972. The ruins have been intelligently refurbished by the Egyptian Antiquities Organization, however, and converted into a museum of the mid-19th Century, when it served as a viceregal *salamlik* (reception) palace.

Below the Muhammad Ali mosque to the northwest, between it and the gateway to the Northern Enclosure, is the great 14th Century **mosque of An-Nasir Muhammad**, the father of Sultan

Festival decor at the Al Hussein Mosque, Cairo.

Hasan. Built in 1318, enlarged in 1335, but stripped of its gorgeous marble by the Ottomans after 1517, it shows Persian-Mongol influence in its unique minarets, which the Antiquities Organization has recovered with green faience, and an incredible variety of Egyptian sources in its columns: levied from pharaonic, Greek, Roman, and Coptic sites, they constitute a survey of Egyptian architectural styles. Behind the mosque are the remains of a well dug under the direction of one of Salah-ad-Din's amirs down through 283 feet of solid limestone. Originally supplied with two water-wheels worked by animals, it provided drinking water for the sultan.

North of the mosque of An-Nasir Muhammad are two gates: one downhill to the left leads into the Lower Enclosure; the other, around a corner to the right, leads into the Northern Enclosure. Within the Northern Enclosure are the Military Museum, which is housed in Muhammad Ali's Harim Palace, built in 1827, and an interesting small Museum of Carriages, displaying a few vehicles transferred here from the large collection of royal and viceregal conveyances at the **Carriage Museum in Bulaq**, which is worth a separate visit. In the far corner of the Northern Enclosure is the first Ottoman mosque built in Cairo (1528). Nestled next to an old Fatimid tomb, it is set in a small garden, which must have afforded a cool and leafy touch of the Bosphorus to the homesick Janissaries who lived there during the centuries after 1517.

Sultanic Serendipity: The Citadel was remote from the city: what did a sultan do when he wanted to know what was really going on? There are no first-hand reports, but presumably he imitated the Harun ar-Rashid of *The Arabian Nights* — or Antony and Cleopatra, who seem to have invented the princely sport of slumming — disguised himself, and went out to "wander through the streets and note the quality of people."

Certainly Cairo can only be known on foot; and one of its most magnificent walks begins at the **Bab al-Gadid**, the northern gate of the Citadel. From inside the Citadel, Bab al-Gadid is reached by going past the mosque of An-Nasir Muhammad and taking the left-hand gate, proceeding down into the lower enclosure. Bab al-Gadid lies straight ahead, and leads into a road that descends in a half circle around the Arc-

hives (1828) to a point just opposite one corner of the Citadel walls, where an old street seems to plunge downhill. From outside the Citadel this point can be reached by leaving a car near the Sultan Hasan mosque and walking up towards the Citadel, then turning left to climb a road that runs parallel to its walls, bearing on to the first intersection it makes with an old street running downhill.

This old street has other names — Al-Tabbana, Bab al-Wazir — but is best known as **Darb al-Ahmar**. Connecting the Citadel with Bab Zuweyla, the southern gate of Al-Qahirah, it runs through an area that had been cleared for pleasure-gardens by Salah-ad-din, then became fashionable during the reign of An-Nasir Muhammad, when many of his sons-in-law began building there. Lined with mosques, palaces, apartment houses and other buildings dating from the late 13th to the mid-19th Century, the Darb al-Ahmar thus represents a good sample of Cairo's medieval richness, the splendor of Misr.

First, on the left down a very short sidestreet, for example, are the ruins of a medieval hospital (1420), the *bimaristan* of Mu'ayyad Shaykh; while on the right appear the *madrasah* and tomb of Amir Aytmish al-Baghasi (1348), the remains of the tomb and *sabil-kuttab* of Amir Tarabay as-Sharifi (1503), and the tomb of Azdumur (early 16th Century). A hundred yards farther down the street on the right (east) is the palace of **Alin Aq** (1293), later occupied and remodeled by the traitorous Amir Khayrbek, who built his tomb (1502), mosque and *sabil-kuttab* (1502) next to it, creating a northward view that is one of the most picturesque and frequently photographed in Cairo.

On the left (west) across the street from Khayrbek's mosque is the beginning of a 14-unit apartment house with several entrances, dating from 1522, which stretches along the street for nearly 210 feet. Just beyond Khayrbek's mosque on the right (east), meanwhile, is a 17th-Century house, with the mosque of **Amir Aqsunqur** (1347), one of An-Nasir Muhammad's sons-in-law, next to it, which tiles from Damascus installed in 1652 by Ibrahim Agha, the first owner of the house, have inspired guides to call it the "Blue Mosque".

Across the street from Aqsunqur's mosque, next to the 16th-Century apartment house, is a 17th-Century *sabil* and

Al Azhar University, founded in 970 A.D., and surrounding districts. On the left are the twin minarets of Bab Zuweyla, one of the city's ancient gates.

tomb, then on the east side comes another of Ibrahim Agha's houses (1652) with his adjoined *sabil* (1639); and beyond the *sabil* is a small Ottoman religious structure, with an Ayyubid minaret (1260) behind it. On the western side of the street at this point are the *madrasah* and tomb that the Sultan Sha-'ban (1368) built for his mother. The adjacent palace, which contains two courtyards and over 100 rooms, with a maze of tunnels underneath, dates largely from 1778, but incorporates a house built by Sultan Qaitbay in 1494. A little farther down the street, after an intersection, another 17th-Century *sabil-kuttab* appears on the left, then a 14th-Century tomb on the right.

Jutting into the street from the left, next comes the **mosque of Altanbugha al-Maridani** (1340), notable for its woodwork and marble, which give some idea of what An-Nasir Muhammad's mosque at the Citadel must have been like before the Ottoman conquest; and farther along on the same side of the street is the **mosque of Ahmad al-Mihmandar** (1325) with still another 17th-Century *sabil-kuttab* next to it. Finally, on the right as the street turns a

corner and Bab Zuwayla comes into view, stands the exquisite funerary mosque of **Amir Qijmas al-Ishaqi** (1481) connected with his *sabil-kuttab* by a bridge over a sidestreet.

Darb al-Ahmar now runs east and west and appropriately leads past **Bab Zuwayla** and the Tentmakers' Bazaar — after a change of name — to the **Islamic Museum**, Cairo's great storehouse and display-case of medieval treasures, which lies 540 yards straight ahead, on the northwestern corner of Shari' Port Said and a cluster of cross-streets, at Maydan Ahmad Maher.

Street Life: All this monumentality, however, represents only a small fraction of what the Misr of *The Arabian Nights* still has to offer: there are hundreds of medieval buildings in Cairo, dotted and clustered over an area that is larger than Venice. To the ordinary man or woman in the Darb al-Ahmar, moreover, the monuments are merely a setting for daily lives: for them — and probably for most foreign tourists — the buildings themselves are less important than the street to which they give so much character.

In Cairo even more than other Arab

The Mosque of al Mu'ayyad makes a quiet sanctuary from the bustling traffic outside.

cities noise is a measure of life. Commerce hums in one-room shops and buzzes around pushcarts selling everything from fresh fruit to second-hand clothes; bakers and tailors ply their own quiet trades to an obbligato of banging hammers, as neighboring tinsmiths and furniture-makers carry on their percussive craft, turning out the aluminum buckets or the gilded chairs that are modern necessities of the traditional life. Schoolrooms roar through open windows with mass recitation, everyone's transistor blares orgasmic *fioriture*, and five times a day loud-speakers crackle cassettes of the call to prayer from every working minaret. Housewives shriek chit-chat at each other from second- and third-floor latticed windows on opposite sides of the street. Chickens cackle from roofs overhead and donkeys bray from the street below. Every few minutes, the scene is punctuated by the growl of a lumbering bus or the wild report of a two-stroke propelling its goggled rider and his overloaded sidecar to someone else's probable death and destruction.

The pungent sweetness of incense wafts from everywhere. It is one of the simple means by which this heavily-peopled street constantly reclaims its own original spirit. Universally believed to dispel all malignancy, whether human or supernatural, incense, like courtesy, does not cost much, but is worth a very great deal. It gratifies friends, wins strangers, and softens the hearts of enemies. In Cairo it thus symbolizes the moral solidarity of an old and confident urbanity, which makes this city the safest in the world to walk through — except for the madcap hazards of construction and traffic — either in broad daylight or after dark. Street crimes, of the kind so familiar in New York, Stockholm, or Rio, are virtually unknown, largely because it is inconceivable that passers-by would not come instantly to a victim's aid. Moral solidarity is the great gift of its medieval quarters to the modern city of Misr as a whole.

Bab Zuwayla and Beyond: Bab Zuwayla was built in 1092 as the southern gateway of Al-Qahirah, the most distinguished of all these old quarters. Originally a palace enclosure, it was opened to commercial development by Salah-ad-Din, who either gave away the accumulated treasures of the Fatimid caliphs or used them to finance his campaigns.

An 18th-Century *Sabil Kuttab* in the Ottoman Baroque style.

Most of the Fatimid buildings disappeared in the course of new construction; and Al-Qahirah rapidly displaced Fustat as the focus of the city's trade and commerce. Through its heart still runs the Qasabah, at once the main artery of the whole medieval city and a single enormous bazaar, straddled momentarily at either end of Al-Qahirah by massive Fatimid gates.

High up on the wall next to the gate at Bab Zuwayla hangs a mysterious trophy of metal objects — weapons, tools, or Sufi instruments — which no one has ever convincingly identified. Directly on top of the gate are two minarets, which have given it such a specific identity that depictions of it were once used as logo-symbols for the modern city. Belonging to the mosque of **Sultan Mu'ayyad Sheikh** (1420), which stands just inside the gate to the left, they also demonstrate that by the end of the 14th Century Bab Zuwayla had ceased to be regarded as primarily a military structure.

It is in this mosque that the splendid doors of Sultan Hasan were finally hung and can still be seen. Across the street, with an attached *sabil-kuttab*, is the facade of a caravanserai-emporium called **As-Sukkariyah** (from the Arabic *sukkar*, the source of the word meaning "sugar" in every European language), which has given this district just within the southern Fatimid walls its name. Built in 1796, it was owned by a woman, Nafisa Bayda, the wife of Murad Bey, chief of the Mamluks at the time of Bonaparte's invasion, who evaded capture and successfully waged guerilla war from Upper Egypt until the French departure.

Cruising Up The Qasabah: The **Qasabah** from here northward has been devoted for eight centuries to buying and selling; and 450 yards up the street is another famous commercial district, the **Ghuriyyah**, named for Qansuh Al-Ghuri, one of the last Mamluk sultans. His *madrasah* and mausoleum (1505) stand on opposite sides of the Qasabah, marking the site of the **Silk Merchants' Bazaar**, a covered street-market that was once the most famous in Cairo. The place is still bursting with trade in other goods.

At this point the Qasabah's north-south axis is suddenly sliced by the modern east-west traffic of **Shari' al-Azhar**, cut through old Misr in 1930 to provide tram service for the greatest and

The Mosques of Rifai and Sultan Hasan at festival time.

158

most long-lived of the Fatimids' foundations, the **University of Al-Azhar**, which continues to attract Muslim students from around the world. Lying a little over 220 yards down Shari' al-Azhar to the east, Al-Azhar's oldest buildings represent a variety of endowments over several centuries from the 10th to the late-19th.

On the other side of Shari' al-Azhar, which can now be crossed safely only by using a pedestrain overpass, the Qasabah continues north, but is soon interrupted, just beyond a 15th-Century *madrasah*, by another modern street, **Shari' al-Muski**, which was begun by the French, extended again by Muhammad Ali in 1845, and finally breached the Qasabah in 1854. Connected with old Christian and European quarters, it soon became favored by foreign merchants and by the end of the 19th Century was lined from end to end with European-owned shops.

The Qasabah itself still maintains its traditional character. Around this intersection spices and scents are sold; beyond are goldsmiths; and the first major street off the Qasabah to the right (east) leads to the **Khan al-Khalili**, famous formerly for Turkish goods and

now the tourists' bazaar, where locals also go to buy jewelry and antiques (see ''Markets and Bazaars''). Best buys in ordinary brassware will still be found in the Qasabah itself, for at this point it becomes the **Suq al-Nahhasin**, the Coppersmiths' Bazaar, an identity it has had since the 14th Century, where brassware is sold at local prices by weight, regardless of its age.

Between the Palaces: A few steps further along, the Qasabah makes a jog to the left around a *sabil*, added in 1326 by An-Nasir Muhammad to the great hospital-tomb-*madrasah* complex that had already been built here by Sultan Qalawun, his father, 40 years earlier. This section of the Qasabah was known even then as **Bayn al-Qasrayn**, ''Between the Two Palaces,'' in commemoration of the two huge Fatimid palaces that had stood facing each other on this site over a century earlier still. Here two *madrasahs* honoring Ayyubid sultans were built over Fatimid ruins; and one of them, the *madrasah* built to house his tomb by the widow of Sultan as-Salih Ayyub, the last real ruler of the Ayyubid line, would later become the seat of the supreme judiciary under the Mamluk state.

Cloth merchant taking a break, Cairo.

159

Incessant attacks by Crusaders had led As-Salih to the wholesale importation of slave-cossacks from Central Asia. He could hardly have foreseen that in 1250, only weeks after his death, they would murder his son and heir and make themselves masters over their own new empire. Next to his tomb-*madrasah*, showing perhaps a kind of belated loyalty, Baybars, the greatest of As-Salih's Mamluks, the acknowledged founder of this empire, built another *madrasah*; and across the street are the tomb-*madrasahs* of Qalawun and An-Nasir Muhammad, two of his greatest Bahri successors, as well as that of Barquq, first of the Burgi Mamluks. Appropriately, Cairo's principal slave-market was also held here in the Bayn-al-Qasrayn, where Mamluks and girls, mainly Circassian and Greek, continued to be bought and sold until the time of Muhammad Ali.

One should imagine the Bayn al-Qasrayn, however, as it might have been after business hours on the night of some Mamluk festival, when it would have been illumined as high as the tops of its six minarets by thousands of lamps and cressets. Silks and satins would have been hung from upper windows, with more spread over the dust of the street for the sultan's horse to tread upon as he came riding down the Darb al-Ahmar and the Qasabah from the Citadel. Preceded by an amir bearing the Saddlecloth, the emblem of state, by two pages in yellow silk and gold brocade mounted on white horses, by a standard-bearer, and by a musician playing a flute, the sultan would have been surrounded by halberdiers uniformed in yellow silk. An amir bearing a Poniard of State accompanied him on either side, the yellow silk royal Parasol surmounted with its Golden Bird was held over his head and he was accompanied by still another amir bearing the Mace, with drummers and chanting poets. He must have felt like considerably more than a million dollars.

To recall some semblance of this splendor, extensive repair work is being constantly carried out in the Bayn-al-Qasrayn by the Antiquities Organization and the German Archaeological Institute, who are responsible for the restoration of both the delightful 18th-Century *sabil-kuttab* that overlooks the area from the north and the 14th-Century palace on the corner nearby.

To the Northern Gates of Al-Qahirah: Far-

The *Haramlik* or ladies' quarters of an 18th-Century Palace, the Bayt Sihaymi.

ther north, in a stretch of the Qasabah where such items as copper bean-pots and finials for mosques are made, stands the **Aqmar Mosque**, one of the few remaining Fatimid monuments; and around the corner at the second turning afterwards, on a side-street called the Darb al-Asfar, stands one of the best examples of an 18th-Century Cairene townhouse, the **Bayt as-Sihaymi**, a merchant's dwelling that was actually inhabited by the owners until 1961. More typical than the Gayer-Anderson house, it illustrates not only the standard division of rooms into a *salamlik* and a *haramlik*, but also the ingenuity with which architects used courtyards, fountains set in sunken floors, high ceilings, and north-facing wind-catchers on the roof to counter the heat of a long Cairene summer.

Just before the Qasabah exits through Bab al-Futuh, one of the two northern gates of Al-Qahirah, a space opens out to form another market, where fine agricultural produce from what were formerly the royal family's experimental farms is sold in its various seasons, the garlic being especially prized. Overlooking this area on its eastern side is the congregational **mosque of the Fatimid Caliph Al-Hakim**, finished in 1013 and restored in 1980 by the Bohora, an Ismaili Shi'ite sect who are based in Bombay, but trace the ancestry of their leaders back directly to the Fatimids, and who have imported features that give the building a touch of India.

Bab al-Futuh, the great "Gate of Conquest," **Bab an-Nasr**, "The Gate of Victory," the other northern gate of Al-Qahirah, and the 360-yard stretch of wall between them — all built by the Fatimids' Armenian general Badr al Gamali in 1087 — have been restored and are worth touring. Few buildings testify better to the sweep of Cairo's cosmopolitan history: Badr's Armenian architects were skilled military specialists; and their work originally made use of blocks quarried and carved under the pharaohs, some of which were scratched in turn, more than seven centuries later, with Napoleonic grafitti.

Outside the two northern gates is an open area, beyond which the Qasabah moves off from Bab al-Futuh northward through the **Husayniyyah district**, known both as a butchers' quarter and as a hotbed of nationalist sentiment; its

Brass merchant in the Coppersmiths' Bazaar, Cairo.

161

patriotic meat-cutters gave the French a great deal of trouble and were bombarded by them more than once from the Fatimid walls. Adjoining the Husayniyyah on the east opposite Bab an-Nasr is a famous cemetery. Ibn Khaldun, the 14th-Century historian so dazzled by the city, is among the celebrated who are buried here, though the area is so built up with dwellings among the graves that it looks thoroughly residential.

Living Among the Dead: This fact, however, makes it a good introduction to Cairo's great **Northern and Southern Cemeteries**, which Western journalists delight in calling collectively ''The City of the Dead,'' though they grew up at different times and have always been separated from each other by the limestone spur on which and out of which the Citadel was built. People live in these two cemeteries, a situation journalists explain by quotations from official statistics indicating that the modern city has a terrible housing shortage. Foreigners made the same observations and offered the same rationale, however, as long ago as the 15th Century; and the fact is that these cemeteries, as far as anyone knows, have always had inhabitants,

because many of the tombs they enclose are large permanent structures.

Permanent structures demand caretakers and guardians and soon have communities around them, the more so if they are used for occasional purposes other than merely housing the dead. The tombs of popular Cairene saints are always thronged, but on Thursday evenings, Fridays, and major feast days the living Cairenes frequently visit their family tombs — as ancient Greeks and Romans did or as modern Europeans used to on All Saints' Day — and have picnics among the graves. This custom was elaborated, especially by the Mamluk sultans and amirs, who used such outings for parties of a kind to which piety, though providing an excuse, was otherwise incidental.

Every guest wore his most extravagant clothes: silks from China (like the cups, bowls and serving dishes) embroidered by the ladies of local *harims*, brocades manufactured in the Mamluks' own workshops, like the inlaid metalwork basins, trays, ewers and cauldrons, or the exquisite fine-knotted carpets and cushion-covers against which each princely guest reclined. Amidst an

Turco-Syrian tiles at the Mosque of Aqsunqur.

abundance of flowers, perfume and incense, eating, drinking, and music received rapturous attention, but if the tomb-site was suitable, there might also be horse-races contests at mounted archery, and even hunting expeditions. The Northern Cemetery actually began in the 13th Century as a hippodrome with viewing stands, evolving quite naturally into a royal necropolis only later.

The Southern Cemetery is larger — it begins as far north as the mosque of Ibn Tulun — and much older. Several of the tombs have been pilgrimage sites for centuries, particularly that of Imam as-Shafi'i, a descendant of the Prophet's uncle and founder of the most influential of the four orthodox schools of Sunni jurisprudence, who died in Egypt in 820. Nearby is the mausoleum built by Muhammad Ali in 1816 for his favorite wife, where her three sons and other family members, including King Faruq, are also interred, alongside many of their retainers. All around in every direction, interspersed with apartment blocks and ranging in date from yesterday to 10 centuries ago, are a multitude of other tombs. The most notable are those of

Burgi Mamluk amirs, set within the remains of complexes that frequently included *khanqahs* and other large residential structures.

What these amirs built in the Southern Cemetery, however, can hardly compare with what their sultans built in the Northern Cemetery. The Burgi period marks the high point in the development of both the carved stone dome and the three-stage minaret — with a square base, an octagonal second storey, and a cylindrical upper storey, elaborately carved and topped by a bulb set on colonettes — features that used to dominate Cairo's skyline and are uniquely typical of it among all the cities of Islam.

Unhampered in this freshly opened necropolis by considerations of space, the Circassian rulers were free here to indulge their tastes for piety and pleasure to the full. The results still visible are the remains of five huge monuments that may represent an epitome in Mamluk architecture and interior adornment. The most important are the complexes built by Farrag, the son of Barquq, the first of the Burgi line, to which Barquq's body was eventually transferred from his own earlier tomb-*madrasah* in Bayn al Qas-

Houses encroach on a medieval cemetery. Debris is thrown on roofs because of inadequate garbage collection.

rayn, and Qaitbay, the longest-lived, most active, and most famous of these Circassians, whose *madrasah* and mausoleum, built between 1472 and 1474, are the jewels of the period.

The domes and minarets of the Circassian sultans are among the first typically Cairene sights that visitors arriving by air are likely to see, situated as they are on the main road leading from the airport to the southern suburbs or, by way of Shari' Al-Azhar, to the modern center of town at **Maydan at-Tahrir** (Liberation Square).

The City's New Center: Maydan at-Tahrir was originally named Maydan Ismailiyyah, for the Khedive Ismail, whose statue was later supposed to be placed on the huge granite plinth at its southeastern corner. An open *place*, it demarcated one end of the new administrative, commercial and residential quarter of Maydan Ismailiyyah, laid out by the Khedive in 1865. Despite a strategic position near the Nile, however, Maydan Ismailiyyah did not achieve its present importance until after the July Revolution. Its name was changed and the mid-19th-Century barracks on its western (Nile) side, occupied throughout

most of their history by British Guards regiments, were demolished, to be replaced by the **Corniche**, two new administrative buildings, and the **Nile Hilton**, the first major hotel built in Cairo since 1910. On the south side of the Maydan the remains of a palace were removed and a gray concrete block was run up to accommodate those portions of several ministries that deal with the administration of permits, licenses, visas, expulsion orders and endless other bureaucratic forms: the **Mugama'a**, a Kafkaesque Castle of Red Tape, notorious not merely for venality, insolence, entrapment, frustration, and delay, but also for the number of suicides that have made use of its 14-story central stairwell. Across the street from this monster at the extreme southeastern corner of the Maydan is the only building left from Ismail's era, a small palace dating from 1878, which now houses the **American University**. On the north side of Maydan at-Tahrir is the **Egyptian Museum**.

The Egyptian Museum: Built in 1902 under Abbas II Hilmi and uniquely dignified with Latin inscriptions that may testify to his education at the Theresianum, the Museum holds the world's

Qasr el Nil Bridge, circa 1910, Cairo.

greatest collection of Egyptian artifacts. It should be an early stop for any intelligent visitor, who would also be well advised not to join a group or hire a guide, "official" or otherwise, but to walk slowly around the building on two or three different occasions. Displays on the ground floor are of large objects arranged more or less chronologically running clockwise, so that a left turn from the entrance foyer leads, for example, to the famous Menkaure triads from Giza, while a right turn leads to Hellenistic painting and statuary.

No one should be advised to miss anything, but visitors in a hurry might turn right and go immediately upstairs to the eastern and northern galleries on the upper floor, where the treasures from the tombs of Tutankhamen and Hetepheres are displayed. Not to be missed, in addition, is Case H in the upper foyer, containing small masterpieces that are the pride of the Museum, many of them famous from photographs that give no idea of their diminutive size: the ivory statuette of Khufu from Abydos; the black steatite bust of Queen Tiyi; the statuette of a Nubian girl with a single earring; the gilded statuette of Ptah; the

dancing pygmies carved from ivory, made moveable by an ingenious arrangement of strings; and the blue faience hippopotami of which reproductions have been made that are sold in boutiques all over the world. Of special interest also are the models displayed in Room 27 on the upper floor, mostly from an 11th-Dynasty tomb in Thebes, showing daily life as it was lived circa 2000 B.C.

Vestiges of Glamor: Running northeast from between the front of the Museum and Maydan at-Tahrir, its entrance demarcated on one side by TWA's main office and on the other by an apparently permanent triangular excavation — where, until 1961, Cairo's two most distinguished private houses stood — is **Shari' Qasr an-Nil**. Still the city's main shopping street, it has vestiges of the glamor that Ismail intended when he planned this part of the city. Up the street 220 yards on the left is the **Automobile Club**, founded in 1924, a favorite haunt of King Faruq, who loved playing poker for outrageous stakes, and 100 yards further on, where the street enters a square, is **Groppi's Corner House** (1924), the second of two luxu-

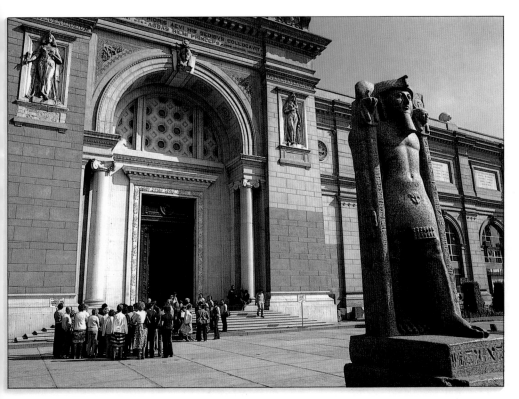

rious catering establishments founded in Cairo by an Alexandrian Swiss family.

In the years before World War II this branch of Groppi's sold Sèvres, Meissen, Lalique and silver as well as afternoon teas, aperitifs, confectionery, patisserie and delicatessen. In the rear were a garden and a rotunda with a stained-glass ceiling, where concerts were given three nights a week during the winter season (November — April), with dinner- and supper-dancing on the other four nights. But in 1952 the rotunda was burned, the dancing stopped, and Groppi's clientele began to change. A dwindling handful of old Turkish ladies, who still arrived for tea out of habit, bundled into pre-War furs, gradually found themselves elbowed out of the way by students, prostitutes, pimps and petty gangsters, though the bar remained popular with local businessmen until the whole place was sold to a teetotalling Arab in 1983.

The Revolution also changed the name and appearance of the square in front of Groppi's. Until then it had officially carried the Arabic name adopted by a Bonapartist officer, Colonel Anthelme Sève, who had entered Muhammad Ali's service after Waterloo, had converted to Islam, and as Sulayman Pasha al-Faransawi ("The Frenchman"), had distinguished himself brilliantly, becoming the founder of a blue-eyed line that was eventually to intermingle with the royal family. The north-south street running through the square likewise carried Sulayman Pasha's name, which is still used for both street and square by senior residents. A statue of the old hussar stood in this square until 1963, when it was replaced by the prosaic figure of a pre-Revolutionary nationalist banker.

Across the square, opposite Groppi's and on the same side of Shari' Qasr an-Nil, where a later building has been handsomely renovated by a foreign bank, stood the townhouse of one of Muhammad Ali's great-grandsons, which became the **Savoy**, second only to Shepheard's in glamor among the capital's hotels during the Edwardian era. Royalty stayed here, for example, and several suites were taken every winter between 1898 and 1914 by Sir Ernest Cassel, the international financier, whose guests would include celebrities such as the Duke and Duchess of Devonshire, Winston Churchill, or Mrs. Keppel, King Edward's last *maitresse en titre*. Evening

Groppi's, a center of cosmopolitan life in the 1920s and 30s, is still a favorite Cairene meeting place.

dress was mandatory for late dining, as it was in all of Cairo's first-class hotels.

Banks and airline offices line most of Shari' Qasr an-Nil in the 550-yard stretch to the next square, with shops in between. Best buys are Egyptian yard goods — cottons, of course, printed and plain, but also silk and wool — and leather goods. Another nationalist adorns this second square and the north-south street that crosses Shari' Qasr an-Nil here again has two names — Shari' Emad ad-Din or Shari' Muhammad Farid — between which Cairenes choose according to age and politics. Down the north-south street to the right another 220 yards is **St. Joseph's**, Cairo's biggest Catholic church, built in 1909; and nearly opposite is its finest neo-Islamic building, the main branch of **Bank Misr**, built in 1922, which has original woodwork and a particularly splendid Mamluk-style marble floor.

The Pleasures of Azbakiyyah: Shari' Qasr an-Nil leads on into **Shari' Gumhuriyyah**, formerly Shari' 'Abdin, which runs north and south and was designed to connect **'Abdin Palace**, the Muhammad Ali family's chief residence, with the main railway station, where their private trains are now on display at a fine **Railway Museum**. An early 18th-Century Ottoman mosque on the corner of Shari' Gumhuriyyah and Shari' Qasr an-Nil indicates the overlapping of Ismail's new quarter with old Misr as it was before the French marched in; and a left turn into Shari' Gumhuriyyah leads to **Azbakiyyah**, which was founded as a pleasure zone in the 15th Century, but had evolved into an upper-class residential area by the time Bonaparte decided to make his headquarters there in 1798. This fact would make Azbakiyyah the center of the city from then until 1960.

When Napoleon moved into the commandeered palace of an unlucky Mamluk grandee, newly-built on what is now Shari' Gumhuriyyah, the focus of the area was a picturesque seasonal lake that filled during the Nile flood. Local resistance and stern punitive measures soon reduced most of the luxurious dwellings along its southern and eastern shores to ruins; and during a revolt of Albanian troops after the French departure, Bonaparte's own palace overlooking the western shore, where his successor had been assassinated by an Egyptian patriot, was also burned.

Under Muhammad Ali, however, who established official residences here for himself and members of his family, Azbakiyyah was soon rebuilt and became dotted with new administrative offices. After 1837, when the lake was drained and its site coverted into a park, hotels began to move their premises into Azbakiyyah from the old European quarter along Shari' Muski to the east. One of them, the New British Hotel, occupying in 1850 a building that Muhammad Ali had erected five years earlier on the site of Napoleon's residence to serve as a Language Institute, was to become world-famous under the name of its first owner — Shepheard's. There was already a French theater, which would soon be joined by restaurants and coffee-houses.

In 1868 Ismail reduced the park to an octagonal garden and the remainder of the old lake-site was opened for development. New squares were created in three of the four corner-spaces left by the octagon's shortest sides and new public buildings were erected, the most striking of which was a theater for opera. Built entirely of wood and completed within five months during 1869, the **Cairo Opera House** saw the premier of *Aida* in 1871 and later became renowned for its collections of manuscripts, scores, costumes and sets, all of which were consumed by fire when the building burned in 1971. Its site is now identified by one of the city's few high-rise parking lots. Commissioned by Ismail, later erected (1882) in the square in front of the Opera, and still standing on the same spot, is a heroic equestrian **statue of Ibrahim Pasha**, however, which has survived both fire and revolution.

Two of Ismail's new streets, both still fashionable — Shari' Abdel Khaliq Tharwat and Shari' 'Adli, where the largest of Cairo's synagogues stands — lead westward from Ibrahim's statue, while Shari' Gumhuriyyah continues north along the western edge of the **Azbakiyyah Garden**. Reduced in size again in 1872, but elegantly redesigned by Ismail's French city-planner as an enclosed English-style garden on the order of the Parc Monceau in Paris, the Garden at present retains its octagonal shape, but otherwise shows the devastating result of 20th-Century priorities. Public-sector construction, including a street driven through the octagon's heart,

Opera Square in 1910. The Opera House, built for the opening of the Suez Canal, has since burned down.

Opera Square.
Place d' Jbrahim Pacha et Théâtre Khédivial.

has eliminated its central pond, destroyed its plan, perverted its intention, and occupied nearly a third of its green space, while Ismail's exotic trees and shrubs have been allowed to die. Only a few neglected 19th-Century buildings — cast-iron gazebos, a band-stand, an elaborate Ottoman-Baroque marble fountain — suggest a time when joys were more elegant, plentiful and cheaper than they are in Cairo now.

Grand Hotels and Further Pleasures: The **Continental Hotel** still stands overlooking the garden from the west, though it has been cut in half and concealed by a row of shopfronts. It was owned at an earlier stage (as the New Hotel) by Ismail himself and came to rank third among Cairo's hotels after the Savoy and, of course, Shepheard's.

Shepheard's itself, destroyed by fire in 1952 — the new Shepheard's on the Corniche has nothing in common with the old one but the name — stood at a site farther north on Shari' Gumhuriyyah now occupied by a public-sector highrise. In Ismail's time there were at least seven other hotels nearby, half a dozen restaurants, and a dozen foreign consulates, which provided the focus for much of native and resident social life, as the city's major hotels continue to do even more so today, when fewer Cairenes own palaces.

The area had also been known earlier, however, for its prostitutes, pedlars, mountebanks, jugglers, acrobats and beggars, a reputation that deservedly did not diminish until long after the second of two world wars, during which the city was occupied by British and ANZAC troops eager for such diversions. **Shari' Clot Bey**, ironically named for Muhammad Ali's chief advisor on public health, was famous until quite recently for its brothels. And there is still something raffish about other streets just north of the garden — where Bimbashi McPherson watched through an open window of the **Eden Palace Hotel** as Johnny Black made love to his Turkish mistress before going out on another murderous job; or where the runaway Princess de Caraman-Chimay (née Clara Ward of Detroit) sauntered on the arm of Janczi Rigo the gypsy violinist, — something that breathes of *Arabian-Nights* huggermugger despite the European appearance of things.

A Truly Traditional Quarter: Farther north and east of Azbakiyyah is an area where tourists never go and that few Cairenes ever visit, the old **Bab al-Bahr quarter**, long identified with Christians, which probably exemplifies the meaning of tradition better than any other in the city. Though it contains very few historic monuments, most of its buildings being less than 100 years old, its streets follow the 15th-Century pattern surveyed in 1800 by Napoleon's *savants*, whose map remains the only accurate guide.

The whole district has always been nourished by working and living and has always been maintained, as their own place, by its residents, who have rebuilt their houses continually on the old sites. Here, as in any truly Eastern city, distinct professions and trades cluster together, to create streets of shops selling and repairing sewing machines, for example, or making and selling electric lamps. Untouched either by decay or redevelopment, the Bab al-Bahr quarter may represent the best of Cairo's old urban spirit and one can only hope that it will remain unspoiled.

Newer districts, however, still have some charm. **Al-Gazirah** (The Island), joined to the mainland by three bridges, two of them near Maydan at-Tahrir,

Minaret and billboard compete for attention in central Cairo.

offers not only **Zamalek**, a suburb popular among European residents, but also several individual attractions for tourists. The **Gazirah Exhibition Grounds**, for example, which were replaced in 1982 as the site of the city's international expositions by the new **Cairo International Fairgrounds** at Madinet Nasr, have since become instead the location of a Japanese-built cultural complex that Cairenes call the **Opera House,** seeing it as a replacement for the old Opera House in Azbakiyyah. **The Museum of Modern Art** has meanwhile been moved from outmoded and overcrowded premises on Maydan Finney in Doqqi to one of the old permanent pavilions; and another permanent pavilion has been set aside for exhibitions of work by contemporary artists. Finally, it was decided to construct a new **Museum of Egyptian Civilization** here as well, to complement the displays of objects at the Egyptian Museum with working models and live demonstrations.

Across the road from the Gazirah Exhibition Grounds, in the park at the southern end of the island, is the **Mukhtar Museum**, housing works by Egypt's greatest modern sculptor, one of the handful of 20th-Century Egyptian artists to achieve international recognition. North is the 500-foot-high **Cairo Tower**, erected in 1957, about which unkind jokes are made, but which is set in a beautiful garden and offers, when the lifts are working, a remarkable view of the city. Farther north are the grounds of two clubs: the **National**, home of the national (*Ahli*) football team, with its own stadium; and the once-famous **Gazirah Sporting Club**, which offers a wide variety of facilities for tennis, riding, swimming and other sports. Temporary memberships are available at the Gazirah Club, especially for good bridge players, who may run into the likes of Omar Sharif at its tables. Arab horses from the best studs in Egypt, which race at the Gazirah track on alternate weeks throughout the season, offer another form of excitement, though official betting is parimutuel and, to some tastes, a little anaemic.

Opposite the northern entrance to the Gazirah Club is the charming house built in 1927 for *Nabil* (Lord) Amr Ibrahim, a great-great-grandson of Ibrahim Pasha, as a *salamlik* in the Khedivial style. Confiscated after the Revolution, it now

houses the Muhammad Mahmud and Emilienne Luce Khalil Collection of paintings and objets d'art, a bequest to the nation moved here when the Khalils' house on the Nile at Giza was absorbed into President Sadat's personal administrative complex. Sixteen of the Khalil collection's Orientalist paintings, which now would evoke great interest, had meanwhile already been given to the **Muhammad Ali Club** near Maydan at-Tahrir, formerly Cairo's most exclusive private institution, rescued after the Revolution by the Foreign Ministry and transformed into a club for diplomats. They can still be seen there. The **Amr Ibrahim house** is worth visiting for its own sake; for the Khalil collection, which is particularly strong in 19th-Century French painting and sculpture and in chinoiserie; and for the **Al-Salam Gallery**, a small exhibition space in the basement where the Ministry of Culture stages one-man and group shows of contemporary artists.

Gazirah Palace: Immediately north, landmarked by a huge old banyan tree, one of Muhammad Ali's imported species, is the **Italian Cultural Center**, outstanding among foreign institutions in Cairo for its support of the arts, where there are also exhibitions. The banyan indicates that the land the Amr Ibrahim house sits on formerly belonged to Ismail's **Gazirah Palace**, whose gardens stretched from one side of the island to the other. The Palace's grounds now survive more or less intact only in two small portions: the **Fish Garden**, 350 yards to the west, between Shari' Gabalayyah and Shari' Hasan Sabri, a public park since 1902, which still has the original estate's grotto-aquarium as its most picturesque feature; and the enclosed garden attached to the **Marriott Hotel**, standing just across Shari' Lutfallah immediately to the east.

The central block of the hotel incorporates Ismail's Palace itself. Legend says it was built for the Empress Eugenie to reside in during the Suez Canal inaugural celebrations of 1869, but it was actually begun in 1863 and opened in 1868. Its chief architect was the German von Diebitsch, a pioneer in modular design, and its grounds were laid out by the Frenchman Barillet-Deschamps, who planned not only Ismail's final version of the Azbakiyyah Garden, but also every large green space that Cairo can still

The Nile in Cairo at sunset.

boast, including the grounds of the present zoo in Giza. There was once a small zoo in Ismail's garden here, as well, with an aviary of African birds, but it has disappeared, along with von Diebitsch's exquisite neo-Islamic **Gazirah Kiosk**, a 20-room one-storey *garconnière* adorned with a cast-iron arcade over 120 yards long and far more admired by 19th-Century visitors than the big three-storey palace itself. When the grounds were laid out in 1867, the Nile was diverted on the western side of the island and the resultant dry channel was turned into an irrigation canal for the gardens. Entire displays of masterworks were meanwhile being bought at the Exposition Universelle in Paris to serve as the palace's major furniture. Many of these pieces can be seen within the present hotel, having somehow survived the palace's later history.

Although the Abdin Palace has been closed to the public for some years, two other palaces elsewhere in the city that once belonged to the Muhammad Ali family have been made into museums and can still be seen: **Shubra Kiosk** on the northern edge of the city and the **Manyal Palace** complex on Rawdah Island, now partially occupied by a hotel. Built in 1826, the Shubra Kiosk's plain square exterior conceals an Ottoman-Baroque fantasy within: an immense marble basin with a marble island in its center, where it was later rumored that Muhammad Ali sat cross-legged on silken cushions smoking a *shibuq*, while his *harim* cavorted naked in the water around him. The galleries and chambers along the basin's four sides and in its corners include a billiard room that still displays balls and cues given to the Pasha by Louis-Philippe; and the original Turkish glass chandeliers still hang throughout, though the surrounding gardens were illuminated with gas from their own plant as early as 1829, making them a great showplace.

The Manyal Palace complex displays another gift of Louis-Philippe: a 1000-piece silver service. Built between 1901 and 1929 and left to the Egyptian nation in 1955 by Prince Muhammad Ali, the younger brother of Khedive Abbas II Hilmi and a first cousin of King Faruq, the complex includes six separate structures, of which the most interesting are a museum exhibiting Faruq's game-shooting trophies; the prince's own resi-

dence with its furnishings; and a 14-room museum housing his collections of family memorabilia, calligraphy, glass, silver, costumes and porcelain. The banyan-shaded gardens, featuring dracaena and philodendron, are also worth a visit.

Zamalek and Other Suburbs: Zamalek covers all of Gazirah north of the Gazirah Sporting Club. Less green, less exclusively residential, and far more crowded than it once was, Zamalek now boasts on its western Nile-side a street (Shari' Abu 'l-Feda) of cheap nightclubs, which have replaced the old house-boat brothels that used to ply this stretch of the river. Similar nightlife can be found along Shari' al-Ahram, the boulevard leading to the Pyramids, while more elegant diversion is available in the nightclubs of the city's major hotels, most of which also have good discos. Arabic-speaking seekers of down-market pleasure may prowl Azbakiyyah and adjacent streets in the center of town, but those in the petro-dollar fast track simply order fresh tarts by telephone: between 5 and 7 p.m. in prosperous seasons the taxi traffic around Cairo's five-stars is as lively as it is in Paris *de cinq à sept*.

For the more sober-minded, the **Akhnaton Gallery** on Shari' Ma'ahad as-Swissri presents exhibitions of art. Zamalek also offers excellent shopping at a number of boutiques. Designer-models for women are a particularly good buy and reflect the conservative *chic* of a district where there are several embassies on every major street. Nearly a quarter of the 140-odd foreign missions in Cairo maintain their chancelleries or ambassadors' residences here. And most of the rest are scattered throughout areas on the Western bank, in Giza, Doqqi, Aguza, or Madinat al-Muhandesin, which were still a rural hinterland as recently as 1970.

One or two embassies have installed themselves in **Heliopolis (Misr al-Gadidah)**, however, the new suburb laid on the city's northeastern desert edge in 1906. Development of Heliopolis began at the wrong end of a boom in land and property values, but was so intelligently planned otherwise that its density has remained low, its traffic has not become unmanagable, its original neo-Islamic architecture still predominates over new slabs of concrete, and it has even enjoyed something of a revival.

Meanwhile the British and Americans

have remained faithful to **Garden City**, laid out at almost the same time as Heliopolis, but on the site of an old estate of Ibrahim Pasha's south of Maydan at-Tahrir. The British Consulate-General—now the **Residency**—had in fact been there earlier, since 1893, and was restored in 1986 to its full late-Victorian splendor. Overcrowded with banks and their customers during the day, Garden City recovers some of its charm at night.

Towards the 21st Century: Unlike the British Ambassador, most Cairenes live in relatively new "informal-sector" housing, which accounts for as much as 80 percent of all residential construction since 1965, when the city had less than a quarter of its present population. Private building activity has thus easily outstripped the government's ability not only to provide an adequate infrastructure, but even to enforce property laws or building regulations.

The result is that the built-up agglomeration we call "Cairo," only six miles (10 km) long in 1965, has been extended some 15 miles and now covers the eastern bank of the Nile solidly for 21 miles (35 km). It has even begun to reach deep into the desert, and in many areas is without such basic services as running water, drainage, electricity, or paved roads. For political reasons the government itself meanwhile created multiple disincentives to maintenance of public and private structures or systems that already existed, while undertaking new projects of its own that were often devastating to the environment. Pollution-heavy industrial zones were thus arbitrarily planted at either end of the new carcinopolis. Thus the resort town of **Helwan**, at the southern terminus of the metro system, formerly a fashionable spa—an Egyptian Saratoga or Tunbridge Wells, famed for its baths, its Casino and its Japanese Garden—rapidly became a third-world industrial slum, sharing the fate that had already overtaken Shubra on the northern fringe, where Muhammad Ali's Kiosk is all that remains of an old and once popular summer retreat.

Midway between Helwan and Maydan at-Tahrir, the planned residential community of **Maadi**, once identified by its groves of trees and the green fields that surrounded it, can now be picked out from any point in the city by 50-storey

Boats in the rare yellow light of a sandstorm.

concrete apartment blocks, built on precious agricultural land in defiance of local ordinances to shelter the more affluent part of a population that is denser than the city's as a whole was in 1970.

Since 1975, and especially since 1980, the government has made enormous efforts, mostly successful, to try to catch up with and correct the course of the city's growth, curtailing wildcat construction while installing new systems for telephones, electricity, water, drainage, traffic and even natural gas. Small new green spaces have been created where formerly rubbish was dumped; and the Egyptian Antiquities Organization has instituted a non-stop restoration campaign (see "Endangered Monuments"). There is plenty of evidence that control has been reestablished and that from the rawness and rubble created by a decade or so of selfish shortsightedness, a more liveable city is emerging.

Frenetic construction testifies to the pinch of Cairo's housing shortage.

How such changes will affect the old spirit of the Mother of the World in the long run, only time, of which she knows so much, will tell. What is certain, however, is that the same qualities that have created her ramshackle charm and made her the most endearing city on earth have also made her the most humane; and that if these qualities are allowed to perish, Egyptians, and indeed the World, will have suffered a major loss.

Naguib Mahfuz, the great Egyptian novelist, winner of the 1988 Nobel Prize for Literature, is a true son of the city: he was born in the Gamaliyyah, less than a stone's throw from Bayn-al-Qasrayn. His most famous work, the *Cairo Trilogy*, is set in the heart of Cairo's historic zone, while later books have had settings in virtually every part of the city. And all his novels radiate a sense that Cairo — the city itself — has its own special morale: not unlike the spirit that travelers and residents found in pre-war Paris or Berlin, but unique in its depth as well as in its appeal.

This morale is linked with Cairo's typical attitudes and lifestyles, which in turn have been shaped and conditioned by the city's streets and monuments. Mahfuz is no longer alone in having seen that these streets and monuments therefore have a moral meaning; and one that is in danger of being obscured and even lost as they are transformed or disappear.

MARKETS AND BAZAARS

The best way to get a feel for the living energy of any city, beyond the epidermis of its monuments and museums or the skeleton of its streets, is to examine its circulatory system: the mainstream and tributaries of its economic life. For Cairo, at the crossroads of continents and the nexus of the Nile, the function of marketplace has always been vital. Like Rome, the city's origin lay in its location at an easy crossing of the river. Commerce grew out of the transit of merchandise. Egyptian Babylon was already a settlement of buyers and sellers; and the coming of Islam in the seventh Century brought a new impetus to business, for despite its Bedouin origins, Islam was an urban-centered religion. The prophet Muhammad had himself been a merchant; and the codes of his revelation called for fair play, respect for property and inheritance, and a communal spirit. Egypt, with the new city of Fostat as its capital, became the center of an enormous area of free trade within the Muslim empire.

Throughout the Middle Ages, as it added more quarters and spread to the north, Cairo boomed. It was an international entrepôt for slaves, ivory, textiles, livestock, spices and luxury goods; and until superceded in the 15th Century by the sequin of the sharp-eyed Venetians, the dinars and dirhems of the Cairo mint were the most stable currency in the Mediterranean. Long before the Mamluks' extortionate monopoly of the spice trade had pushed Europeans to search for new routes to the East and led indirectly to Columbus' discovery of America, crafts such as metalworking, ceramics, weaving and glassmaking had also turned the city into an industrial center. Fatimid lustre-ware, glass, and textiles were enlisted early among the treasures of European cathedrals, while Mamluk metalwork and carpets have become prizes for museums. Egyptian taste, however, was even more sophisticated: as eary as the 14th Century, for example, the kilns of Cairo were turning out quantities of imitation Chinese pottery, a fact that shows not only the extent of Egypt's trading links, but also indicates the city's thirst for cosmopolitan luxury.

The coming of Ottoman rule in 1517 brought coffee to replace spices, but marked a rigidification of the economic structure and a slackening of the entrepreneurial pulse-beat. Guilds and other professional organizations came to dominate the city's economic life. Cairo was divided along ethnic and economic lines into strictly defined districts, each with its own specialization. Over generations, trades were kept within the hands of a few families, so that by 1800 over 300 professional unions occupied 12 bazaars and 80 marketplaces.

The industrial age came to Egypt in fits and starts. The legacy of the medieval marketplace has therefore had time to adapt to, as opposed to being swallowed up by, modern mass-production and marketing. It is this fact that makes Cairo's market life so interesting. Even Nasser's socialist experiment and mammoth bureaucracy spawned traditional offshoots, as the booths of photographers, scribes, and fixers outside many government offices attest. The zone of boutiques and department stores in the modernized center of town is still ringed with distinct market areas catering to specialized trades. Cairo remains the Oriental City *par excellence*.

In and Around the Khan al Khalili: Situated at one corner of a triangle of markets that stretches south to Bab Zuwayla and west to Azbakiyyah, the Khan al-Khalili is a good place to begin exploring older parts of the city. Founded by a Mamluk Amir in 1382, the original *khan* or caravanserai grew into the headquarters for merchants of Turkish wares. By the present century, it had become the center for retailing the products of traditional crafts. Today, while souvenirs, trinkets and assorted *gris-gris* continue to make headway on the shelves, the narrow lanes of the Khan still conceal articles of fine workmanship and occasionally true works of art, though many things, such as carpets, papyrus, antiques, appliqué work, and caftans (*gallibiyas*), are best procured elsewhere. Within the Khan, the better bargains are leather goods, inlaid boxes, silver, gold, jewelry (the stones are mostly artificial as the dealers will readily tell you), brass and copper.

Haggling is called for in most transactions in the Khan, though not in all other *suqs*. Some people are born bargainers, while others botch the business miserably. A few tips: Relax and take your time. Shop around and *never* spend money for politeness' sake. Keep up a cheerful banter and maintain eye contact as much as possiblee. In Egypt nearly everyone is a softy at heart, so charm is essential. Be sure of what you want and calculate how much it is worth to you before entering negotiations. Couples should be particularly prudent — best to let one person do the talking while the other maintains silence and a sour expression: when husband turns to wife and says, ''Do you really think we should, dear?'' the merchant has his cue to home in for the kill.

The Khan al-Khalili strictly speaking is bordered on the south by Shari' Muski and on the west by the Qasabah, the main street of medieval Cairo, here called Shari' Muizz li Din. Northwards along the Qasabah from the Khan are gold and silversmiths, then the *Suq an-Nahhasin*, the Brass and Coppersmiths

extends westward for two miles through mat-makers, glass recyclers and dye-makers to Ramses Station. The Qasabah meanwhile leads on northward through garlic, onion and lemon markets to Bab al-Futuh. On Fridays a market for pigeons convenes outside this gate, while five minutes walking further north along an insalubrious lane into the Husayniyyah quarter leads to a pair of traditional glass-blowing shops, where colored hand-blown glass is sold at rock-bottom prices.

Southwards from the crossroads of Shari'

Market. Shops here cater more to local needs and much of the work is now done in aluminium, but better bargains are to be had than in the Khan. A zone of monumental buildings, Bayn al-Qasrayn, comes next, beyond which are a dozen shops specializing in water pipes, cafe accessories, and cooking pots.

Running left off the Qasabah at a small vegetable market, is Shari' Amir al Guyushi, where the cacophonous bang and clash of hammers announces the presence of dozens of metalworking ateliers: this ancient street

Textile merchant in no hurry to sell his goods.

Muski and the Qasabah, a turning to the right alongside the mosque of Sultan Al-Ashraf Barsbay brings us into the *Suq al-Attarin*, the picturesque Spice Bazaar. Its flagstoned lanes are mere corridors among scores of tiny booths stocked with bottles of essences and bags of spices. Slats of sunlight pick out swirling spice dust kicked up by shuffling feet, as black-clad women of the older quarters procure herbal remedies, perfumes, aphrodisiacs, and fertility potions.

A few shops further on, a pedestrian overpass crosses bustling Shari' al-Azhar. On the other side, where the Qasabah plunges into what was the famous Silk Merchants' Bazaar, is the Ghuriyyah. Passages to the right under the mosque of al-Ghuri lead to a lane parallel to the Qasabah. On this tiny street, more of the Spice Bazaar, truncated with the cutting of Shari' Al-Azhar, merges with a market selling carpets, blankets and finally shoes, all at fixed prices.

Bab Zuwayla: Southwards towards Bab Zuwayla, the shops along the Qasabah bulge with all manner of useful household goods, from teapots and brooms to prayer mats. One of the few remaining manufactories for tarbooshes stands here: new fezzes can be bought or old ones reblocked. Beyond the massive 11th-Century gate of Bab Zuwayla itself, with its spectacular twin minarets, lies a charming square where the Qasabah is crossed by Darb al-Ahmar, which changes its name here to Shari' Ahmad Maher. On the far side of this square the Qasabah dives into

small streets between Shari' Port Said and Maydan al-Atabah provides a fascinating glimpse of the internal mechanics of Cairo's furniture industry: wholesale wood merchants give way to vendors of upholstery, stuffing and springs until, towards Atabah, the final flashy product emerges in full gilt glory.

Maydan al-Atabah itself is the true hub of Cairene market life. In its vicinity just about anything from transistors to bulk paper, timber, or a whole side of beef can be found. Shari' Muski leads from it eastward parallel to Shari' Al-Azhar back to the Khan al Khalili. Its length crawls with shoppers and wares, street hawkers, porters and black marketeers in a ceaseless buzz of commerce. Just off Shari' Muski, beginning at the Atabah end, are watches, shoes, paper, confectioner-

the tunnel of the *Khayamiyyah*, the covered Tentmakers' Bazaar. A shop on the right just at the entrance specializes in colorful canvas bags, one of the best bargains in Cairo. Under the bazaar's wooden roof, the only one currently surviving, are the alcoves where artisans fashion applique tent panels, cushion covers, bedspreads and wall hangings. The most beautiful are the calligraphic and geometric designs.

To the west Shari' Ahmad Maher leads through an assortment of saddles and bridles, colorful tin lamps, butchers' blocks, garden chairs, rat-traps, beach umbrellas, marble and pesticides to Shari' Port Said and the Islamic Museum.

Maydan al-Atabah: Following one of the

ies, hardware, pipes and hoses, luggage, beads, buttons and textiles.

Bulaq: Far from the crush of central Cairo, on the Nile north of Shari' 26th of July, lies the district of Bulaq. Untouched by the tourist trade, this former river port, transformed into an industrial center by Muhammad Ali, offers an exemplary microcosm of a traditional economy's adaptation to modern needs. Still dotted with Mamluk warehouses as well as small machine works and welding shops, Bulaq is also a huge junk market, which found its niche during World War II dealing in military surplus. The alleys back from the main streets are crammed with arm's-width stalls selling car parts cannibalized from wrecks. An astonishing degree of specialization has been achieved, so that a shop may stock only 1950 Cadillac fenders or a variety of radiator caps. Further inside is the used clothing market, a jumble of colorful streets packed with America's and Europe's cast-offs, which are auctioned daily by the sack-full.

Further northward is the *Wikalat al-Balah*, a district named for a former date warehouse, which now serves as a market for all kinds of refuse, from bits of old iron grillework to antiques pilfered from collapsed buildings. Nowadays the rich don blue jeans to pick through the junk, so prices are not what they used to be. Beyond Wikalat al-Balah is the district of Rod al-Farag, which houses Cairo's wholesale fruit and vegetable market.

The Camel Market: Students of native life

bringing the animals as far north as Aswan, where they are loaded onto trucks for a 24-hour ride to the Cairo market. Here hundreds of the noble yet troublesome beasts are hauled off the trucks, examined, and haggled over by dozens of rustic traders, most of them Nubians or hot-headed Upper Egyptians. Once sold some will be loaded back on trucks, while others will be herded across one of the city's southern bridges, all of them destined for Cairo's *abattoirs*. Tourists at the camel market are therefore not expected to buy the merchandise there, but to wait until it emerges in finished form: camel flesh is closely textured but prized as *basturma*, the dried spiced meat that is apparently the origin of pastrami.

Another market that was the terminus of a

may find the Suq al-Gimal, or Camel Market, more diverting. Held early on Friday mornings on the edge of the city beyond the west bank district of Mohandiseen, this teeming market presents an extraordinary spectacle.

Though some of the camels come from the Western Desert — small Bedouin herds may be seen there and in the Eastern Desert and Sinai — most come from the Western Sudan and used to be herded north on an arduous 40-day trek called the *arba'in*. Nowadays only the first 30 are done on foot or hoof,

Some rustic types in a rustic setting. Boxes made from palm fronds carry fruits and live animals.

trek is at the village of Kirdassah, north of the Gizah pyramids (see the chapter "Cairo, Mother of the World").

Legend notwithstanding, there has been a great deal of traffic across the Western Desert for centuries, since desert routes avoided the impassable Delta and provided useful shortcuts. One of them entered the Nile Valley at this village, which is situated at a point where one of the largest wadis emerges from the desert. Formerly specialized in textiles woven for the Bedouin trade, Kirdassah now offers cloth, ready-made clothing, (including a huge selection of *gallibiyas*), carpets of all sizes, colors and textures, and their usual accompaniments of copper and brass.

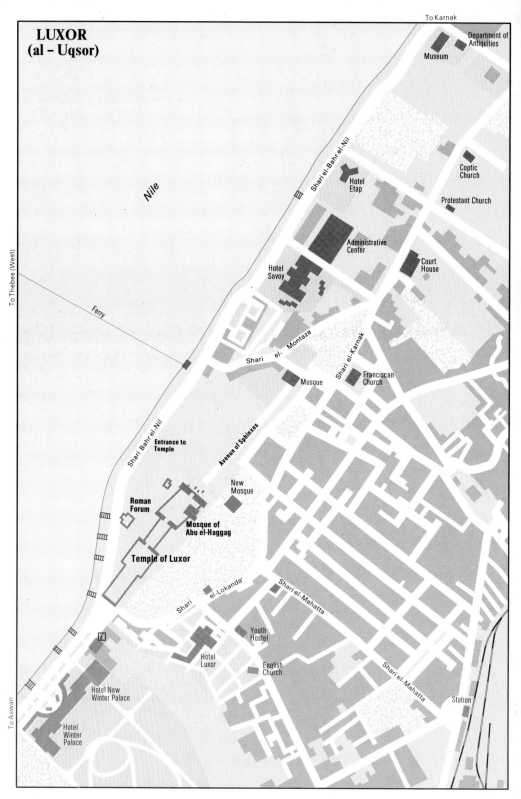

LUXOR
(al – Uqsor)

To Karnak

Department of
Antiquities

Museum

Coptic
Church

Protestant Church

Nile

Hotel
Etap

Shari el-Bahr el-Nil

Administrative
Center

Court
House

Hotel
Savoy

To Thebes (West)

Ferry

Shari   el-   Montaza

Shari el-Karnak

Mosque

Franciscan
Church

Shari Bahr el-Nil

Entrance to
Temple

Avenue of Sphinxes

Roman
Forum

New
Mosque

Mosque of
Abu el-Haggag

Temple of Luxor

Shari   el-Lokanda

Shari el-Mahatta

Youth
Hostel

Hotel
Luxor

English
Church

Shari el-Mahatta

To Aswan

Hotel New
Winter Palace

Station

Hotel
Winter
Palace

UPPER EGYPT

If one thinks of Egypt as a lotus flower with the Delta as the blossom, Upper Egypt is the long narrow stalk, extending from Lake Nasser in the south to Cairo, with the oasis of the Fayoum growing out to the left like a leaf. This stalk is 550 miles (800 km) long, and never more than 12 miles (20 km) across. Throughout its whole length are remains of Egyptian civilization including such famous sites as **Abydos, Karnak,** the **Valley of the Kings** and **Philae**, dating from the very earliest times. To explore it properly would take months of leisurely travel and study.

During the 19th Century, as more and more archaeological discoveries were being made and the mystery of hieroglyphics unravelled, wintering in Egypt became fashionable for the well-to-do. They would hire a private sailing houseboat, complete with crew and cook, at the port of Cairo, and proceed upstream, stopping here and there to explore the ruins and visit local dignitaries. Their impressions were conscientiously set down day by day in letters home or in morocco-bound diaries, as they sat under the awning on deck, glancing up every once in a while to watch the palm-fringed shore slipping peacefully by and ponder on the wonders of antiquity.

A river trip between November and March is still the ideal way to visit the magnificent monuments of Upper Egypt. Sightseeing can be interspersed with delicious idleness. Most of the luxury cruise boats run three-, five-, or eight-day trips starting from either Luxor or Aswan. Passengers fly or take the train to meet the boat and go straight on board. Facilities and services are comparable to those in the best hotels and most boats have well-trained guides speaking several languages. For the Egyptology buff, there are select tours led by university lecturers and archaeologists. True romantics can hire a *felucca* (the indigenous sailing boat with tall lateen rig) for the trip from Aswan to Luxor for a fraction of what tourist steamers charge, but these boats are more picturesque than comfortable.

There are certain advantages, however, to seeing Upper Egypt by private car or by taxi. Out-of-the-way sites can be visited and alternate routes can be taken for the return trip, either through the Western Oases or over the mountains and up the Red Sea coast.

Whichever way the visitor may choose to travel and whatever his particular predilections, the monuments of Upper Egypt are breathtaking. They have to be seen to be believed. They also require a certain amount of study to understand and the more reading done beforehand the better. For anyone but an expert, a good guidebook or, better still, a good guide is essential.

Sightseeing can be both exhilarating and exhausting, so be prepared. Comfortable shoes, not sandals there are too many stones to stub the toes — a hat, sunglasses, and a flashlight for dark corners, are useful additions to light cotton clothes. Sweaters and wraps may be needed for evenings, which can be cold. Parties in the big hotels and cruiseships can be dressy and romantic, but not risqué — remember Egypt is a Muslim country.

Luxor: Luxor, 420 miles (675 km) south of Cairo, is the most important and dramatic site in all Egypt. *Al-Uqsur* (the Palaces) is the Arabic name for **Thebes**, the capital city of the New Kingdom (1550-1070 B.C.), whose glory still glowed in the memories of classical writers a thousand years later. Here the booty of foreign wars, tribute and taxes poured into the coffers of the pharaohs of the 18th and 19th Dynasties, each of whom surpassed his predecessor in the construction of more and more gorgeous temples and tombs, creating a concentration of monuments that rivals that of any imperial city before or since.

Amun, once just a local god, took on the qualities of Re, the sun god of Heliopolis, when Thebes became the seat of power, becoming Amun-Re and rising to a position of ascendancy over all the multifarious gods of Egypt. With his consort Mut and his son Khonsu he formed the Theban Triad.

Two tremendous temple complexes were established in honor of these gods, the temple of Karnak and the temple of Luxor. Both were built over extensive periods of time and can best be understood when the visitor grasps the fact that they were constructed from the inside outwards; the original founders built sanctuaries on spots that had probably been venerated for centuries, and successive pharaohs added progressively more grandiose courtyards, gateways and other elaborations.

Preceding pages: Naive children's tapestry conveys the well ordered nature of the Egyptian countryside; a heavily laden *felucca* catches a breeze. Left, map of Luxor.

Cosmic Symbolism: Temples in general all followed the same principles. For the ancient Egyptians the precinct represented a little replica of the cosmos at the time of the creation. It was set apart from the everyday world and demarcated by a mudbrick girdle wall. Usually, but not always, the temple had an east-west axis, so that the rising or setting sun could strike right into its innermost recesses. Giant wedge-shaped pylons or gateways flanked tall gold-plated doors and were decorated on the outside with enormous reliefs of the pharaoh symbolically subduing his enemies and safeguarding the sacred place from malevolent forces.

Within the gates were courtyards, with small kiosks or barque-stations for visiting gods. Other shrines appeared in later times, including Birth-Houses in which the divine progeniture of the pharaoh was established. Before the entrance of the covered part of the temple stood enormous statues of the pharaoh in human or animal form and/or obelisks. Inside was a hypostyle hall, where giant columns, usually with vegetal bases and capitals shaped like papyrus reeds or lotus buds, clustered thickly together to represent the marsh of creation. The conception was completed by the ceiling overhead which was adorned with depictions of heavenly bodies, to recreate the sky. All was lavishly decorated with reliefs and brightly painted.

In the outer parts of the temple, the reliefs record historical events: the foundation and dedication of the temple itself and details of processions and ceremonies. The pharaoh is very much in evidence, leading the activities. He always faces the interior, while the resident god or goddess, often shown together with a consort and attendant gods, faces the outside world.

Proceeding through a vestibule into the offering court and then the inner parts of the temple, the ground rises by degrees, the roof gets lower, the brilliant daylight is shut out, until the sanctuary, which cosmically represents the mound of creation, is quite dark. Only the pharaoh and the priests were allowed into this holy of holies, where a gold-plated image of the presiding god was kept.

From time to time the god would be brought out from his seclusion, suitably dressed and perfumed, to receive offerings of bread and beer, or to pay visits to other gods carried on his sacred barque.

Upper Egyptian elegance on the Luxor Corniche.

186

Certain rites and offices were performed daily, others at set intervals. Probably the image could be made to move its hand or bow its head, and its movements were no doubt accompanied by mysterious sounds.

The rooms surrounding the sanctuary were used as storerooms for cult furniture, vestments, perfumes and incense, as laboratories and as libraries. Some temples had crypts and secret passages and ducts under the floor.

Karnak: The temple complex of Amun-Re at Karnak and its concomitant accretions constitute the most overwhelming of all the Egyptian monuments. Apart from the immense conglomeration of elements that make up the temple proper, the vast precinct covers an area of 60 acres (25 hectares) and contains no fewer than 20 smaller temples and shrines. It incorporates 10 pylons, six on an east-west axis and four on a north-south axis, which, together with intervening courts, halls and enclosures, surround the nucleus of the sanctuary. Behind the sanctuary to the east is a great Festival Hall; to the north is a temple of Ptah and an older enclosure of Montu, and to the south are a sacred lake, temples of Mut and Khonsu,

and avenues of sphinxes connecting the enclosures with each other and with the Luxor temple.

The origins of the Karnak temple as we now see it are attributable to the royal family of the 18th Dynasty, whose rise to power brought Thebes to the heights of glory. Three Tuthmosis and Hatshepsut, whose relationships are still not satisfactorily sorted out, were responsible for most of the inner parts of the temple. Hatshepsut dominated the family from the time of Tuthmosis I's death in 1492 B.C. She was Tuthmosis III's unfavorite wife/aunt, however, and as soon as she was out of the way he proceeded to hack her name away from cartouches, substituting his own, and to wall up the chamber and the bases of the 320-ton obelisks that she had had erected. Thus unwittingly he preserved her work in pristine condition, protected from the wear and tear of the passing centuries.

The third Tuthmosis (1479 B.C.-1425 B.C.) proceeded to reign long and brilliantly, waging 17 successful campaigns and extending the Egyptian empire from Syria to the Sudan. He brought back thousands of prisoners and immense quantities of booty, as well as new

The Temple of Karnak seen from across the Sacred Lake. It is one of the largest religious complexes in the world.

varieties of trees and plants, new ideas, new fashions. The annals of his career are inscribed on the walls surrounding the sanctuary and extend to his great Festival Hall and to the southern courts and pylons.

Succeeding generations added new pylons, new courts and subsidiary temples, all lavishly and colorfully illustrating their conquests, like a great stone history book. Amenhotep III added a pylon and the temple of Mut. Akhnaten, and built another temple to the east, but it was demolished by the soldier-pharaoh Horemheb. Its block were used for the cores of three more pylons.

The complex was thus already enormous at the advent of the 19th Dynasty, when Seti I (1306 B.C.-1290 B.C.) conceived the idea of constructing the **Great Hypostyle Hall** with its 137 huge columns, covering an area of 6,000 square meters. This mighty work was completed by Ramses II (1290 B.C.-1224 B.C.), who placed the appropriate colossi of himself at the entrance.

Though the capital moved away to the Delta and the importance of Thebes declined thereafter, Karnak continued to be expanded and embellished, such was the awe in which Amun Re was held. Ramses III added a complete small temple and at the end of the Ramesside line the temple of Khonsu was built, in which reliefs show clearly the rise to kingly status of the priests.

In the sixth Century the Persians did a certain amount of damage when they sacked Thebes, but the incoming Greeks set things to rights. Alexander, his brother Philip Arrhidaeus (who replaced the original sanctuary with one of rose-granite), and subsequently the Ptolemies restored and continued to make additions to the temple. The entrance pylon by which it is approached from the west to-day, and the enclosure of the first great court were their work.

Since the beginnings of Egyptology and the deciphering of hieroglyphics, Karnak has yielded endless fascinating material to generations of archaeologists. It was and still is one of the wonders of the world.

Luxor Temple: The Luxor temple is relatively long (780 feet/230 meters) and narrow. It is also dedicated to the Theban Triad, but Amun of Luxor had a slightly different form and function, as a divinely fertile figure, and in this particular con-

Hypostyle hall of the Temple of Amun, Karnak, Luxor.

text assumed his ithyphallic aspect. The temple was built on a north-south axis, sometimes off kilter to accomodate older structures. The major part was built by Amenhotep III (1414 B.C.–1397 B.C.) with substantial later additions by Tutankhamen (1333 B.C.–1323 B.C.), Horemheb (1319 B.C.–1307 B.C.), Ramses II (1290 B.C.–1224 B.C.), and Alexander the Great (332 B.C.–323 B.C.).

The sanctuary area dates from the reign of Amenhotep III. In one room called the Birth Room, his mother Mutemwia is shown being impregnated by Amun and giving birth to the infant pharaoh, whose body and spirit are formed on the potter's wheel by the ram-headed creator-god Khnum. The facts of life are indicated with delicate symbolism. The inner parts of the temple issue into an extensive peristyle court from which a tall processional colonnade with papyrus-bud columns leads northwards.

Amenhotep was succeeded by his son, the revolutionary pharaoh who took the name of Akhenaten (1353 B.C.-1335 B.C.) and rejected all forms of religion except the worship of the Aton, symbolized by the sun disc, and moved the capital away from Thebes to Tell el-Amarna. His reforms collapsed immediately after his death however, the capital returned to Thebes, the old hierarchy of priests was re-established, and his successors Tutankhamen and Horemheb dutifully took up the embellishment of the Luxor temple again. On the walls of the colonnade their skilful sculptors depicted the annual Opet festival, showing the gods of Karnak, accompanied by a cheerful procession of priests, musicians, singers, dancers and sacred cows, parading down to Luxor on the west, and going back to their own temple on the east. The great peristyle court, which today incorporates a medieval mosque, was added by Ramses II, who redefined the structure in his usual Cecil B. de Mille style, with a gigantic pylon on which were displayed his triumphs. He also had vast colossi of himself erected within the gates.

The invading French and 19th Century diarists, noted the glorious city of Thebes had shrunk to a miserable cluster of villas and squalid mudhuts on top of the meters of dirt and debris which cluttered the Luxor temple. Only the heads of the colossi of Ramses, half the granite obelisk of

A medieval mosque, known as abul Haggag, left high and dry by 20th-Century excavation of the temple it sits on.

Amenhotep, and the capitals of the columns were visible; and these remains were battered and blackened with smoke. The temple of Karnak was not much better, with columns, pediments, and pieces of colossi and obelisks lying every-which-way in a seemingly inextricable jumble.

A century of digging, clearing, cleaning, recording and reconstruction has revealed much of these temples' former majesty and visitors come in thousands from all over the world to see them. The riverside road called the Corniche, along which the cruise boats tie up and the ferries to the West Bank dock, runs parallel to the courts and colonnades of the Luxor temple, which still form the nucleus of the modern town.

Strung out to the north are hotels, shops, an excellent small museum and other public buildings. To the south are bigger and more luxurious hotels, some old and venerable and others very up-to-date. The rest of the town spreads to the east towards the station, and the small international airport.

Wonderfully dilapidated old calèches clatter up and down the corniche, the drivers cracking their whips and vocifer-ously soliciting business. The sound and smell of the horses and some of the old facades give Luxor a faintly raffish air, as of a gold-rush town in the Wild West.

The West Bank: The Nile valley is wide here at Luxor and the mysterious pink limestone mountains hovering to the west above the lush green plain are so honey-combed with treasures and secrets, legends and curiosities, that the average day or two spent among them is not enough.

An early start is recommended. For one thing the mornings are crisp and delicious, the ferries are less crowded then, the donkeys are fresher, the bicycles have not been picked over, and the monuments themselves are better seen by oblique sunlight rather than direct vertical rays. Taking advantage of the cool crystalline air, one can savor the sounds and scents of the countryside: beanfields, cassias and acacias in bloom, birds twittering and singing, and children wandering along to school.

The fringes of the desert hills lie about 2.5 miles (four km) to the west of the Nile across the plain; and here the great mortuary temples of the pharaohs of the New

The Valley of the Kings and, beyond it, the Nile Valley, seen from the desert.

Kingdom are spread out over a shallow arc. The **Valley of the Queens**, the **Tombs of the Nobles** and the **Workers' Village** are in the foothills behind them. The road leading to the **Valley of the Kings** skirts the cliffs before climbing a rocky defile to the northwest.

Mortuary Temples: The innovative pharaohs of the 18th Dynasty broke with the pyramid tradition and began to have their tombs tunneled deep into the mountainside, hoping that they would thus avoid the depredations of tomb robbers. On the edge of the valley, at some distance from their final resting places, each one built his individual mortuary temple. Those of Hatshepsut, Seti I, Ramses II, and Ramses III still stand. Two colossi in the fields by the side of the road are all that remains of the Temple of Amenhotep III, the famous Memnon.

The architecture and decoration of these mortuary temples follows essentially the same lines as those of the temples already described, except that in the sanctuary area there is a false door through which the *ka* or spirit of the deceased king could pass freely back and forth to enjoy the offerings and ceremonies in his honor, as he became a deity at his death.

Questionable Queen: The temple of Hatshepsut (1492 B.C.-1458 B.C.) is somewhat different from the others, being set back in a spectacular natural amphitheater of soaring pinkish purple cliffs. Three gracefully proportioned and colonnaded terraces are connected by sloping ramps. The sanctuary areas are backed right up against the mountain and partially hollowed out of the rocks.

Probably the daughter, sister/wife and aunt of the first three Tuthmoses, Hatshepsut was a lady of great character. She succeeded her father when she was 24 years old and assumed royal powers and regalia, including the false beard, reigning until her death 34 years later. Her divine birth and exploits are recorded on the walls behind the colonnades. They include a famous expedition to Punt in Somalia, whence incense trees, giraffes and other exotica were brought back to Egypt. The cutting and transportation of the two great obelisks set up by Hatshepsut at Karnak are also recorded. The temple was designed by an architect named Senenmut, evidently a great favorite of the queen. His portrait is discreetly hidden behind a door; and his own tomb is nearby, connected by a tunnel.

The Temple of Hatshepsut at the foot of the same mountains (as in 196) Deir al Bahari, Luxor.

"Ozymandias King of Kings": A large part of Ramses II's (1290 B.C.-1224 B.C.) mortuary temple is in ruins, but like other monuments of this long-lived and most prolific pharaoh, who reigned for over 60 years and had no fewer than 80 children, what remains is majestic indeed. Parts of what is the largest granite colossus on record lie collapsed before the entrance of the hypostyle hall. The foot alone measures 11 feet. The famous battle of Kadesh is depicted on the pylons. More interestingly there is a representation of Thoth, the ibis-headed secretary-god writing Ramses' name on the leaves of the sacred tree. Both here and at Ramses III's temple, there are vestiges of adjoining palaces where the kings came to spend a few days supervising work on their ''Mansions of Eternity.''

Medinet Habu: Ramses III (1194 B.C.-1163 B.C.) however, is not eclipsed by his famous forebear. His mortuary temple is the largest building in a complex surrounded by a massive mudbrick girdle wall, known as **Medinet Habu**. The battle reliefs on the exterior of the Ramses temple are particularly interesting: this pharaoh fought off invading sea peoples from the west and vivid naval engagements are depicted. The reliefs in the interior are also outstanding and retain suggestions of their original color.

Valley of the Kings: After being embalmed and mummified, the New Kingdom pharaohs were transported in solemn cortège to the Valley of the Kings. Gorgeously bedecked with gold and jewels, surrounded with treasures and replicas of all they would need in the afterlife, they were buried in their rock-cut tombs. There are 62 of these sepulchers, though only a few are open to the public. In most, long, elaborately decorated corridors lead down through a series of chambers and false doors to the burial vault. The entrance passage is painted with texts and illustrations from mortuary literature and the Book of the Dead. As the pharaoh takes his last journey he passes through the the 12 gates of the 12 hours of the night, beset by serpents, crocodiles and other malevolent beings. He arrives at the Court of Osiris where he is met by a delegation of gods; he makes his confession and his heart is weighed for its truthfulness and purity. A hideous monster waits to devour him should he fail the test, but evading the torments of hell, he is at last received into the company of

The Temple of Medinet Habu. The niches in the facade were for huge banners.

heaven.

The Tomb of Tutankhamen: Only one of these tombs miraculously escaped the attention of the tomb robbers, who were already ransacking them, sometimes within a few years of their construction. The famous small tomb of the boy-king Tutankhamen (1333 B.C.-1323 B.C.) was not discovered until 1922, when Howard Carter, under the patronage of Lord Carnarvon, chanced upon it after a search of seven years. The dramatic story has been told many times. A treasure of over 5000 precious objects was buried with the young pharaoh, whose embalmed remains were still in situ in a complex system of gold and jeweled mummy cases and coffins within coffins. A gilded chariot, beds, chairs, stools and headrests covered in gold leaf, alabaster lamps and vases, weapons, sandals, statues of servants, and all manner of other objects in perfect condition were crammed into the relatively small space of the tomb. The excitement generated by this discovery was tremendous. The treasure has been exhibited in Europe and America, but its permanent home is in the Egyptian Museum in Cairo.

Valley of the Queens: The royal wives were buried in the Valley of the Queens in the hills behind Medinet Habu. Very few are open to the public. The nine-year old son of Ramses III is buried in the same valley. The young boy is shown being led by his father to meet the gods.

Tombs of the Nobles: Unlike royalty, who were buried with somewhat ominous solemnity, the scribes and dignitaries of the court, whose tombs are scattered in the sandy foothills, departed this world surrounded with scenes of the joyous good living to which they had apparently been accustomed during their lifetime. There are 414 private tombs, ranging in date from the fourth Dynasty to the Roman period, but the majority are from the golden age of the New Kingdom. Compared with the tombs of the kings they are small and intimate. Many of them are vividly painted with naturalistic scenes of agriculture, fishing, fowling, feasting and junketing, and they constitute a fascinating record of everyday life. One lady diarist, Amelia Edwards, was so delighted when she visited them that she wrote: "It seemed to me that I had met those kindly brown people years ago, perhaps in some previous existence; that I had walked with them in their gardens; lis-

Feet of a colossal statue of Ramses II at the Ramesseum, Luxor.

tened to the music of their lutes and tambourines; pledged them at their feasts."

Workers Village: There are records of more humble workmen's lives in the tombs of the village of **Deir al-Madina**, where the masons, painters and decorators were kept segregated from the rest of the population for generations, in an effort to keep the whereabouts of the treasure-filled royal tombs a secret. They too felt the importance of the afterlife and prepared their own tombs in advance.

Even today the country folk on the West bank, known for their independence and their secretiveness, cannot be persuaded to move down from the hills to the plain. World-famous architect Hassan Fathi designed a model village for them at **New Qurna**, but they would have none of it. It still stands beside the road, rather the worse for wear, and the wily villagers still guard their secrets.

Abydos: Since there are no accommodations or facilities for tourists in the immediate vicinity of Abydos, it is usually visited on an all-day excursion from Luxor or from one of the longer boat trips. It is among the most spell-binding spots in the whole country and is well worth the extra time and trouble.

In the dawn of history, Wepwawet, the local jackal deity, roamed the edge of the desert guarding the ancestral burial grounds below the dip in the western hills. At sunset the ancients imagined it to be the dusty golden staircase to the afterworld and they wished to be buried at its foot.

The Osiris Legend: Later Abydos became closely associated with the legend of Osiris. The story relates how the just ruler Osiris was killed by his evil brother Seth (the brothers represented the fertile land and the barren desert, respectively). Isis the weeping sister/wife faithfully searched the banks of the Nile for the dismembered body of Osiris, which she at length managed to reassemble. He revived sufficiently for their son Horus to be conceived. Thereafter the pieces of Osiris were buried at different places in both Upper and Lower Egypt, but his head was supposed to have been buried at Abydos; and it was at Abydos that he was resurrected and assumed his powers as the lord and judge of the afterlife. His son Horus grew up and resumed the struggle with Seth.

Every January the great drama of Osiris' death and resurrection was reenacted

Titi alabaster shop, painted by a local talent, Luxor.

as a sort of miracle play with a caste of thousands and crowds of pilgrims came from all over Egypt to participate. A gold-plated image represented Osiris during this play, the pharaoh himself took the part of Horus, and the priests and priestesses masqueraded as Wepwawet, Seth, Isis, Nephthys and supporting cast, wearing headdresses and masks and carrying appropriate attributes.

From the Middle Kingdom onwards, every pharaoh as well as hundreds of thousands of pilgrims left some token of their presence at Abydos, hoping to gain favor for themselves and their relatives with Osiris in his capacity as Judge of the Court of the hereafter. The area is a mass of funeral stelae, burial grounds, former temples and memorials. But it was Seti I (1306-1290) of the New Kingdom who was responsible for the most extraordinarily beautiful tribute to Osiris in his seven-sanctuaried temple.

Seti came to power in 1306 B.C., just 29 years after the monotheistic regime of Akhnaten at Tell al-Amarna, some miles to the north, had collapsed. The nation was still recovering from the shock of this apostasy, and Seti wished to reaffirm his faith in the traditional gods and restore them to their former preeminence. To this end he rallied all the resources of the land to build and adorn a new temple at Abydos, in which he recorded his devotion to Osiris and his wife and son, as well as to Amun-Ra, Ra-Hor-Akhty and Ptah. He also honored his forebears by recording their names in a List of Kings, an assemblage of cartouches which has been of immense importance to subsequent researchers and historians.

Exquisite reliefs on fine white limestone, which has sometimes taken on the shade of old ivory, show Seti engaged in performing a multitude of rites in honor of Osiris and the company of gods. Devotedly the young king dedicates the temple, washes the golden offering table, waters the lotuses, kneels beside the tree of life, and communes with the gods, who respond with dignity and graciously bestow their blessings in return. Seti himself died before the temple was completed, leaving his son Ramses II to finish the decoration of the courtyards and colonnades.

The cult of Osiris and Isis later moved south to the Cataract Region, but the annual festival of Abydos continued through Egyptian history, lingering for

Inside the Temple of Ramses II at Abydos.

almost 400 years into the Christian era. It was the Christians themselves who finally sacked the temple in 395 A.D., but mercifully failed to spoil its essential beauty. Vestiges of powerful magic still cling to the sacred precincts. Local women can be seen circling the pool of the mysterious building, probably the burial place of Osiris, called the **Osireion**; and quite recently an English mystic deeply versed in Egyptian history and religion spent the last 25 years of her life living at Abydos and working daily in the temple. She was known as Umm Seti, or the Mother of Seti.

Dendera: The longer boat trips visit the **Temple of Dendera** on a bend in the river about halfway between Abydos and Luxor. The Temple of Dendera like those of Esna, Edfu, Komombo and Philae, and others further south that have been lost under Lake Nasser, is approximately a thousand years younger than the New Kingdom temples, and its construction was initiated by the Ptolemies.

It is dedicated to Hathor, the cow goddess, known as "The Golden One," goddess of women, who was also a sky and tree goddess, sometimes equated to Aphrodite by the Greeks and a great favorite with them. She was supposed to have had healing powers, and the sick journeyed here, as to Kom Ombo and Philae, to be cured.

Despite being damaged by the Christians, who chipped out the faces and limbs of many figures, Denderah is one of the best preserved of all Egyptian temples and its adjunct structures can all be easily identified. It has retained its girdle wall, its Roman gate, two birth houses and a sacred lake, as well as its crypts, stairways, roof and chapels.

Its most immediately distinctive feature is its hypostyle hall, with its 24 Hathor-headed columns and a ceiling showing the out-stretched Nut, the sky-goddess, swallowing the sun at evening and giving birth at morning. The hall was decorated during the reign Tiberius and is dated 34 A.D. The dark courts and crypts in the interior give evidence of various festivals in whch Hathor was involved. Her symbol of the sistrum occurs frequently. The most important of these feasts was the annual New Year Festival, during which the goddess was carried up the western staircase to a kiosk on the roof for the ritual known as the "Union with

The Sacred Lake at the Temple of Dendera.

the Disc," returning down another staircase to the east. On the walls of the stairways the order of procession of the gods in full regalia is clearly shown. There are interesting graffiti on the roof including names of Napoleon's soldiers. On the back of the temple is a large sunk relief of Cleopatra with Caesarion, her son by Julius Caesar.

Esna: The town of Esna lies 30 miles (50 km) south of Luxor and is built over the ruins of the temple of Khnum. Only the hypostyle hall has been excavated and its foundation level is 27 feet below that of the street. It contains most interesting reliefs and inscriptions, however, and is of great historic importance. The names and activities of Ptolemies and Roman emperors up until the time of Decius, who was murdered in 249 A.D., are recorded. French archaeologists have recently deciphered many details of the rituals of the worship of Khnum, as well as a precise calendar specifying when and how they should be celebrated.

Edfu: By contrast, the Ptolemaic temple of Horus at Edfu, another 30 miles to the south, is the most completely preserved in Egypt and is in near-perfect condition, with its great pylon, exterior walls, courts, halls and sanctuary all in place. Its walls are a veritable textbook of mythology and geopolitics. Building is recorded as having been begun in 237 B.C. by Ptolemy III Euergetes (246 B.C.-221 B.C.), and continued until the decoration of the outer walls was finally finished in 57 B.C. Several great annual festivals are depicted: the mock battle commemorating the victory of Horus over Seth; the joyful annual wedding visit of Hathor, who journeyed up the river from Denderah to be reunited with her spouse, and the annual coronation of the reigning monarch, identified with Horus, which took place in the great forecourt. Regal granite sparrow-hawks still stand sentinel at the doors.

Kom Ombo: The temple of Kom Ombo, dedicated jointly to Horus the sparrow-hawk and Sobek the crocodile, is situated right on a sweeping bend of the Nile 24 miles (40 km) north of Aswan, near a sandy bank where crocodiles used to sun themselves. Part of the front of the temple has fallen into the river and the back parts are roofless. It is built on a double plan with twin sanctuaries for Horus to the north, and Sobek to the south. Each has a black diorite offering table. Most of the

The Northern Palace at Tell el Amarna.

reliefs were executed by Ptolemy XII (80 B.C.–58 B.C. and 55 B.C.–51 B.C.) and have some fine details including the personifications of the four winds and an interesting set of medical instruments. At one side a small shrine dedicated to Hathor is used for storing some rather unpleasant crocodile mummies.

The Ptolemies evidently had more than religion in mind when they subsidized the building of these temples, as each one is placed in a strategic position both economically and militarily, commanding the river and the routes to east and west.

Aswan: Ivory, ebony, rose, and gold are the colors of **Aswan**. Here, a wild jumble of glistening igneous rocks, strewn across the Nile, suddenly create narrows between the highlands of the Eastern Desert and the sandy wastes of the Sahara. The barrier to navigation is known as the First Cataract, and was once where the civilized world stopped. Beyond this treacherous reach of the river lay a less familiar and hospitable land.

During the Old Kingdom a few travelers ventured further up the Nile in quest of gold, slaves and the occasional pygmy, leaving records of their missions inscribed on the rocks among the islands, but most expeditions were to **Elephantine**, the island in the middle of the river at the foot of the cataract, which was the capital of the first Egyptian nome. They came to man the garrison and defend the frontier, to construct and maintain the temples to the important local god Khnum and his consorts, upon whose benevolence the well-being of the land depended, and to exploit the abundant wealth of building materials and minerals in the geological formations of the area.

Quarries: Colored granites, graywacke, syenite, alabaster, ochre and other minerals were quarried and transported down the Nile when the river was in flood to the royal cities of the north. Obelisks that later made their way, by hook or imperial crook, to Rome and Istanbul, Paris, London, or New York were ingeniously cut from Aswan granite. In a quarry just south of the present town of Aswan, an unfinished obelisk can still be seen, attached to the bedrock. It would have weighed an incredible 1,100 tons had it ever been completed, but it developed a crack. The sophisticated technology and organization of the ancient Egyptians can readily be appreciated when one considers that Queen Hatshepsut of the New

Heads of the goddess Hathor at the Temple of Dendera.

Kingdom ordered two of these giant needles as part of her contribution to the temple at Karnak and received them within the space of seven months.

Nilometer: From the Old Kingdom onwards a strict watch was kept on the rise and fall of the Nile. Its measurement was one of the important functions of the resident governor of Elephantine and later Aswan, an office that was originally hereditary. Up until the last century, when western technology started to revolutionize the management of the water, frequent and regular readings were taken from the Nilometer at the southern end of Elephantine Island and the in-

formation was communicated to the rest of the country. Those responsbile for the cultivation of crops and the maintenance of embankments and canals would thus know in advance what to expect; and other administrators could calculate tax assessments.

According to an interesting text at Edfu, if the Nile rose 24 cubits at Elephantine, it would provide sufficient water to irrigate the land satisfactorily. If it did not, disaster would surely ensue. Just such a failure, which lasted for seven years—though it is not the drought mentioned in the Bible—is recorded on a block of granite a short way upstream:

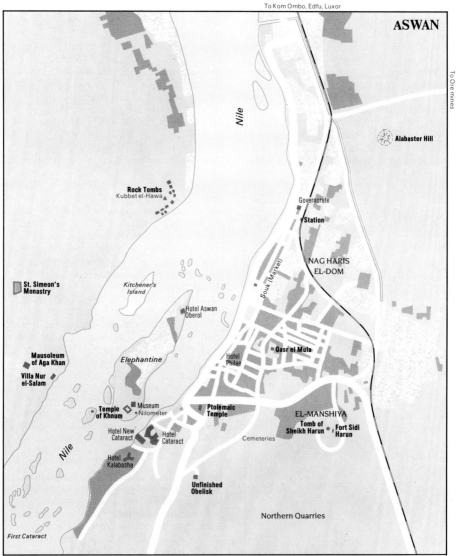

To Kom Ombo, Edfu, Luxor

ASWAN

To Ore mines

Nile

Alabaster Hill

Rock Tombs
Kubbet el-Hawa

Governorate

Station

St. Simeon's Monastry

Kitchener's Island

Souk (Market)

NAG HARIS EL-DOM

Hotel Aswan Oberoi

Mausoleum of Aga Khan

Elephantine

Hotel Philae

Qasr el Mula

Villa Nur el-Salam

Temple of Khnum

Museum
Nilometer

Ptolemaic Temple

EL-MANSHIYA
Tomb of Sheikh Harun

Fort Sidi Harun

Hotel New Cataract

Hotel Cataract

Cemeteries

Hotel Kalabasha

Nile

Unfinished Obelisk

Northern Quarries

First Cataract

To Airport, Aswan Dam

To Airport, High Dam

"By a very great misfortune the Nile has not come forth for a period of seven years. Grain has been scarce and there have been no vegetables or anything else for the people to eat." The king sent a message to the governor, asking for information about the god or goddess who presided over the behavior of the Nile; when he was told that it was Khnum, he ordered rich sacrifices to be made and promised all manner of offerings, if only the ram-headed god would bring back the flood and the abundant harvests. Khnum complied, temples were built to him and his consort Satis, and shrines were erected to the river god Hapi, who was supposed to live in a cave on one of the islands.

Archaeological remains of the temples on the southern end of Elephantine are sketchy, but there is evidence that Tuthmosis III, Amenhotep III, Ramses III, Alexander IV (the son of Alexander the Great), Augustus Caesar and Trajan all had a hand either in their construction or maintenance. Parts of them were still standing when the French expedition arrived in 1799, but were demolished about twenty years later by Muhammad Ali's son Ibrahim, at this time viceroy of Upper

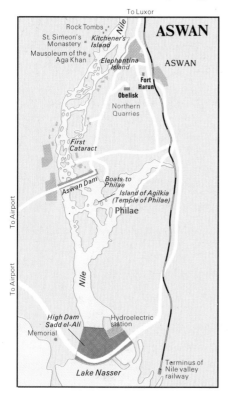

Egypt, who used the fine white stone to build himself a palace.

Outpost of Empires: The excellent winter climate and beautiful setting of Aswan were well-known in the classical world and were described by several writers. They mentioned the temples, the garden and the vineyards of Elephantine, which were supposed to produce grapes all the year round. Both the Ptolemies and the Romans maintained garrisons at this distant southern outpost. The greatest geographer in antiquity, Eratosthenes (c. 273 B.C. – 192 B.C.) who held a post as librarian at Alexandria under the Ptolemies, established the approximate circumference of the earth from astronomical observations made at Elephantine and Alexandria. He noted that the sun's rays fell vertically to the bottom of a well at Elephantine at the summer solstice, whereas on the same day in Alexandria an upright stake cast a shadow indicating that the sun was seven degrees from its zenith. Since he knew the distance between the two cities, he could then proceed to work out the total circumference of the earth; and he came within a few miles of the truth. He presumed that the earth was a sphere and guessed that it moved around the sun.

Juvenal, the satirical Roman poet, died here in exile at the age of 80 towards the end of the first Century A.D. But it was the merchants rather than the scholars, scientists, poets and soldiers, who left the greatest quantity of humble reminders of their passage, in the form of *ostraka*, or potsherds, inscribed with records of their commercial transactions. Nineteenth-Century travelers were able to pick up a pocketful within a few minutes.

Some of these remains can be seen in a small museum on Elephantine, which is to be replaced by a more ambitious one just south of Aswan. A gold-plated ram, ram mummies, precious stones, jewelry and amulets, as well as artefacts salvaged from sites in Nubia, are on display.

Dome of the Winds: As in so many places in Egypt, there are a multitude of burial grounds and memorials from the different eras of Egyptian history. The hereditary governors of Aswan and other high-ranking officials had their tombs cut out of the cliffs on the west bank of the Nile at a spot called *Qubbat al-Howa* in Arabic, or **Dome of the Winds**. They were decorated in traditional style, and, combined with a visit to the Aga Khan's mausoleum and the well-preserved Coptic Monastery of St. Simeon, make an interesting morning's expedition.

Aga Khan III, the grandfather of Kerim Aga Khan and distinguished leader of the Ismaili sect of Islam for many years, loved Aswan for its timeless tranquillity and had his domed mausoleum built high up on the bluffs overlooking the river. He was buried there at his death in 1957. The building is a close relative of those of his ancestors the Fatimids, whose followers' mausoleums are on the east bank. There are also many gravestones from the long period of Turkish occupation, during which Aswan continued its role as a frontier and trading post and as a convenient stopping place for travelers and explorers.

In February 1799 a contingent of Napoleon's invading army arrived, footsore and exasperated, having chased the Mamluk Murad Bey, a survivor from the Battle of the Pyramids, all the way up the Nile Valley. He infuriated them further still by slipping away up the cataract under cover of darkness. The French occupation lasted for less than two years, but it nevertheless brought a long era of somnolence to an end. Aswan was to wake up to great schemes, envisioned by Napoleon himself and set in motion first by the reforming Muhammad Ali and his son Ibrahim, then later by the British and other European powers.

Aswan from a *Dahabeyya*: In the second half of the 19th Century tourists began to arrive by way of Thomas Cook steamers and *dahabeyyas*; and there were plentiful observations to be noted in morocco-bound diaries. Amelia Edwards gives a description of the hustle and bustle of the waterfront, which probably had not changed much in hundreds of years, although slaves and gold were no longer the chief items of merchandise. "Abyssinians like slender-legged baboons; wild-looking Bishariya and Ababdeh Arabs with flashing eyes and flowing hair; sturdy Nubians . . . and natives of all tribes and shades, from Kordofan to Sennar, the deserts of Bahuda and the banks of the Blue and White Niles. Some were returning from Cairo; others were on their way thither . . . Each was entrenched in his own little redoubt of piled-up bales and packing cases, like a spider in the center of his web; each provided with his kettle and coffee pot, and an old rug to sleep and pray upon . . . great bundles of lion and leopard skins, bales of cotton, sacks of

Aswan seen across the Nile from the West.

henna-leaves, elephant-tusks swathed in canvas and matting, strewed the sandy bank.''

Elegant hotels were built to accommodate the fashionable travelers who came to spend the winter at Aswan or to plan the future development of Egypt and the Sudan. The terraces of the **Cataract Hotel** must have been the scene of many a portentous discussion by cigar-smoking Victorian empire-builders. The construction of the first **Aswan Dam** was successfully financed and the project completed in 1902. Edward VII's younger brother the Duke of Connaught came out from England to be present for the opening with Lord Cromer and a host of onlookers, among whom was the young Winston Churchill. He foresaw many future developments in Egypt, though perhaps he could not predict the demise of the British occupation or the later tussle between two young superpowers that would overshadow the building of the even more ambitious High Dam in the troubled 1960s.

Modern hotels have replaced the grand old ladies of the past, though the Old Cataract survives and the happy hour can still be enjoyed, to the accompaniment of splendid sunsets, from its terrace. Below on the shore, the *feluccas*, which are one of the prettiest sights of Aswan, tie up for the night after a busy day sailing up and down and around the islands.

The *suq* retains a hint and a whiff of Africa, where small shops sell cotton, baskets, dates, hibiscus-blossom tea (*karkadé*), ebony canes and crocheted skull caps. Soft-spoken Nubians while away their time in front of coffee shops, and shy women carry home the day's shopping on their heads, still wearing the thin black dresses with flounces that trail behind them. Not so long ago, when they walked across the Nubian sand-dunes, these flounces used to brush away their footprints in the sand. Nowadays they return to their neat stone-built villages in the area, which are quite a contrast to the untidy-looking mudbrick and brick villages further north.

Rescued From a Watery Grave: During Ptolemaic times the cult of Isis and, to a lesser extent, that of Osiris moved south and were established on the islands of **Philae** and **Biggeh** respectively lying at the head of the cataract about five miles (eight km) south of Aswan. A particularly beautiful temple was built and dedicated to Isis on Philae; and many subsidiary

Elephantine Island, Aswan.

temples, shrines and gateways were added to enhance the glory of the original. Some of the reliefs bear witness to the fact that under the Ptolemies the Egyptian and Meroitic kingdoms were briefly united (220 B.C. – 200 B.C.) Pilgrims came from both north and south to invoke the healing powers of Isis and continued to come long after Christianity had been adopted further north.

The construction of the first Aswan Dam in 1902 resulted in the partial submersion of Philae during eight months of the year. There had been strong objections by the conservation-minded but, as Winston Churchill caustically observed, to abandon plans for the dam would have been "the most senseless sacrifice ever offered on the altar of a false religion." The dam was built, Philae was indeed inundated, and more so in 1932, when the dam was heightened for the third time. But visitors were able to row and even swim about among the foliated capitals of the long colonnades and glimpse the ghostly reliefs on the walls in the water below.

Sixty years later, when the **High Dam** went up, Philae was threatened with total and permanent immersion. This time it was rescued by a huge international mission. A mile-long coffer dam was constructed round the island, and all the water within was pumped out. Stone by stone the temples were dismantled, and transported to nearby **Agilkia Island**, which had been leveled and remodeled to receive the masterpiece of reconstruction that visitors see today. The total cost was in the area of U.S.$30 million.

The massive bulk of the **High Dam** straddles the Nile eight miles (13 km) south of Aswan. Beyond it **Lake Nasser** stretches for 500 miles (800 km) deep into the Sudan. The dam was built with help from the Russians between 1960 and 1971, after negotiations with the United States had broken down, and it was hoped that it would be an answer to many of Egypt's economic problems.

Taming the Nile: The taming of the river's unpredictable moods, sometimes bountiful and sometimes enraged, and the year-round conservation of its waters has been at the core of Egypt's history and civilization since its earliest beginnings. In primeval times, the unharnessed flood roared down annually from the Ethiopian Highlands, swamping the valley for three months before it receded, leaving behind

Tomb of the Aga Khan at Aswan.

the thousands of tons of fertile silt, which, accumulating over the millennia, created the 10-meter-thick blanket of soil which constitutes the Valley and the Delta. An ecosystem favorable to primitive agriculture was thus set up. Seeds planted in the mud after the recession of the flood at the end of October germinated during the cooler winter months, grew to maturity during the spring, and crops were ready for harvesting by the early summer. During the hot months of June and July, the land lay fallow, baking and drying out and ridding itself of salts and parasites.

The flood, however, was unpredictable and occasionally failed to appear. The consequences were disastrous; and the coordinated planning required to deal with the recurring problem was an important factor in the development of ancient Egyptian civilization. By systems of dykes and channels, water could be trapped in basins. These systems were improved by the waves of conquerors who tried their hand at governing Egypt: the Persians, the Ptolemies and the Romans, who built bigger and better canals, introduced the water wheel, and doubled the land under production.

Barrages and Dams: Few advances were made and methods of irrigation remained essentially the same for hundreds of years until the advent of Muhammad Ali in the 19th Century. He set about repairing and extending the canals and building barrages, which conserved enough water for a limited year-round supply. They made feasible the production of summer cash crops such as sugar, rice and cotton, which enormously increased the country's revenue.

Continuing this pattern of development, the British in their turn built the first Aswan Dam in 1902 at the head of the Cataract, creating a reservoir 140 miles (225 km) long. At the time it was acclaimed as a great feat of engineering, and there was another marked increase in the well-being and prosperity of the country. It was heightened twice, in 1912 and 1932.

With the demise of the British occupation and the takeover of Egypt by Colonel Nasser's revolutionary government in 1952, the Nile Valley became a testing ground for international rivalries. The new regime focussed its aspirations on the construction of a High Dam that would generate enough electricity for new industry, as well as for wide rural

Toothache victim and the colonnade at Philae near Aswan.

electrification, and provide enough water to bring millions of new acres under cultivation, but they needed financial and technical assistance to realize the project. The United States was ready to help, but withdrew its offers abruptly when Nasser refused to compromise his non-aligned status. The Soviet Union stepped in with the necessary loans and technology.

For 10 years 30,000 workers labored on the enormous dam, which was built on a new principle of soil mechanics. Hundreds of tons of rubble and rock were shoveled into the Nile to make a barrier 2.5 miles wide, 300 feet high, and 900 yards long. Four huge channels were cut through the granite on the west side to divert the water while 12 turbines (which have since had to be replaced with the help of the United States) were installed on the east. By 1972 the dam was finished; and at last Egypt had a predictable guaranteed water supply.

The beneficial effects of the dam were immediately apparent, though it has fallen short of being the hoped-for panacea for all Egypt's ills. Had it not been for the water stored up behind it, however, Egypt would have suffered as disastrously as Ethiopia and the Sudan during the droughts of 1972 and 1984.

The hydroelectricity produced was sufficient to power new fertilizer, cement, iron and steel plants, and to make electricity available throughout rural areas, though it is recognized that the dam will not be able to produce enough to satisfy the country's ever-increasing demands in the future and other sources of energy have to be tapped.

New Lands: The addition of three million *feddans* (1.2 million hectares) to Egypt's cultivable lands, irrigated by the new assured water supply, was planned. But the leaders were so closely identified with the project that they turned a deaf ear to seasoned advice. The new lands were on poor soil, which took years to attain marginal productivity at exorbitant cost. Eventually Sadat had to admit that grandiose schemes for land reclamation were unrealistic and further plans could only be undertaken slowly.

The total containment of the flood has had other results. Houses can now be built in places that used to be under water for three months of the year; and as a result of vastly improved incomes from the oil boom, together with the pressure of the population explosion, the private

The Kiosk of Trajan, Philae.

sector has responded by a rash of building on precious agricultural land. Moreover other land is being lost through the constant use of excessive amounts of water, causing waterlogging and salinity, and the projected drainage system that would remedy this defect is proving to be more costly than the dam itself.

Though technological terminology is now applied to the forces of nature, which the ancient Egyptians so aptly personified, it seems as though the struggle between Horus and his wicked uncle Seth over the blessed patrimony of Isis and Osiris is still going on and, indeed, may go on forever.

Middle Egypt: Middle Egypt is more readily accessible by car or train than by cruise boat. Cruises generally pass through only twice a year, at the beginning and end of the winter season, on their way between Cairo and the more glamorous sites of Upper Egypt. Except for Tell al-Amarna, there are few royal monuments in this region, but there are some very interesting tombs of provincial governors and dignitaries.

Minya, which is a sizable town with an important university, is 153 miles (245 km) south of Cairo. One does not see the Nile from the road, for between it and the river are the railway and the Ibrahimiyyah Canal. Except for the occasional fantastic pigeoncote, rising like a mudbrick palace among the palms, or the odd camel loaded with a swaying peacock tail of palm fronds, the road is not particularly interesting. Minya has a couple of decent hotels and is a good place from which to make various excursions. Crossing the Nile by a ferry, and driving 12 miles (21 km) north on the east bank of the river brings the curious traveler to an extraordinary monastery, the **Deir al Adhrah** (*Monastery of the Virgin*) perched on top of a cliff and approached by 66 steps hewn into the rock. It is said to have been founded in 328 A.D. by St. Helena, a dubious attribution, but one that corresponds in date at least with the archaeological evidence and the plan of the church. Coptic pilgrims flock here on the feast of the Virgin every August 22 and make the precipitous ascent.

On the east bank of the Nile 11 miles (18 km) south of Minya, approached by a battered old ferry with a competent young man of about nine as a pilot, is the village of **Beni Hassan**, above which 39 Middle Kingdom tombs are cut in the cliffs. After

Monument to Soviet-Egyptian Cooperation and generators at the Aswan High Dam.

disembarking from the Nile crossing, one can ride up through the clover fields on a donkey to visit them.

Powerful feudal lords, who ruled the local Nome of the Oryx almost independently of the central government and of the pharaohs of the Middle Empire, were buried here. Twelve of the tombs are decorated with scenes similar to those at Saqqarah, but painted in fresco rather than carved in relief. Biographical accounts describing the military and administrative pursuits of the aristocratic owners are depicted, as well as occupations and trades such as hunting, fishing and dyeing cloth. From the cliffs of Beni Hassan the view across the reedy meandering Nile to the checkerboard of the valley on the opposite side, punctuated by the occasional minaret and church spire, is itself worth the climb.

Ten miles (16 km) further south is the site of the town of **Antinoe** (*Antinoopolis*), founded by Hadrian in memory of his friend and favorite, the beautiful boy Antinous, who drowned in the river here, perhaps willingly, as a human sacrifice.

At **Mallawi**, a few minutes further on, a road leads to the right, bending northwards through fields of sugarcane, where a little railway runs in and out to transport the crop to a smoky redbrick Victorian molasses factory nearby. The road passes through the village of **Ashmunayn**, which partially covers the ruins of ancient **Hermopolis**, city of the moon god Thoth, the reckoner of time, and therefore equated by the Greeks with Hermes. It is worth taking the time to wander around the rather confusing overgrown hummocks, which are all that remains of this once flourishing provincial capital. The ruins of a huge temple of Thoth and a church of the Virgin are about all that can be identified. Across the fields on the edge of the desert is the necropolis called **Tuna el Gebel** with some interesting graves, in particular that of a man named Petosiris, the decorations of whose family tomb provide a vital link between Egyptian and Greek art.

Petosiris belonged to a family of high priests of Thoth during the time that Alexander liberated the Egyptians from the hated Persians at the end of the fourth Century B.C. In the decoration of his fine tomb, which is actually more like a small temple, he chose to have the conventional offering scenes depicted in the fashionable new Greek style. The

Mudbrick domes of a cemetry in Middle Egypt, near Minya.

stiff virgins of the New Kingdom are replaced by a parade of buxom young matrons in fluttering see-through draperies, who carry their babies and turn to chatter with ploughmen and shepherds in the procession. The men are clad in hitched up *gallibiyas* and straw hats.

As you make your way back through the countryside at evening, in fact, you will see very similar frieze-like processions swinging in single file along the canal banks in the rays of the setting sun. Women bring water on their heads, brightly dressed girls and boys drive home cows, water buffaloes and goats, dignified elderly peasants trot along on donkeys, their toes turned up, their stout sticks lying across the animals' withers.

This idyllic scene may be betrayed by a Toyota or a tractor, for the countryside is changing fast. For the last 25 years electricity has been reaching nearly every village of any size; and with the influx of money from labor in other Arab countries, families are now able to buy washing machines and television sets, to set up small workshops with power tools, or at least to throw parties with strings of lights and loud *microfonat*. Much tut-tutting goes on in Cairo over the effects of all this modernization; and one may be told that the peasants no longer get up at the crack of dawn to tend their fields, that village headmen are losing their authority, and that the storytellers in coffee-houses are forgetting their tales. A century of change is being telescoped into a dozen years.

Tell el-Amarna: Returning to the main road and heading south, another six miles (10 km) will bring the motorist to the turn-off for **Tell el-Amarna**, the open plain on the east bank of the Nile where Akhenaten and Nefertiti made their brief bid to escape from the stuffy and overbearing establishment at Thebes in the 14th Century B.C. Though their story is appealing, the hot dusty bowl of the Amarna plain is rather a disappointment. Archaeologically, however, it has yielded a great deal of information and some beautiful objects, including the famous head of Nefertiti now in the Berlin Museum. After the collapse of their 15-year idyll, there was no further building of any significance on the site, so that the original outlines of the great temple to the supreme Aten, the palace and the houses of the courtiers and workmen are still discernible.

Ping pong on the Nile, somewhere between Luxor and Aswan.

From what remains of buildings and frescoes, Akhetaten seems to have been a bright and cheerful place reflecting the king's delight in his family and the everyday world. "Because Thou hast risen" he says in his wonderful 'Hymn to the Sun,' "all the beasts and cattle repose in their pastures; and the trees and green herbs put forth their leaves and flowers. The birds fly out of their nests; and their wings praise Thy Ka as they fly forth. The sheep and goats of every kind skip about on their legs; and feathered fowl and birds also live, because Thou hast risen for them. The boats float down and sail up the river . . . likewise, for their path is opened when Thou risest. The fish in the stream leap up towards Thy face; and Thy beams shine through the waters of the Great Sea."

The city of Akhetaten was spread out over a distance of nine miles (14 km) from north to south. To the north, outlines of a palace and courtiers' villas can be traced. Incorporating reception rooms, bedrooms, bathrooms with basins and toilets, kitchens, and storerooms, the houses were surrounded by gardens with trees and pools. Air conditioning was effected by wind catchers which faced the northerly breezes. These architectural details can be seen in paintings in the Egyptian Museum. Remains of the official palace and the **Temple of Aten**, situated in the middle of Tell al-Amarna, are discernible south of the present day village of **El Till**.

A few miles further on, **Asyut**, the most important town in the region, stands on a bend in the river. Thanks to the cotton boom during the late-19th and early-20th Century, its millionaires built themselves palatial villas and lived on a grand scale, with black-tie dinners and weekly races. Most of these families eventually moved north, however, and Asyut is now rather provincial, though it has a university, a huge cement plant and rug factories. A Presbyterian Mission has been established here for over a hundred years; and there are many Coptic churches and communities in the area.

Continuing southwards through what is the heartland of the Nile Valley, one passes several early monasteries and many rather interesting ancient remains, arriving eventually at Sohag, Akhmim and Baliana, the turn-off place for Abydos, a standard stop for the longer tourist cruises of Upper Egypt.

Aswan ferry.

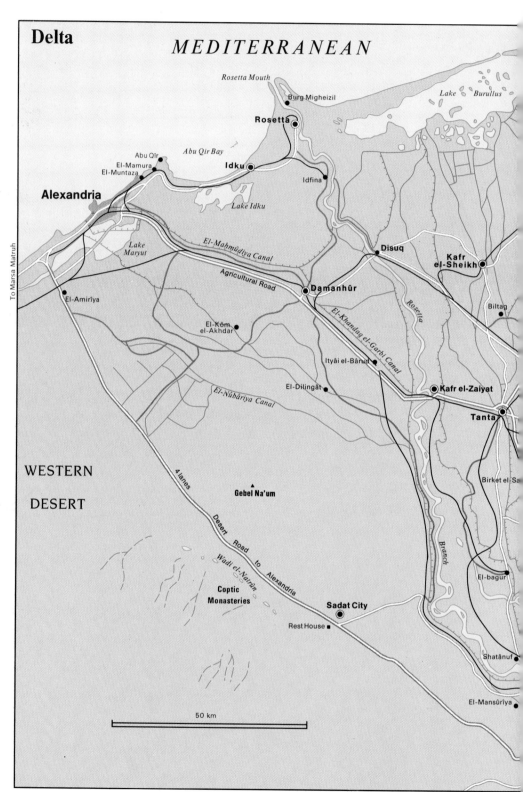

Delta

MEDITERRANEAN

Rosetta Mouth

Burg Migheizil

Lake Burullus

Rosetta

Abu Qîr

Abu Qir Bay

El-Mamura
El-Muntaza

Idku

Alexandria

Idfina

Lake Idku

Disuq

**Kafr
el-Sheikh**

El-Mahmûdiya Canal

*Lake
Maryut*

Biltag

Agricultural Road

Damanhûr

El-Amirîya

Rosetta

El-Khandaq el-Garbi Canal

El-Kôm
el-Akhdar

Ityâi el-Bârud

El-Nûbârîya Canal

El-Dilingât

Kafr el-Zaiyat

Tanta

WESTERN

Birket el-Sa

DESERT

4 lanes

Gebel Na'um

Desert Road to Alexandria

Wadi el-Natrûn

Branch

El-bagur

Coptic
Monasteries

Sadat City

Rest House

Shatânuf

50 km

El-Mansûrîya

To Fayyum

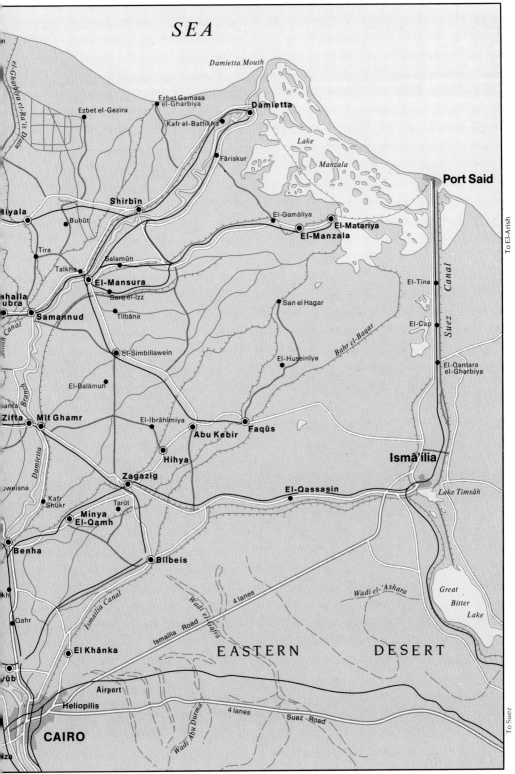

SEA

Damietta Mouth

el-Ghārbīya el-Ra'īs Drain

Ezbet el-Gezira

Ezbet Gamasa el-Gharbiya

Kafr el-Battikha

Damietta

Lake Manzala

Port Said

Fâriskur

Shirbîn

Buhût

siyala

El-Gamâliya

El-Matariya

El-Manzala

San el Hagar

Tira

Talkha

Salamûn

Suez Canal

El-Tina

El-Cap

El-Mansura

Barq el-Izz

Tilbâna

ahalla ubra

Samannud

El-Huseinîya

Bahr el-Baqar

El-Qantara el-Gharbiya

El-Simbillawein

El-Balâmun

anta

Zifta

Mît Ghamr

El-Ibrâhîmiya

Abu Kebir

Faqûs

Ismâ'ilia

To El-Arish

Suez Canal

Damietta Branch

Jweisna

Hihya

Zagazig

Lake Timsâh

El-Qassasin

Kafr Shúkr

Tarût

Minya El-Qamh

Benha

Bîlbeis

Wadi el-'Ashara

Great Bitter Lake

kh

Qahr

Ismailia Canal

Wadi el-Gafra

4 lanes

Ismailia Road

EASTERN

DESERT

El Khânka

Airport

Heliopilis

4 lanes

Suez Road

CAIRO

Wadi Abu Durma

ûb

iza

To Suez

ALEXANDRIA AND THE NORTHERN COAST

When Emperor Alexander died in 325 B.C., his mortal remains were brought to Memphis for burial, but the priests of Memphis sent the funeral cortege away. "Do not settle him here," they said, "but at the city he built at Rhakotis. For wherever his body must lie, that city will be uneasy, disturbed by wars and battles." So the conqueror of Asia was returned to the city he had founded eight years earlier, where he was buried in a grave now lost somewhere below the foundations of modern Alexandria. And the priests were wrong: Memphis today is a sand heap waiting for future archaeologists, while Alexandria, though buffeted by many wars and battles, has somehow stood the test of time.

Visitors to modern Alexandria must be prepared, however, for some disappointment. A search for physical testimonies to the Alexandria of antiquity will be largely in vain. There is very little left of the buildings and monuments that graced it during the Hellenistic and post-Hellenistic period, making Alexandria the most renowned city of the ancient world after Athens and Rome. An odd column or two on the skyline, dank catacombs deep under modern pavements, a Roman pillar propping up the gateway to some pre-Revolutionary patrician villa are all that is left of this glorious past, though there was a miraculous revival of sorts, during the hundred years before 1952.

Modern Alexandria is the second largest city in Egypt, with a population of about six million inhabitants. Set as it is on the shores of the Mediterranean, it has long been a summer holiday spot, a refuge from landlocked Cairo's searing summer heat. During the summer season, which usually begins in early June and ends in September, a million or two more people crowd into the city, filling the beaches, taking over apartment blocks especially built for their needs and haunting the streets in the cooler hours between dusk and dawn. As autumn heralds winter, however, and the vacationers depart, the Mediterranean churns crossly against the littoral, hotels pull in their awnings, and outdoor cafés retreat indoors. Then the city takes on a resigned air and seems to go back into hibernation, tired, it would appear, of competing for prominence in a changed world. Having twice been the busiest and most cosmopolitan commercial center in the Eastern Mediterranean, Alexandria now seems to exist largely as a city of memories.

A Magnificent Entry: E. M. Forster observed that "few cities have made so magnificent an entry into history as Alexandria. She was founded by Alexander the Great." When the 25-year-old Macedonian conqueror arrived in Egypt in 332 B.C., he realized that he needed a capital for his newly conquered Egyptian kingdom and that, to link it with Macedonia, it would have to be on the coast. Early in 331 he sailed northward from Memphis down the Nile; and on the site of a small fishing village, with a splendid harbor, a perfect climate, fresh water, limestone quarries and easy access to the Nile, he founded his city. Being a young conqueror and no doubt in a hurry to do more conquering, Alexander gave orders to build his metropolis and promptly departed. He never saw the city.

The deaths of powerful rulers are often followed by division of their empires and Alexander's was no exception. Egypt fell to a Macedonian general named Ptolemy who had been present at the foundation of Alexandria. He made it his new capital and founded a dynasty that ended when Queen Cleopatra, who needs no introduction, clutched an asp to her burnished bosom and expired on the glorious wreck of her love for Mark Antony.

As is so often the case with a post-conquest generation of rulers, the first Ptolemies had busily set about adorning their city. They also encouraged scholarship; and under their rule Alexandria became a haven and refuge for intellectuals. It nurtured not only outstanding scientists and mathematicians, such as Archimedes, Aristarchus, Hipparchus, Hierophilus, Erasistratus, Ctesibius, Euclid and Eratosthenes, but also poets like Callimachus, Apollonius Rhodius and Theocritus. The first two Ptolemies meanwhile decided that they needed a great monument in their new city, which could be seen by ships at sea and provide a guide for sailors through the limestone reefs that line the shore. Thus the Pharos, one of the Seven Great Wonders of the ancient world, came into being. A fortress as well as a beacon, this huge lighthouse stood at the eastern end of Pharos island, where it dominated both the Eastern Harbor, which sheltered the royal fleet, and the Western Harbor. Nothing remains today of the Pharos, but it represented the greatest practical achievement of the Alexandrian mind.

The Mouseion: The Ptolemies' intellectual achievement was epitomized by the Great Library attached to the Mouseion in Alexandria. The Mouseion was founded by Ptolemy I Soter, who invited a follower of Aristotle to organize an institution on the lines of the Lyceum in Athens, Aristotle's school, where a *mouseion*, a shrine to the Muses, had contained his library. The Mouseion developed quite differently from its Athenian model. Essentially a courtly institution, it enjoyed both the advantages and disadvantages of royal patronage. In many ways, it resembled a modern uni-

versity, but the scholars, scientists and literary men it supported were under no obligation to teach. They could devote their entire time to their studies. The Great Library, alas, was burned during Caesar's wars and the Mouseion's buildings have disappeared under subsequent rubble. Indeed, the very site of the Mouseion is conjectural, though it is known to have been vast, with lecture halls, laboratories, observatories, a dining hall, a park and a zoo, as well as the library.

The Ptolemaic dynasty received its death blow when the imminent might of Rome turned its stolid, censorious march away from the western Mediterranean, which it had already swept into the folds of its empire, and came trundling east-

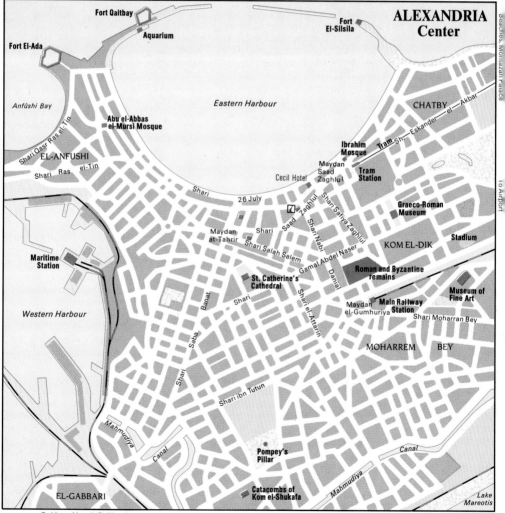

wards. By 89 B. C., thanks to the large debts it owned to this new power, the Ptolemaic dynasty was under Roman control. It would not be long before she annexed Egypt and deprived Alexandria of any lingering autonomy. In 51 B. C., while rivals squabbled in the Roman Senate, a 17-year-old girl was crowned queen in Alexandria as Cleopatra VI. This great seductress possessed all the attributes of an accomplished courtesan and came down from her gilded throne to play the temptress, first at Caesar's, then at Mark Antony's feet. In all fairness to the legendary Queen, however, it could be observed that her dalliances with powerful Romans were also the shrewd and calculated moves of a politician attempting to thwart the ambitions of men who had designs on her kingdom. And as long as she lived, Alexandria preserved its autonomy. At her death, it became a Roman city and its story as a Graeco-Egyptian capital came to an end.

Centuries of Decline: As Rome acquired increasing sway over its new colonies in the East, Christianity, a brand new religious movement, began to find adepts and disciples among the poor of Palestine. More than any other city in the Roman Empire, Alexandria may claim to have won the battle for the new religion, raising its doctrines to the level of a philosophy, while the Egyptian tradition provided the new faith with some home-grown images. Depictions of the god Osiris or the goddess Isis with her child, Horus, for example, parallel the images of Christ on the one hand, and the Virgin and Child on the other; and the Pharaonic *ankh,* which reminds one of a looped cross, actually appeared as such on many early Christian gravestones.

The conflict between Church and State came to its height in the first years of the fourth Century under the emperor Diocletian, who demolished churches, demoted all Christian officials and enslaved or killed the rest, as many as 60 a day for five years, according to the traditions of the Coptic Church. This persecution prompted flight to the desert, which led to the founding of the first monasteries, and made such an impression on the Egyptian church that it dates its calendar from the Era of Martyrs.

Although the emperor Constantine soon made Christianity the official state religion, centered in his new city of Constantinople, Alexandria still thought of

Alexandria in a 19th-Century engraving.

itself as the spiritual capital of the East, where bishops, priests and monks vied to have the last word in doctrinal disputes. This displacement of Alexandria was in part the source of the Monophysite controversy, a disagreement over the nature of Christ. Alexandrian theologians decided that although Christ had been born of Mary, the man in him had been entirely absorbed into the divine. Adherents of this view were *monophysites* and "single nature" became the national cry of Egypt. Accepted at Nicea in 325, the Egyptian view was condemned at the Council of Chalcedon in 451, where a majority of churchmen agreed that Christ had two natures, unmixed and unchangeable, but at the same time indistinguishable and inseparable. This is the definition officially accepted by Western Christians. The Copts and Ethiopians are still Monophysites, though these days the issue doesn't receive much discussion.

In 641, Alexandria fell to the Arab General Amr, who rode into Egypt with 3,500 Bedouin horsemen. It still retained some of its former glory. Islam, the new religion that Amr brought with him, would have been hostile to a pagan Alexandria and was uneasy with a Christian one, but the Arab Conquest was a humane affair and no damage was done to property. The two great libraries, which the Arabs are often accused of destroying, had already been burned by pagans and by Christians. It was Cairo that would develop and blossom under Egypt's Arab masters, however, while Alexandria gradually dwindled, especially after a Frankish raid in 1365, when all the public buildings were destroyed and 5000 people were carried off to slavery. By the time Napoleon landed on Alexandria's shores in 1798, the city was hardly a shadow of its former self.

Renaissance and Revolution: Modern Alexandria really dates from the early 19th Century and the reign of Muhammad Ali, who was responsible for introducing cotton and for building the Mahmudiyyah canal, which once more linked Alexandria to the hinterland, forcing Egypt to look not only towards the Mediterranean again, but beyond it, to Europe. The later 19th Century witnessed the creation of great wealth in the cotton trade and a steady influx of Greeks, Italians, French and English, who turned Alexandria into a pseudo-European city, complete with wide, grid-planned streets, foreign

The Mosque of Abul Abbas.

schools, clubs, restaurants, casinos, businesses and banks. It is hard today, strolling down the city's pocked and dusty boulevards, to believe that behind the grimy, peeling walls of its once elegant buildings the aspirations of a whole cosmopolitan society were played out in vast, ornate rooms lit by pendulous chandeliers. For while the poor — and there were plenty of them — lurked somewhere out of sight in the back streets, the rich and even the not-so-rich enjoyed an incomparable Dolce Vita in what was then not only one of the foremost port cities of the Mediterranean basin, but also the country's summer capital.

The 1952 Revolution changed all that. The new government eventually expelled most foreigners and confiscated their lands or nationalized their businesses, while Egyptian capital and enterprise fled abroad. Much of both went to Beirut, and helped transform that active little port, for two decades, into a new Alexandria. Meanwhile Alexandria's own star was once more on the wane; and despite steady population growth, it sank into a torpor from which it has still fully to emerge.

Using the Mind's Eye: Modern visitors to Alexandria will get the most out of the city if they possess lively imaginations. That is not to say that there isn't plenty to look at, for the city is still enchanting, but the visible glories of its past are few and far between and for the most part must be almost reconstructed in the mind's eye. The city is best explored on foot, but taxis, painted in distinctive black and orange, are plentiful and cheap and can be hired by the hour or the day for sightseeing purposes. A more leisurely pace can be achieved by hiring a horse-drawn carriage or *arabiya*.

A good place to begin your tour of Alexandria is the **Cecil Hotel**, located at the heart of the former European zone, overlooking the sea. The entrance to the hotel is on the west side of **Maydan Saad Zaghlul**, a large square between **Ramleh** (*Ar-Raml*) **tram station** and the **Corniche**. Here, in the lee of a few straggling palm trees, where the Romans built a temple to honor Julius Caesar, Cairo buses disgorge their passengers. The two obelisks that once stood here, the famous ''Cleopatra's Needles,'' are now in London and New York. In the center of the *maydan* is a **statue of Saad Zaghlul**, the nationalist hero who tried to negotiate

The Eastern Harbor and the 15th-Century Fortress of Qaitbay, which stands on the site of the ancient Lighthouse.

the independence of Egypt after World War I. As you stand facing the sea, let your gaze follow the sweep of land to your left and come to rest on the solid mass of the **Fort of Qaitbay** at the western tip of the headland. The best time to see the fort is just before dusk, when the warm reds and oranges of an Alexandrian sunset turn the old sandstone building the color of rich honey.

The Fortress and the Pharos: The trip out to the tip of the promontory where the fort of Qaitbay stands is of no great interest. On the Corniche side, you pass some dilapidated apartment buildings, gaily festooned with washing. On the sea side is the modern Yacht Club and a small fishing port, where brightly painted boats bob up and down on a dirty-looking sea and nets are hung along the jetty to dry. The fort is at the end of a breakwater and has been restored since the British bombardment of Alexandria in 1882, the preliminary to their invasion and occupation. It stands on the site of the ancient **Pharos lighthouse** and, if only for this reason, draws the curious.

The lighthouse took its name from the **island of Pharos**, where it was built in around 279 B.C. It gave its name in turn

to future lighthouses, called *phares* in French, *fari* in Italian, while its form inspired the classic Cairene minaret. The Pharos was a marvel of its day. It was over 400 feet (120 meters) high and hydraulic machinery may have been used for hauling fuel to the top. Within its square base were as many as 300 rooms, to house mechanics and operators; above were an octagonal story and a circular story, topped by a lantern with a beacon, the workings of which are still a mystery. It has been described as a mirror of polished steel, to reflect the sun by day and a fire by night, or as made of glass or transparent stone, so fashioned as to enable a man sitting under it to see ships at sea that were invisible to the naked eye. This latter device would suggest some kind of lens, of which Alexandrian mathematicians might well have discovered the secret, lost or destroyed when the Pharos fell. The lantern collapsed as early as the eighth Century, followed by the circular story. In 881 Ibn Tulun did some restoration, but in 1100 an earthquake toppled the octagonal story and nullified his efforts. The Pharos still served as a lighthouse, however, until the square base was finally ruined in another earthquake

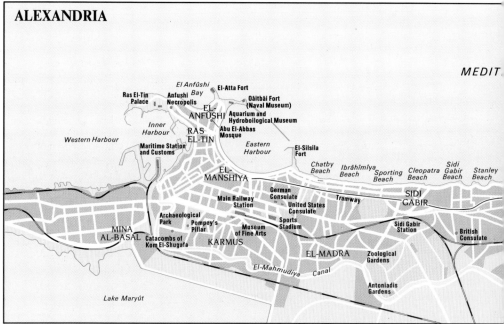

ALEXANDRIA

MEDIT.

El Anfûshi Bay
Ras El-Tin Palace
Anfushi Necropolis
El-Atta Fort
Qãitbãi Fort (Naval Museum)
EL ANFÛSHI
Aquarium and Hydroboilogical Museum
Inner Harbour
Abu El-Abbas Mosque
Western Harbour
RAS EL-TIN
Maritime Station and Customs
Eastern Harbour
El-Silsila Fort
EL-MANSHIYA
Chatby Beach
Ibrãhîmîya Beach
Sporting Beach
Cleopatra Beach
Sidi Gabir Beach
Stanley Beach
German Consulate
Main Railway Station
United States Consulate
Tramway
SIDI GABIR
Archaeological Park
Pompey's Pillar
Sports Stadium
Sidi Gabir Station
MINA AL-BASAL
Museum of Fine Arts
Catacombs of Kom El-Shugafa
KARMUS
British Consulate
EL-MADRA
Zoological Gardens
El-Mahmudiya Canal
Antoniadis Gardens
Lake Maryût

To Airport   To Cairo 208kms. via Delta Road

in the 14th Century. Enter Sultan Qaitbay, who in 1480 built the fort that still stands on the site, which incorporates some of the debris from the Pharos. You can make out granite and marble columns, for example, in the northwest section of the enclosure walls. The fort itself is an impressive piece of defensive architecture and inside is a newly revamped **Naval Museum** open to visitors.

Ras at-Tin and Anfushi: Westward along the sea front, a mile and a half (three km) from the Fort, is the **Palace of Ras at-Tin** (Cape of Figs). Built by Muhammad Ali, but altered by later rulers of Egypt, it is the site where King Faruq abdicated on July 26, 1952, and from which he embarked a few hours later to sail away on his yacht, **Mahrusa** — just as his grandfather, the Khedive Ismail, had done in the summer of 1879. This enormous pile is still used for official Egyptian government functions and cannot be visited. East of the Palace on Shari' Ras at-Tin, near the end of the tramline, and worth a look, are the **tombs of Anfushi**. Ptolemaic, with decorations that marry Greek and Egyptian styles, their stucco walls are painted to imitate marble blocks and tiles and are interesting, though inferior to those in the Kom ash-Shawqafah catacombs.

At this point, you can turn into the old Turkish quarter of **Anfushi** at the heart of what was once the island of Pharos. Going southeast along Shari' Ras at-Tin, then turning north on Shari' Sidi Abu'l-Abbas al-Mursi will bring you to a square where the large and imposing **mosque of Sidi Abu l-Abbas al-Mursi** stands, built in 1943 on the site of an earlier mosque over the tomb of this 13th-Century saint. At the northern end of this square, which was the chief *maydan* of the 18th-Century Turkish town, is the little **mosque of Sidi Dawud**.

Continuing southeast along Shari' Ras at-Tin you will reach **Shari' Faransa** (*Rue de France*). You are now in one of the most 'native' parts of the city, where you may stop briefly to look at the 17th-Century **Terbana mosque**. It has a pale yellow exterior, plaster overlying a red and black Delta-style facade of bricks and wooden beams. On the left side note the ancient columns at the entrance to the cellars. Two huge Corinthian columns mark the entrance to the mosque itself and support its minaret. More antique columns inside prop up various other parts of

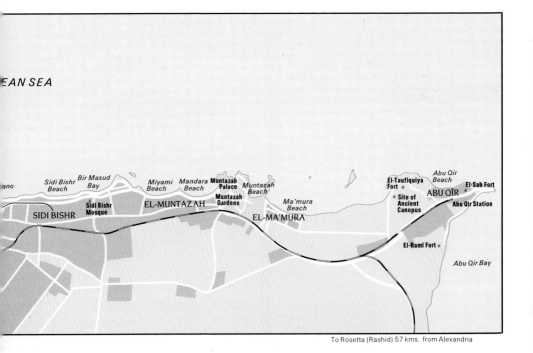

To Rosetta (Rashid) 57 kms. from Alexandria

the building.

In ancient times Pharos was connected to the mainland by a causeway called the **Heptastadion**, which gradually became a permanent broad neck of land. Along it to the south Shari' Faransa runs into **Maydan at-Tahrir**, formerly *Place Muhammad Ali*. A statue of the Pasha on horseback (by Jacquemart) still graces the *maydan*. The southern end of the square marks approximately the former mainland coastline and the seafront of the village of Rhakotis.

The Southern Quarter: To reach the center of **Rhakotis**, the hub of ancient Alexandria, you must be prepared for a detour, armed with a map and on foot, through a particularly insalubrious part of town. Rhakotis is about a mile southwest from the Corniche along Shari' Salah ad-Din and Shari' 'Awud as-Sawari. Simplest, perhaps, is to hail a taxi and tell the driver to take you to **Pompey's Pillar** (*Al-'Awud as-Sawari*, "The Horseman's Pillar"). If you survive the drive, which bumps over busy tram tracks, you will reach the bottom of a rather shapeless hill surrounded by a wall. Believe it or not, this is what is left of the acropolis of the Ptolemies.

Long before Alexander arrived on the scene, this hill was the citadel of Rhakotis, dedicated to the worship of Osiris. The Ptolemies in their turn built a temple of Serapis on its summit. Here, with a collection of 200,000 manuscripts given to her by Mark Antony, Cleopatra endowed the second great Alexandrian library, which was to remain attached to the **Serapeum** until the temple itself was destroyed by a Christian mob; and thus here, for 400 years, was the most learned spot on earth. Today not much of the Serapeum remains: some tunnels in the rocks with crypts and niches and a few marble pillars. What the Christians wiped out in 391 A.D. later vicissitudes have put paid to. But the principal attraction, a solitary 72-foot (22-meter) high pillar of pink Aswan granite, seems to touch the sky defiantly and when European travelers arrived in the 15th Century it caught their attention. No scholars they, but since they had heard of Pompey, they named the pillar after him and said his head was enclosed in a ball at the top. It actually has nothing to do with Pompey: according to an inscription on its base, it was dedicated to the Emperor Diocletian in 297 A.D. and it may once have had an

Late Roman council chamber excavated in down – town Alexandria.

equestrian statue on top, which would explain its Arabic name. Even less is left of the temple to Isis that once stood on the hill than of the Serapeum. You can see a **statue of Isis Pharia**, found near the site of the Pharos, as well as two granite sphinxes.

This once famous site has been encroached upon by a brash and often ugly modern city: hideous buildings loom around its perimeter, trams bump, screech and grind their way noisily along the street below. But children come to play among the ruins, a solitary kite can sometimes be seen soaring above the hillside, and a certain sense of dignity and charm lingers about the place. Pompey's pillar still stands, in any case, straight and tall above the noise and bustle of the city.

The Catacombs at Kom esh-Shawqafa: A short distance south of the site of Pompey's pillar and not to be missed are the **catacombs of Kom esh-Shawqafa.** Come out of the enclosure of Pompey's pillar, turn right up a small crowded street and at the top you will come to a small crossroads. Just beyond it is the entrance to the catacombs. Immediately inside the entrance are four very fine sarcophagi of purplish granite. You are now on the Kom esh-Shawqafa (Hill of Tiles) and the tombs here are the most important in the city and quite unique. They also constitute the largest Roman-period funerary complex in Egypt. They date from about the second Century A.D., when the old religions began to fade and merge with one another, a fact demonstrated in the curious blend of classical and Egyptian designs here. It is not known who was to occupy these tombs, although there is a theory that they began as a family vault and were later taken over by a burial syndicate. Certainly, one's first visit to this underground complex is otherworldly, spellbinding and eerie. The catacombs are on three levels, the lowest being flooded and inaccessible. The first level is reached by a wide circular staircase lit by a central well, down which the bodies were lowered by ropes. From the vestibule you enter the Rotunda, with a well in its center upon which eight pillars support a domed roof. To the left is the Banquet Hall, where friends and relatives of the deceased held ceremonial feasts in honor of their dead.

From the Rotunda, a small staircase descends to the second level and the amazing central tomb is revealed. Here the decorations are fantastic and in a hodgepodge of styles. Bearded serpents on the vestibule wall at the entrance of the inner chamber hold the pine-cone of Dionysus and the serpent-wand of Hermes, but also wear the double crown of Upper and Lower Egypt, while above them are Medusas in round shields. Inside the tomb chamber are three large sarcophagi cut out from the rock, Roman in style, decorated with fruits, flowers, Medusas and filleted ox-heads. None of them has ever been occupied and their lids are sealed on. Over each sarcophagus is a niche decorated with Egyptian-style reliefs. Turn and face the entrance. On your right stands the extraordinary figure of Anubis — with a dog's head, but dressed as a Roman soldier, with sword, lance and shield. Left is the god Sobek, also dressed in military costume, with cloak and spear. There is much more to gaze at in this Disneyland of death; and if you do not suffer from a case of the spooks, it is worth taking your time at this site, one of the most interesting in Alexandria.

In Search of Alexander: Start at Maydan Saad Zaghlul and walk south along **Shari' Nebi Danyal.** The point where it meets **Shari' Hurriyyah** has been the chief crossroads of the city for over 2300

years. Here once, from east to west, the **Canopic Way** (Shari' Hurriyyah) ran from the **Gate of the Sun** to the **Gate of the Moon**. From north to south ran the street of the **Soma** (Shari' Nebi Danyal). In ancient times both were lined from end to end with colonnades.

A short walk up Shari' Nebi Danyal will bring you to the mosque of that same name, on the left side of the street with an entrance somewhat set back from the street. Mistakenly believed to be the tomb of the prophet Daniel, it is named for Shaykh Danyal al-Maridi, who died in 1407; more importantly, it stands on the site of Alexander's tomb, the Soma, where he and some of the Ptolemies were buried in the Macedonian manner. Inside the mosque, an ancient caretaker will beckon you over to peer down a great square hole into the crypt where Danyal and one Luqman the Wise lie and where presumably, somewhere lie Alexander and some of his successors. The cellars have never been properly explored, although there is the dubious account of a dragon man once attached to the Russian consulate, who claimed in 1850 to have descended into the gloom and seen through a hole in a wooden door "a hu-man body in a glass cage with a diadem on its head, and half bowed on a sort of elevation or throne. A quantity of books and papyrus were scattered around."

As you return to the street, notice that almost immediately opposite the mosque are some antique columns propping up the gatepost of what is now a French Cultural Center, but which may once have been the site of the Mouseion, the great intellectual center of the Ptolemaic Dynasty.

Kom ad-Dik and the Greco-Roman Museum: One block east of Nebi Danyal, on the south side of Shari' Hurriyyah lie the **excavations of Kom ad-Dik**. Here, Polish archaeologists have been digging up Alexandria's past since 1959. Below Muslim tombs dating from the ninth to 11th Centuries, they have found baths, houses, assembly halls, and the site where Christian mobs burnt objects from the Serapeum. Continue east along Shari' Hurriyyah and you will come, on your left, to the Rue du Musée and the entrance to the **Greco-Roman Museum.**

For those visitors who have been satiated by the hieratic wonders of ancient Egyptian civilization, the Greco-Roman Museum can only come as a delightful

Monument to the Unknown Soldier was originally a gift of the Italian community in Alexandria.

relief. Filling the historical gap between the country's several museums of pharaonic antiquities and Cairo's museums of Coptic and Islamic art, it has recently been renovated and a charming new sculpture garden has been laid out in its grounds. Among its many treasures are some very fine pieces of Hellenistic sculpture, but special attention must be paid to the wonderful collection of Tanagra figurines. Likewise not to be missed is a masterpiece of fresco-painting that is also the earliest depiction of an ox-powered waterwheel.

Modern Pleasures: This might be the time to take a break from sightseeing and to stroll back down Shari' Hurriyyah towards the sea, stopping off at **Pastroudis**, one of the last Greek cafés. Here you can sit at a sidewalk table overlooking the ruins of Kom ad-Dik and ponder Alexandria's more recent cultural past. For during the earlier part of this century, as countless ships, furrowed the harbor and ticker tape made mad confetti in the bustling halls of the Bourse, a literary revival was also taking place. Its luminary was Constantine Cavafy, called "the poet of the City" by Lawrence Durrell. E.M. Forster, who lived in Alexandria

and wrote its history, first met Cavafy in 1917 and was responsible for introducing him to the English-speaking world. The Greek poet's apartment has been recreated as a museum on the top floor of the **Greek Consulate** in Alexandria and can be visited.

Lawrence Durrell's *Alexandria Quartet*, largely inspired by Cavafy's poetry, can be and has been used as a guide to the city. The narrator of the Quartet, Darley, first catches sight of Justine at the Cecil Hotel and shares a flat with the Frenchmen Pombal on Shari' Nebi Danyal. Clea's studio is in the *rue* St. Saba, Scobie lives in rooms in Shari' Tatwig, and Melissa dies in the Greek Hospital. All the characters meet at least once at Pastroudis for an *araq*. But modern traveler, beware: Durrell's Alexandria is in many ways just as elusive as Mark Anthony's.

Alexandria is a Mediterranean city and still has a Mediterranean café life. **Pastroudis,** the **Trianon** and the **Delices** (the last two are on Maydan Saad Zaghlul) are fine examples, if somewhat down at the heel, of fin-de-siècle coffee houses. Alexandria has a reputation for good food, particularly seafood. **Greek** *tavernas*, such as the **Diamantakis Taverna** on the

Alexandria in 1930.

Alexandria   The Boulevard Fouad I   106

south side of **Maydan Raml** (*Ramleh Square*), offer fried or grilled fish and Greek salads. The **Santa Lucia** is the best known restaurant: the food is good and the atmosphere lively. It is on Shari' Safiyya Zaghlul, not far from Pastroudis. Relic of the past is the **Union**, on Shari'al-Bursa just off Maydan Muhammad Ali near where the charming Anglican **church of St. Mark's** is situated. As for hotels, romantics will probably favor landmarks such as the Cecil or the **Windsor Palace**, overlooking the sea. But there are many more to choose form.

West to Burg al-Arab: Although a train runs westward just inland from the Mediterranean coast, it is unreliable and anyone interested in exploring the region west of Alexandria would do best to hire a car by the day.

The coast road is unprepossessing for the first 18 miles (30 km) until you pass the resort town of **Agami**, which began some years ago as a few bathing huts and simple beach houses in a grove of trees, but has now mushroomed into the Marbella or St. Tropez of Egypt's Mediterranean coast, complete with swimming pools, discos, fast-food joints and a section of villas known as "Millionaire's Row." Several hundred thousand people now congregate here during the summer months. Beyond Agami, the coastline improves, although a private-sector construction boom has conspired with government-sponsored development of tourist resorts to leave ugly marks upon what used to be unspoilt beaches and shapely dunes, studded with a few palms and fig trees.

Before the turnoff to the **village of Burg al-Arab** on the hill on your left, is the ancient **temple of Taposiris Magna**, whose name is preserved in the modern Abu Sir. It is contemporary with the founding of Alexandria and was dedicated to the cult of Osiris. The ruined tower to the east is a Ptolemaic lighthouse, the first of a chain that stretched from Alexandria all the way down the North African coast. It looks, in miniature, very much as its big brother, the Pharos, would have looked and for this reason is of interest to historians and archaeologists.

It is no longer possible to ascend to the top of the lighthouse — a great pity, as the view from the top is magnificent: To the north, the brilliant turquoise blue of the sea is offset by its bleached white

"The Bride of the Sea" from across the Eastern Harbor.

beaches, while to the south lies the dun-colored **lake-bed of Mariut** (ancient **Mareotis**), vibrantly alive with wildflowers in the spring. If you leave the coast and drive south across the lake-bed, you will be able to make out the remains of the ancient causeway, to your left, which connected ancient Taposiris with the desert. Over the crest of the hill, you will come to the curious little village of Burg al-Arab, the brain child of W.E. Jennings-Bramley, governor of the Western desert under the British, who decided in the early '20s to build a Bedouin capital, using stone from the ruins of Roman villas, which dotted the area. Modeling his village as a fortified medieval Italian hill town, he invited friends to build vacation houses within its turretted walls. When Egypt could no longer tolerate its foreign overseers, our good Englishman departed and his utopian ideals were abandoned. Today the village looks like a crumbling set for a remake of *Beau Geste*, though one or two of the houses are still in private hands and the Egyptian president has built himself a rest house at this spot.

At this point, you might want to continue your inland route and visit the ruins of the **monastery of Abu Menas**. Drive north out of Burg al-Arab and turn left at the first crossroad you come to. This road will take you to **Bahig** and the turnoff to the monastery. Before long you will spot the twin towers of the new monastery, founded in 1959, on the horizon, an ugly concrete pile much favored as a pilgrimage spot by modern Copts. Drive on by and very shortly you will see a low line of hillocks to your right. You have arrived at the site of the ancient monastery of Abu Menas and the hillocks are the scrap heaps left by several generations of archaeologists.

Menas was a young Egyptian officer, martyred in 296 A.D. during his service in Asia Minor because he would not renounce Christ. When his troops returned to Egypt, they carried his remains with them, but at this spot a miracle occurred: the camel carrying the remains of the saint refused to go any further. Here, then, he was buried and forgotten for a while. Some time later, a shepherd noticed that a sick lamb passing over the burial spot became well; so did another sick lamb, then a sick princess. The saint's powers were quickly recognized. A church was built over his grave by

The Palestine Hotel at Muntazah, Alexandria.

Athanasius in the fourth Century and was incorporated into a great basilica, erected by Emperor Arcadius, at the beginning of the fifth Century. The site became the Lourdes of the Western Desert.

The reason for this rapid popularity was probably the local water, which must have had real curative powers, for in the shrine's heyday pilgrims flocked here by the thousands, filling little flasks, stamped with the saint's image, from the sacred source by his tomb. Houses sprang up, baths were built, the land nearby was irrigated, and the settlement soon grew big enough to need its own cemeteries. The cult of Menas was meanwhile carried across the desert by traders and over the Mediterranean by sailors, extending as far as France and Spain, where the distinctive little flasks have also been found, with their stamped depictions of the saint standing between two kneeling camels. Conversions to Islam eventually put an end to the cult of St. Menas, but as late as the year 1000 an Arab traveler saw the great double basilica still standing in the desert: lights still burned day and night at the shrine and there was still a trickle of "the beautiful water of St. Menas that drives away pain."

The site has been excavated and the foundations of the primitive church and the basilica of Arcadius may be clearly discerned. The crypt where St. Menas was buried lies at the foot of a marble staircase in the church, which was incorporated into the portico of the basilica, but his relics rest in the modern monastery. A baptistry with a font can be seen to the west. North of the basilica are the hospice and the baths, with cisterns for hot and cold water.

Pursuing the Desert Fox: Further along the coast road is **El Alamayn** (*Alamein*) the site of a series of battles that began in the summer of 1942 and turned the tide of war in favor of the Allies. When the Afrika Korps under Rommel pushed as far as Alamayn on July 1, 1942, the British fleet left Alexandria and withdrew through the Suez Canal to the Red Sea. In Cairo, British Military Headquarters burnt their files and steeled themselves for a German victory, cautioning any remaining nationals to flee. But Rommel had problems of his own: his troops were exhausted and the British navy had succeeded in torpedoing ships carrying badly needed supplies. In October 1942, Britain's General Montgomery launched a

Near Alexandria.

third and final counteroffensive against Rommel, defeating the German army and driving it westward out of Egypt. His victory was the first in the successful Allied campaign to control all of North Africa.

Battle sites are often dull and uninteresting — as well they might be, since the drama that gave them momentary life is long over by the time they receive casual visitors. One does not come here to gaze upon the landscape of battle, however, but to honor its dead. Of the three main war cemeteries here, the British cemetery is the first one you come to, on your left as you enter the town from the east. A walk around its simple tombstones, each with its own inscriptions, cannot fail to move.

In the center of town, is a **Military Museum**, housing artifacts of the battle. Beyond stands the massive stone monument to Germany's fallen in a beautiful setting overlooking the sea. Further down the coast is the Italian memorial, a huge impressive white marble pile, and curiously reminiscent of a railway station in a provincial Italian city.

From this point on, the coast is startlingly beautiful. On the left are the duns and ochres of the desert, with the occasional flash of color from a gaily painted house or a Bedouin tent; to the right, the sea and sand stretch towards infinity. A word of caution: Do not attempt to swim off these beaches unless specifically permitted to do so. There is still grave danger from unexploded landmines and the area is, in any case, out of bounds except to the military who patrol it.

If you long for a day on the beach, keep going to **Sidi Abdul Rahman**, about 15 miles (25 km) beyond Al-Alamayn; some claim it's the best beach on the coast. There is a perfectly adequate hotel here with camping facilities. Or you can go all the way to **Mersah Matruh**, 45 miles (72 km) farther, 175 miles (280 km) from Alexandria, which has long been a seaside resort and has some fine beaches. Its hotels are simple but good and the town is still picturesque. There you can visit **Rommel's Cave**, now a museum containing, amongst other things, the Desert Fox's own armory, donated by his son.

The road south to Siwah leaves from here and there are several excellent beaches open to an almost non-existent public scattered intermittently along the 18-mile (30-km) stretch of coast road

Girl near the desert monastery of St. Menas. Tracks are for excavations of a Fifth-Century A.D. city.

leading farther west.

Eastward to Rosetta: Alexandria's **Corniche** extends some 10 miles (16 km) eastwards and there are a number of public beaches along the seafront between the Eastern Harbour and Montazah. But they are crowded and often dirty and Egypt's incessant building has turned most of the Corniche into an ugly string of high-rise buildings, lashed into premature decrepitude by salt sea-winds. At Montazah, where a former summer residence of the royal family is set within extensive closed grounds planted with Italian pines. No longer open to the public, **Montazah Palace** was built in the Turco-Florentine style by Khedive Abbas II and E.M. Forster worked there when the Red Cross took it over as a hospital during World War I. A walk in its gardens, open to the public for a small fee, is very pleasant.

Five miles (eight km) east of Montazah is **Abu Qir**, famous for the two battles fought here in 1798 and 1799. The first was the Battle of the Nile, Nelson's great victory, which destroyed Napoleon's fleet and left the French army stranded in Egypt, so named because Nelson reported that the engagement had taken place not far from the Rosetta mouth of the Nile. The second took place on land a year later under the command of Napoleon himself, who had rushed down from Cairo with 10,000 men, mostly cavalry, to repel an Ottoman force of 15,000. Underway since 1985 has been a joint Franco-Egyptian project aimed at raising the sunken French fleet from the seabed.

Abu Qir therefore ought to be a romantic spot, but it isn't. The only real reason to come to this seaside shanty town is its excellent seafood restaurants. One in particular, the **Zephyrion**, is worth a visit. It is a large barn-like structure with an open air terrace right on the sea. The fish is fresh and best eaten grilled or fried. Wash it down with the local anise drink, *zibib*, or cold bottles of Stella beer. A nice touch is supplied by the Piper, an ancient mariner (Egyptian) who was apparently taught to play the bagpipes by an itinerant Jock during the last war and now struts below the restaurant eagerly indulging in requests that range from ''Scotland the Brave'' to the *Marseillaise*.

Nearby is the site of ancient Canopus, but there is little to see. The next spot of interest is **Rosetta** (*Rashid*), 40 miles (65 km) from Alexandria on the western branch of the Nile near the sea. It was

Italian War Cemetery at El Alamayn, one of the key battlesites of World War II.

here that the Rosetta stone, which enabled Champollion to decipher the language of the pharaohs was discovered by a French soldier. Rosetta is famous for its fine 17th- and 18th-Century houses, built on its prosperity under the Ottomans as the most important port city in Egypt. The surviving red and black brick buildings, their facades decorated in the Delta style, are reminiscent of the Terbana mosque in Alexandria. Many of them incorporate ancient stones and columns, as well as elaborate wooden carving. The finest example is the **house of 'Ali al-Fatairi**, a residence on the main street, which has inscriptions above its lintels that date it to 1620. At the end of the same street is the most important building in Rosetta, the **Mosque of Zaghlul**, which is in fact two mosques that have been joined together. The eastern one is painted white, with arches running around a courtyard, and the western one has a wonderful cluster of columns.

The Delta and Wadi Natrun: Lush with vegetation and veined with canals, the **Nile Delta** is the flower of the Egyptian lotus. From the Barrage at **Qanater al-Khayriyya** in the south, where parks surround locks and sluices built under the British occupation, to the marshy waters of **lakes Edku, Burullus and Manzala,** where smugglers and fugitives live among the reeds, the Delta fans out like a broad palm reaching for the Mediterranean. To both the west and the east, deserts are receding in the face of vast land reclamation projects, while in the Delta's heartland sons of *felaheen* pack their bags for Cairo or the oil-rich Gulf.

The *Saidis* or people of Upper Egypt are renowned for their pride, generosity, spontaneity, and hair-trigger tempers. Their Delta cousins, less independent, more attuned to the hard labor of perennial irrigation, and lacking the wild inspiration that may come from living close to the desert, are sober, thrifty and sharp-witted. Natives of **Menufiyyah,** in particular — among them Presidents Sadat and Mubarak — the Delta's richest orchard country, are famed for their craftiness.

Indeed, each section of the Delta has its recognized particularity. **Mansurah,** the 'victorious' city, was founded on the site of the Mamluks' triumph over invading Crusaders under Louis IX. With its elegant Nileside villas from the age when cotton was king and its light-skinned,

Sunbath-
ing cows,
Mersa
Matruh.

fair-haired inhabitants, the city is regarded as Queen of the Delta. The men of **Mahalla al-Kubra,** center of the textile industry, are known for their hardworking habits, while the women of **Zagazig,** capital of Sharqiyyah Province and home of a university, are famed for their ''gazelle-like'' eyes and classic Bedouin beauty. **Dumyat** (*Damietta*), an ancient port that rivaled Alexandria in the Middle Ages, is recognized as the home of Egypt's furniture industry; and **Disuq,** on the Rosetta branch of the Nile, is identified with the famous annual festival, or *mulid,* it stages in honor of its patron saint, Ibrahim ad-Disuqi. It is the Delta's largest town, sprawling **Tanta,** that is renowned as the home of Egypt's greatest *mulid.* In the month of October, as many as two million thrill-seekers gather to celebrate the festival of Ahmad al-Badawi, continuing a tradition of wild revelry that was chronicled by Herodotus in late Pharaonic times.

The prehistoric Delta was a swampy tidal estuary interspersed with islands. Centuries of Nile effluvia built up a silty land mass that eventually split the river in two. Diligent canal building after the union of Lower and Upper Egypt in the Old Kingdom, tamed the swamp and sedentarized the region's original inhabitants. With the growth of Mediterranean trade and rivalry between Egypt, Phoenicia, and the Greeks, the Delta grew in importance, encouraging later Pharaohs to abandon the old capitals of Thebes and Memphis and establish headquarters in the Delta near the sea.

Sadly, the region's muddy soil and lack of solid building materials conspired to reduce the glory of its ancient cities. Of **Buto, Leontopolis, Mendes, Naukratis, Piramesse** and **Athribis** little remains but mounds of earth. **Bubastis,** near the modern town of Zagazig, once the home of the cat goddess Bastet, is now reduced to a few chunks of stone. **Tanis,** a great port long before Alexander founded his city, is nothing but a huge mound. Graced with an enormous temple of Amon when it was the capital city of the 21st and 23rd Dynasties, none but the most astute archaeologists can now make sense of its acres of fallen obelisks, headless statuary, and hunks of engraving, though many important individual objects have come from there.

The Monasteries of Wadi Natrun: To the

One of King Farouk's palaces at Muntazah, Alexandria.

232

west of the Delta, beyond the ridge of desert and just off the Cairo-Alexandria desert road, the **Wadi Natrun,** or *Valley of Natron*, snuggles below sea level. An early center of Christian monasticism, the valley was once home to over fifty monasteries. Hundreds more monks lived in the total isolation of desert caves.

Europeans who are unused to seeing Christianity as a vital, living faith, will find the *wadi* a strange, perhaps even unsettling place. Dour, bearded monks in black robes with gilt-embroidered hoods appear in the middle of the waste atop shiny new Massey Ferguson tractors. On the occasion of religious festivals, hordes of devout pilgrims descend on the valley's four extant monasteries. A religious revival has swept across the Middle East in recent years; and Coptic Christians like everyone else, have been caught up in the religious fervor.

Deir Abu Maqar, the largest and most active of the monasteries, has in recent years been the seat of the Coptic Pope, who was exiled to the desert by the late President Sadat. Its oldest remains date to the 9th Century. **Anba Bishoi,** founder of another monastery, was a disciple of Abu Maqar (St. Macarius). A third monastery,

Deir as-Suryan, has some of the best preserved buildings. Its church of al Adhra' has 10th-Century paintings and ivory panels. **Deir Baramus** is the smallest and most remote of the four.

Although the monasteries' foundation dates back to the 5th and 6th Centuries, extensive restorations throughout their history have left very little of the original work and indeed testify more to the decline in taste that has beset Egypt since the Ottoman occupation. Note that Wadi Natrun's Coptic churches, like Pharaonic temples, have three distinct areas. The outer is reserved for laymen, the middle for initiates, and the inner for clergymen. Ordinary visitors to the monasteries should therefore on no account venture into the curtained inner sanctuaries. Aside from numerous churches and chapels, each monastery has a hospice, living quarters for monks, a refectory and a keep where monks could shelter from Bedouin raids.

Monasteries are closed to visitors during periods of fast: Sexagesima Monday to Orthodox Easter (61 days), Advent (November 25-January 6), before the Feast of the Apostles (June 27-July 10), and before Assumption (August 7-21).

By the sea at Damietta.

233

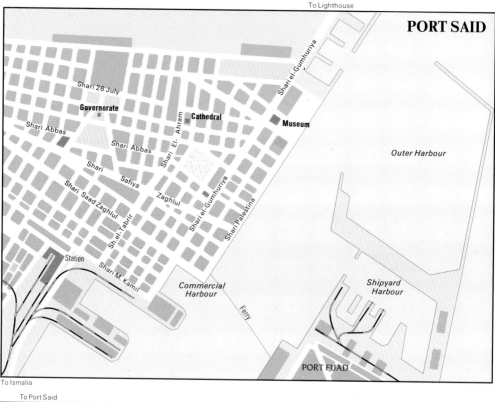

PORT SAID

Shari 26 July

Governorate

Shari Abbas

Shari Abbas

Shari

Safiya

Zaghlul

Sh. el-Tahrir

Shari Saad Zaghlul

Station

Shari M. Kamil

Shari El- Ahram

Cathedral

Shari el-Gumhuriya

Shari el-Gumhuriya

Shari Palestina

Museum

Outer Harbour

Shipyard Harbour

Commercial Harbour

Ferry

PORT FUAD

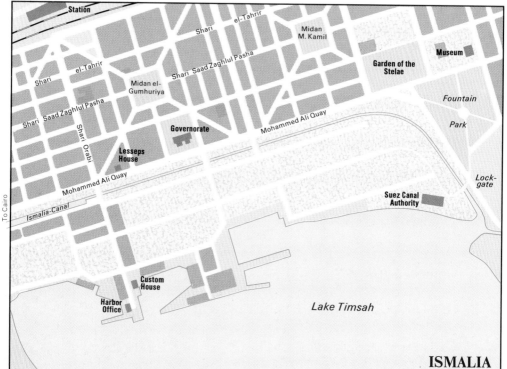

Station

Shari

el-Tahrir

Midan M. Kamil

Museum

Shari

el-Tahrir

Shari Saad Zaghlul Pasha

Midan el-Gumhuriya

Garden of the Stelae

Fountain

Shari Saad Zaghlul Pasha

Shari Orabi

Governorate

Mohammed Ali Quay

Park

Lock-gate

Lesseps House

Mohammed Ali Quay

To Cairo

Ismalia-Canal

Suez Canal Authority

Custom House

Harbor Office

Lake Timsah

ISMALIA

234

SUEZ CANAL

Picture a huge ocean-going ship drifting through a sea of sand. Seen across flat desert, the hallucinatory effect of the Suez Canal underlines the revolutionary impact the waterway has had not only on Egypt, but on the structure of international commerce. The Suez Canal is arguably the single most vital traffic artery in the world.

"Laboring for the Barbarians": The idea of building a canal to link the Mediterranean with the Rea Sea is ancient indeed. The 26th Dynasty pharaoh Necho II first aired such a proposal at the end of the seventh Century B.C., with a project to join the Gulf of Suez to the Nile, down which ships could continue to the Mediterranean. According to Herodotus, an oracular pronouncement that he would merely be "laboring for the barbarians" dissuaded Necho from completing excavations. The job was therefore left to Egypt's Persian conquerors a century later; and their work was followed by Ptolemaic and Roman re-excavation.

During the centuries before the Arab conquest, however, this old canal silted up and the Muslims' brilliant general Amr ibn al-'As suggested that a new and better one should be cut across the narrow isthmus of Suez. Cautioned by the Caliph Omar that it would be hard to defend and that Greek pirates might use it as a route to attack the holy city of Mecca, he had to be satisfied instead with renovating the old canal. It flourished for another century before being blocked on orders of the Abbasid Caliph al-Mansur, who feared its use as a route of supply to the Shi'ite rebels then ensconced in Medina. Briefly re-opened under the next Caliph, it later fell into disuse.

It was not until the 19th Century, with the growth of European power and the energetic promotion of a French engineer, Ferdinand de Lesseps, that Amr's idea could be brought to fruition. A Suez Canal Company was opened by public subscription in Europe and an agreement was reached with the Viceroy Said and his successor the Khedive Ismail whereby Egypt provided both capital and labor for the job itself.

Construction began in 1859. It took 10 years, with 25,000 laborers working three-month shifts, to cut the 100-mile

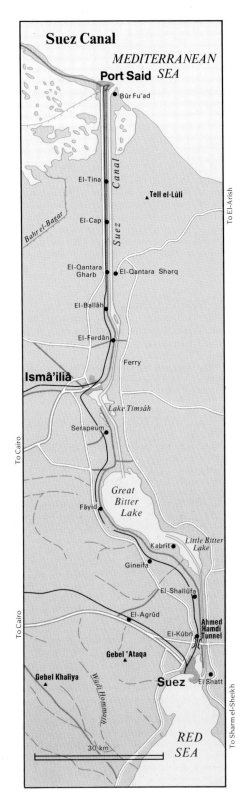

Suez Canal

MEDITERRANEAN SEA

Port Said
Bûr Fu'ad
El-Tina
Tell el-Lûli
El-Cap
Suez Canal
El-Qantara Gharb
El-Qantara Sharq
El-Ballâh
El-Ferdân
Ferry
Ismâ'ilìa
Lake Timsâh
Serapeum
Great Bitter Lake
Fâyid
Little Bitter Lake
Kabrìt
Gineifa
El-Shallûfa
El-Agrûd
Ahmed Hamdi Tunnel
El-Kûbri
Gebel 'Ataqa
Gebel Khaliya
Wadi Hommath
Suez
El Shatt
To Cairo
To Cairo
To El-Arish
To Sharm el-Sheikh
RED SEA
30 km

(160 km) channel. The total cost of the operation, including the building of the Sweetwater Canal for drinking water from the Nile, reached £25 million, of which Egypt put up more than two-thirds. Amidst extravagant fanfare, with assorted European royalty in attendance, the Canal was opened to shipping in November of 1869, transforming trade and geopolitics as dramatically as the Portuguese and Spanish discoveries of the 15th Century. Distances from Europe to the Far East were cut by a third, distances to India by half. Unfortunately for Egypt, the pharaonic oracle proved to be extraordinarily clairvoyant. The country's mounting debts, compounded by usurious creditors, forced the sale of Egypt's stake to the British government for a paltry £4,000,000 sterling. As London's *Economist* drily commented in the year of its opening, the Canal was "cut by French energy and Egyptian money for British advantage." The strategic importance of the Canal to Britain's empire provided one of the excuses for occupying Egypt in 1882.

The Fortunes of Five Wars: Britain imposed draconian measures on Egypt while fighting to defend the Canal in both the Arabian campaign of World War I and the North African campaign of World War II. For Egyptians, foreign possession of the Canal came to represent the major reason for anti-imperialist struggle. Not until 1954 did Nasser arrange for the withdrawal of British troops occupying the Canal Zone.

In 1956, hard up for cash and seeking to finance the High Dam, Nasser turned as a last resort — having been refused financing at the last minute by the United States — to nationalizing the Canal, from which Egypt received only a tiny portion of the revenue. Apparently unreconciled, despite the loss of India, to the rapid decline of its empire, Britain responded by invading, with the collusion of Israel and France. Only the intervention of the two superpowers resolved the ensuing crisis, which marked a turning point in world affairs. Ten years later, all that remained of Britain's empire were Gibraltar, Hong Kong and a few remote islands, while Egypt had become dependent upon the Soviet Union.

In 1967, the Israelis again attacked Egypt, and occupied the Sinai Peninsula up to the edge of the Canal. Heavy bombardment during the "War of Attrition"

Mecca-bound pilgrims relax by the Suez Canal.

that followed the Israeli conquest shattered the canal cities and made refugees of their half million inhabitants. For six years, until the successful Egyptian counterattack of 1973, the waterway remained closed to traffic. Reopened in 1975, it has since been widened and deepened. More earth was moved, in fact, than when the Canal was dug originally; and it will now accommodate all but the largest fully-loaded supertankers.

The Canal Cities: Port Said sits on an artificial landfill jutting into the Mediterranean. From here convoys of ships pass the green domes of the Suez Canal Authority building to begin the journey to the Red Sea. Once the major point of entry for tourists stepping off the great Peninsular and Orient (''P and O'') passenger liners, Port Said is now the Hong Kong of Egypt, where Cairo consumers flock to spend on duty-free goods. Despite the damage of three recent wars and the current emporium atmosphere, this resilient town retains a good deal of character.

Situated on **Lake Timsah** halfway between Port Said and Suez, **Ismailia** is the queen of the canal cities. With its tree-shaded avenues and genteel colonial-style houses, it is the cleanest city in Egypt. There are a number of fine hotels and restaurants; and from uncrowded lakeside beaches ships transiting the canal can be watched. These attractions make Ismailia very popular with week-ending Cairenes.

South of Ismailia the canal enters the **Great Bitter Lake**, a small inland sea bordered by holiday villas and military installations. Halfway between the lake and Suez, the three-mile (five-km)-long **Ahmed Hamdi tunnel** provides the only permanent bridge across the Canal, the other crossings being made by ferry.

Suez, the canal's southern terminus, was Egypt's major Red Sea port for hundreds of years. Its harbor is now at **Port Tawfiq**, an artificial peninsula where the canal meets the **Gulf of Suez**. Israeli bombardments flattened the town in the 1967 war; and hasty rebuilding after 1973 has not enhanced its beauty. Nor has its oil refinery, fed on petroleum pumped up from the floor of the Gulf of Suez. Suez is best observed from the Sinai side of the canal, where scores of ships can be seen lining up in the turquoise waters of the Gulf ready to make the northward passage.

Wreckage from a recent war in the Sinai Desert.

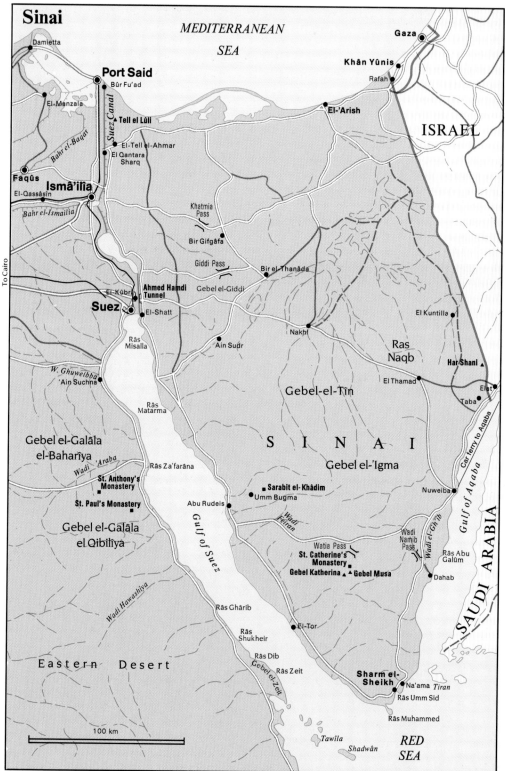

Sinai

MEDITERRANEAN
SEA

Gaza

Khân Yûnis

Rafah

Damietta

Port Said

Bûr Fu'ad

ISRAEL

El-Manzala

Tell el Lûli

El-'Arish

Bahr el-Baqar

El-Tell el-Ahmar

El Qantara Sharq

Faqûs

Ismâ'ilîa

El-Qassâsîn

Bahr el-Ismailia

Khatmia Pass

Bir Gifgâfa

Giddi Pass

Bir el-Thanâda

El-Kûbri

Ahmed Hamdi Tunnel

Gebel-el-Giddi

To Cairo

Suez

El-Shatt

El Kuntilla

Râs Misalla

Ain Sudr

Nakhl

Ras Naqb

Har Shani

W. Ghuweibba

'Ain Suchna

El Thamad

Elat

Râs Matarma

Taba

Gebel-el-Tîn

S I N A I

Gebel el-Galâla el-Baharîya

Wadi 'Araba

Râs Za'farâna

Gebel el-'Igma

Car ferry to Aqaba

St. Anthony's Monastery

Sarabit el-Khâdim

Umm Bugma

St. Paul's Monastery

Gebel el-Galâla el-Qibilîya

Abu Rudeis

Wadi Feirân

Nuweiba

Gulf of Aqaba

SAUDI ARABIA

Wadi Namib Pass

Watia Pass

Wadi el-Gh'îb

Râs Abu Galûm

St. Catherine's Monastery

Gebel Katherina ▲   ▲ Gebel Musa

Dahab

Gulf of Suez

Wadi Hawashiya

Râs Ghârib

Râs Shukheir

El-Tor

Eastern   Desert

Râs Dib   Râs Zeit

Gebel el-Zeit

Sharm el-Sheikh

Na'ama   Tiran

Râs Umm Sid

Râs Muhammed

100 km

Tawila

Shadwân

RED SEA

To Hurgada

240

SINAI

"Take off thy shoes from off thy feet, for the ground on which thou standest is holy ground," the Lord admonished Moses (Deuteronomy 3:13). And ever since, whether treated as holy ground or as battleground, fought over by people of different religions, classical empires, and modern nation states, the Sinai peninsula has been special.

Most other available words have been repeatedly used in descriptions that range from the Bible's "great and terrible wilderness" to 20th-Century scuba divers' rhapsodies over its incredible coral reefs. Volumes have been dedicated to this small jewel of a desert poised delicately but obstinately between two continents. As a passage between Asia and Africa, it has weathered far more military crossings than peaceful occupations, thanks in part to a climate that precludes all but the sparsest settlement. Even its few prehistoric, ancient and medieval remains, however, have only been scratched at by archaeologists, while Biblical geographers' controversies over problematical routes and sites have created an academic kaleidoscope of fact and fantasy.

It is only in the few short years since the latest of more than 50 recorded invasions and incursions that Sinai has finally ceased to be regarded by non-inhabitants as an empty buffer zone, as a dangerous crossroads where native Bedouins or foreign powers controlled all access, as a natural outwork for the defense of the Suez Canal, or as a barrier separating the two halves of the Arab world. Used four times for bitter tank battles, this physical tiny pile of rocks and sand has at last been robbed by modern weaponry of all its old isolation.

Sinai's 10,000 square miles (25,000 sq km) of pristine desert, ranging from the spiky granite mountains of the south to the central plateau of At-Tih, then to the rolling dunes of the northern coastal plain, are now fair game to backpackers, camel trekkers and camera-happy busloads of tourists. The shock of the recent occupation and the Israelis' opportunistic development of the peninsula's tourist potential prodded Egypt towards a fierce determination to bind Sinai once again to the Nile Valley, this time

inextricably. Although some of the hotel infrastructure, originally geared to low-budget kibbutzniks rather than staid middle-class Cairenes, has grown a trifle rusty, the Sinai now boasts Egypt's best maintained roads and most efficient bus services. The latter tie all the major centers to each other and to Cairo, while daily flights connect the capital to Al-Arish, St. Catherine's and Sharm ash-Shaykh. While public transport is reliable, however, distances are great and many of the peninsula's attractions are remote. There is no substitute for having one's own car — preferably with four-wheel drive.

The Sinai is divided administratively into two governorates, the Northern and the Southern. Visitors are recommended not to try to cover all of Sinai at once, but to go to one of the governorates at a time.

North Sinai: Aside from seasonal Bedouin encampments, North Sinai's population is concentrated around the provincial capital of **El-Arish.** From Cairo the main Ismailia highway leads to the Suez Canal. At **Qantara**, north of Ismailia, crossing to Sinai is made by ferry. The road continues across the desert to the northeast, skirting the marshy lagoon of **Lake Bardawil** to reach Al-Arish after 85 miles (130 km). This town of 40,000 is the biggest in the peninsula and much recent effort has been made to turn it into a tourist center. Its main attraction is the palm-fringed and unspoiled beach. There are plenty of reasonably priced hotels and restaurants. Bedouin crafts and jewelry are on display at the local museum.

Just east of the town, the bare dunes along the coast begin to sprout five o'clock shadow. A few olive trees appear, marking the decline of the desert and the beginning of the fertile Palestine coastal plain. At 30 miles (50 km) the town of **Rafah** marks the current border. Beyond lies the **Gaza Strip**, a Middle Eastern Soweto occupied by Israel since 1967. Rafah's population is a mixture of local Bedouin and Palestinian refugees. Their camp — built with Canadian government aid and consequently called "Canada" — was brutally bisected by the border fence erected after the area's return to Egypt in 1983.

Between El-Arish and Rafah a number of *wadis*, seasonal watercourses, lead back from the sea into the desert interior. The laid-back Bedouin graze their goats and camels extensively in this region.

Preceding pages: the view from Mt. Sinai. Left, map of Sinai.

Friendly and hospitable, they are wont to invite travelers into their ramshackle settlements — shacks slapped together with cans, boxes and the debris of four wars — for a glass of tea. The desert-dwelling women of North Sinai wear gorgeous embroidered dresses and heavy silver jewelry, so the opportunity to mingle should not be missed.

South Sinai: With its two coasts, oases, mountains and historic sites, the South Sinai is a more popular destination. North of Suez, the **Ahmed Hamdi tunnel** carries traffic under the Canal. Turning south, the main road follows the Canal, veering eastwards opposite Suez. From here it descends 200 miles (320 km) along the breezy Gulf of Suez to Sharm ash-Shaykh.

Along this route are **'Uyun Musa**, the "Springs of Moses" where the prophet is said to have rested with his flock, a palm grove fed by brackish water reached after 25 miles (40 km). Twenty miles (33 km) farther on the road nears the coast at the wide sandy beach of **Ras as-Sidr**, a favorite stopping place, and for some people worth the day trip from Cairo. Unlike the Gulf of Aqaba on Sinai's east coast, the Gulf of Suez is shallow and sandy-bottomed; the marine life is abundant, but there are no major coral reefs this far north.

Beyond Ras as-Sidr the road bends away from the coast up into the mountains. A track to the right at this turn leads after a few hundred yards to **Hammam Fara'un**, the hot spring known as the *Pharaoh's Bath*. The spring's boiling hot waters, said by local Bedouin to cure rheumatism, bubble from the base of the mountains right into the sea.

About ten miles (16 km) into the mountains above Hammam Fara'un, a track leads left among palm trees. Negotiable only by four-wheel drive vehicles, it continues for 20 miles to the site of **Sarabit al-Khadim**, a 12th-Dynasty temple that serviced workers in the region's extensive mines and was dedicated originally to the goddess Hathor. A second shrine, for the patron god of the Eastern Desert, Sopdu, was later added. Dozens of New and Middle Kingdom stelae commemorate Egyptian rule. Chief among them are those dedicated to Hatshepsut and Tutmosis III. Inscriptions at the **mines of Wadi Maghara**, south of Sarabit al Khadim, date back to the fourth Dynasty and the reigns of Snefru and

Bedouin in the northern Sinai.

Khufu, builder of the Great Pyramid. Turquoise, malachite and copper were mined in the region and the extant remains show that exploitation was prolonged and intensive.

From Wadi Maghara a track running down the **Wadi Sidri** for 15 miles (24 km) rejoins the main road at **Abu Zeneima**, where it descends again from the mountains to the coast. Beyond this ramshackle frontier settlement, where manganese from local mines of recent date is processed, the road continues to **Abu Rudeis**. The Gulf of Suez is at this point dotted with beetle-like rigs shooting flame into the haze: this is the center of Sinai's oil fields, most of them offshore. Pipes, fences, tanks and prefabricated housing clutter the shore down to **Balayim** thirty miles farther on.

The road again leaves the coast, heading inland towards the high mountains of the Sinai range. A checkpoint marks the turnoff to St. Catherine's monastery, while the main road continues south to **Al-Tur** and Sharm ash-Shaykh. Tur, the capital and largest town in South Sinai, is reached after 45 miles (75 km) of hot driving through a wide valley. Settled in ancient times because of its good water supply and excellent harbor, it was the chief quarantine station for pilgrims returning to Egypt from Mecca. Modern Tur, despite scattered palm groves and a beautiful beach, retains this way-station atmosphere. A peculiarity of the town is the racial mix of its inhabitants, many of them descended from Berber and African immigrants. From Tur it is 60 miles (100 km) to Sharm ash-Shaykh.

Going to St. Catherine's: Turning instead up towards St. Catherine's, we enter the **Wadi Feran.** Narrowing as it mounts, after 20 miles (33 km) the dry gulch suddenly blossoms into a river of date palms. This is the **Oasis of Feran**, the largest patch of cultivation on the peninsula. Parched for most of the year, winter rains and melting snow send down short-lived torrents to water the valley, whose steep sides are bordered by jagged reddish cliffs. Scattered throughout the palm groves are clusters of Bedouin huts. Colonies of Christian anchorites inhabited the oasis long before the foundation of the monastery at St. Catherine's, and the remains — for the most part scanty — of their constructions abound. South of the oasis, approached most easily up the **Wadi 'Aleyat**, rises the peak of the **Jebel**

Litho-glyphs at Ain Hora, Sinai.

Serbal. At 7,000 feet (2,100 meters) it is not high for the Sinai range, but its isolation makes the view from its summit extensive. One school of Biblical speculators claims it as the true **Mount Sinai**.

From Feiran the road climbs into an open plain and after 20 miles reaches the settlement of **Santa Katarina**. Here there are hotels, a campsite and the bus stop. The famous monastery sits in a *wadi* between **Jebel Musa** — most popular candidate for the site of the delivery of the Ten Commandments — and the **Jebel ad-Deir** just up the hill to the south.

The Roman emperor Justinian ordered the building of a fortress monastery on the site in 537 A.D. in order to protect the Sinai passes against invasion. Originally dedicated to the Transfiguration of Christ, the church built within the fortress was renamed for St. Catherine, a fourth-Century Alexandrian martyred for her derision of Roman idol-worship, when her body miraculously appeared atop the Sinai's highest peak — now **Jebel Katarina** — five centuries later, apparently looking none the worse for wear. This miracle, coupled with the Crusaders' occupation of nearby Palestine, ensured the support of Christian rulers. The monastery's fame spread, so that by the 14th Century as many as 400 monks lived there, as the grisly collection of skulls in the ossuary attests. In recent centuries Russia was the chief benefactor, having styled herself, until the Revolution, the protector of the Greek Orthodox Church, to which the monastery belongs. The dozen or so monks who now inhabit the monastery are mostly Greek.

The Monastery and Its Treasures: The path to St. Catherine's leads past a walled orchard and an outer complex of buildings before reaching the monastery itself. An old basket-and-pulley system of entry has been abandoned and visitors now enter by simply walking through a portal. (Note that the monastery is closed on Fridays and religious holidays and that modesty of attire is required. The best time for a visit is between 9:30 a.m. and noon.) A small building on the left inside the wall is one of the original structures, diplomatically converted into a mosque in the 12th Century. The **Church of St. Catherine** is down the steps to the left just behind the mosque.

Within the narthex note the wooden doors leading to the church. Their panels, brilliantly carved in the Byzantine style,

The Church of St. Catherine's, founded by the Emperor Justinian.

are original. Inside, the church is basilical in form, with great granite columns supporting the nave. The marble inlay floors will be familiar to anyone who has visited the mosques of Cairo. The wooden bracing beams of the reconstructed ceiling are original and beautifully carved, one of them with a foundation inscription dating to Justinian. The doors leading to the sanctuary are flanked by two silver chests inlaid with precious stones. Both were donated by members of the Russian royal family, one in the 17th Century, the other in the 19th. The sanctuary is adorned with mosaics that are the monastery's greatest treasure. Within the arch and semi-dome of the apse is a portrayal of the Transfiguration of Christ. To his left stand Moses and St. James, and on his right are Elijah and St. John the Apostle. Various biblical scenes surround this ensemble, as well as 31 portraits, some of them astonishingly lifelike, of other prophets and saints. The mosaics are sixth-Century and equal those of Ravenna or Istanbul in quality.

Side aisles lined with chapels dedicated to varied saints and decorated with ancient and modern icons lead off from either side of the church. At the sanctuary end of the building a small alcove opens into the **Chapel of the Burning Bush**. Here, on a site marked by a small silver plate God spoke to Moses disguised as a flaming shrub.

The monastery's other treasures are off limits to run-of-the-mill tourists. They include a library whose collection of 2,000 Greek, 700 Arabic and various Georgian, Armenian, Slavonic and Latin manuscripts is among the finest in the world, and a museum stocked with a superb collection of icons dating back to the sixth Century. Enthusiasts should arm themselves with a letter of introduction from the Greek Patriarchate in Cairo to gain admittance.

Just behind the monastery a well worn path begins, leading ultimately to the summit of **Jebel Musa**. Steps mounting the cliff to the right should be avoided for the ascent. Instead, continue on the gently sloping main track, which curves behind the southern slope. All but the most feeble should be able to manage the way up — coming down is trickier. The view from the top is terrific, particularly at dawn or sunset. Desertscapes play tricks with depth perception, so the vista of range after range of battle-worn crags

leaves even the most strait-laced awed and a little mystical. **Jebel Katarina**, the highest point in Egypt at over 8,500 feet (2,600 meters), has an even better view. It is approached up the *wadi* on Jebel Musa's western side.

Sinai's mountains are geologically very ancient, and their variety, in terms of texture, color, shape and vegetation, is fascinating. The descent from St. Catherine's to the east traverses enthralling landscapes all the way to the sea. Here along the **Gulf of Aqaba** one of the earth's most dramatic interfaces has yet to be ruined by commercialization. The Gulf itself, only 10 miles (16 km) wide, is in places as much as six thousand feet (2,000 meters) deep. Indeed, it marks a long geological fault, running from the Dead Sea in the north to Africa's Great Rift Valley in the south. Coral reefs — according to many, the world's most varied and beautiful — line the shores of the Gulf from Ras Muhammad at the peninsula's extremity to Taba on the Israeli border. Teeming with life and color, they provide a striking contrast to the desolation of the land.

The Gulf of Aqaba: Ras Muhammad, a peninsula jutting into the Red Sea, has the best diving of all. Luckily for professionals and unhappily for amateurs, it is a nature conservation area and difficult to reach. A permit is required for camping. **Shark Reef** off the eastern shore is the favorite swimming hole.

North of Ras Muhammad, on a beautiful natural harbor much damaged by the ill-planned building of successive occupants, is the town of **Sharm ash-Shaykh**. Five miles farther on, **Na'ama Bay** is the local tourist center, with hotels, restaurants, camping grounds and a grocery. Unattractive in itself, it makes a good base for visiting local beaches. Some of the best for diving and snorkeling are **The Tower**, **Ras Umm Sid**, **Ras Nasrani** and **Nabq**. Equipment can be rented at one of several diving centers, where boat trips to **Gazirat Tiran**, an island in the middle of the straits with superb corals, can also be arranged.

The next coastal settlement lies 50 miles (85 kilometers) north at **Dahab**. Sediments washed down from the mountains have created a broad sandy plain here. A model Israeli-built town on a sandy cove, it boasts a hotel, a cafeteria, and camping and diving facilities. Across the plain a mile to the west, a Bedouin village sits next to a perfect palm-lined horseshoe bay. Here low-budget travelers stay in reed huts on the beach and live on grilled fish. Since the locals are very laid-back — frequently horizontal in fact — outsiders are often surprised to find that many of them speak perfect English. Camel treks into the interior can be arranged on a few days notice. Fees are dirt cheap and some of Dahab's fertile *wadis* are stunningly beautiful.

Nuweiba is the last major town before the frontier. This is a slightly up-market resort, although the reefs are not as good as farther south. There is a wide sandy beach, a hotel and a campsite. The hotel offers tours by Land Rover to the **Oasis of 'Ayn al-Furtaga**. If the preferred vehicle is the camel, arrangements can be made with the Bedouin at their settlement a few miles south of the hotel, where palms mingle with shacks along the beach. Ferries from Nuweiba's new port leave daily for Aqaba in Jordan, three hours distant, from which excursions to the rock city of **Petra** can be arranged.

There are beautiful beaches north of Nuweiba, although many are littered with archaeologically uninteresting artifacts attesting mainly to the beer-drinking habits of the modern Israelites. Near the border at **Gazirat Fara'un**, an island just offshore, is a recently-restored 12th-Century fortress. Smack in the middle of the peninsula and difficult of access lie the ruins of a second medieval fortress, **Qalaat al-Gindi**. Built by Salah-ed-Din to protect trade and pilgrimage routes, these fortifications attest to the importance Muslim rulers attached to Egypt's Asian gateway.

Although no one needs to be warned of the danger of sharks, swimmers should be aware of a few facts. For centuries, the word 'coral' has evoked images of beauty and color, while the word 'reef' is not nearly as well-received. Coral reefs can hide unpleasant as well as pleasant surprises. The spine of a sea urchin is most unfriendly on the feet and the sting of the well-camouflaged stone fish can be fatal. Wear shoes or flippers in the water at all times. Always swim in pairs and keep calm in the water no matter what happens. Above all, be aware that corals take thousands of years to form and so should be handled with due care and respect. They should be able to be appreciated by everyone, and should never be removed. Anyone seen damaging them should be reported to authorities ashore immediately.

Right, ancient steps to the summit of Mt. Sinai.

246

RED SEA AND EASTERN DESERT

The **Red Sea coast** of Egypt runs for a thousand miles (1,600 km) in a south-easterly direction from Suez. Despite the many offshore oil wells and frequent oil depots, gas-stations — as in Sinai — are few and far between and trips by car must be planned with foresight. Once assured of freedom from mechanical worries, however, the happy motorist is rewarded with a glorious sense of infinite space. For most of its length, beautiful but desolate limestone and granite mountains border the coast. Range rises upon range as a thousand peaks harmonize their purples with the blue of the sky. Sandy coves and beaches edge a brilliant sea. Within its coral reefs the water is a light blue-green, while beyond them a deep dark blue shimmers to the distant coasts of Sinai and Arabia, even further away.

In the vicinity of Suez, this deep dark blue is rather liberally strewn with tankers and other ships converging on the canal, and the road along the coast has received a good deal of wear and tear from heavy trucks. Both sea and land traffic soon thin out, however, and the beaches improve near 'Ayn Sukhna, where a pleasant bay makes a day's picnic or an overnight camping trip from Cairo quite feasible.

South of 'Ayn Sukhna the rocky skirts of the North Galala Plateau come right down to the edge of the sea and the drive is spectacular. A new highway has recently been constructed on which one can proceed comfortably and swiftly to **Zafarana** (50 miles/80 km) south of 'Ayn Sukhna, the checkpoint and junction for a road coming across the desert from the Nile Valley 180 miles (290 km) to the west. Gas can be bought here or a little further south at the rather unattractive oil town of **Ras Gharib,** which will be sufficient to carry a car on down the coast, past some sandy headlands opposite the tip of Sinai, until **Hurghada,** approximately 250 miles (420 km) south of Suez is reached.

Hurghada (Arabic *Ghardaqa*), is fast becoming Egypt's most popular seaside resort. Its pleasures are the ideal antidote to an overdose of monuments. It has none. Instead it offers golden sands and a sea teeming with exquisite tropical fish, which swim in and around the plentiful

Preceding pages: the not-so-red Sea. Left, Bedouin chic, Sinai.

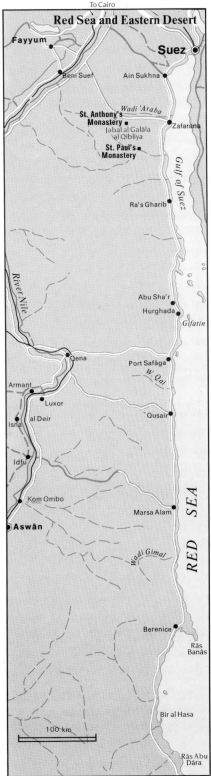

To Cairo

Red Sea and Eastern Desert

Fayyum

Suez

Beni Suef   Ain Sukhna

Wadi 'Araba

St. Anthony's Monastery ■   Zafarana
Jabal al Galâla
al Qibliya

St. Paul's ■
Monastery

Gulf of Suez

Ra's Gharib

River Nile

Abu Sha'r

Hurghada

Gifatin

Qena   Port Safâga

W. Qai

Armant

Luxor

Qusair

Isna   al Deir

Idfu

Kom Ombo

Marsa Alam

Aswân

RED SEA

Wadi Gimal

Berenice

Râs Banâs

Bir al Hasa

100 km

Râs Abu Dâra

To Port Sudan

coral beds. The water is warm all the year round except for a few weeks in December and January; the sun is always shining and even in the hottest months there is a breeze. Anyone who can swim and cope with a mask and snorkel can get a glimpse of the marvelous marine life, but those who are able to scuba dive get an even better view.

Hurghada has an airport and is only an hour's flight from Cairo. Its hotels are much in demand and at least three are of international standard. There is a deluxe Sheraton standing on a point overlooking a magnificent bay; and two tourist villages, **Giftun** and **Magawish**, with chalets and buffet meals, are staffed by cheerful youngsters of many nationalities. These young people do double duty as instructors in diving, snorkeling, sailing, surfing, archery and other sports. For the fisherman, all-day or overnight fishing trips to the offshore islands can be arranged through the hotels or privately with individual boat owners at the harbor. More modest accommodations are available and many people camp on the beach. For those who simply want to rest and sunbathe there are endless sands for pottering about and picking up shells.

Further on down the coast, famous ancient ports, which were thriving even after the discovery of the Cape route in the 15th Century, but were made redundant by the cutting of the Suez Canal in the 19th Century, have largely fallen into disuse. Some are little ghost harbors with the skeletal hulls of old wooden boats beached up and whitening in the sun; and others have completely disappeared under the sand.

Safaga, however, which is 45 miles (70 km) south of Hurghada, is still very much alive. Its deepwater facilities have recently been expanded and it has retained the role it played in the past as the nearest port to **Qena** (110 miles/177 km) to the west. The old caravan trail leading through the mountains is now covered by an excellent paved road that carries truckloads of the wheat and raw aluminium off-loaded at Safaga to the Nile Valley. It is also convenient for those who want to make the round trip from Cairo down the Nile to Luxor, across the mountains to the sea, returning north up the coast.

"Where My Caravan Has Rested": In antiquity and even in Ottoman times the ports of **Qusayr**, **Mersa Alam**, **Berenice** and **Halayib** were of more importance than

Windsurfing at Hurghada on the Red Sea.

they are today. Like Suez and Safaga they were connected to important points in the Nile Valley by caravan routes, along which the laden pack animals brought the spices, silks, pearls and precious woods from Arabia, Persia, India and the East African coast. Muslim pilgrims from the hinterlands thousands of miles away, sometimes en route for years, embarked at these ports for Mecca. One can still see traces of the old wells and way stations and decipher the graffiti carved on the rocks from earliest times by pharaohs, soldiers, merchants and pilgrims.

Except for the remote mountainous area known as Gebel Elba on the Sudanese border in the far south, which receives monsoon rains and has a unique ecosystem supporting forest and pasturage, the coastal plain and the Red Sea mountains are almost entirely devoid of vegetation. What rain there is falls only a few times a year and then often in the form of violent storms, which carry all before them as water pours off the mountains into the sea. Some water gathers in pools and pot-holes among the granitic rocks and together with the ancient wells amounts to enough to support the scattering of *bedu* and animals that inhabit the region. Until very recently freshwater for the little towns along the coast had to be shipped in, and the natives lived miserably without fruit or vegetables, on a diet of bread and fish.

Realms of Gold: In pharaonic times the Eastern Desert, particularly the mountains, was thoroughly searched for gold and other precious metals, for ornamental stone and for building materials. These resources contributed greatly to the wealth and prestige of the pharaohs and were later coveted by Assyrians, Persians, Greeks and Romans.

Thousands of prisoners in chains were used for the extraction of these riches. More often than not they died in the mines and quarries, as the hazards of escape were almost insurmountable. The gold was arduously mined and smelted, and the limestone quarried and transported to Thebes for the construction of the temple of Amun-Re.

The indefatigable Romans established permanent quarrying camps in the mountains, visible from the stretch of road between Hurghada and Safaga. They were particularly partial to the purple stone known as porphyry, which comes from **Gebel Abu Dukhan** ("Father of

Tourists at sunset, Hurghada.

Smoke"). It was in great demand for the adornment of palaces and temples and was brought out of the Egyptian mountains until as late as the fifth Century A.D. Great blocks were quarried and then dragged the 112 miles (180 km) through the mountains and over the desert to Qena, whence they were transported down the Nile and then across the Mediterranean to Rome. Hunks of abandoned porphyry have been found near the ruins of the stone-built Roman encampments 2,000 feet (610 metres) above sea level on the flanks of the mountain.

Another famous mountain nearby, known as **Mons Claudianus**, yielded superlative white granite. Remains of animal stalls in the ruins of a quarrying encampment indicate that the huge lumps of stone were hauled out by bullocks.

Ships of the Desert: Desert roads that we now speed across in hours or fly over in minutes were laboriously traversed by camels. For the amateur this mode of transport could be tiresome. One enthusiastic but baffled traveler comments: "It is unpleasant to ride an animal which not only objects to being ridden but cherishes a strong personal antipathy to its rider . . . His paces are more compli-cated than his joints and more trying than his temper. He has four: a short walk, like the rolling of a small boat in a chopping sea; a long walk which dislocates every bone in your body; a trot that reduces you to imbecility; and a gallop that is sudden death."

More hardened veterans of the desert, however, were wholeheartedly in favor of camels, who have the capacity to keep going for four or five days without water and can carry loads in difficult places. "Only those who have traveled in the desert," wrote an English devotee at the beginning of this century, "can understand the joy of returning there; a joy which, strangely enough, has only one equal and that is the pleasure of returning to water, to flowers and trees after a spell of some days or even weeks in the wilderness."

The transition from the teeming green valley is abrupt: suddenly the lush green cultivated land gives way to the stony wilderness, where the rocks rise up in extraordinary formations, strangely reminiscent of the pyramids and sphinx, the sand blows and spills, and there is scarcely a sign of life for hundreds of miles. The one exception to this dramatic change is

Keep at the Monastery of St. Antony's near the Red Sea in the Eastern Desert.

east of Cairo, where semi-suburban industrial zones sprawl out to the east, eventually joining up with the pock-marked battlegrounds of recent wars in the canal area.

Desert Flora and Fauna: Interesting excursions can, however, be made from Cairo into the Eastern Desert. The geological formations are endlessly various and strange, yielding stones and sands of amazing shapes and colors. The flora and fauna, though sparse and timid, are all the more wonderful for their tenacious hold on life. A variety of plants, some of them aromatic, grow on the flanks and bottoms of the wadis; once in a while a lone tamarisk or wild fig casts a bit of shade. There are numerous species of birds, some resident and some migratory, and occasionally in spring and autumn a skein of migrating cranes can be seen high overhead, their conversations with each other quite audible. Once in a while a gazelle or a wild goat streaks across the open plain and disappears among the rocks; and often a sandy picnic place can be criss-crossed with the embroidery of bird and animal tracks. Jerboas, jackals and foxes leave dainty padmarks, while rabbits, gazelles and hyenas leave heavier prints.

One hundred and thirty-one miles (200 km) east of Beni Suef in the rugged hills at the foot of the South Galala Plateau, looking out over the desolate Wadi Araba stands the **Monastery of St. Antony**, the fifth-Century Christian hermit whose temptations are so enthusiastically illustrated by European painters of the Renaissance. An hour's drive further on by car, or a hair-raisingly difficult and dangerous 40-mile (65-km) scramble on foot, brings one to the Monastery of his contemporary **St. Paul**, tucked into a fold of the Red Sea Mountains.

These two monasteries are the object of pilgrimage for thousands of Egyptian Christians on certain feast days during the year and are also visited by many curious tourists. Both were founded on the sites chosen by the hermits in the fourth Century A.D., when Egyptian Christians were being persecuted by the Romans, and the influence of their way of life spread far and wide throughout the Christian world.

The monks lead a quiet life of work and prayer, very much as they did 15 centuries ago, when the original Desert Fathers retired from the fever and injustice of the world to seek a better way of life.

A typical desert monastery.

SCUBA DIVING AND WATER SPORTS

Egypt is only just waking up to the marvels that fringe her Red Sea Coast, the eastern coast of Sinai, and the handful of scattered islands offshore. Snorkeling and scuba diving are becoming increasingly popular with young Egyptians as more hotels and facilities are opened up.

Coral Reefs: The climatic and geographic position of Egypt's eastern coasts is ideal for the formation of coral, which cannot grow at temperatures of less than 18.5°C or at depths of more than 70 feet (22 meters). Though the Gulf of Aqaba and the Red Sea attain a depth of 6,000 feet (1,850 meters) in the middle, where the tectonic plates of Africa and Asia have drawn apart to form a great rift, relatively shallow seas cover the continental shelf that runs along the shores, which are interrupted only by occasional *wadis*, formed by infrequent but torrential rains. The sunshine that penetrates the very salty water for many hours each day enables the coral to build up its formations.

There are basically four types of reefs. Fringing reefs and barrier reefs run parallel to the coast, usually with shallow sandy-bottomed lagoon between the land and the coral, which then drops steeply as much as 70 feet in a cliff-like formation. Atolls are reefs that have formed around islands that have since disappeared. There are no atolls in the Egyptian part of the Red Sea, but the fourth type of reef, roughly distinguished as a patch formation, occurs quite frequently. Mounds of coral build up on the sandy floor of the sea like islands, the tips of which are barely skimmed by the waves. Patch formations occur at Nuweiba on the Sinai coast, off Hurghada and at other spots further south.

Living on Skeletons: Each coral accretion consists of numerous minute anemone-like individual polyps, growing together in a colony. When one colony dies, a new colony grows on top, attached to the skeletons of their defunct ancestors, so to speak. Two thousand species have been identified and christened with complex names. Even the amateur can find as many as 100 types on most reefs or patches in the fantastic profusion that meets his eye the minute he looks under the water.

Delicate pinks, purples, yellows and beiges

are dappled by the flitting shadows of waves. Some corals are soft and undulating, like the sea anemones; some are hard and solid, squat and rounded like brains or mushrooms; some branch like elkhorns, or stack up like fortifications, spires and pinnacles; others are fan-shaped and perforated like Elizabethan lace collars. The almost miraculous forms are at the same time familiar and strange.

Ecosystem: The corals feed, mostly at night, on organisms trapped on their multiple surfaces. These organisms in turn are nourished by sunlight, which is the base of an ecosystem that supports a rich variety of marine life and furnishes a living laboratory for both professional and amateur biologists. Some creatures live off algae and plankton trapped by the coral, others actually eat and digest the coral itself. These characters are in turn hunted and eaten by a progressive chain of predators, the biggest of which are the prowlers of the open sea.

Slugs, snails, shellfish, shrimps and crabs live in the nooks and crannies of the coral or in the sandy patches within the lagoons. But it is, above all, the fish that liven the coral beds, with their beauty and variety, their curious relationships and habits, as they suddenly dart about or circle, idly waving their fins, either singly, in pairs, or in schools. Their vivid colors contrast with the coral: black against rose, orange against indigo, lemon yellow against lacy white.

The most common inhabitants of the reefs are the thousands of little damsel fish, including green chromis and blue fusiliers, which graze peacefully or shoot up suddenly in a great sparkling cloud. Flame-colored coral fish, only about an inch long, hover close to the shadows in ones and twos. Butterfly and angel fish form a large and easily distinguishable family because of their oval shape, snub noses, and gorgeous lemony coloring, enhanced with blue and black stripes and patches: they swim im pairs and stick to the same territory. Other easily distinguishable types are the disc-shaped sergeant-major, who sports appropriate stripes, and his cousins the dascylus and bi-color chromis, who parade in regiments, turning together like lazy pieces of a Calder mobile.

More gorgeous greens and blues occur in the families of wrasses and parrot fish, which can reach a fair size if they manage to survive the hazards of predatory society; the giant humphead wrasse can be as big as five feet long. These families actually eat coral with their beaks and the crunching of their nibbling jaws can be heard as they chew up the madrepore. Grinding plates in their throats break down the coral; and once the nourishing material is extracted, great quantities of coral sand are excreted.

The parrot fish also have a very noisy sex-life, in which dominant males preside over a harem of females. Something very curious happens when the boss of the harem succumbs or is eaten by a passing prowler: rather than a younger male taking his place, the leading lady in his entourage changes sex, and with it her colors, assuming the leadership of the pack. Shades of that other great Egyptian lady, Hatshepsut!

The adaptive and dissimulating mechan-

teau and his colleagues, who spent many months in the Red Sea, engage in debates with moray eels, lionfish, barracuda, sting rays or sharks.

Whales and sea-cows (or dugongs) rove the deep sea also and are not carnivorous, but ingest gallons of plankton. The only danger from these species is that they may accidentally give a small boat a mighty wallop.

In spring one may observe some extraordinary aspects of the mating season from a boat or even from the beach. The sea may suddenly boil with a million sardines laying eggs, or one may be lucky enough to see the dance of the manta rays, who compete for the favors of the female and court her by making great leaps out of the water.

Diving Centers: Several of the modern hotels

isms of other varieties of small fish are just as fascinating, but too numerous to mention here. Each one has his distinctive character, coloring, shape and habits.

Predators: Next up the ecological ladder come the groupers, jacks, skates and other predators, who feed on the little fish. Their bodies are usually mottled or blotched brown, red, or blue, and they have big mouths, which can stretch wide to swallow their dinner. They hunt singly, swimming with their pectoral fins and hovering stealthily, ready to pounce on their prey.

The more scary monsters of the deep are not normally encountered by the ordinary snorkeler and rarely by a prudent scuba diver. Only experienced professionals like Jacques Cous-

on the Sinai and Red Sea coasts have affiliated diving centers with resident diving instructors, boats and equipment for hire. One does not have to stay in the hotel, however, to use facilities in all cases: Nuweiba, Dahab and Sharm el Sheikh, for example, have diving centers with hotels and camping grounds in the vicinity. The Hurghada Sheraton, Giftun Village, and the Club Méditerranée at Magawish are all well-equipped. Diving and fishing trips are organized daily as part of these hotels' sports programs: the trained professional supervisors can initiate the novice into what to look for, where to see it, and how to manage his gear.

Gear: Reasonably efficient snorkeling equipment — mask, snorkel and flippers —

can be rented by the day, but not purchased in Egypt. For those who want to take the sport seriously, it is advisable to buy and test out gear before coming. Test the mask for a perfect fit by placing it over the upper part of the face and breathing in gently. If the mask stays in place it fits; if it drops off, it is too big or too small. Simple masks are the best. The snorkel should not be more than 12 inches long, because of the possibility of carbon dioxide back-up, and the rubber mouthpiece should be firm. Flippers should be the kind that completely cover the foot, are flexible without being floppy, and about one size larger than one's normal shoe size. Old tennis shoes are useful if one simply wants to put one's feet down and peer at the wonders from a more static position.

and a weight belt, comprise the essential equipment. A wet suit, or part of one, may be advisable, particularly during the winter months, when the water can be chilly and the wind cold. It has the added advantage of protecting the wearer from the coral.

Training: No one should attempt to scuba dive who has not completed a course of proper training consisting of at least 15-20 hours of theoretical study, followed by 20-30 hours of practical diving experience. There are dangers of running out of oxygen, going too deep, and coming up too suddenly, which can be fatal. Certificates of competency are granted after a sufficient course of training. For those who are able to invest enough time and money, the Red Sea is an ideal setting for gaining mastery of this sport.

Scuba: Scuba is an acronym for "self-contained under-water breathing apparatus" which enables the diver to submerge completely for up to 30 minutes at a time, to depths of 70 feet or more, and leaves him free to drift at ease, unfettered by gravity, and able to send himself up or down, backwards or forwards, by a movement of his flipper. Besides the mask and flippers, a dive tank, consisting of two cylinders of compressed oxygen, attached to a harness generally worn on the back and connected to the mouth by tubes, a regulator,

Trophy-hunting is severely discouraged, as every effort is being made to protect the delicate environment, which has already suffered from fishing with explosives, vandalism and oil spills. The best souvenirs of snorkeling and scuba diving are photographic; and special high quality waterproof cameras are available, enabling divers to share their unique experiences with less fortunate souls.

For the less adventurous there are trips in glass-bottomed boats, sailing, wind-surfing and fishing, not to mention beachcombing, sunbathing and just doing nothing. The Red Sea beaches are a wonderful playground and can be enjoyed all year round, though the optimum months are October, November, February and March.

Left, some aquatic exotica. Above, diver with find, the Red Sea.

259

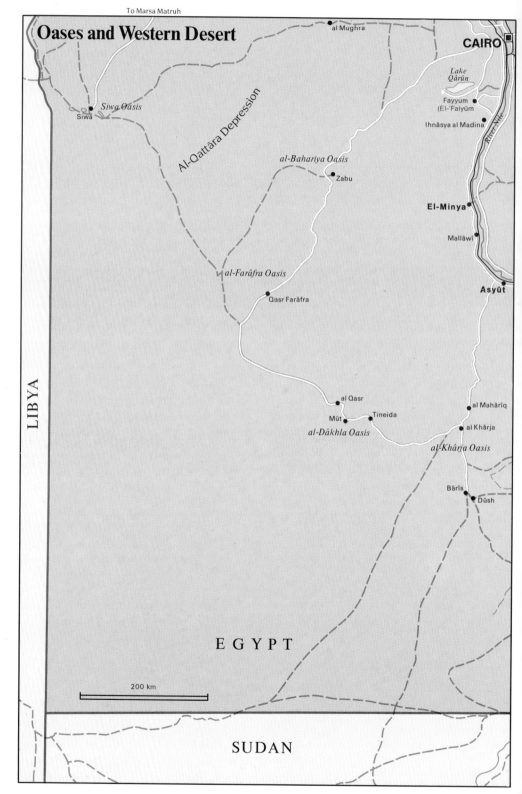

Oases and Western Desert

To Marsa Matruh

al Mughra

CAIRO

Lake
Qârûn

Fayyum
(El-'Faiyûm)

Ihnâsya al Madina

Siwa Oasis

Siwâ

Al-Qattâra Depression

al-Bahariya Oasis

Zabu

El-Minya

Mallâwî

al-Farâfra Oasis

Qasr Farâfra

Asyût

LIBYA

al Qasr

al Mahârîq

Mût

Tineida

al Khârja

al-Dâkhla Oasis

al-Khârja Oasis

Bârîs

Dûsh

E G Y P T

200 km

SUDAN

THE OASES AND
THE FAYYUM

Oasis: The very word conjures a string of images — swirling sands, blue-veiled Tuaregs, mirages, the thirsty caravan stumbling into a pool of sweet water set amidst swaying palms.

As always, little of this vision has any foundation in modern reality: the caravans have all but vanished, banditry has been suppressed, and the Bedouin have traded in their camels for 4WD Toyotas. Not even the vestiges of modern man, however, in the form of asphalt, high tension wires and water pumps, are capable of concealing the truths of a harsh climate, where shifting sands can block roads for days and where the foolhardy can still meet death by thirst, exposure, or the sting of a scorpion. Nor have 20th-Century wonders obscured the essential miracle of water, gushing hot or cold from barren rock to irrigate acres of garden in the midst of a wasteland.

From the Nile, the Sahara stretches 3,000 miles (5,000 km) westward to the Atlantic. The world's greatest expanse of desert is broken only by some several score dots of green, where human habitation has survived the spread of sands. Contrary to popular imagination, which sees verdure sprouting incongruously from dunes, oases generally lie in rocky lands where wind and time have scratched out vast depressions whose depths allow natural underground aquifers to reach the surface.

In Egypt's Western Desert a single aquifer flows north from Sudan, running in an arc more or less parallel to the Nile Valley to water five oases. Prehistoric remains show that man has been exploiting nature's gift since at least 5000 B.C. Under the pharaohs the four Nileward Oases — Kharga, Dakhla, Farafrah and Bahariyya — formed a line of defense against marauding Libyan tribes, their inhabitants shifting between autonomy and subservience depending on the strength of the central government.

The camel, the only beast capable of five days' march without water, was introduced by invading Persians in the 6th Century B.C. and provided the oases their first great leap forward, matched in importance only recently with the introduction of electricity and the automobile. The camel helped to revive the desert

economy, on a decline since the last Ice Age, and to ease the penetration of Egyptian authority. The new beast was no help to the Persian emperor Cambyses, however, when he dispatched his army from Kharga across the desert to Siwah in 525 B.C. According to Herodotus, all 50,000 men were buried in a sandstorm.

The Ptolemies, who ran the country like a vast estate, set about improving desert agriculture. Archaeological remains show that cultivation grew to its furthest extent under their rule; new wells were dug with Alexandrian technology and the complex systems of water distribution that still persist were brought into use. Roman conquest led to a reversal of fortunes. The internal unrest of the late Roman period saw banditry increase at the expense of sedentary agriculture, while persecutions forced Christians into desert refuge, as the many Christian remains in the oases testify. Wells that had been regularly repaired and cleaned were allowed to dry up, as a general decline in population, lasting up to the present century, set in.

Although the date of the last Christian conversions to Islam is not known — the present inhabitants of the oases being

263

solidly Muslim — it is likely that the new religion, so well suited to desert ways, made easy headway in the oases. A millennium of Islam, with periodic revivalist uprisings, such as the Libyan Senussi revolt, has shaped the character of the oases dwellers to a greater extent than it has valley folk. The charm, generosity, and peaceability of the inhabitants owe much to Islam. In a landscape seemingly touched by God — abundance amidst waste — a touching humility of outlook is so appropriate as to seem unsurprising.

Al-Kharga Oasis: Al-Kharga (*The Outer*) Oasis is the most frequented of Egypt's oases, by virtue of its proximity to the Nile and because it is the seat of the New Valley Governorate. Although it is linked by twice-weekly flights from Cairo and Luxor, most travelers prefer the overland route. Three miles (five km) north of Asyut, a fine paved road leads past a new industrial complex up into the desert. One hundred twenty miles (200 km) of barren gravel later, the road descends suddenly down a magnificent cliff into the **Kharga Depression**, which extends southwards, narrowing at its extremity, for 60 miles (100 km).

As one crosses the flat bottom of the depression, a few straggly trees appear on the roadside, inauspiciously announcing the beginning of cultivation. Then Nasserite housing blocks begin to sprout, marking the entrance to **Kharga** town. Visitors to the oases should not be too disappointed by the town. It is merely an administrative center and a showpiece of the New Valley project, initiated by Abdul Nasser in the later 1950s. The project, the aim of which was to utilize the vast potential of the oases' waters for land reclamation and new settlement, has met with considerable success. Much of Kharga's population consists of resettled Upper Egyptians; and the new hotels, duck farms, and packaging industries point to a fair degree of prosperity. With the exception of its old market there is not much to see in the modern town, however, and the fields surrounding it provide little of the scenic delight found elsewhere in the oases.

Just northeast of the town, not far from the main road, lies a cluster of monuments. Chief among them is the **Temple of Hibis**, important as one of the few remnants of Persian rule. Built of local sandstone, it was begun under Cambyses' successor Darius I, but not completed un-

Camel herd in the Western or Sahara Desert.

til the reign of Nectanebo II in the fourth Century B.C. The temple lies in a palm grove beyond the remains of a ceremonial pool and an avenue of sphinxes. The carving style within shows local influence, while the content of the reliefs — deities, the burial of Osiris, a winged Seth struggling with a serpent — follows a standard pattern.

At the edge of cultivation to the north of the temple lies the Christian necropolis of **Al-Bagawat**, a huge area of mudbrick domes and vaults, some of which preserve decoration. A kilometer's hike across the sand leads to the ruins of a fortified monastery.

South of Kharga town a paved road extends through a string of smaller oases, past some minor antiquities, to **Baris**, the village designed by renowned architect Hassan Fathi. Not far from here is a temple of the Roman period dedicated to Isis and Serapis.

Dakhla Oasis: With 30,000 acres (12,000 hectares) under cultivation and a population of 60,000, **Dakhla** (*The Inner*) is the largest of the oases. The New Valley project has more than doubled its size in recent years, but Dakhla retains more of its original charm than Kharga, to which it is connected by a 120-mile (200 km) road and daily buses.

The first village of importance in the depression is **Balat**. Here a direct caravan route from Asyut had its terminus and a hive of mudbrick dwellings testifies to medieval prosperity. Using only mud and straw, builders attained a sophistication in architecture that combines utility, beauty and harmony with natural surroundings. Balat was the seat of the oases, pharaonic governors; and a French expedition is currently excavating the extensive remains to the northwest of the village.

Dakhla's current capital is at **Mut**, some 18 miles (30 km) farther west. The town contains Dakhla's only hotels, as well as the police station where foreign visitors must register. Most necessities may be obtained here and there are a number of decent restaurants, but little to see — the old town's mudbrick citadel has been allowed to fall into ruins. Outside the town to the northwest are the **Tourist Springs**, which visitors are expected to admire. In fact many of the other springs — most in Dakhla are warm — are equally pleasant.

No trip to Dakhla would be complete,

Coptic cemeteries at Al Bagawat in the Kharga Oasis.

however, without a walk through its fields and gardens. The main field crop is wheat, while in the gardens grapevines vie for space with date palms, mulberry trees, figs and citrus. Dakhla is the only place in Egypt where new *saqiyas* — huge buffalo-driven waterwheels constructed of palm timber and clay jars — are still made; and their gentle moaning makes a pleasant accompaniment to a walk through the shady groves.

Eighteen miles beyond the Tourist Springs, the town of **Al-Qasr ad-Dakhla** perches on a mound between the desert and the fields. Like Balat, Al-Qasr is a honeycomb of little lanes that run in, out, under and between multistoried mudbrick houses. A 13th-Century mosque and a less ancient *madrasah* show the degree of refinement reached. Although cement is gaining ground, many locals still prefer the older material, since mudbrick walls retain heat at night and coolness in the day.

In the desert beyond Al-Qasr to the west are some well preserved Hellenistic tombs, one with a brightly painted zodiac on the ceiling. Farther along the main road lie the ruins of the Roman temple at **Deir al-Hajar**. This first-Century wreck is a picturesque landmark.

Farafrah: Farafrah is the farthest of this group of oases from the Nile valley. Although it is also the smallest, with little over 2,500 acres (1,000 hectares) under cultivation, it has the greatest potential for land reclamation.

Only recently has Farafrah been connected to the rest of Egypt by decent roads. One now leads south, past the isolated settlement of Abu Mungar and through a 120-mile stretch, justifiably called the Sand Sea, to Dakhla. The other, a more traveled route, goes northeast, through 150 miles (250 km) of some of Egypt's most spectacular desert, to the Bahariyya Oases and then to Cairo.

Al-Qasr al-Farafrah is the only town in Farafrah. It has a three-room resthouse, one shop and a coffee-house: note that food here is not obtainable. The village, many of its houses gaily painted by a talented local artist, clusters on the leeward side of a hill. Farafrah's beautiful gardens, famous for apples and apricots, lie on the windward side. A small natural bath-house at the gardens' edge is a good place for a scrub, while a Roman well within the gardens is of archaeological interest. At the bottom of the hill is a

Wind sculptures in the Western Desert.

small lake stocked with river fish. The gentle *Farfuris* are not entirely accustomed to foreigners and prefer to avoid them.

Bahariyya: The **Bahariyya Oases** are reached from Cairo by an excellent road that leads westward off the Fayyum desert road behind the Giza pyramids. About 200 rather dull miles later we reach the new settlement attached to Egypt's only iron mines. Not far beyond the mines the road descends into the **Bahariyya Depression**. The major town, **Al-Bawiti**, lies in the center of the depression, which measures 45 miles (75 km) from north to south. Visitors should not be put off by Bawiti's uninviting aspect, as the town has only very recently emerged from being a self-sufficient agricultural village and is suffering growth pangs brought about by the arrival of electricity in 1986. Accommodations at the town's only hotel leave much to be desired, but there are some decent eateries.

Bawiti sits atop a rock outcrop. To the north, cliffs drop abruptly into a sea of palms. Bawiti's gardens, spread for three miles (five km) along the base of this cliff, are among the most beautiful in all

the oases. The view from the cliffs at the spring called **'Ayn Bishmu** is breathtaking. Here the water emerges from a gorge to flow into the orchards. Within the gardens, land is so precious that there are few walkways and one must often paddle through the irrigation channels. Dates, olives, oranges, apricots, lemons, pomegranates and tiny apples grow in jungle-like proliferation, set in gardens fenced with mud walls and palm fronds. Farmers shout friendly greetings as they splash by on donkeyback.

Around Bawiti and its sister village of Al-Qasr are numerous ancient sites, not all accessible and not all interesting. More to the taste of tourists are likely to be the hot springs, which range in temperature up to a scalding 115 degrees (47°C). The waters vary in content, some reeking of sulphur, others tinged with iron ore. Few things in life are more memorable or more relaxing than a moonlit bath under palm trees in the crisp air of the desert.

Siwah: **Siwah** is the most mysterious, the most remote, and until recently was the least visited of Egypt's oases, as troubles along the Libyan border, to which it is adjacent, prevented foreign tourism. At present, half an hour's bureaucratizing at

A casaulty of the desert.

Mersa Matruh is all that is required to obtain a visitor's permit. Daily buses now ply the tarmacked 190 miles (300 km) between Siwah and Matruh, while ten years' heavy military presence have contributed to gradual Egyptianization. A number of shops now cater to basic needs, while a large government-run hotel provides lodging.

Siwah is unique in Egypt in that it has a distinct culture — formed over thousands of years of isolation — and its own language. The *Siwi* dialect, related to the Berber languages of North Africa, still holds out against the massive inroads made by Arabic through state education and military service. Unusual customs, such as homosexual marriages, have altogether died out, although the reclusive women of the oasis cling to traditional dress.

The oasis' main population center is in **Siwah town**, to which the Siwis moved from the **fortress of Aghurmi** in the earlier part of this century. On the rock of Aghurmi, 2.5 miles (four km) distant from the town center, sit the remains of the **Temple of Jupiter-Amon**, home of the famous oracle which confirmed Alexander the Great in his status as a god. In the palm groves below the rock stood a second temple, unfortunately destroyed by dynamite in 1887. The other major historical site is at **Gabal al-Mawta**, a mile or so northeast of Siwah town. Here tombs have been cut out of the rock of a conical ridge. Paintings cover some of the walls, especially in the tomb of Si-Amun, but much was destroyed when the tombs were used as shelters during the Italian air raids of World War II.

The most impressive sight in the oasis, however, is undoubtedly its agriculture. Siwah is the major producer of dates in Egypt. Some 250,000 palms fill the cultivated area; and their production is prized as the finest in the country. Olives also grow in abundance, as well as various other fruits and vegetables. Among the groves lie numerous springs, such as the **'Ayn al-Gubah**, the ancient **Well of the Sun**, whose waters were said to have purifying properties. Indeed, water is in such abundance that large salty lakes have formed and drainage is a major problem.

Fayyum: The Fayyum, which sprouts from the west bank of the Nile like a tender leaf, is referred to by some as Egypt's largest oasis. Others deny that it

is an oasis at all, fed as it is by the **Bahr Yusef**, an ancient canal flowing from the Nile just north of Asyut.

In prehistoric times the Fayyum was a marshy depression that collected the Nile's overflow in flood season. Its wetlands were a favorite hunting ground of the Old and Middle Kingdom Pharaohs until the 12th Dynasty's Amenemhet I (1991-1962 B.C.) drained the swamps, building a regulator at Al-Lahun, the point where the river periodically breached its banks, and allowing a permanent reservoir to form, **Lake Moeris**, to the Greeks, now called *Lake Qarun*.

With this lake at the depression's northern end stabilized, agriculture could be introduced; and the Fayyum began to flourish. It received a further boost under the Ptolemies, who reclaimed more than 450 sq miles (1,200 sq km) of fertile land, reducing the lake to about twice its present size. Improved agricultural methods were introduced and new-fangled Greek hydraulics — waterwheels of a unique type still in use today — permitted extensive terracing. The population, reinforced by new towns filled with Greek and Jewish settlers, exploded during this Ptolemaic Golden Age.

The Fayyum, then, was an early and highly successful effort at land reclamation. Further improvements under the Mamluk Sultan Baybars and Muhammad Ali in the 19th Century turned it into the "Garden of Egypt," as it is sometimes called. This century has unfortunately brought with it the twin evils of over-population and salinization. Lake Qarun now measures only 24 by five miles (40 by nine km) and is as salty as the Mediterranean, while the population surge has transformed Madinat al-Fayyum, the capital city, into a sprawling slum.

Day trips from Cairo to the Fayyum (two hours away) are practical and pleasant as an excellent road connects them across the desert, leaving Cairo from behind the Giza pyramids but the main road along the Nile to Upper Egypt is more attractive. Thirty miles (48 km) south of Cairo's edge the road draws parallel to the **Pyramid of Meidum,** a huge two-stepped tower silhouetted on the western horizon. A signposted turn-off leads up to the pyramid.

Dating from the end of the third

The collapsed pyramid of Meidum.

Dynasty, Meidum represents the transition from the Saqqarah-type step pyramid to the 'true' pyramidal forms of Giza. Its present shape resulted from the collapse of the smooth outer casing; it is sometimes called the Collapsed Pyramid. A descent into Meidum's murky interior will charm the intrepid non-claustrophobe, while a walk down its funerary causeway into the fields below emphasizes the contrast between stone encased death in the desert and the timeless bounty of the valley.

Continuing southwest for 10 miles (16 km) across the desert the road leads over train tracks and along the edge of an army camp. Eventually we arrive at a forking: the road to the right enters cultivation and ultimately goes to Madinat al-Fayyum; the road to the left goes on towards the **pyramid complex of Amenemhet III** (1832-1797 B.C.) at Hawarah. Having lost its outer casing of limestone, Amenemhet III's pyramid survives as a huge pile of mudbrick. It is easily climbed and the view from its top is superb. Below the pyramid are a number of ruinous tombs and very patchy remains of a mortuary temple that rivaled those at the pyramids at Giza in its splendor. This

was the great **Labyrinth**, which received a rave review from that globe-trotting Greek of the fifth Century B.C., Herodotus, and was a "must" among ancient tourists. It was Hawarah that Flinders Petrie excavated, sometimes up to his neck in water, to discover the first of the famed Fayyum portraits, the extraordinarily moving and lifelike paintings of the Roman era now displayed in Cairo, London, Moscow and elsewhere.

Southwest of Hawarah the road crosses a canal to reach the main Fayyum-Beni Suwayf road. Five miles (eight km) to the left, on a peninsula of desert, stands the 12th-Dynasty **pyramid of Al-Lahun**, the southernmost in the Fayyum pyramid field. Turning right we reach **Madinat al-Fayyum** after six miles (10 km).

This town of half a million is the site of ancient **Crocodilopolis** and the hub of Fayyum province. Strung out along the Bahr Yusef, it has lost most of its evidently considerable former charm. In the central square a fine example of the Fayyum waterwheel groans away, bemoaning its fate. There is one 15th-Century mosque of interest and the main *suq*, its tortuous lanes cluttered with wares, has an untouched rustic simplicity surpassing that of any other major provincial market.

Between Madinat al-Fayyum and Lake Qarun to the north lie 18 miles (25 km) of agricultural land, which slopes gently downward to the surface of the lake, 150 feet (45 meters) below sea level. The town of **Fidimin** at the halfway point marks the center of the Fayyum's orchard district. As one approaches the lake, the increasing salinity of the soil begins to thin the vegetation, so that the south shore is only sparsely planted. The northern shore is stark desert.

The lake itself is the Fayyum's greatest tourist attraction. It has a peculiar aura of mystery, especially at dusk on a windless day, when the pale sky and stripe of sand on the far side melt into their own reflection. The beaches at its eastern end, where the hotels and an excellent fish restaurant on a pier are located, fill up with mobs of Cairenes on holidays. The western end, approached from inland through the villages of **Sanhur** and **Ibshawai**, is more peaceful: the Ptolemaic **temple at Qasr Qarun**, the site of ancient Dionysias, is an attraction and the lovely countryside makes the drive worthwhile. At Lake Qarun's eastern end the lake-side road joins the main desert road back to Cairo.

Life in the desert, right.

ABU SIMBEL AND NUBIA

Nubia, the arid sun-seared land of about 8,500 square miles (22,000 square km) between Aswan and the northern Sudan, now lies beneath the waters of the High Dam reservoir. Nubia's entire population of some 100,000 people were uprooted from their ancestral homes, half to be relocated in Egypt (in Kom Ombo, about nine miles north of Aswan), the other half in the northeastern Sudan (in Kashem el-Girba). Nubia's major monuments, like its people, were transported to new locations, one as far afield as New York. Both the tragedy of the uprooting of the Nubian people and the technological achievement in saving the monuments can best be understood in the context of Nubia as it was before the deluge.

Old Nubia: Nubia was the link between Egypt and Africa, but it was not a regular trade corridor because of its inhospitable environment. It was a largely barren land, while Egypt, on the other hand, had an abundant agricultural surplus. Even in ancient times Nubians turned to their rich northern neighbor for vital food supplies, especially grain. And Egypt was ready to fulfill the Nubians' requirements in return for the right to exploit their rich mineral resources.

Despite its stark and barren nature the Nubian people had a strong attachment to their land. In the 20th Century their working men went northwards to Egypt to find employment as bargemen, doorkeepers, cooks, or government clerks, but they seldom married Egyptians and inevitably returned to Nubia, bearing cloth, clothing and food for their families, as well as pictures cut out of magazines and newspapers — mostly portraits of political leaders, athletes and film stars — which were used to adorn the walls of their houses.

In the years before the High Dam, Nubian houses were made of sun-baked brick, a mixture of clay and straw. The facade of each house was different from the next, not only individually shaped, but uniquely decorated by laying bricks at angles, in steps, or in lattice designs. Houses were painted, both inside and out, with finger paintings of trees, chickens, boats, flags and sacred symbols,

and most had porcelain plates (brought from Cairo) inserted into the clay before it dried. Colored baskets woven from palm fronds hung around the inner doorway or adorned the spacious rooms: Nubia's date-palm groves provided the people not only with food, but also with no fewer than 40 other commodities, such as fiber for ropes, timber for heavy construction, and palm "spears" for a variety of uses.

Sailing southwards from Egypt before the land was flooded, one could see Nubian settlements grouped near the banks of the river. Whitewashed shrines of local saints and sheikhs broke the skyline. The groaning of ox-driven waterwheels echoed along the Nile as tiny fields, planted with barley, beans and castor plants, came into view.

In the vast distances from village to village, ancient temples could be seen: the great fortress of Kubban which once guarded the Wadi Alaki, one of the richest gold-mining areas in Nubia; the temples of Debod and Tafa, now reassembled in Madrid and Leiden, or the temples of Kertassi, Kalabsha, and Beit el Wali, now re-assembled on a new site near the High Dam, all originally built atop jutting sandstone cliffs. And, of course, the great Temple of Ramses II at Abu Simbel, a symbol of Egyptian power in Nubia in ancient times.

The End of Old Nubia: The trauma for the Nubians, faced with the news that their land was doomed, was compounded by the fact that this was not the first, but the fourth time they had watched their homes being submerged by the River Nile. An old man at Darau, near Kom Ombo, for example, recalled when the first Aswan dam was built, between 1899 and 1902. It formed an artificial lake 140 miles (225 km) upstream and the Nubians had to move back from the fertile strip at the edge of the river to rebuild their homes. Less than five years after the dam was completed, it was seen to be inadequate to meet the growing needs of the country and was heightened by about 15 feet (five meters). The reservoir now created by the thwarted Nile backed upstream 185 miles (300 km) and the Nubians had to move a second time. Between 1929 and 1934 the Aswan dam was raised again, another 30 feet and this time the water extended as far south as Wadi Halfa in northern Sudan. When the Nubians were told that a new dam would be built and that they would have to move again, this time out of Nubia completely, they therefore found it difficult to understand. Some of the older generation refused to leave; and with the water lapping at their feet they finally had to be helped or even carried, to the waiting vessels.

Saving the Nubian Monuments: Meanwhile, the Egyptian and Sudanese governments launched an international appeal to save and record as many of the monuments of Nubia as possible. The response was immediate and Nubia was subjected, between 1960 and 1970, to the most concentrated archaeological operation ever mounted. Scholars, engineers, architects and photographers from over 30 countries fought against time to preserve what they could. Twenty-three temples were saved. Many of them were left in Nubia but moved or lifted out of harm's way: the **temple of Amada**, for example, was raised as a unit of 800 tons (tonnes), put on rails and dragged up a hill to safety, while the **temple of Derr** was re-assembled nearby. A temple built by Queen Hatshepsut was dismantled, crated, loaded on 28 lorries, and transported to the Sudan, where it was rebuilt in the National Museum at Khartoum. Three temples were re-assembled at **Waai as-sebua**, three more were moved to a single site near the High Dam, and others were transported to museums in New York, Leiden, Turin and Madrid.

The Temples of Abu Simbel: The famous **Temple of Ramses II** at Abu Simbel, the largest and most magnificent monument in Nubia, presented a formidable challenge. Unlike other temples, Abu Simbel was not freestanding. The temple facade was, in fact, the cliff face itself hewn in imitation of a pylon, dominated by four seated statues of a youthful Ramses II. The central hall was flanked by eight more statues of the king in a double row facing each other, against a corresponding number of square pillars. The northern wall of the hall was decorated with the Great Battle Scene, which is one of the most extraordinary and detailed reliefs to be found in the Nile Valley. There are over 1,100 figures and the entire wall, from ceiling to bedrock, is filled with activity: the march of the Egyptian army with its infantry and charioteers, its engagement in hand-to-hand combat, and the flight of the vanquished prisoners, leaving overturned chariots

The Temple of Abu Simbel before excavation.

276

behind them. There are also scenes of camp life, showing an inspection by officers, and of farmers anxiously driving their cattle into the hills.

Beyond the court, carved out of the mountain to a depth of 180 feet (55 meters), was the sanctuary, which contained seated statues of four gods, Ptah of Memphis, Amon-Ra of Thebes, the deified Ramses II and Ra-Harakhte, the sun-god of Heliopolis.

Countries from all over the world offered technical and financial aid to save this unique monument. The project finally chosen entailed sawing the temple into over a thousand transportable pieces, some weighing as much as 15 tons and placing them safely above the water level until they could be reassembled at a new site 200 feet (60 meters) higher than their original site. While these blocks of stone were being treated and stored, the new site on top of the mountain was levelled. Explosives could not be used for fear of damaging the temples, so compressed-air drills were utilized. Studies were carried out on the bedrock to ensure that it could support the enormous weight it was destined to bear forever, not only the mass of the

reconstructed temple, but also a great reinforced concrete dome that would cover it. The dome would be 400 feet (125 meters) high and the cylindrical part was designed with a free span of some 200 feet, which would bear a load of about 100,000 tons.

The small **temple of Queen Nefertari**, which lay to the north of the Great Temple at Abu Simbel, was also saved. Nefertari was the most beloved of the wives of Ramses II; and throughout the temple, on pillar and wall, even in the sanctuary, the names of the royal couple are linked in their shared dedication to the goddess Hathor.

Salvage Archaeology: By 1970, with the water of the High Dam lake constantly rising, engulfing more and more of what had once been Nubia, considerable portions of known temples and shrines had been salvaged. But how much unknown archaeological evidence, in the form of town sites, tombs, temples, churches, and documents, had been lost forever can never be ascertained.

Ironically, however, it is due to its disappearance that we now know more of Nubia than we do of many important sites in the best of Egypt. We know, for

The Queen's Temple at Abu Simbel.

277

example, that when the civilization of ancient Egypt was in its decline, a kingdom of Upper Nubia prospered, and that around 600 B.C. the Nubians moved their capital from Napata southwards to Meroe (Shendi). In the fertile bend in the river, free from invasion, well-placed for trade, rich in iron ore and in wood for iron-smelting, they developed a culture that was at once a continuation of the Egyptian-influenced Napatan culture and a totally individual African culture. What is known as the Meroitic script is a corruption of Egyptian hieroglyphic.

The Meroitic Kingdom spread northwards until, by the reign of Ptolemy IV (181 B.C.), the king of Meroe, Argamanic, controlled the Nile to within sight of Elephantine. There the Nubians remained until the Roman conquest of Egypt in 30 B.C., when the Romans signed a treaty with them, turning all northern Nubia into a buffer zone. Despite this treaty, however, there is evidence of conflict between the proud and independent Meroites and the Roman army.

Nubia embraced Christianity between the fifth and the sixth centuries, when numerous churches were built and some

ancient temples were converted into churches. When Egypt was conquered by the Arabs in the seventh Century, they concluded a treaty with the Christian Nubian king and Nubia officially remained Christian until the 12th Century, when many Nubians embraced the Muslim faith. Mass conversion to Islam came when tribes from Arabia settled in Lower Nubia and began to impose their religion and their political organization on the people. They intermarried with Arabs and their children came to be called *Beni Kanz*, or the Kenuz tribe. This tribe forms the bulk of the resettled Nubian population in Kom Ombo. By the end of the 15th Century, Nubians, with the exception of only a few settlements, were Muslim.

Digging at Qasr Ibrim: Surviving documents in a host of languages, including 'Old Nubian' (which has yet to be deciphered), Arabic, Coptic and Greek, provide a wealth of information about the Nubian people in the form of private and official letters, legal documents, and petitions, which date from between the end of the eighth to the 15th centuries. Most of these documents come from a site about nine miles (15 km) north of Abu Simbel called **Qasr Ibrim**. Now an island, it was situated on the eastern bank of the Nile where three massive peaks of rock rose from the river. Crowning the middle peak was a ruined town and fortress, whose imposing position commanded the valley for miles around in all directions. This *qasr* (castle) is all that emerges above the level of the lake today and it must have been a striking landmark in Roman times when the first fortress was built.

Qasr Ibrim is the only site in Nubia where archaeologists are still at work. A joint American/British excavation started in 1986. This military frontier post, which separated Meroe from Egypt in Roman times, was both an artillery base and a religious center; and its ruins contain an ancient temple and a large cathedral. Restoration of the cathedral is one of the long-term projects envisioned by the team.

Nubia did not, then, "pass into history" when the High Dam was completed in 1971. Excavations continue, visitors can fly or drive to Abu Simbel from Aswan, and a new life has started again for some of the Nubian workers who stayed on at Abu Simbel, Amada and as-Sebua.

Left, the draping of a turban shows a typically Nubian casualness. Right, inscriptions on a boulder at Elephantine Island, Aswan. Following page, skull caps for sale, Aswan.

TRAVEL TIPS

GETTING THERE

BY AIR

Cairo is the link for air travel between Africa, Asia and Europe therefore most major international airlines stop regularly at **Cairo International Airport**. With over 45,000 flights yearly, servicing six and a half million passengers, Cairo International Airport is an active air terminal. Its safety record and airport security are excellent. A new international terminal was opened in 1986 to handle mainly European and American traffic. Of the former terminals, **number one** is for Middle Eastern and African traffic, **number two** is the Egyptair and Air Sinai terminal and **terminal three** is for traffic to Saudi Arabia.

Egypt has two national carriers for internal flights—**Egyptair** and **Air Sinai.** Distances are short and fares are low. Egyptair flies daily from Cairo to Alexandria, Luxor, Aswan, Abu Simbel and Hurghada and twice a week to Kharga Oasis. Air Sinai flies from Cairo to El Arish, Sharm el Shaykh, St. Catherine's Monastery and to Tel Aviv in Israel.

Both airlines can be booked through travel agents and Egyptair offices are at:
Cairo: 6 Adly St., Tel: 920000; 12 Kasrel Nil St., Tel: 750600; Nile Hilton, Tel: 759703; Cairo Sheraton, Tel: 985408; 22 Ibrahim el Lakani, Heliopolis, Tel: 668552.
Alexandria: 19 Midan Saad Zaghloul, Tel: 4920778 (in the process of moving).

There are **non-stop service flights** from most major African, Asian and European cities. Egyptair has a non-stop Cairo/New York service twice a week. Airline tickets must be confirmed for departure. Check with a travel agent in your hotel or contact the airline office in Cairo. (For a listing of all airline offices in Cairo, *see* Appendix).
Daily flights: British Airways, Egyptair, Trans World Airlines.

Other Airports in Egypt: Alexandria, Asyut, Luxor, Aswan, Abu Simbel, El Arish, Sharm al Shaykh, St. Catherine's, Kharga Oasis, Siwah Oasis.

BY SEA

The ports of Egypt are visited by passenger ships at Alexandria and Port Said on the Mediterranean Sea and Suez on the Red Sea.

FROM THE MEDITERRANEAN

Adriatic Lines:(Italian). 5 World Trade Center, New York, Sealink UK Limited. Victoria Station P.O. Box 29, London SW1. Castro and Company, 12 Talaat Harb, Cairo and Saad Zaghloul Square, Alexandria. Car and passenger ferry connects Piraeus, Iraklion, Crete and Venice with Alexandria. Red Sea ferry service El Arish, El Tor, Suez, Jeddah and Aqaba.
Danish Seaways:199 Regent St., London W1. Links Ancona, Rhodes and Crete to Alexandria.
Black Sea Shipping Company: (Russian). Agents: CTC Lines 1-3 Lower Regent St., London SW1. Operates from Alexandria to Beirut, Istanbul, Larnaca, Latakia, Odessa, Piraeus and Varna.

FROM THE RED SEA

The Egyptian Navigation Company, 1 El Hurreya Ave., Alexandria, Tel: 4920824; 26 Sherif St., Cairo Tel: 758278. Connects Suez to Jeddah, Aqaba and Port Sudan and runs a new daily service (in cooperation with Jordan) from Nuweiba to Aqaba and return. Average sailing time is about three hours.
Misr Edco Shipping Company, Menatours, 14 Sharia Talaat Harb, Cairo. Connects Suez to Aqaba and Jeddah.
Saudi Maritime Transport Company, 2 Tulumbat St., (corner of Kasr il Aini) Garden City. Suez to Aqaba and Jeddah.

There are three ways of entering Egypt by land: from the sea ports via ferry, overland from Israel in the east and overland from the Sudan in the south. (The border with Libya is closed.) For cars, motor cycles, scooters, mini-buses (up to nine seats), caravans, commercial passenger buses and taxis, the following rules apply:

Vehicle must have a triptych or *carnet de passage en douane* from an automobile club (i.e. AAA), or pay customs duty (as high as 250 percent).

Entry is valid for 90 days and includes a multiple entry. Renewal (additional 90 days) via **Automobile Club of Egypt**, 10 Sharia Kasr el Nil, Cairo, Tel: 743355. In Alexandria, it is on Sharia Sherif. This procedure takes time.

Owner must possess an International Driver's License and car must have an International Motor Vehicle License. (Again from a local automobile club.) Owner must not have a residence in Egypt.

Owners must buy insurance on arrival and leave a deposit against road tax and customs duty. (Portion refundable).

For more information contact your local automobile club or an Egyptian State Tourist Office. For motoring in Egypt contact the Automobile Club of Egypt (See above).

ROAD ADVICE

Some roads in Egypt are quite dangerous, so take heed of these warnings.

Night driving is dangerous, especially on the Agricultural Road (through the Delta) between Alexandria and Cairo, the river road that connects Cairo with all points south to Aswan, and the road from Helwan to Hurghada.

Large expensive cars do not wear well on Egyptian roads. Leave them home. Bring spare parts with you if possible, Egyptian dealers only carry parts of the authorized agencies in Egypt: General Motors, Madza, Mercedes, Fiat, Opel, Peugeot, Volkswagon and Toyota.

From Israel (bus or taxi): From Tel Aviv and Jerusalem via bus to the border at **Rafah**, passengers have to leave the Israeli bus,

go through customs, walk across the border and take an Egyptian bus or taxi. There are no facilities for issuing visas at the Rafah border.

Also note that at the present time private vehicles cannot enter Egypt from Israel without special permission. Contact the Egyptian consulate nearest your home for details.

From Eilat: Via bus, through the Taba border to the Sinai beaches of Nuweiba, Dahab and Sharm al Shaykh on the Gulf of Aqaba on the Red Sea. The bus does not go beyond Sharm al Shaykh and must re-exit the country at Taba.

From Sudan: Twice weekly there is a steamer (which ferries cars) from Wadi Halfa to Aswan. Information from **Nile Navigation Company Limited**, Ramses Square, Cairo (in the train station) and **The Nile Company** for river transport, 7 Atlas Building, Aswan. All arrangements to enter Sudan including visas must be made in Cairo.

Distances between Cairo and other cities		
	miles	km
north to Alexandria (delta)	140	225
north to Alexandria (desert)	138	221
north to Damietta	119	191
north to Barrages	15	25
south to Minya	151	236
south to Asyut	224	359
south to Luxor	415	664
south to Esna	449	719
south to Edfu	484	775
south to Kom Ombo	521	835
south to Aswan	550	880
east to Port Said	137	220
east to Ismailia	87	140
west to Fayoum	64	103
west to Bahriyya Oasis	197	316
west to Farafrah Oasis	262	420
west to Dakhla Oasis	431	690
west to Kharga Oasis	366	586

TRAVEL ESSENTIALS

VISAS AND PASSPORTS

All travelers to Egypt must have valid visas. To obtain a visa you must go, or write to an Egyptian consulate. Applying in person will require a 24-hour wait. Applying by mail will require a·self-addressed stamped envelope and a waiting period of two weeks. In either instance you will need: one passport photo, your passport, and the required fee.

Single entry visa is good for one entry into the country for one month. If you require a longer stay, request for it at the time of application.

Multiple-entry visa should be requested if you plan to exit and re-enter Egypt during your visit.

Visa extension must be obtained in Egypt at the **Passport Department**, Government Building (Mugama'a) Room 16. Midan Tahrir (near the Hilton Hotel) Cairo; or 136 El Saraya St., Alexandria.

Student visas for people studying in Egypt are valid for one year. For information contact an Egyptian consulate near you.

Business visas are for people who plan to work in Egypt. For more information contact an Egyptian consulate or the **Egyptian Commercial Office**, 2715 Connecticut Ave., N.W. Washington, D.C.

It is also possible to obtain a visa at the Cairo International Airport or the Port of Alexandria.

EGYPTIAN CONSULATES

United States: 2310 Decatur Pl. N.W. Washington, D.C. 20008; 1110 Second Ave., New York, NY 10022; and 3001 Pacific Ave., San Francisco, CA 94115.

Canada: 3754 Côte de Niéges, Montreal, and 454 Laurier Ave., M.E. Ottawa.

Great Britain: 19 Kensington Palace Gardens, London.

EGYPTIAN TOURISM INFORMATION CENTRES

Athens: 10 Amerikis St., Tel: 360-6906.
New York: 630 Fifth Ave., Tel: 246-6960.
San Francisco: 323 Geary St., Tel: 433-7562.
London: 168 Picadilly, W1, Tel: 493-5282.
Rome: 19, Via Bissolati, Tel: 475-1985.
Geneva: 11, Rue de Chantepoulet, Tel: 3291 32.
Paris: 90, Avenue de Champs Elysees, Tel: 562 9442.
Frankfurt: Kaiserstrasse 64, Bürohaus A, Tel: 25 23 19.

MONEY MATTERS

Airport Exchange: Banks are available at the airport for currency exchange. Egyptian money, identified in both Arabic and English, consists of the following denominations:

Pound notes: 100, 20, 10, 5, 1.
Piaster notes: 50, 25, 10, 5.
Coins: 10, 5, 1, 1/2.

Currency declaration: Visitors must declare all money brought into the country. The form you will receive at the airport should be presented to the bank teller each time you exchange money at a bank. Upon departure, if requested, this form should be presented for inspection.

Credit cards are used in most major hotels, but not always in shops. Do bring some **traveler's checks.**

HEALTH

Health certificates: Arrival from most areas is free of health restrictions, but a valid (at least six days in advance) cholera and yellow fever certificate is necessary if one comes from an infected area. Check with the closest Egyptian consulate. Egyptian quarantine is not a pleasant experience. In Egypt, certificates and vaccination shots are available at the **Public Health Unit**, Continental-Savoy Hotel, Opera Square, Cairo.

Uncooked fruits and vegetables often leave visitors with *"Pharaoh's Revenge."* Even a change of water can upset your system. Mineral water is cheap and readily available. Bring something with you like *kaopetate*. Pharmacies in Egypt will have something to help you.

WHAT TO WEAR

If you are coming to Egypt, leave your synthetics at home as they will prove to be too hot in summer and not warm enough in winter— you need materials that breathe. It is advisable to wear cotton in summer as the heat can be like a furnace. Egypt is primarily a desert so you will almost always need a wrap at night. Wear layers that can be taken off during the day. Hotel rooms will be nice and warm, but winter nights in Luxor or Aswan can be bitterly cold.

Above all, bring modest clothes to Egypt. Keep your shoulders and upper arms covered and your skirts below the knee. Both men and women should not wear shorts in public. Don't plan on any nude bathing. A one-piece bathing suit is preferred instead of a bikini.

Bring comfortable walking shoes. Temple floors are not made for dress shoes. In summer, you should carry a hat, or bring an umbrella, to protect yourself from the heat of the Egyptian sun.

If you are going into the desert, cover up, the less skin showing the better. Wear layered and flowing garments so the wind can circulate between them. Look to the Bedouin, they know what they are doing.

Travel light. Preferably get wheels for your luggage and leave heavy items like irons at home. You'll be on the move a lot, so the less you carry the better. But don't forget to bring a candle or a small flashlight for the tombs.

ON ARRIVAL

Registration: Every visitor must register with the police within seven days of arrival and thereafter re-register in each new city. Hotels provide this service automatically. The traveler will have to relinquish the passport, but there is no worry, it will be returned. When staying with friends, one must report to the nearest police station. The procedure will take a few minutes. One may also go to the Mugama'a (see above) in Cairo or Alexandria.

CUSTOMS

The visitor is permitted to enter the country with 200 cigarettes, 250 grammes of tobacco or 50 cigars, one liter of alcohol and personal effects free of tax. Animals must have a veterinary certicate attesting to their good health, and a valid rabies certificate.

Duty Free: Cairo International Airport is one of the few airports that has a duty free shop upon arrival in the country.

ON DEPARTURE

Departure regulations: Egyptian currency is not permitted to be taken out of the country. There is a LE 5.00 **departure tax** at Cairo Airport. When leaving Egypt by road the **departure tax** is LE 10.50.

GETTING ACQUAINTED

The **official name** of Egypt is the Arab Republic of Egypt, (A.R.E.) and the **president**, Hosni Mubarak, is Commander in Chief of the Army and leader of the National Defense Council. The Prime Minister and cabinet are appointed by the President.

The **National Assembly** is composed of representatives from all districts of the country. Fifty percent must be from the working class or farmers. Copts and women are represented according to a quota. The **Shura Council** is an advisory council with 140 elected members and another 70 appointed members.

Economy: The good old days—when there were a tenth as many Egyptian mouths to feed and when private-sector export of long-staple cotton was the mainstay of the economy—can never return. During the past 25 years remittances from individual Egyptians working abroad have clearly emerged as the single most important source of foreign currency and of investment capital, as well as that of personal, private sector income. Major importance, economically and politically, has been attached to aid from more developed countries—the U.S. most significantly, followed by the Soviet Union, Japan, China, the Arab OPEC members, and nearly every country in Europe, including Albania—which provides not only the basic support, but usually also the initiative for most development projects in Egypt. Of some considerable importance are the U.S. dollar receipts of the public-sector Suez Canal Authority, the revenues from sales abroad (usually in U.S. dollars) by Egypt's public-sector armaments and petroleum firms, and the hard-currency income from

foreign tourism, which is earned by firms in both the public and the private sectors.

Tourism is thus a major industry in Egypt. It receives careful nurture, and is due to receive more emphasis as the country leaves further behind its agricultural past.

GEOGRAPHY

Egypt has her feet planted on two continents, the north-eastern corner of Africa and the south-western edge of Asia.

Area: Egypt is approximately 626,000 square miles (1,002,000 square km) in size. Its longest distance north-south is 640 miles (1025 km) and widest distance east-west is about 775 miles (1240 km).

Borders: Egypt's northern border is the Mediterranean Sea and her southern boundary is the Sudan, at latitude 22 degrees north. Israel (in the northern tip), the Gulf of Aqaba and the Red Sea flank her eastern border, while on the west is Libya at longitude 25 degrees west.

DESERTS

The deserts of Egypt comprise over 90 percent of the land surface and are inhabited by less than one percent of the population. They are part of an arid region that stretches from the Atlantic coast in the west to Central Asia in the east.

The **Eastern** or **Arabian Desert** is east of the Nile Valley. Extending to the Red Sea, it is bisected by the Red Sea Mountains. It is approximately 86,101 square miles (223,000 square km), or 21 percent of the land mass of Egypt. The Arabian desert has two distinct areas, the northern Al Ma'aza Plateau, composed primarily of limestone, and the southern Al 'Ababda Plateau. Water is very scarce in these areas.

The **Western** or **Libyan Desert** is much larger than the Arabian Desert, covering 332,434 square miles (681,000 square km) and comprises two thirds of Egypt. Contrary to common belief, it is not a part of the Sahara Desert, but separated from it by highlands. It is composed primarily of Nubian sandstone and limestone. South of the Qattarah depression there is a band of north-south sand dunes, continuing as far south as the Kharga Depression where they become a flat sea of land. The Western Desert is the most arid region of Egypt.

OASES

There are six inhabited depressions in the deserts of Egypt. There is the **Al-Kharga Oasis Depression** which is west of the Nile Valley town of Asyut and joined to it by a roadway. Evidence of tectonic plate movement can be seen in the escarpment walls. North to south the depression is 115 miles (185 km), east to west 9-18 miles (15-30 km). Only one percent of the total area is cultivated. One of the most distinctive features of the Kharga Oasis Depression is the escarpment that one must descend before arriving at the town of Kharga.

Dakhla Oasis Depression is 75 miles (120 km) west of Kharga. Unlike all of the other depressions, 45 percent of its land is cultivatable. Its primary water source is the deep artesian wells saturated Nubian sandstone. This water is from rainfall in Equatorial Africa and is believed to take 500 years to reach the oasis.

Farafrah Oasis Depression is connected to Dakhla by a road that crosses the chalk escarpment at Bab al Qasmand Pass. There is one major village in the depression, **Qasr el Farafrah,** supported by 20 freshwater springs. There is a large area of sand dunes in the eastern and south-eastern section of the depression which extends for some 93 miles (150 km).

Bahariyya Oasis Depression differs from the other depressions in the Western Desert in that it is surrounded by an escarpment. The depression is 26 miles (42 km) long and eight miles (14 km) wide. Dolorite and quartzite rock hills are scattered along the depression floor.

Siwah Oasis Depression has the saltiest water of all oases. Although this water also comes from Equatorial Africa, the water passes through salty strata on its long journey north to Siwah. The entire floor of the depression is below sea level. The area is 680 square miles (1088 square km). The southern part of the depression is covered by a 312-mile (500-km) sea of sand.

Fayyum Oasis Depression. Because it is joined to the Nile by the **Bahr Youssef,** a man-made canal, one does not think of the Fayyum as a depression. Even the soil is composed of Nile silt brought in since the Middle Kingdom when it was first used as a catchment basin for the Nile overflow.

SINAI AND THE RED SEA

Sinai: The Sinai peninsula juts into the Red Sea creating the **Gulf of Aqaba** on the east and the **Gulf of Suez** on the west. It is 38,125 square miles (61,000 square km) in area (6 percent of Egypt) with desert in the north and granite mountains in the south. Its highest mountain peak is **Gabal Katrina** at 8715 feet (2641 meters). The central part of Sinai is the Tih Plateau.

The Red Sea: The Red Sea is 7785 feet (2359 meters) deep, 1207 miles (1932 km) north-south and 191 miles (306 km) east-west. Cutting through the Gulf of Aqaba from the Dead Sea and continuing south through the Red Sea and on into East Africa is the **Great Rift Valley,** the juncture of the African and Arabian Tectonic plates. The Red Sea is highly saline with small tides and exquisite coral shelves and reefs.

LAKES

The Lakes: The two seas that border Egypt in the north and east have left a string of five saltwater lakes across the northern border of Sinai and the Nile delta basin; **Lake Bardawil** in Sinai; **Lake Manzalah,** the largest of the northern lakes; **Lake Burullus,** at the extreme northern border of Egypt; **Lake Idku,** west of Alexandria and **Lake Maryut,** the only lake of the five not directly connected to the sea by a natural channel.

Lake Maryut was once a freshwater lake with agricultural land around its shores. In 1801 the commander of the first British expedition to Egypt cut the dike between it and Lake Abu Kir, a saltwater lake, in order to gain an advantage over the French troops. The British were successful, but the land was destroyed.

There are three saltwater lakes that connect the Suez Canal, the **Great Bitter Lake, Little Bitter Lake** and **Lake Timsah.** Saltwater lakes also exist in Siwah oasis and the Fayyum (**Lake Qarun**). Today, the **High Dam Lake** is the only freshwater lake in

Egypt. Truly a reservoir, it was created by the High Dam at Aswan backing up the Nile waters in the land of Nubia.

TIME ZONES

Egypt is two hours ahead of GMT and six hours ahead of Eastern Standard Time. When it is noon in Cairo it is:

2 a.m.	in San Francisco
5 a.m.	in New York
10 a.m.	in London
10 a.m.	in Paris
11 a.m.	in Rome
3.30 p.m.	in New Delhi
4.30 p.m.	in Bangkok
7 p.m.	in Tokyo
8 p.m.	in Sydney

CLIMATE

The climate is one of Egypt's joys, especially the mild winters. The **Northern Coast** has a Mediterranean climate with an average rainfall of 7 inches (18 cm). This weather continues through the Delta. **Cairo** and **Southern Egypt** are in the Arid Zone, with hardly any rainfall at all. They have chilly desert nights and hot desert days. Of late, the humidity has risen considerably in Cairo and summer nights can be quite uncomfortable.

Average Year Round Temperatures

city	winter	spring	summer	fall
Alexandria	69/51	80/58	86/69	86/62
Cairo	69/51	90/51	96/6	89/57
Luxor	79/42	103/50	107/72	103/54
Aswan	79/49	103/57	108/7	103/51

The Khamsin (Sand-storms) are high winds that arrive from the desert in April and May. They have been known to sandblast the paint off a car. They are uncomfortably hot and blow sand everywhere. Such storms can last for a few hours or can continue for several days. If you are caught in one, go to the nearest shelter. Don't go out to the desert if a Khamsin is brewing.

CULTURE AND CUSTOMS

Etiquette: Egyptians are a friendly and warm people who will go out of their way to please. However, be patient. Things may not always go according to plan. Egyptians also take time to greet each other before they ask a question. It is rude to be abrupt.

Although alcohol is permitted in Egypt, do remember that this is a Muslim country. Drink moderately, and don't drink and drive. The penalties are severe and in Egyptian traffic, one's reflexes must be tip- top.

Warnings: There are several "dos" and "don'ts" which should be observed by all tourists:

* Don't touch, lean against or ship away pieces of the monuments.
* Don't pick up rocks in the desert without checking underneath for snakes or scorpions.
* Don't go barefoot around the coral reefs.
* Don't touch anything in the reefs: it may shock or bite you.
* Pyramid climbing, once a must for every tourist in Egypt, is now strictly forbidden.

Women: Before the famous Egyptian feminist Hoda Shaarawi deliberately removed hers in 1919, the veil—which had no religious significance—was worn in public by all respectable middle-class and upper-class women, Muslim, Jewish, or Christian. By 1935, however, veils were a comparative rarity in Egypt, though they continued to be worn as an item of fashion in neighboring countries like Syria and Jordan for thirty more years and have remained obligatory in the Arabian Peninsula to this day.

Nowadays in Egypt veils are worn only by Bedouin women, who are the inheritors of the urban fashions of a century ago, or by younger middle-class urban women demonstrating either modesty or Muslim piety. Feminine modesty alone—not necessarily identified with any religion—is shown by wearing a covering over the head or even a sort of wimple. The chief reason for the latter, favored by many young professional women, is that it tends to discourage male advances, physical or verbal.

From the 1930s onwards, Egyptian

women began to enter into businesses and professions. Thus by 1965, thanks in part to social changes effected in the course of the July Revolution, Egypt could boast a far higher proportion of women working as doctors, dentists, lawyers, professors, diplomats, or high officials than might have been found in the U.S. or in any European country outside of Scandinavia. Egyptian women still do not have equality with Egyptian men, however, either in law or by custom; and no matter how much they may rule within the bedroom, the kitchen, the shop or even the office, Egyptian public places, including streets, coffeehouses, and popular cinemas, are still fundamentally male preserves.

BUSINESS HOURS

Banks usually open from 8.30 a.m. to 1.30 p.m. daily except Friday and Sunday. Most hotels also exchange money..

Commercial offices in general operate from 8 a.m. to 2 p.m., daily in winter and 9 a.m. to 1 p.m. and 5 p.m. to 7 p.m. in summer. They close Thursday afternoon and Friday.

Government offices function from 8 a.m. to 2 p.m. except Friday (maybe Saturday) and holidays.

Stores are open for business from 9 a.m. to 1 p.m. and 5 p.m. to 7 p.m. in summer. 10 a.m. to 5 p.m. in winter. Closed on Sunday.

CALENDARS

Calendars: Four calendars, used for different purposes, are used in Egypt. The **Western** (solar, Gregorian) calendar, with years designated as B.C. and A.D. and months bearing the usual Roman names, is commonly employed for all practical purposes, though many people refer to the months by number rather than by name.

The **Islamic** (lunar) calendar designates dates according to their distance in lunar years from the Hijrah (A.H.), the Prophet's withdrawal with his followers to Medina from Mecca in A.D. 622. Used for official governmental and religious purposes, it regulates the Muslim religious year, which consists of 12 lunar months of 29 or 30 days and is thus 11 days less than the solar year. In relation to the Western/Gregorian solar calendar, the Muslim calendar therefore moves forward 11 days each year, completing a full cycle (and thus "losing" a solar year) every 33 years.

The **Coptic ecclesiastical** calendar (solar, Julian), indicates dates according to the solar year in an Era of Martyrs that is reckoned as beginning 29 August/11 September A.D. 284. Used to regulate the religious year of the Coptic Orthodox Church, it is an adaptation of the pagan calendar of Roman Egypt and consists of twelve months of thirty days each, which bear their ancient names almost unaltered and an intercalary period of five days. The **Coptic agricultural** calendar, a popular version of the latter, is often used as a kind of almanac for planning agricultural activities and predicting seasonal changes in the weather.

Holidays therefore are national, Coptic or Islamic. The following is a listing.

HOLIDAYS

NATIONAL

* Union Day
February 23
* Liberation of Sinai Day
April 25
* Labor Day
May 1
* Anniversary of the 1952 Revolution
July 23
* Armed Forces Day
October 6
* Suez Day
October 24
* Victory Day
December 23

Sham il Nassim ("Sniff the Breeze"), the Monday after Orthodox Easter, is a holiday for all Egyptians, Muslim and Christian, and dates back to Pharaonic times. The entire population goes to the counttryside or to some urban green spaces for a day-long outing the picnic basket filled with hard-boiled eggs and pickled fish.

FESTIVALS

COPTIC

Coptic New Year
September 11
Christmas
January 7
Epiphany
January 19
Annunciation
March 21
Easter
Pentecost
Feast of the Apostles Peter and Paul
July 12
Feast of the Assumption
August 22

ISLAMIC

Islamic New Year's Day. The first day of the month of Moharram, which marks the the beginning of a new year in the Muslim calendar.

Ashurah. 10 Moharram, the lunar anniversary of the martyrdom of Sayidna Hussein, the Prophet's grandson, which is a day of special significance to Muslims of the Shi'i sect though they are a minority in Egypt.

Mulid en Nabi. The Prophet's Birthday, 12 Rabi' al Awal. Its eve is marked by a parade of Sufi orders (see page 151).

Laylat al Esraa wa al Mi'rag. 27 Ragab. Commemorates the Prophet's miraculous journey to Jerusalem.

Laylat al Qadr. 26 Ramadan. Occurring near the end of **Ramadan**, the month of fasting, during which business hours are curtailed, while the hours of darkness are spent in social activities. This night commemorates the revelation of the very first verse of the Qur'an.

'Id al Fitr (Ramadan Bairam). 1-3 Shawwal. Marking the end of the Ramadan fast, this feast is celebrated for the first three days of the following lunar month.

'Id al Adha (Qurban Bairam). 10-14 Dhu''l-Higga. Commemorating Abraham's willingness to obey the divine call to sacrifice his only son and heir, this feast traditionally begins with prayers and the slaughter of a sheep.

COMMUNICATIONS

MEDIA

Communications have greatly improved in Egypt over the past 10 years.

Radio: Egyptian broadcasting began in 1934. Egypt has both AM and FM radio stations. The European station of **Radio Cairo** is at **FM95** on the dial from 7 a.m. to midnight.

0730	News in English
0800	News in French
1400	News in French
1430	News in English
1500	News in Greek
1600	News in Armenian
1800	News in German
1900	News in French
2000	News in English
2100	News in French

From 8.30 a.m. to 8 p.m. the FM95 programs primarily consist of classical music.

TELEVISION

The Egyptians love soap operas. There are always three or four mini-soaps running in Arabic. There are also movies made for television. Children's programs run in the afternoon from 4-6 p.m. Educational programs run from 6 p.m. to 7.30 p.m. Commercials are run between programs in special segments. **Channel 1** is on the air from 1.30 p.m. to midnight and is primarily in Arabic. The dial number is 5. **Channel 2,** on the air from 2 p.m. to midnight, carries many foreign programs. News in French is at 7 p.m., English at 8 p.m. and usually followed by a foreign serial. There is usually a foreign film around 10 p.m. The dial number is 9. Also, dial 3 for **Channel 3** which is a new station that broadcasts in the early evening.

POSTAL SERVICES

Mail is reliable and fast, The **Central Post Office** in Cairo is at Attaba Square and is open from 8 a.m. to 7 p.m. daily, except Friday. There are post offices in every section of Cairo. In Alexandria, the **Central Post Office** is at Kom el-Dikka (next to the train station).

Postage: for internal mail: 3 piasters, **Middle East:** 6 piasters, and **other:** 30 piasters. **Express mail:** The Egyptian government runs the **Express Mail Center** in Attaba Square. It takes longer than the overnight mail service but it is reliable.

Parcels: All parcels entering the country from abroad are subject to customs regulations which are often more of a bother than they are worth. If you purchase something that must be mailed out of the country, allow the shopkeeper to handle it for you. Be sure to get a receipt. For airmail allow several weeks; for surface mail allow six months.

COURIERS

DHL, 20 Gamal el Din Abul Mohassin. Garden City, Tel: 355-7301/ 355-7118/354-6710.

Federal Express, 1079 Cornicheal Nil, Tel: 354-5465.

IML Air Couriers, 2 Mostapha Kamel, Maadi, Tel: 350-1160/350-1240/350-1241.

Middle East Courier Service, 1 Mahmoud Hafez, Heliopolis, tel: 45-9281.

SOS Sky International, 45 Shehah St., Mohandessin, Tel: 3460028/346-2503.

TELEPHONE AND TELEX

Telephones can be found in all hotels, railroad stations, airports and public buildings. Overseas calls may be made from any telephone exchange. There are no collect calls in Egypt

Telephone systems have been re-designed and are efficient, and special services have been intoduced all over the country. The telephone system is undergoing a major restructuring. A seven digit number is a new number. If a six digit number clicks off during dialing add a prefix of **2 in Cairo**, and a prefix of **3 in Heliopolis**.

The Alexandria phone system is also in the midst of being restructured, so note the prefixes which have to be added to the old numbers. If the number begins with a 7, prefix with a 59 and :

6	58
2	49
3	49
84	587

Telex and Telefax: Telexes may be sent from hotels, business centers, and government centers. Telefax facilities are available in hotels and some post offices.

Telegraph: Internal and overseas telegrams and cables may be sent from any major hotel.

Government Telephone Telex, Telefax and Telegraph Centers:

Main Office, Cairo Main Railway Station.

Tahrir Office, Tahrir Square.

Zamalek Office, 25th of July St., corner of Mansour Mohamed Street.,

Maadi Office, Maadi Central, Road 9.

EMERGENCIES

SECURITY & CRIME

For either a foreigner or a local, male or female, by day or by night and in any district, Cairo is safer than any large Western city, partly becauseit is thoroughly and effectively policed and partly because the Cairene ethical standard is very high. Tourists generally bring back tales of lost valuables returned not of crime, though carelessness with personal possession is not recommended. Nor is carelessness in wandering about anywhere alone: some parts of Upper Egypt are known for vendetta or sectarian violence, while in others, most notoriously the West Bank at Luxor, it is not advisable for any women or even a pair of women to travel unaccompanied by an able-bodied male companion.

MEDICAL SERVICES

It is useful for visitors to take note of the hospitals in the cities as they can come in handy in event of an emergency.

ALEXANDRIA

Al-Moassat Hospital, Tel: 5972888.
Coptic Hospital, 4 el Maamoun Moharram Bey, Tel: 4921404.
Victoria Hospital, 18 Philip Galad St., Midan Isfaar, Tel: 5868590.

CAIRO

Al Salam Hospital, 3 Syria St., Mohandessin, Tel: 3407561.

Anglo American Hospital, Zumalek, Tel: 3418631.
Arab Contractors Medical Center, El Gebel Akhdar, Nasr City, Tel: 832534.
Al Salam International Hospital, Cornicle el Nil Maadi, Tel: 3638050/3634194/3638424.
Cairo Medical Center, Roxy Square, Heliopolis, Tel: 680237.
Nile Badraw Hospital, Cornicke el Nil, Maadi, Tel: 3638688/ 3638167/8).

Pharmacies are usually open from 10 a.m. - 10 p.m. and will sell many drugs over the counter that require a prescription in the United States. All pharmacists speak some English. Some 24-hour pharmacies are :

ALEXANDRIA

Downtown, 42 Saad Zaghloul, Tel: 805154.

CAIRO

Attaba, Attaba Square, Tel: 910831.
Isaaf, tel: 743369.
Essam, 101 Road 9 Maad, Tel: 3504126.

GETTING AROUND

FROM THE AIRPORT

Taxis, (black and white) are available, but you must bargain. Fix the price before you leave the airport. There is a **limousine service** called Limo Misr which has a fleet of blue Mercedes. Fixed fares are available. Ask to see their rates. Approximate fares are:
From airport to:

Heliopolis	L.E. 6.00
Downtown	6.00
Giza	12.00
Pyramids	12.00
Maadi	12.00
Digla	12.00

Airport buses: Special buses to the city center leave every 20 minutes stopping at the Nile Hilton, Ramses Hilton and Meridien hotels. (LE 2.50). **Public bus** (red and white) number **400** will also take you into town.

Upon exiting the airport your taxi number, name and destination will be recorded by the police for security purposes.

PUBLIC TRANSPORT

Trains are another good bargain in Egypt. They are inexpensive, leave on time and link Cairo with the Nile valley, delta and canal cities. With recent rail improvements, the train to Alexandria has cut an hour off its traveling time. Reservations should be made in advance and can be booked through a travel agent, or by going to the station a day or so before. There are four types of services: First Class, Second Class, Third Class and Wagon.

Stations
Alexandria: Sidi Gaber Station. Mehatta Misr. (main station)
Cairo: Ramses Station, Ramses Square.
Luxor: Maydan al-Mahattah.
Aswan: Maydan al-Mahattah.

The sleeper to Luxor and Aswan is the most luxurious train system in Egypt. A one-way single is approximately 70 dollars and a double is about 40 dollars per person. The train stations have special windows for each type of ticket and lines are segregated: women in one, men in the other. They alternate moving toward the teller. Be sure your car, seat number and date of departure are written on your ticket.

Fares from Cairo

	First Class	Second Class
Alexandria	LE 5.00	LE2.50
Luxor	LE13.00	LE6.50
Aswan	LE14.00	LE7.00
Suez		LE1.75
Ismailia		LE2.50
Port Said		LE3.50

Schedules

	Alexandria	Cairo
Train.	DEP	ARR
905	0750 hrs	1025 hrs
901	0810	1115
907	0920	1200
911	1030	1320
913	1130	1420
917	1410	1640.
795	1530	1815.
923	1710.	2000.
925	1825	2100.
936	1925	2250

	Cairo	Alexandria
	DEP	ARR
905	0800	1030
901	0855	1105
907	0930	1210
911	1120	1400
913	1130	1420
917	1400	1630
795	1545	1835
923	1750	2130
925	1900	2140
936	2000	2255

Cairo	Luxor	Aswan
DEP	ARR	ARR
1945 hrs	0605 hrs	1000 hrs
2120	0830	1445
Aswan	**Luxor**	**Cairo**
1425	1930	0650
1740	1020	2150

THE METRO

Updated and extended between 1983 and 1987 with development aid from the French, Cairo Metro system resembles the Paris Metro. A rapid transit rail line running parallel to the Corniche for most of its length, it currently links the main railway station at Rameses Square with Matariyyah and Marg, to the northeast, and the former resort town of Helwan, to the south. There are stops at intervals of about half a kilometer or so along the way. (Note: Contrary to what is shown on some new maps, the transverse connecting lines over the Nile to Imbabah and Gizah have not yet been built. Other new maps continue to show the line as it was between 1900 and 1985, before the radical new improvements, when it terminated at a station in Bab al Luq, behind the American University.

On the new underground portion running through the center of the city, clean and attractive stops are named after nationalist leaders. Rameses Station stop is thus called *Murbarak* and the stations southwards from it, in order, are: Shari Galaa *(Urabi)*, Maydan Tawfiqqiyyah *(Nasser)*, **Maydan at-Tahrir** *(Sadat)* and the People's Assembly *(Saad Zaghlul)*. Further stops likely to be useful are: Munira *(Sayeda Zaynab)*, Shari Salah Salem *(Malik as-Saleh)*, **Old Cario** *(Mar Girgis)*, Dar as-Salam, Zohraa, Hedayeq al-Maadi, **Maadi,** and Thakanat al Maadi (note that there are three stops in Maadi).

Entrances at Metro stations are indicated by prominent signs consisting of a red M on a black octagonal background and these signs are placed where they will be most visible. At Mayadan at-Tahrir, for example, where there are ten entrances, each is marked. Fares are either 25, 40 or 50 piastres, depending on the destination. In every station, except Dar as-Salam the trains are boarded from the left.

TAXIS

It may be doubted that Egyptian drivers are the world's worst, but they are certainly lethally dangerous, which means that to survive on the road as a professional, a driver must be very alert and adroit indeed. Most Egyptian taxi-drivers are skilled, though they range from the courtly and sedate to the abusive and hair-raising, while their vehicles may be elegant and well-maintained, dirty and nearly moribund, or anything in between.

A conscientious traveler owes it to himself, in any case, to try one or two, just as he would an item of local cuisine.

Two kinds of cars are used for taxis: small cars of any make, usually with identifying lights on the roofs which are painted black and white in Cairo and black and orange in Alexandria; and bigger ones, usually Peugeot 504 "breaks" (stationwagons), which are painted in standard factory colors. The former are metered, the latter are not, but both kinds are "official," carrying distinctively license plates and are marked with logos on the front doors. Unmarked and unmetered private cars are also occasionally used as taxis, and there is at least one so-called "limousine" service, which does not use limousines, but black Mercedes sedans.

Meters may represent suggested "official" fares but they are ignored by everyone since it is recognized that such fares are unrealistically low. Passengers in metered taxis must therefore either know what the going rate is, take a guess at it, or bargain. Standard daylight fares in early 1989, for example, from Maydan at-Tahrir to a few common destinations were as follows: Zamalek or Ramses Square: LE 1-1.50; Maadi: LE 4-5; Heliopolis: LE 3-4; Cairo Airport: LE 10-15.

In an unmetered taxi *(servis)* standard fares do not pertain unless it is on a regular run to your dsetination with a car full of passengers, in which case any of the other passengers will tell you what the fare is (probably less than a pound). If not, you will have to bargain.

Bargaining is required for all taxis, metered or otherwise. This particularly necessary when using the cab after midnight, as the fares asked may go up by at least 50 percent over daylight norms.

BUSES

Egypt has a network of buses that travel all over the country. It is a good way to see the landscape, mingle with the people and be kind to the pocket.

In Cairo, public buses (red or blue and white) are very crowded and often an unpleasant experience, but there are a few routes for the adventurous tourist:
no. 400—from the airport to downtown.
no. 66— from the Nile Hilton to the Khan il Khalili.
no. 72— from the Nile Hilton to the Citadel.
no. 800 and 900—from Mugamma (Tahrir Square) to the Pyramids.

A new bus service has been recently started, It leaves from various destinations in the city and guarantees each person a seat. It's size is between the large buses and the small Toyoto vans which are also used as transport.

To Alexandria By Bus: Operated by the West Delta Bus Company, Midan Tahrir, Tel: 759751 as well as the Federal Arab Land Transport Company, in Tahrir Square next to Hilton Hotel, Tel: 772663. First class (air-conditioned) bus tickets cost about LE4.00 and LE6.00 respectively. Buses leave from Tahrir and take the desert route (three and a half hours) to Saad Zaghloul Square in Alexandria.

From Alexandria By Bus: There is a direct service to Cairo International Airport. Ramleh Bus Terminal (near Cecil Hotel). Advance booking is required. In Alexandria, there are also trams travelling east from Ramleh Station:
Tramway 1: Bacos line, Ramleh Station to Sidi Bishr.
Tramway 2: El Nasr Line. Ramleh Station to Sidi Bishr.
Tramway 3: From Ramleh Station to Sidi Gaber al-Sheikh.
Tramway 4: Sidi Gaber al-Mahata, Ramleh to Sidi Gaber.
Tramway 5: To San Stephano via Bacos.
Tramway 6: To Sidi Bishi via Glym.

COACH TOURS

These are possible to all sites in the Nile valley. Consult a local travel agent.

To Upper Egypt and the Oases: The Upper Egypt Bus Company, from Midan Ahmad Hilmi (north of Ramses Station), Tel: 746658. Operates daily services to Beni Suef, Minya, Asyut, Sohag, Qena, Luxor and Aswan. At Asyut change for Kharga and Dakhla Oases.

To the Suez Canal: From Midan el Ulali (front of Ramese Station) to Ismailia, Suez and Port Said.

To the Red Sea: From Midan Ahmad Hilmi. Two buses ply daily, one at 7.30 a.m. and another at 8 a.m. The trip takes eight hours and tickets cost LE8.00.

To Sinai: From Tahrir Square, the East Delta Bus Company, Sinai Terminal, Abbasiyya Square. operates two buses daily to St. Catherine's, Nuweiba and Taba. 7.30 a.m. (air-conditioned) LE8.00 and 10.30 a.m. (not air-conditioned) LE6.50. Four buses daily to Sharm al Shaykh, 7 a.m. and 10 a.m. LE7.00; 1 p.m. (air-conditioned), LE9.00; and a super express night bus, leaving at midnight. LE12.00.

To the Oases: Siwah: Daily bus to Alexandria, change buses there to Mersa Metruh, and change again to Siwah. A **permit** is needed to visit Siwah. You can get one in Mersa Metruh at the Security Police and Military Police.

Bahriyyya: A daily bus operates from station on Shori' Port Said near Shori' Al Azhar, Cairo.

Kharga and Dakhla: Daily bus service from Asyut leaving from railway station.

PRIVATE TRANSPORT

Driving a car in Egypt allows you a great deal of freedom. There are few road restrictions and the country is yours to explore. Traffic is congested in the cities, especially Cairo, but the authorities have been hard at work to alleviate the problem. The government has erected dozens of flyovers across busy intersections, limited heavy vehicle traffic to late night hours and opened a new ring road to prevent north-south traffic from passing through the center of the city. Despite all of these measures, heavy traffic still remains a problem in Cairo. However, outside the highly populated areas of the Nile valley, the serenity of Egypt awaits you. The open roads have little traffic, the air is clear, and the only sounds are the wind and your motor. You can loop the four oases of the western desert (six days), drive to the beaches of Sinai (a day or a week), or take off for the Fayoum (an hour from Cairo).

Highways: The arteries that link Egypt's major cities have been greatly improved in the past few years. Roads from Cairo to Alexandria, Port Said, Ismailia and Suez are all four-lane. Most desert roads linking major points are now paved. The roads to Upper Egypt and to Hurghada are still very dangerous, especially at night. Be alert and watch for stalled cars parked on the road without lights.

CAR RENTAL

One must have an **International Drivers License** and be at least **25 years old** to rent a car in Egypt. Rental agents are at all major hotels. Car rental companies are:

Avis, 16 Ma'amal el Sukar St., Garden City, Cairo,Tel: 740777.

Cecil Hotel, Alexandria.

Hertz, 15 Nabatat St., Garden City, Cairo, Tel: 814172.

Bita, 15 Mahmoud Bassiouni St., Cairo, Tel: 746169.

Budget, 5 el Marqrizi St.,Zamalek, Cairo, Tel: 409474. 59 El Geish St., Alexandria.

If you don't want to drive, you can rent a car with a driver:.

Misr Limousine, in Cairo, Tel: 2599813/ 2599814.

Alexandria Limousine, 25 Sharia Talaat Harb, Tel: 806502.

MOTORING TIPS

In the city, flow with the traffic. If you're too slow cars will weave around you from both sides.There is no right of way. The first person at an intersection goes through it. If you wait, you only puzzle the other drivers. You have to be aggressive. The speed limit for cars is 56 miles (90 km) per hour.

Accidents: If you hit a pedestrian or domestic animal, other than a dog or cat, do not stop. Drive to the nearest police station to report the incident. For your own safety, do not attempt to linger around to help.

Parking is bumper to bumper and there is usually an attendant who will watch your car. Keep the brake off when you park so that he can move it. Tipping is 10 - 15 piasters.

Checkpoints exist on many roads in Egypt. Slow down and continue through unless the officers indicate you should stop. You will be asked for your passport or your license and car registration. This is a formality. Be polite and patient.

Bridges across the Nile exist at Helwan, Beni Suef, Asyut, Nag Hammada, Qena and Edfu. There is a new and long awaited car ferry at Luxor, which means that travelers can now explore the west bank in their own vehicles. Pedestrian ferries exist in all cities and towns. Just ask.

Gasoline is very inexpensive and is sold by the liter. It has a low octane rating. Gas stations are well marked and easily found on main roads. Two identifying signs are a triple pyramid or the famous Mobil oval in red, white and blue (Mobil is written in Arabic). If the only gas station is miles away and you're out of gas, do not despair. There is a good chance a villager has a jerry can or two squirreled away. You may have to pay a bit more, but he deserves something for his business foresight.

Repairs are inexpensive compared with the American and European rates. Gasoline stations do not necessarily repair cars or sell tires, however, even on-the-street mechanics can often get a car moving. The mechanics of Egypt even keep 1930s cars on the roads by making their own spares.

DESERT TRAVEL

Use common sense. Bring a compass. Check your car. Be sure to have a good spare tire. Drive on loose sand as you would on snow. If your wheels get stuck in soft sand, put a rug under the back tires and move out slowly. If you spin your tires, you will sink deeper into the sand. If your car breaks down along the road, don't abandon your vehicle; even in remore areas another vehicle will pass by. If you break down on a desert track (you should never leave the main road for long distances with only one vehicle), hike to the nearest road and wait. Bring water and shade with you. On all desert travels, have ample food, water and sunglasses. Cover the head and the back of the neck.

Top your gas tank at every gas station as

the next station may be hundreds of miles away. If your gas tank is small, carry a jerry can on long hauls like Dakhla to Farafrah (390 km, 243 miles). Dehydration can sneak up on you in desert travel. Cover your head and the nape of your neck. Carry plenty of water and salt tablets. In an emergency one teaspoon of salt and two tablespoon of sugar in a cup of water will revive you.

Desert driving is very monotonous. Remember you are still on a highway. When you wish to pass, sound your horn. One of the most annoying habits of Egyptian drivers is over-using the horn. There is no escaping it, they even do it when no one is around. Just ignore it. Another is blinking the high beam at night. When a car is approaching he will blink and blink, blinding you. Blink back and he may stop. He may be checking to see if you are awake.

WHERE TO STAY

HOTELS

Hotels in Egypt are officially classified as belonging to one of six categories, which have more to do with prices, set by the government, than with accommodation. They range from "five-star" (i.e., expensive) to "unclassified" (i.e., very cheap). Prices also vary from place to place and according to the nature of the booking: they are much higher for individuals than for groups. Charges to cover several taxes will appear, as small percentages of the price, on your final bill. In the lists below hotels ranked as **five-star** and **four-star** are designated with a **"1"** or a **"2,"** respectively, while "3" covers less expensive hotels belonging to several official categories, many of them well known to specialists or seasoned travellers and quite commendable. Note, however, the variations in standards from place to place. In 1988 the role of the government in operating hotels was reduced and the management of many was handed over to private firms, nearly all of them large international organizations with solid financing and decades of experience in creating customer satisfaction. New training programs were introduced and employment practices were made more in line with international standards, which are centered upon service. Outside of major cities and resort areas, where there are no real hotels, government guest houses may frequently be found.

ALEXANDRIA

3 Amon. 32 Sh. Al Nasr, Manshiyyah. Tel: 80713/ 807126.
2 Cecil Hotel. 16 Maydan Saad Zaghlul, Tel: 480-7055/480-7758.

3 Delta. 14 Champollion, Mazarita, Tel: 482-5542/482-9053.

3 Desert Home. Umar Mukhtar, King Kmariut, Tel: 484-4434/494-3572.

3 El Haram. 162 Al Gaysh, Cleopatra, Tel: 953-984/9633-974.

3 El Mehrek. 173 Al Gaysh, Sporting. Tel: 960-737.

2 Landmark. 10 Abdel Salam Aref. San Stefano.Tel: 587-7850/ 586-7850.

2 Maamura Palace Plaza. 394 Al Gaysh, Zizinia. Tel: 86-2723/ 587-5399.

3 Makka. 88 Al Gaysh, Camp César, Tel: 597-3923/597-3935.

3 Metropole. 52 Saad Zaghlul, Ramleh, Tel: 482-1467/4821466.

1 Montazah Sheraton. Corniche, Montazah. Tel: 969-220/968-550.

1 Palestine Hotel. Montazah Palace Grounds. Tel: 861-799/958-554.

3 Plaza Hotel. 394 Al Gaysh, Zizinia. Tel: 586-2723/587-5399.

1 Ramada Renaissance. 544 Al Gaysh. Tel: 866-111/866-112.

2 Salamlek. Montazah Palace. Tel: 860-585.

2 Vauizia. 21 Maydan Al Nasr, Manshiyyah. Tel: 802-698/802-322.

2 Windsor. 17 Al Shuhada, Ramleh. Tel: 808-700/808-123.

Sidi Abdel Rahman

2 Hotel El Alamein. Tel: 492-1228/29/30. Tlx 55372 ALMTLUN

CAIRO

3 Ambassador. 31 26th July Zamalek. Tel: 75-3342/74-3354.

3 Atlas. 2 Mohamed Roushdy St., Opera Square. Restaurant: Seven Stars. Tel: 91-8311.

2 Atlas Zamalek. 20 Gamiet El Dewal El Arabia Mohadessin. Tel: 346-4175/346-5782/346-6569.

3 Balmoral. 157 26th July Zamalek. Tel: 340-0543.

2 Baron Metropole. Off Oruba St., Heliopolis. Restaurant: The Terrace. Tel: 66-8701/291-5757/291-2467.

2 Belair. Mokkatam Hills. Restaurant: Mashrabeya. Tel: 91-0000/91-6177/91-6375.

3 Cairo Inn. 26 Syria St., Mohandessin. Restaurant: Spanish. Tel: 70-1258/349-0661/349-0662.

3 Capais Palace. 117 Ramses St., Cairo. Tel: 75-4219/75-4188/75-4029.

3 Carlton. 21 26th July Cairo. Restaurant: Kamar (the Moon). Tel: 75-5232/75-5022/75-5181.

3 Cleopatra. 2 Bustan St., Tahrir Square. Restaurant: Palisiar. Tel: 75-9798/75-9712/75-9900.

2 Club Mediterranee (Sales & Reservations). Manial Palace Roda Island. Tel: 348-5594/349-2094/349-2093.

1 Concorde Airport. Tel: 664-242.

3 Concorde. 146 Tahrir St., Dokki. Tel: 70-8751/71-0768/71-7261.

3 Dreamers. 5 Gahd St., & Gamaa Arabia St., Dokki. Tel: 70-9540/70-9526.

3 Egyptel. 93 El Merghani St., Heliopolis. Tel: 66-2258/66-2304.

3 El Borg. El Gezira at Tahrir Bridge Gezira. Tel: 341-6827/340-9978.

3 El Hussein. Hussein Sq. & Al Azhar Khan El Khalili. Tel: 91-8089/91-8479/91-8664.

3 El Nil. 16 Ahmed Ragab St., Garden City. Restaurant: Abdul Zara. Tel: 354-2800.

1 El Salam Hyatt. 61 Abdel Hamid Badawi St., Heliopolis. Restaurant: El Cafe Jardin.Tel: 245-2155/245-5155.

1 Flameco. 2 Sh al Gazirat al Wasta Zamalek. Tel 340-0815/16/18. Tlx 22025 FLAMN UN.

3 Garden City House. 23 Kamel El Din Salah St., Garden City. Tel: 354-8126/354-4969.

3 General. 28 Shagaret El Dorr St., Zamalek. Tel: 340-3490.

3 Grand. 17 26th July St., Cairo. Restaurant: Valley of Kings. Tel: 75-7700/75-7509.

2 Green Pyramids. Helmiat Alahram St., Off Pyramid Rd. Restaurant: Bodega Coffee Shop. Tel: 85-6778/85-6887/85-2600.

3 Green Valley. 33 Abdel Khalek Sarwat St., Cairo. Tel: 75-6317.

3 Heliopark. 100 El Hegaz St., Heliopolis. Tel: 245-1346/244-4617.

3 Horris. 5 26th July St., Cairo. Tel: 91-0478.

3 Indiana. 16 El Saray St., Dokki. Restaurant: El Saray. Tel: 71-4222/71-4503.

1 Intercontinental Semiramis Cairo (3 Restaurants). Corniche El Nil Cairo. R's: The Grill, The Brasserie, Night & Day. Tel: 355-7171.

3 International. 3 Abdel Aazim Rashad St., Dokki. Tel: 71-0243/71-2159.

3 Kanzy. 9 Abu Bakr El Sedik St., Mohandessin. Restaurant: Nona Coffee Shop. Tel: 70-9461/70-9443.

3 Khan Khalili. 7 Bousta St., Attaba Square. Tel: 90-0271.

3 La Liberté. 14 Al Horia St., Heliopolis. Tel: 66-3472/66-7496.

3 Longchamp. 21 Ismail Mohamed St., 5th Fl. Zamalek. Restaurant: The Horus. Tel: 340-2311/340-3977.

3 Lotus. 12 Talaat Harb St., Cairo. Tel: 75-0966/75-0627.

2 Maadi. 53 Misr Helwan Rd. Maadi. Restaurant: Pauvilion. Tel: 350-5050/350-6555/350-6334.

3 Maadi Residence. 11 Rd. 18 Maadi. Restaurant: Palma. Tel: 351-0825.

2 Manial Palace (Club Mediterranee). 1 Roda St., Manial. Tel: 84-6014/84-4083/84-4524. Tlx: 92353 MSA UN.

1 Marriott. Saray El Geizira St., Zamalek. R's: Omar's Cafe, Geira Grill, Roy Rogers. Tel: 340-8888. Tlx: 93464/65 MAR UN.

1 Mena House Oberai. Pyramids Road Giza. R's: Rubayyat, Mogul Room, 3 Coffee Shops. Tel: 85-5444/7999.

1 Meridien. Corniche El Nil Garden City. Restaurant: Champollion. Tel: 84-5444.

1 Meridien Heliopolis (Restaurant: Marco Polo) El Oruoba St., Heliopolis. Restaurant: Marco Polo. Tel: 290-1819/290-5055.

1 Movenpick Heliopolis Hotel. Airport. Tel: 66-4083/66-4977/67-9799.

3 New. 21 Adly St., Cairo. Tel: 74-7124.

3 New Horus House. 21 Ismail Mohamed St., 4th Fl., Zamalek. Tel: 340-3977/340-3182.

3 Nile Garden. 131 Abdel Aziz Saoud St., Manial. Tel: 98-5767/98-3931.

1 Nile Hilton. Tahrir Square. Restaurant: Nile Rotisserie. Tel: 75-0666/74-0777/77-6771. Tlx: 92222.

Nile Zamalek Hotel. 9 Sarat El Ghezira St., Kasr El Nil. Restaurant: The Queen. Tel: 340-0220.

3 Noran. 13 Mohamad Khalaf St., Dokki. Tel: 70-7086/70-9696.

2 Novotel. Cairo International Airport Rd. Tel: 66-1330/67-2916/67-9080.

3 Odeon Palace. 6 Abdel Hamid Said St. Tel: 77-6637/76-9080.

3 Pearl. Corner of Rds 7 & 82 Maadi. Tel: 350-5385/350-5313/350-4153.

3 Pension Suisse. 26 Mahmoud Bassiouni St., Cairo. Tel: 75-9191/74-6639.

3 Pharaohs. 12 Lotfi Hassouna St., Dokki. Tel: 71-2233/2314/0281/7807.

2 Radisson Oasis. Alexandria Desert Rd. Pyramids Giza. Restaurant: Palm Garden. Tel: 5-6916/86-6350.

3 Raja, Mohi bl Dinalre Elezz St., Dokki. Tel: 70-0096.

1 Ramada Renaissance Cairo-Pyramids. Cairo-Alex Desert Rd 3 km Pyramids. French Restaurant, Sultan Coffee Shop. P.O. Box 70. Tel: 53-8111/53-8996/53-8944. Tlx: 93595 RAMPP UN.

1 Ramses Hilton. 1115 Corniche El Nil Cairo. R's: The Grill, Terrace Café. Tel: 74-4400/75-8000/77-7444.

3 Rahab. Fawakeh St., Mohandessin. Restaurant: Marhaba. Tel: 70-7664/70-3112/70-3559.

3 Safa Inn. Madinet Nasr Abbas El Akad St. Tel: 60-4326/60-6917.

1 Safir Hotel Cairo. Midan El Misaha Dokki. Restaurant: Gazirat al Dahab. tel: 48-2828/348-2424. Tlx: 20350 SAFIR UN.

3 Salma. 12 Mohamed Kamel Morsi St., Mohandessin. Restaurant: Jackson. Tel: 70-1482/70-6232/70-0901.

3 Sand. 103 Pyramids St., Giza. Tel: 85-6549/85-0113/85-5479.

2 Shepheard's. Corniche El Nil Garden City. Restaurant: El Caravan. Tel: 355-3800/1/2/3/355-3829.

1 Sheraton Cairo. Galaa Square Giza. R's: La Mama, Coffee Shop. Tel: 348-8600/348-8700. Tlx: 22382 SHERSA UN.

1 Sheraton Gezira. El Gezirah Zamalek. R's: El Kabadry, El Paradis. Tel: 341-1333/341-1336/341-1555. Tlx: 20179 GEZEL UN.

1 Sheraton Heliopolis. Orouba St. Heliopolis. R's: Zahira, Vienna, Der Stuba, Alfredo, K. Tut. Tel: 66-7700/66-5500. Tlx: 20179 GEZEL UN.

Sheraton Hotels - Central Reservations. Tel: 348-8215/348-7422/348-7311.

1 Siag Pyramids Penta. 59 Sakkara Rd. Tel: 85-6022/85-7399.

1 Sonesta. 4 El Tayaran St., Nasr City. Restaurants: Rib Room, La Gondola. Tel: 80-9444.

3 Sphinx. 8 Magles El Omma St. Tel: 354-8258/355-1641.

3 Spring. 5 Wagler St., Rd. El Faraq Corniche El Nil. Tel: 94-4776.

3 Sweet. 28 Rd 13 Maadi. Tel 350-0573/350-4544.

3 Tulip. 3 Midan Talaat Harb Cairo. Tel: 76-2704/75-8433.

5 Vendome. 287 Pyramid St., Giza. Tel: 85-0977.

3 Victoria. 66 El Gomhouria St., Cairo. Tel: 91-8869/91-8966.

3 Windsor. 19 Alfi Bey St., Cairo. Tel: 91-5277/91-5810.

LUXOR

2 Akhenaton Village. Khalid ibn Walid. Tel: 777-575.

2 Etap Luxor. Corniche al Nil. Tel: 82-160/82-011.

1 Isis Hotel. Khalid ibn al Walid. Tel: 82-7750/63-366.

2 Luxor Hotel. Opposite the Luxor Temple. Tel: 82-400/82-405.

1 Luxor Sheraton. Corniche Al Nil, Awamiyyah. Tel: 84-472/84-463.

1 Mövenpick Jolie Ville. Crocodile Island. Tel: 3400/3600.

1 New Winter Palace. Corniche al Nil. Tel: 755-216/774-116.

2 Winter Palace. Corniche al Nil. Tel: 82-222/82-000.

ASWAN

2 Amoun Hotel. Amoun Island. Tel: 322-555/322-816.

1 Aswan Oberoi. Elephantine Island. Tel: 323-455/752-835.

2 Isis Hotel. Corniche al Nil. Tel: 324-0905/324-744.

2 Kalabsha Hotel. Abtal al Tahrir. Tel: 322-999/322-666.

1 PLM Azur New Cataract. Abtal al Tahrir. Tel: 323-343/323-222.

1 Pullman Cataract (Old Cataract). Tel: 323-455/23-222.

1 Tut Amoun Village. Sahara City. Tel: 322-555/322-816.

HURGHADA (GHARDAQA)

3 El Ghardaqa. Tel: 40-393.

3 Giftun Holiday Village. Tel:40-665/40-666.

3 Gizira Hotel. Tel: 41-708.

3 Gobal Hotel. Tel: 40-623.

2 Megawish. Tel: 40-253/40-759.

3 Shedwan Tourist Village. Tel: 40-041.

2 Sheraton Hurghada. Cairo. Tel: 987-200/988-607/40-785.

SINAI

3 Dahab Holiday Village. Dahab, Cairo. Tel: 770-220/770-301.

3 El Salem Hotel. St. Catherine's. Cairo. Tel: 240-2832.

3 El Sayadeen Tourist Village. Nuwayba. Cairo. Tel: 757-398.

2 Fayrouz Village. Sharm El Shaykh. Cairo. Tel: 758-000/769-400.

2 Gazala Resort. Cairo. Tel: 663-890.

3 Marina Sharm. Cairo. Tel: 770-200/770-301.

3 Nuweiba Holiday Village. Cairo. Tel: 770-200/770-301.

3 St. Catherine's Tourist Village. St. Catherine's. Cairo. Tel: 830-242/834-356.

FOOD DIGEST

WHAT TO EAT

Major influences on Egyptian food during the past ten centuries have wafted from the classic cooking pots of Persia, Syria and especially Ottomon Turkey, as well as from Italy, France, and even England. Truly native dishes are based upon an ancient indigenous tradition of stewing vegetables, but even they make extensive use of the tomato, the New World's irreplaceable contribution to Old World cookery. Menus in all hotels are international in outlook .

Mezze, which Egypt owes to the Levant, are hors d'oeuvres, salads, or garnishes, but may be served as a meal. They are eaten with the fingers, scooped up in pieces of flatbread. The most common is *tahinah*, sesame paste mixed with water and lemon juice to form a dip or dressing. It is eaten with flatbread either by itself or mixed with other things, such as white cheese, parlsey, or chopped tomatoes. *Babaghanoug*, *tahinah* mixed with roasted eggplant and crushed garlic, is a Lebanese speciality, as is *hommos bi tahinah*, tahinah mixed with crushed chickpeas and garlic. Often found among *mezze*, however, are stewed brown beans, *ful medames*, Egypt's national dish, which may be offered with *tahinah* , yoghurt, white cheese, cottonseed or olive oil, fried or boiled eggs. Dried white broad beans are the basis for the deep-fried beancakes called *ta'amiya*, known elsewhere as *felafel*. Other vegetables served as *mezze* are likely to be stuffed with a rice mixture, in which case they are called *mahshi*, and range from vine leaves, tomatoes and small eggplant to zucchini or green peppers. Meat served as mezze usually appears in the form of meatballs or meat fingers (*kofta, kibbeh*, or

kobayha) made of ground beef, veal, or lamb.

Street foods, delicious, but normally almost certain to cause distress in an unacclimatized stomach, include: *ta'amiya*, flatbread sandwiches of *ful medames* or *shawirma* (the Turkish *çevirme*—slices of lamb stacked and broiled vertically—better known internationally by its other Turkish name, *doner kebab*), *kusheri* (pasta, rice, and lentils with a hot sauce), *fattah* (hot broth poured over crumbled bread), roast corn or sweet potatoes, and various kinds of bread. Every major hotel now serves refined and hygenic versions of these dishes from elegant counters or carts.

WHERE TO EAT

Most five-star hotels have a restaurant offering variety from elegant dining to snacks at the poolside. In addition to their regular fare hotels often fly in European chefs for week-long extravaganzas. Recently a host of new restaurants have opened in the country and one can have a choice of foods from around the world.

ALEXANDRIA

This is a city famous for seafood and for its coffee-houses (see pages 225-226), but there are those who claim that it also offers the best pizza in the Mediterranean. Included in the list below are establisments in:

Abu Qir (for seafood)

Agami (for social life).

Bella Vista. (Seafood). Abu Qir. Tel: 560-0628.

Délices (Coffeehouse). Maydan Saad Zaghlul

Gelati' Aziz. (The only place in Egypt that still serves *dondurma*, the gorgeously white and sticky Turkish ice-cream which older Egyptians remember with nostalgia) Corniche.

La Pizzeria. (Pizza) 14 Sh. Horreya. Tel: 483-8082.

Lord's Inn. (International) San Stefano Hotel. San Stefano. Tel: 586-5664.

Michael's. Agami.

Pastroudis. (Coffeehouse) 374 Al Gaysh,

Glym, tel: 586-4470.

Qaddura. (Seafood). Anfushi.

Santa Lucia. (International. Alexandria's most famous restaurant, a favorite of many celebrities) 40 Sh. Safeya Zaghlul. Tel: 482-0332.

The Hole in the Wall. Agami.

Tikka. (Speciality: grilled chicken) Corniche, near Maydan Muhammad Ali.

Trianon. (Coffeehouse) Maydan Saad Zaghlul.

Union. Sh. al Borsa.

Zephyrion. (Seafood) Abu Qir.

CAIRO

A city of 14 million or so, Cairo offers a wide variety of choices. The following list is a representative selection of popular establishments in all price ranges.

Abardeen Steak House. 76 Rd 9/Corner Rd., 83 Maadi. Tel: 350-8730.

Al Fanous (Moroccan). 5 Wissa Wassef, Borg Riyadh 6th Fl., Giza. Tel: 73-7595/73-7592.

Andrea's. (Speciality: grilled chicken). 14 Mariyutiyyah Canal (Kirdassah Road). Tel: 851-133. 47 Road 7, Maadi. Tel: 351-1369.

Angus Chargrilled Specialities. 34 Yehia Ibrahim St., Zamalek. Tel: 341-1321.

Arabesque. 6 Kasr El Nil St., Cairo. Tel: 75-9896.

Balmoral (Chinese). 157 26th July St., Zamalek. Tel: 340-6761/340-5473.

Bon Apetit. 21 Wadi El Nil St., Mohandessin. Tel: 346-4937

Borsalino. 1 Latin America St., Garden City. Tel: 54-0168.

Cairo Inn. 26 Syria St., Mohandessin. Tel: 349-0661/349-0662.

Cairo Tower. Gexira. Cairo. Tel: 74-6434.

Cellar. 22 Taha Hussein (Pres. Hotel) Zamalek. Tel: 341-3195/341-6751.

Chandani (Indian). 5 Wissa Wassef, Borg Riyadh 6th Fl. Giza. Tel: 73-7595/73-7592.

Chantilly. 11 Baghdad St., Heliopolis. Tel: 66-9206/66-5820/66-0518.

Cho's (Korean/Chinese/Western). 7A Rd 252 Digla. Tel: 352-6118.

Citadel Grill. Ramses Hilton Hotel. Cairo. Tel: 75-8000/77-7444.

Da Boffo (Italian). 142 Pyramids St., Nirvana Bldg. Giza. Tel: 341-0323. 15 El

Batal Ahmed Aziz Mohandessin. Tel: 346-7490.

Don Quichotte (French/International). 9A Ahmed Heshmat St., Zamalek. Tel: 40-6415.

El Dar (Egyptian/Lebanese). Sakkara Rd. Tel: 85-2289.

El Patio. 5 Sayed El Bakry St., Zamalek. Tel: 40-2645.

El Patio Mediterranean Restaurants. 5 Sayes El Bakry St., Zamalek. Tel: 340-2645.

Eltekia (Take-Out & Deliver/Egyptian Food). 12 Ebn El Walid Square Dokki. Tel: 71-1470.

Estoril. 114 Talaat Harb (passage behind Air France). Tel: 743-102.

Falafel. Ramses Hilton Hotel Cairo. Tel: 77-7444/75-8000.

Fast Food (Cash & Carry Stores). 64 Lebanon Square Mohandessin. Tel: 346-5350/347-1686/346-6891.

Felfela (Egyptian). 15 Hoda Sharawi St., Cairo. Tel: 74-2751.

Flying Fish. 166 El Nil St., Agouza. Tel: 349-3234.

Fouquet's. El Nasr St & Rd 257 New Maadi. Tel: 352-3450.

Fu Ching (Chinese). 28 Talaat Harb St., Cairo. Tel: 75-6184.

Gazirat al Dahab. Safir Hotel, Maydan Missaha, Dokki. Tel: 348-2828/348-2424.

Good Shot. Corniche El Nil Maadi. Tel: 350-3327.

Grill Gezira Marriott Hotel. Zamalek. Tel: 340-8888.

Groppi. 46 Abd El Khalek Sarwat St., Cairo. Tel: 91-1946/91-1948/91-1949. Talaat Harb Square, Cairo. Tel: 74-3473.

Happy Joe's (We Deliver). 67 Rd. 9 Maadi. Tel: 350-1526.

Il Camino (Italian). 5 Wissa Wassef, Borg Riyadh 6th Fl. Giza. Tel: 73-7595/73-7592.

Il Capo (Italian/International). 22 Taha Hussein, Zamalek. Tel: 341-3195/341-6751.

Justine, The Four Corners. 4 Hassan Sabri St., Zamalek. Tel: 341-3961/340-1647.

Kentucky Fried Chicken. Rd 9 (In front of Metro Station) Maadi.
Tel: 350-4714.

La Brasserie Meridien Hotel. Corniche El Nil Garden City. Tel: 84-5444.

La Charmerie (Opposite Margaret Boutique). 26th July St., Zamalek. Tel: 340-

2645. 157, 26th St., Zamalek. Tel: 340-9640.

La Cloche d'Or. 3 Abu al Feda, Zamalek. Tel: 340-2314/340-2268.

La Piazza, The Four Corners. 4 Hassan Sabry St., Zamalek.Tel: 341-2961/340-4385.

La Terrine. 105 Higaz. Heliopolis. Tel: 257-8634.

Lolita Italian Restaurant & Take Away Service. 15 Rd. 9B Maadi. Tel: 351-5465/351-5587.

Maadi Hotel. 55 Misr Helwan Rd Maadi. Tel: 350-3432/350-5050/350-5903.

Mama Lola, 15 Rd 9B Maadi. Tel: 351-5465.

Matchpoint, The Four Corners. Hassan Sabry St., Zamalek. Tel: 341-2961/340-4385.

Maxie's, The Four Corners. 4 Hassan Sabry St., Zamalek. Tel: 341-2961/340-4385.

McBurger. Corniche, opposite Cairo Sheraton, Dokki. Tel: 344-2410.

Mermaid. 77 Rd 9 Maadi. Tel: 350-3964.

Moghul Room, Mena House Oberoi Hotel (Indian). Pyramids Rd. Giza. Tel: 85-5444/85-7999 ext 661.

Naniwa (Japanese). Ramses Hilton Annexe. Tel: 752-399. 3 Lebanon St., Dokki. Tel: 346-5943/346-6154.

Nile Pharaoh (luncheon and dinner cuisine). 31 El Nil St., Giza. Tel: 73-8957/73-8914.

Okamoto (Japanese). 7 Ahmed Orabi St., Agouza. Tel: 349-5774.

Omam Restaurants (See Al Fanous, Chandani, Il Camino, Sakura).

Paprika (Lebanese). 1129 Corniche El Nil Cairo. Tel: 74-9447.

Paxy's (Korean), Amoun Hotel. 26th July St. Sphinx Sq., (Maydan Abu Khor) Agouza. Tel: 346-1434.

Petit Swiss Chalet. 9 Rd 151 Maadi. Tel: 350-4941.

Portofino (Italian/Continental). #5 Rd 204 Digla. Tel: 352-2138.

Pub 28. 28 Shagaret El Dorr St., Zamalek. Tel: 340-0972.

Rex. 14 Abdel Khalek Sarwat St., Cairo. Tel: 74-5763.

Roy Rogers (Marriott Hotel). Zamalek. Tel: 340-8888.

Sakura (Japanese). 5 Wissa Wassef, Borg Riyadh 6th Fl. Giza. Tel: 73-7595/73-7592.

Scarbée. (Floating restaurant, luncheon and dinner cruises) Docks at **Shepheard's**. Tel: 984-967.

Seahorse. Corniche El Nil (In front of As Salam) Maadi. Tel: 351-6830/351-6686.

Silver Fish. 39 Mohy El Din Abu El Ezz St., Dokki. Tel: 349-2272/349-2273.

Sphinx House. Sound & Light Bldg., Pyramids Area Giza. Tel: 85-6006.

Sweet Hotel. 39 Rd.,13 Maadi. Tel: 350-4544.

Swiss Chalet. 10 Al Nakhil St., Mohandessin. Tel: 70-7799.

Swissair Restaurant: Le Chateau & Le Chalet. Nile St., El Nasr (Swissair) Bldg., Giza. Tel: 72-8488/72-9487.

Tandoori (Indian). 11 Shehab St., Mohandessin. Tel: 48-6301.

Tia Maria. 32 Jeddah St., Mohandessin. Tel: 71-3273.

Tikka Grill. 47 El Batal Ahmed Abdel Aziz Mohandessin. Tel: 340-0393.

Tirol (Austrian). 38 Geziret El Arab St., Mohandessin.

Tokyo (Japanese). 2 Said El Bakry St., Zamalek.

Vienna (Austrian). Al Batal Ahmed Aziz St., Mohandessin. Tel: 346-6940.

Wimpy (Hamburgers Fast Food). El Emoubilya St., Off Sherif St., Downtown. Tel: 76-9754. Hoda Sharawy St., Off Talaat Harb, Downtown. Tel: 75-0484. 102 Merryland St., Heliopolis. 7 Dr. Sayed Abd El Wahed St., Heliopolis. El Khalifa El Maamoun St., Heliopolis. 49 El Batal Ahmed Abdel Axix Mohandessin. Pyramids St., Giza. El Manial St., Giza.

DRINKING NOTES

The **traditional hot and cold drinks** served in coffeehouses, delicious and thought to be health-giving, are already described in "Egyptian Coffeehouses". Many of the cold drinks described there were until recently also served by street vendors and are now offered in major hotels by waiters dressed in the traditional 'erqsusi costume.

Fruit Juices

Fresh juices such as orange, mango, strawberry, pomegranate, lime or whatever--depending on the season—are available everywhere *except* in major hotels.

The usual idea of American coffee is instant Nescafé. If you want decaffeinated coffee, you have to bring your own.

Bottled Drinks

Internationally formulated drinks made and bottled locally under license include a range of Schweppes and Canada Dry mixes, Coca-Cola, Seven-Up, Sport, and Pepsi-Cola.

Beers

The local beer is Stella, a lager that comes in four varieties: Stella Export or ordinary Stella, which is less sweet and therefore usually preferred to Export; the increasingly rare Stella Aswali, a dark beer from Aswan; and seasonal Stella Marzen, a bock or Märzenbier. The adventurous may encounter a mild home-brew called *buza*, which is recorded to have been made as long ago as the Third Dynasty.

Wines

Egyptians were making wine even earlier. Since 1986, however, Egyptian wine has deteriorated disastrously, despite the importation of new hardware. Whereas previously bottles varied unpredictably in quality, they are now almost uniformly unfit even for cooking purposes, thanks to heavy-handed introduction of chemical preservatives. Reds include Omar Khayyam, Pharaons, and Château Gianaclis; there is one one rosé, called Rubi d'Egypte. Among the whites—Gianaclis Village, Cru des Ptolemées, Castel Nestor, Nefertiti, and Reine Cléopatre—one label or other is occasionally drinkable for a brief period. Caution is therefore advised when dining out: no bottle is likely to be good, but if there is a risk of spoiling an evening, the worst should be sent back immediately. Imported wine is available in the major hotels, of course, but are sold at preposterous prices.

Imported liquor is also available. Local liquors are quite popular among Egyptians, they include several kinds of brandy and various versions of **zibeeb** or **araq**, the Arab World's heady equivalent to *ouzo, raki, anisetta*, or *pastis*.

Most crucial to know are the two brands of **mineral water**, that are popular and available in hotels: **Baraka**, bottled in association with Vittel, and **Mineral**, bottled in collaboration with Evian.

THINGS TO DO

TOURIST ATTRACTIONS

Luxor, Aswan, Abu Simbel and St. Catherine's can all be visited within a day by tourists with minimum time by flying in the morning and returning in the evening. Book through a local travel agent.

ALEXANDRIA

Roman Sites

Pompey's Pillar. Dedicated in 297 A.D. to Emperor Doicletian, the pillar is made of Aswan rose granite. It rises to a height of 84 feet (25 meters) and stands on the site of the ruins of the **Serapium**, one of the greatest temple complexes of the ancient world.

Roman a'Byzantine Remains (1/2 hours). Council-chambers, lecture halls, baths and the foundations of houses are visible dating mostly from the 4th century A.D.

Catacombs of Kom esh-Shwqafa. Discovered in 1900, the catacombs are dug one hundred feet into the rock bed and date back to second century A.D. The reliefs blend Greek and Egyptian symbolism.

Medieval

The Fort of Qaythbety. Located at the northern end of the harbor entrance, the fort stands on the site of the Pharos. Built in the 15th century, it is now a naval museum.

Modern

Montazah Palace (1 hour). Built in 1926 as a summer residence of the royal family. The women's quarters are now a hotel. The main building is closed, but the gardens and beach are a summer playground.

In and Around

Abu Qir (Morning trip from Alexandria): Once within the ancient city of Canopus, the sites to see are the **public baths** and the **Temple of Serapis**. The current name means St. Cyril and this is where the ancient Coptic Basilica of that name was located. More modern are the relics of **The Battle of the Nile**. Nelson destroyed Napoleon's fleet here in 1798. Currently, a French salvage team is exploring the bay in the hopes of refloating some of the ships. **L'Orient**, the French flagship, has been located and plans to bring it to the surface are underway.

Al Alamayn: (Day trip from Alexandria-Sixty two miles (104 km) west of Alexandria lies the World War II site of a major battle between the Afrika Corps led by General Rommel, and the Allied forces under Montgomery. The preliminary battle took

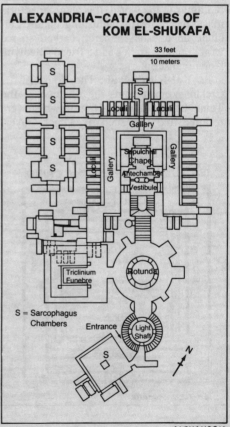

ALEXANDRIA–CATACOMBS OF KOM EL-SHUKAFA

33 feet
10 meters

S = Sarcophagus Chambers

ALEXANDRIA

place in July 1942 when the British stopped the German advance. The final battle, raging between October 23 and November 4, 1942 forced the Germans out of Egypt. Today the area is a war memorial with a museum and four cemeteries dedicated to the men who died there. At **Sidi Abdul Rahman**, the El Alamein Hotel on the beach of Sidi Abdul Rahman is open the whole year round.

CAIRO

Islamic Sites

Mosque of Amr ibn al-Aas: Bearing his name a mosque was built here by the Muslim conqueror in 641 A.D. The first in Egypt, it was the hub of the city of al-Fustat, which became transformed into Cairo. Little remained of the original mosque.

Mosque of Ibn Tulun: (2 hours): Graceful and serene, this mosque, built between 876-879, is the oldest intact mosque in Cairo and one of the most impressive religious buildings in the world. It is an architectural masterpiece. Its distinguishing features include an unusual minaret, carved stucco work, pointed arches and a frieze filled with Koranic inscriptions.

Bayt al-Kiridliyyah: The House of the Cretan Woman abuts the Mosque of Ibn Tulun. It is two medieval houses which were restored and furnished by Major Gayer-

Anderson in 1935-42.

Southern Cemetery (1 hour): The **Mausoleum of Imam al Shafi'i** built in 1211 as a Sunni madrassa (religious school) to counter the Shi'i teachings of al-Azhar, it is still a functioning mosque. The tourist may mingle with the faithful here but might be asked to leave at the hour of prayer. Note the dome, made of wood covered with lead, the boat on top of the dome, the latticework, screen and teak cenotaph in the interior.

Hosh al Basha or **Tomb of the Family of Mohammad Ali:** Near Imam al Shafi'i can be found the multiple-domed tomb of many members of the dynasty founded by Mohammad Ali, who is himself buried at the Citadel. Some family members originally buried in Alexandria were moved here.

The **Mosque of Ibn Tulun** is the greatest architectural monument in a city of monuments (see pages 148-149). The adjoining **Gayer-Anderson Museum (Bayt al-Kiriliyyah)** is open daily from 9 -3.30 p.m., Fridays from 9-11 a.m and from 1-3.30 pm.

The Citadel (3 hours) overlooks the **Madrasah of Sultan Hasan**, the greatest of the Bahri Maluk monuments, and the **Rifa'i Mosque** finished in 1912, an impressive dynastic shrine containing the tombs of Khedive Ismail, Sultan Husayn, King Fuad, and Muhammad Reza Shah Pahlevi, the late Shah of Iran (see pages 150-152). The most obvious feature of the Citadel itself is the **Muhammad Ali Mosque**, built between 1830 and 1848, but not really completed until 1857 (see page 153) , an Ottoman-style congregational mosque in which the great Muhammad Ali himself is entombed.

Other attractions at the Citadel include the **Police Museum**, the **Military Museum**, the **Gawharah Palace**, the **Mosque of Sultan An-Nasir Muhammad**, the **Well**, the **Mosque of Sidi Sarya**, and a small museum of wheeled vehicles (see pages 152-154).

Darb Al Ahmar: This colorful area of the city, studded with monuments, is discussed on pages 154-157. It includes the **Mosque of Mardani:**, one of the most exquisite monuments of the 14th century. Its greatest treasure is a large wooden screen of turned wood. Then there is **The Khayamiyyah** which is the last existing example of a covered bazaar. It now houses the Tentmakers' Bazaar (see page 178).

Al Qahirah (4 hours) see pages 156-162.

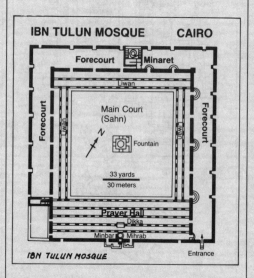

IBN TULUN MOSQUE CAIRO

Forecourt   Minaret

Liwan

Forecourt   Liwan   Main Court (Sahn)   Forecourt

N

Fountain

33 yards
30 meters

Prayer Hall
Dikka
Minbar   Mihrab

Entrance

IBN TULUN MOSQUE

Fatimid City :Bab al Nasr, Bab al Futuh and Bab Zuwaylah: are constructed in 1087 by Badr al-Gamali, are the three remaining gates of the Fatimid city. The first two gates break the northern walls. Bab Zuwaylah, where criminals were punished during the Middle Ages, is separated from them by the entire length of the city. Things to see **within Fatamid City** include:

Wikalatal-Ghuri: This *wikalah* is one of the few intact caravanserais. Foreign merchants sold their wares on the ground floor and stored them in the upper stories where they also rented sleeping quarters. It is now mainly used by artists. In the evenings, concerts and plays are sometimes presented in the courtyard.

The Ghuriya: Here are two buildings built by the last important Mameluk sultan, Qansuh al-Ghuri madrasah. The mosque is on the eastern side of the Qasaba and the mausoleum and sabil-kitab (fountain and school) on the west. The latter is currently used as a cultural center.

Qasabah: The high street of Cairo, the Qasabah, runs from Bab el Futuh in the north to Bab Zuwaylah in the south. (see pages 140, 157-162).

Mosque of al-Azhar: Built by the Fatimids, it was established as a Shi'i teaching mosque. Classes have continued for the past 1000 years, making it one of the oldest universities in the world. Although the enrollment is now over 90,000 and the campus includes many facilities, some classes are still held in the mosque where students gather around their professors to study the Koran and the Hadith (sayings of the Prophet).

Mosque of al-Hakim: Recently reconstructed by the Bohras, a Shi'i sect from India, the mosque is built for congregational use.

Mosque of al-Aqmar: This mosque is a jewel of Fatimid design and a model from which later Islamic art developed. Decorative features include shell motifs as well as stalactites.

Complex of Qalaun: The maristan (hospital), madrassa (school) and mausoleum of Qalaun typify the monumental architecture of the Mameluk era.

Northern Cemetery (3 hours):This is one of the few places in Cairo where one can still see an Islamic skyline. The domes and minarets are an impressive sight and one can wander amid the tombs to explore for hours.

Complex of Faray ibn Barquq: This was the first massive monument built in the Northern Cemetery. Everything is in duplicate: two minarets, two domes, and, on either end of the qibla wall, two delicate wooden screens.

Complex of Qaitbay: The perfect expression of Islamic architecture in Cairo, it is a balance of geometric forms.

Christian

The section of the city that contains most ancient Christian structures is called **Old Cairo**. The **Fortress of Babylon**, not to be confused with the remains of the Babylon on the Euphrates, it houses the following churches:

Convent of St. George: A reception hall in the convent should be seen.

The Hanging Church: The most impressive features of this church are the screens from the 13th and 14th centuries.

The Church of Abu Serga: Dating from the fifth century A.D., this church was built above the cave where the Holy Family allegedly took refuge in their flight from Herod

The Church of Saint Barbara: The wooden portal of this church is a masterpiece in woodwork.

Modern

Camel Market (2 hours): It begins at dawn on Fridays and Sundays. Men from the Sudan trek their camels over lonely caravan routes through the Western Desert to sell them here.

Cairo Zoo (2 hours): Established in 1890, it is one of the oldest in the world with a most comprehensive collection of animals. The zoo is a favorite outing place for Cairenes especially on Friday.

SAQQARAH PLATEAU

Pharaonic Sites

Near Saqqarah, 16 miles (27 km) southwest of Cairo, is a major part of the Memphate necropolis (cemetery) that runs from above Giza in the north, to below Maydum in the south. Begun before the advent of the Old Kingdom, its monuments span some 5000 years. The important sites to see are:

The Funerary Complex of Zoser. Built by the architect Imhotep in the third dynasty, the funerary complex of Zoser contains the **Step Pyramid** is the first attempt at pyramid building and was a precursor of the famous **Giza pyramids**.

The Pyramid of Unas. The exterior of this pyramid looks like a heap of rubble, but the interior walls are covered with Pyramid Texts, the mortuary literature of the ancient Egyptians.

The **Tombs of Ptah-Hotep, Ti** and **Mareruka**. These tombs contain the finest tomb reliefs of the Old Kingdom. They give us an interesting and comprehensive insight into the daily lives of the ancient Egyptians.

The **Serapeum** is the underground burial gallery of the sacred Apis Bulls. Discovered by Mariette in 1851, the Serapeum dates from the Ptolemaic period.

Memphis, the capital of the Old Kingdoms never lost its importance to the ancient Eygptians; yet there is little to see. In the museum compound are the **Alabaster Sphinx** and the **Colossus of Ramses II**.

The Pyramids of Abu Sir (2 hours). A few miles north of Saqqarah and visible from the Saqqarah plateau are three pyramids of the pharaohs of the Fifth Dynasty.

The Pyramids of Dahshur needs special permission to visit. South of Saqqarah, it is part of the Necropolis with four pyramids. The two Old Kingdom pyramids, both be-

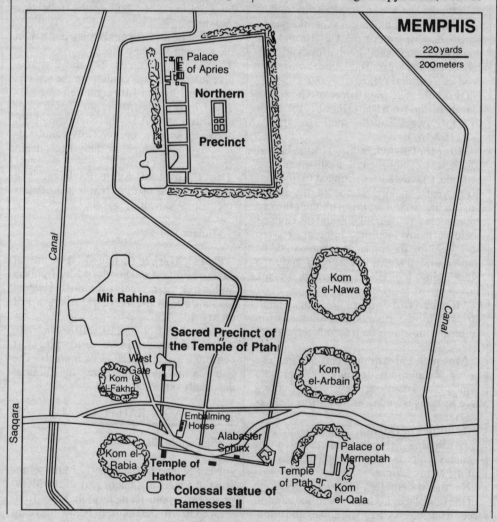

MEMPHIS

220 yards
200 meters

Palace of Apries

Northern

Precinct

Kom el-Nawa

Canal

Canal

Mit Rahina

Sacred Precinct of the Temple of Ptah

West Gate

Kom el-Fakhri

Kom el-Arbain

Saqqara

Embalming House

Alabaster Sphinx

Kom el-Rabia

Temple of Hathor

Colossal statue of Ramesses II

Temple of Ptah

Palace of Merneptah

Kom el-Qala

longing to the Pharaoh Snefru, are in much better condition than the two Middle Kingdom pyramids. The northern pyramid has the largest base of any pyramid in Egypt.

GIZA PLATEAU

The monuments of the Giza plateau, built during the fourth dynasty, are the most famous monuments in Egypt.

The Pyramid of Khufu is the greatest pyramid ever constructed by the ancient Egyptians.

The Pyramid of Khafre: The second pyramid on the Giza plateau gives us the best picture of a mortuary temple complex of the Old Kingdom. Near the **Sphinx** is the valley temple where the pharaoh's body was brought after mummification. Leading up the hill is the causeway by which the priests would carry the body of the pharaoh to the moartuary temple. Here prayers for release of the pharaoh's soul took place. Then the body was placed in the tomb chamber.

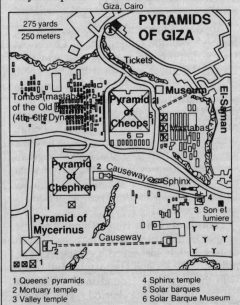
Giza, Cairo

1 Queens' pyramids
2 Mortuary temple
3 Valley temple
4 Sphinx temple
5 Solar barques
6 Solar Barque Museum

The **Sphinx** is the largest of many to be found in the Nile valley, but the only one in the Giza necropolis.

The Pyramid of Menkaure: The smallest pyramid of the Giza trio, it is the last great pyramid of the age. All later pyramids were of inferior quality.

The audio-visual shows at Giza are presented in the area in front of the Sphinx in various languages - Saturday: English and French; Sunday: French and German; Monday: English and French; Tuesday: French and German; Wednesday: English and French; Thursday: Arabic and English; Friday: English and French.

The Nile Barrage (Day trip from Cairo)
It is found some fifteen miles (24 km) north of Cairo, just before the Nile branches into the Canopic and Dumyat streams. Very crowded on Friday, but a pleasant place to end a ride on the Nile. A public water-taxi leaves from the **Maspero** stop next to the television building on Fridays and Sundays. Do not ride on it during hot weather it is like being in a sauna.

BENI SUEF

The Pyramid of Meidum: (Day trip from Cairo). The pyramid is the first true pyramid of Egypt. It was built after the Step Pyramid and is the second stage in pyramid building.

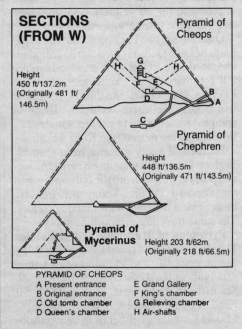

PYRAMID OF CHEOPS
A Present entrance
B Original entrance
C Old tomb chamber
D Queen's chamber
E Grand Gallery
F King's chamber
G Relieving chamber
H Air-shafts

Today only the core remains, but it still an impressive sight. The Pyramid of Meidum is south of Cairo off the main highway to Upper Egypt. It can be seen from the distance. The turn off is posted and appears to be beyond the pyramid. Bring a picnic lunch.

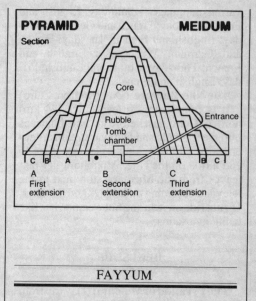

PYRAMID — MEIDUM

Section

Core

Rubble
Tomb
chamber

Entrance

A	B		C

A
First
extension

B
Second
extension

C
Third
extension

FAYYUM

Traveling to the historic sites in Fayyum is not always easy as many sites are unpaved, unmarked desert tracks; but the drive is pleasant, the air is clean and the green fields and the lakes are worth seeing.

Qasr es-Sagha: Far into the desert to the north of Lake Qarun is the Middle Kingdom temple of Qasr-el Sagha. It stands on a rocky hill commanding an exquisite view of the Fayyum. One should take this trip in at least two four-wheel-drive vehicles. Bring a compass for it is easy to get lost. Guides can be found at the museum in Kom Aushim.

Dimayh: Twenty minutes from Qasr el-Sagha is Dimayh. It was once a caravan town and port for traders from the Nile valley and the Western Desert. Today the treasure hunters visit its ruins with metal detectors. The same traveling precautions apply.

Pyramids of Hawarah and **el-Lahun:** The Pyramid of Hawarah was built by Amenemhct III. The Pyramid of el Lahun was built in the 12th Dynasty by Pharaoh Sesostris II. Both were excavated by Sir Flinders Petrie in the 1880s. Built during the Middle Kingdom, neither of these pyramids is impressive except for sheer size

AL-MINYA

Most of the sites here are an hour's drive south of Al-Minya. One can hire a taxi for the day at reasonable rates. Do bring your candle or flashlight since the tombs are dark.

BANI HASSAN

On the east bank of the Nile, are the 39 noblemen's tombs of the 11th and 12th Dynasty (Middle Kingdom). The interior decoration is painted on plaster and depicts scenes of sports, crafts and farming in ancient Egypt. The most interesting tomb is that of **Kheti**, a governor during the 11th Dynasty. The wall paintings show scenes of fishing and birding, hunting, wrestling and weaving.

TUNAH AL-GABAL

The interesting sites of Tunah al-Gabal are the **Tomb of Petrosiris**, the **necropolis** of mummified ibis and baboons, and an important sculpture, the **Boundary Stela of Akhet-Aten**. It depicts Akhnaten, Nefertiti and their children worshipping the sun god Aten.

ABYDOS

Abydos, which existed "at the dawn of history" was the cult center of Osiris. As Osiris' importance grew, so did Abydos'. By the Middle Kingdom it had become a place of pilgrimage. By the New Kingdom all Egytians tried to visit Abydos before they died. Those who did not, often had their mummies transported to Abydos before burial. The earliest monuments of this site are in total ruin and the New Kingdom Temple of Ramses II has little left of what must have been a magnificent temple. However, New Kingdom Temple of Seti I is among the finest in Egypt.

Temple of Seti I: Built of limestone, the temple is dedicated to no less than seven deities and holds seven sanctuaries. The reliefs of the second **Hypostyle Hall** break with the rigid style found in Egyptian art before the Armana Period. The **Seven Shrines** are from right to left: Horus, Isis, Osiris, Amon-Ra, Ra-Harakhte, Ptah and Seti I. **The Corridor of Kings** lists 76 cartouches of the pharaohs of Ancient Egypt. This list was the beginning of a chronology of Ancient Egypt.

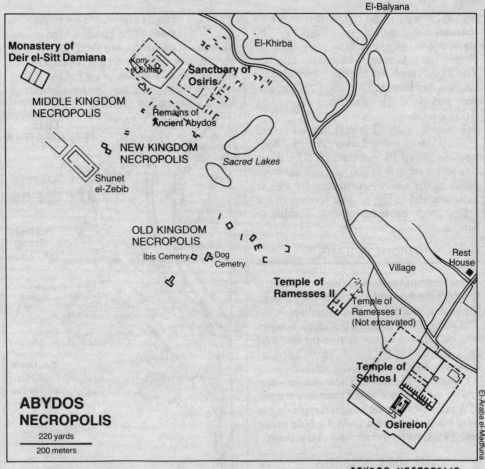

El-Balyana

El-Khirba

**Monastery of
Deir el-Sitt Damiana**

Kom
el-Sultan

**Sanctuary of
Osiris**

**MIDDLE KINGDOM
NECROPOLIS**

Remains of
Ancient Abydos

**NEW KINGDOM
NECROPOLIS**

Sacred Lakes

**Shunet
el-Zebib**

**OLD KINGDOM
NECROPOLIS**

Ibis Cemetery

Dog
Cemetery

Village

Rest
House

**Temple of
Ramesses II**

Temple of
Ramesses I
(Not excavated)

**Temple of
Sethos I**

Osireion

El-Araba el-Madfuna

**ABYDOS
NECROPOLIS**

220 yards
200 meters

ABYDOS NECROPOLIS

LUXOR

Luxor is ancient Thebes, the heart of the New Kingdom and of rural Egypt, where the pace is slow and nature is at its best. The winter sunsets are breathtaking. Awaiting the tourist are glimpses into traditional everyday lives of the people and some of the most impressive monuments of ancient Egypt, including **Karnak** and the **Valley of the Kings**.

Great Temple of Amunat Karnak (4 hours minimum) This sacred area saw 1300 years of pageantry. Pharaohs from the Middle Kingdom to the 30th Dynasty built temples, oblisks, pylons and shrines at Karnak, primarily in honor of the God Amun Ra, his consort Mut and their son Khonsu.

The First Pylon: The largest at Karnak, not added until the 25th Dynasty. In front of it, forming an impressive entrance, is the

Avenue of the Sphinx.

The **Temple of Ramses III** is a typical New Kingdom temple in a good state of general repairs.

Great Hypostyle Hall: Erected by Seti I and Ramses the II, the hypostyle hall is the largest and most magnificent in Egypt. Inside there are 134 massive columns decorated with reliefs. On the outer southern walls are records of Ramses II's **Battle of Kadesh** and on the outer northern walls are Seti I's battles in Lebanon and Syria.

Obelisks of Hatshepsut: Of the two obelisks erected by Hatshepsut at Karnak, one remains standing. The second was toppled centuries ago. The top of the second obelisk has been placed near the **Sacred Lake**. The relief shows Hatshepsut being crowned Pharaoh by the God Amun.

One of the best audio-visual shows you will see and hear. Two performances nightly, at 6 p.m. and 8 p.m. It lasts for 90 minutes and requires some walking. The show are in various languages - Sunday: French and German; Monday: English; Tuesday: French and German; Wednesday: English and French; Thursday: Arabic; Friday and Saturday: English and French. Bring a wrap.

Luxor Temple (2 hours) In the heart of modern Luxor stands **Luxor Temple**. Built by Amenhotep III and Ramses II, it is the southern sanctuary of god Amun. The colonnades of the Court Amenhotep III are the most graceful in Egypt. The Avenue of the Sphinx once connected Luxor Temple to Karnak.

THE WEST BANK

One can cross to the west bank on a tourist ferry or take the local ferry with the farmers. There is also a new long-awaited car ferry. Tickets available at all the landings. You can rent bicycles in Luxor to ride on the west bank and take in the sights. Taxis and donkeys will await to offer their services.

Colossi of Memnon. These statues once graced the entrance to the mortuary temple of Amenhotep III, the largest temple on the west bank. As you go from the Nile to the necropolis, take 10 minutes to view them.

TELL EL AMARNA

One must cross the Nile by local ferry to visit the west bank of Akhet-Aten. At first glance, little remains of what was the capital of Ancient Egypt during the short reign of Amenhotep IV, the Pharaoh Akhnaton. The temple complex on the plane is a mere outline. But the rock tombs above the vanquished city exemplify the mannered art of the Armana period which is vastly different from other art of Ancient Agypt. There are 25 tombs cut into the rock cliffs.

There are 25 tombs cut into the rock cliffs. Tombs one-six are in the north and seven-25 in the south. They are separated by **Darb el Malik** where the tombs of the royal family are found (closed to the public).The **Tomb of Aye** is the most important tombs in Tell el Amarna. On the right side of the entrance is found the most complete version of the famous Hymm to the Sun. On the interior walls the activities in the streets, palaces and

women's quarters of Amarna are brought to life. On the walls of the Tomb of Meri-re, the high priest of Amon, are the floor plans of the temples, palaces and government buildings of the city on the plain below. It was through these plans that the foundations of the city were uncovered.

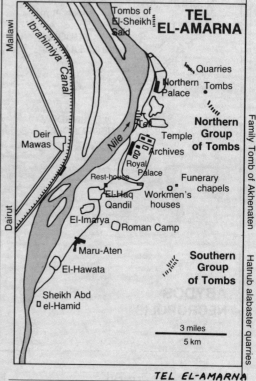

TEL EL-AMARNA

VALLEY OF THE KINGS

There are 62 known tombs in this desert valley; only 11 have electricity and fewer are open to the public on a continuous basis. Among the most famous tombs are:

Tomb of Tutankhamen: Discovered by Howard Carter in 1922, this is the smallest tomb in the Valley of the Kings. If you have seen the great treasures of Tutankhamen in the Egyptian Antiquities Museum, you may find the tomb disappointing. Fortunately the sarcophagus and gold mummy case are still on site for viewing.

Tomb of Ramses VI: The vaulted ceiling in the tomb chamber is the most outstanding feature of this tomb. Painted primarily in blue and gold, it represents the heavens. The Goddess Nut circles the sky enclosing the representations of the day, the year and the entire zodiac.

Tomb of Seti I: This is the largest and finest tomb in the valley. Features of special note are the unfinished room used as a decoy to fool tomb robbers and the burial chamber with a black and gold astronomical ceiling.

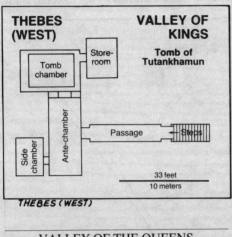

THEBES (WEST) — **VALLEY OF KINGS**

Tomb of Tutankhamun

Tomb chamber

Store-room

Ante-chamber

Passage

Steps

Side chamber

33 feet
10 meters

THEBES (WEST)

VALLEY OF THE QUEENS

Over 70 tombs of the queens and royal children of the 18th-20th Dynasties are found in this valley. Only a few are open to the public, but not the best: the **Tomb of Nefertari**, the wife of Ramses II. This tomb has become a victim of the ravages of salt erosion and is currently under restoration.

Tomb of Amun-her-Khopshef: In the small tomb are reliefs depicting the son of Ramses III being escorted by his father into the underworld. The colors are spectacular and the light is very good.

QURNAH

There are over 400 **noblemen's tombs** which cut into the Thebian hills. They give us an intimate portrait of the men who served the pharaoh. Many are closed to the public, but those not to be missed are:.

Tomb of Nakht: Nakht was a scribe of the 18th Dynasty. His tomb, although small, is the finest nobleman's tomb, and some say, "the best on the west bank." The scenes of harvesting, banqueting, hunting and fishing are all known for their detail and brilliant colors. The three female musicians so often reproduced on postcards are found here.

Tomb of Menna: Menna was the Scribe

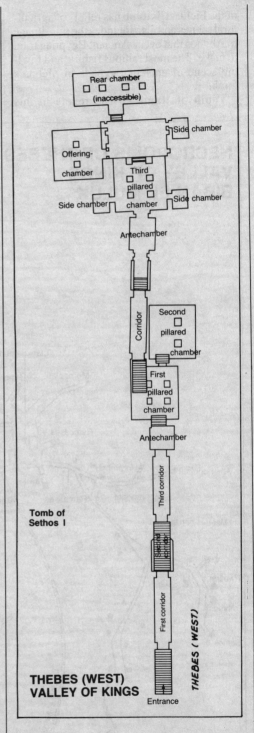

Rear chamber (inaccessible)

Side chamber

Offering-chamber

Third pillared chamber

Side chamber

Side chamber

Antechamber

Corridor

Second pillared chamber

First pillared chamber

Antechamber

Third corridor

Second corridor

First corridor

Tomb of Sethos I

THEBES (WEST) VALLEY OF KINGS

Entrance

THEBES (WEST)

of the Fields. His tomb has reliefs of agricultural scenes and also includes the pilgrimage to Abydos that every Ancient Egyptian tried to make. The most famous fishing and fowling scene of ancient Egypt is in Menna's tomb.

Tomb of Ramose: The reliefs in this tomb, one of the largest in Qurnah, are wonderful. The details are realistic and worth close attention. Outstanding is the mourning scene on the left wall.

Mortuary Temple of Seti I: On the northern end of the Thebian plateau, this temple is often missed by the traveler. Built

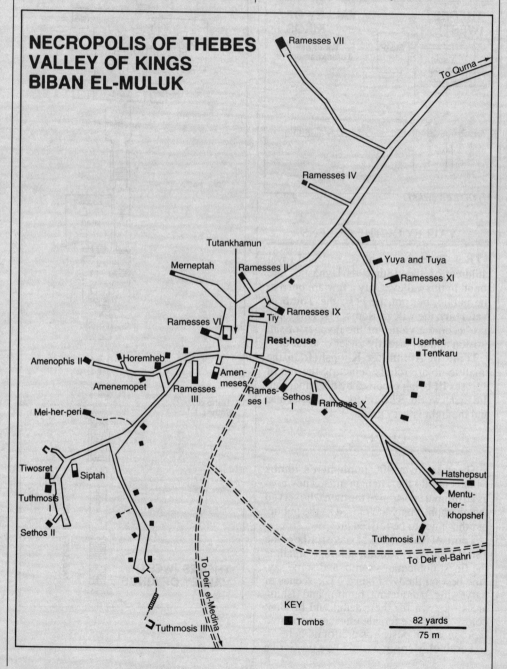

NECROPOLIS OF THEBES
VALLEY OF KINGS
BIBAN EL-MULUK

Ramesses VII

To Qurna

Ramesses IV

Tutankhamun

Yuya and Tuya

Merneptah   Ramesses II   Ramesses XI

Ramesses IX

Ramesses VI   Tiy

Rest-house   Userhet
Tentkaru

Amenophis II   Horemheb

Amenemopet   Amen-
meses
Ramesses   Rames-   Sethos   Ramesses X
III   ses I   I

Mei-her-peri

Tiwosret   Hatshepsut
Siptah   Mentu-
her-
Tuthmosis   khopshef

Sethos II

Tuthmosis IV   To Deir el-Bahri

To Deir el-Medina

KEY

Tombs   82 yards
75 m

Tuthmosis III

314

during the same period as the Temple of Abydos, it contains fine reliefs depicting the the life and times of Egyptian royalty.

THEBIAN PLATEAU

Mortuary Temple of Ramses II: The Ramsesseum was built in honor of the great propagandist of ancient Egypt and the walls depict his wars and conquests. In the courtyard is the fallen collossus that Shelley used as a subject in *Ozymandias*.

Mortuary Temple of Ramses III: Located at Medinet Habu, in the southern part of the Thebian Plateau, this mortuary temple is the best preserved on the west bank.

These temples shouldn't be visited as a single unit of the tour.

Deirel Bahri: Below the cliffs that form the barrier between the desert and the Nile stands the graceful **Mortuary Temple of Hatshepsut**. This elegant building, so different from any other building in the Nile valley, forms a graceful symmetry with its surrounding environment. Be sure to view the Punt Colonnades.

ESNA TO KOM OMBO

The Temple of Esna (Morning trip from Luxor). Built during the Ptolemaic period in honor of Khnum, the God of the Cataract region, this temple is the least impressive of the later temples built along the Nile. The last Roman name to appear in a cartouche is found here.

The Temple of Edfu (Day trip from Luxor or Aswan) Dedicated to Horus the elder and taking two centuries to complete, this temple is the best preserved in Egypt.

The Temple of Kom Ombo (Morning trip from Aswan) This temple stands on a picturesque knoll at a bend in the Nile and is particularly striking when approached from the river. The temple is a double temple dedicated to two gods, Horus and Sobek.

ASWAN

Dry and warm with a splendid location on the first cataract of the Nile, Aswan forms the barrier between Egypt and Africa. It has played a major role in the history of the region for over 5000 years. It also offers a glimpse into the Nubian culture.

Abu Simbel (Morning trip from Aswan) Abu Simbel is south of Aswan on the High Dam Lake. You can fly from Cairo, Luxor or Aswan, take a hydrofoil, or go overland on a newly paved road. Air flights usually allow a two-hour stay at the temples. The methods used to dismantle the temples and move them to a new location above the former site are depicted in the interior of the man-made mountain that now houses the **Temple of Ramses II**. The **Temple of Nefertari** is the second temple at Abu Simbel. It is dedicated to Nefertari, the favourite wife of Ramses II, as well as to the Goddess Hathor.

Elephantine Island (2 hours) One gets to the island by sail boat and docks at the quay of one of the few remaining villages in Nubia. At the southern end of the island are the **Nilometer,** the ancient gauge for measuring the height of the flood each year; the temple dedicated to the god Khnum and a museum.

Tombs of the Nobles (4 hours) are across the river from Aswan, high on a hill. There are two rows of tombs belonging to local rulers of the Old and Middle Kingdom. The journey is difficult and the tombs are not all that impressive, but the view is magnificent.

PHILAE

The original island of Philae became susceptible to flooding by the Nile after the first heightening of the dam at Aswan. The final drama was played out in the 60s as coffer dams surrounded the island while salvage work was in progress. Piece by piece the temple was dismantled, moved to the nearby island of Agilkia which had been contoured to resemble Philae, and reconstructed as we see it today. In Greco-Roman times Philae was to become the cult center of Isis and the most important shrine in the whole of Egypt. Apart from The **Temple of Isis** there are several others.

The **Arch of Hadrian** with reliefs about the source of the Nile as understood in Pharaonic times. The God Hapi is pouring the waters of the Nile from a pot.

The Temple of Hathor: Depicts scenes of the God Bes dancing, laughing as well as playing musical instruments.

The **Kiosk of Trajan** is the most famous

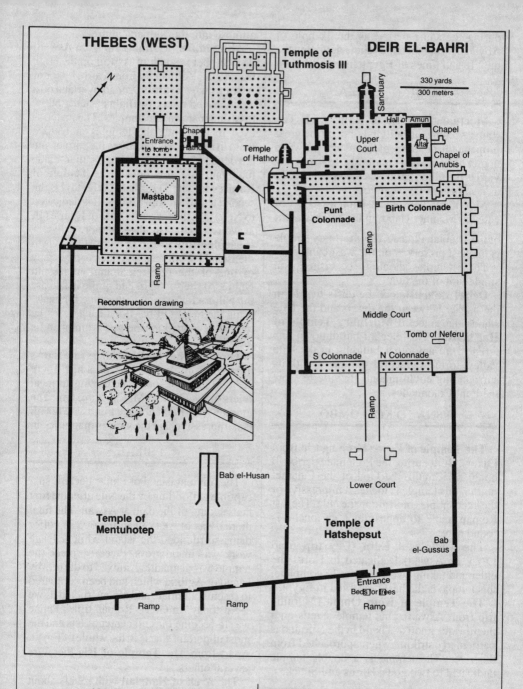

THEBES (WEST)

DEIR EL-BAHRI

Temple of
Tuthmosis III

Sanctuary

330 yards
300 meters

Hall of Amun

Chapel
Chapel

Entrance
to tomb

Upper
Court

Altar

Chapel of
Anubis

Temple
of Hathor

Mastaba

Punt
Colonnade

Birth Colonnade

Ramp

Ramp

Reconstruction drawing

Middle Court

Tomb of Neferu

S Colonnade

N Colonnade

Ramp

Bab el-Husan

Lower Court

**Temple of
Mentuhotep**

**Temple of
Hatshepsut**

Bab
el-Gussus

Entrance
Beds for trees

Ramp

Ramp

Ramp

monument of Philae. It was the only monument on the island that was visible above the water surface when the island was flooded during the first part of this century. There is an audio-visual show in the evening.

The Temple of Kalabsha (2 hours) is another salvage miracle. Dismantled block

by block, it was removed from the fate of a watery grave in Nubia and re-erected close to the High Dam.

Roman Sites

The current Temple at **Dendera**, dedicated to Hathor the Goddess of Love and

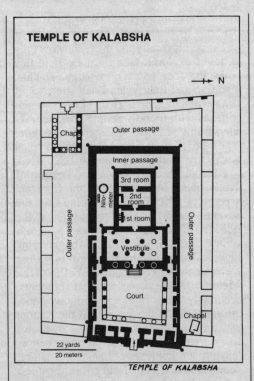

TEMPLE OF KALABSHA

Chapel

Outer passage

Inner passage

3rd room

2nd room

1st room

Nilo-meter

Outer passage

Outer passage

Vestibule

Court

Chapel

22 yards
20 meters

N

TEMPLE OF KALABSHA

Joy, dates from the Ptolemaic and Roman periods. The zodiac on the ceiling of the great hypostyle hall is the best preserved in Egypt. The Crypts below the temple have excellent reliefs dating from the reign of Ptolemy XIII. The relief of Cleopatra VI and Caesarion, her son by Julius Caesar, is found on the south outer wall. It is the only place in Egypt where Cleopatra VI is depicted.

Kom Aushin in Fayyum is the best preserved Roman city in Egypt. Called Karanis in Roman times, it contains the ruins of domestic architecture, two temples and a nearby museum of antiquities. The museum has an excellent Fayyum portrait.

Christian Sites

Ain Musa: Nine miles (15 km) south of Suez is the oasis of Ain Musa, believed to be the spot where Moses struck the rock to find water for the thirsty Israelites. There are no facilities available.

Basilica at Dendera: One of the earliest structures of the Christian era, this bascilica, built of sandstone, is now in ruins. It is beside the birth house of the Temple of Dendera. A beautifully carved niche from the Christian

period can be seen by looking just inside.

Monastery of St. Anthony and St. Paul: (Overnight from Cairo) These two monasteries are 12 miles (20 km) apart as the crow flies over the Red Sea Mountains. The distance is much greater by the road that runs along the plateau and Red Sea Coast. St. Anthony's lies off the **Zafarana-El Wasta** desert road that links the Nile valley to the Red Sea. The turn off to the monastery is marked by a sign. The monastery is at the base of the mountains. There are resthouses inside, but they provide accommodations for men only. St. Paul's, deep in the mountains, is even more picturesque. South of Zafarana by 12 miles (20 km), the turn off is marked. The monastery, perched atop a hill, is approached by a wadi.

Monastery of Saint Simeon: (3 hours) The most beautiful and famous monastery in Upper Egypt, it is a fine example of an early monastery. Begun in the seventh century, it was inhabited until the 1100s when it was vanquished by Salah il Din.

St. Catherine's Monastery: Started in the sixth century, the monastery lies in the valley between the Mount of Moses (Mt. Sinai), where Moses allegedly received the 10 commandments from God, and **Mount Saint Catherine's**. Still a functioning monastery of the Greek Orthodox Church, its main features are: the **Basilica Church** built by Justinian in 527 A.D., the **Crusader's Church** and the **library** with thousands of rare manuscripts (special permission required. for looking at them). Treks up the mountain are arranged by the monks each day before dawn. It is possible to ride a camel part of the way. Near the summit hundreds of steps await. The view from the top is astounding. Although the monks provide sleeping accommodations, you must bring your own food and water. There is a hotel nearby.

Wadi Feran: At the foot of **Gebel Serbal** is the largest wadi in Sinai, which may have been the site of the battle between the Amalakites and Israelites. Within the mountain are the remains of monasteries, chapels and hermit cells of the early Christian monks who believed this to be the **Elim** of the Bible. The oasis is the most fertile in Sinai, with many tamarish trees that some scholars argue are the source of the manna spoken of in Judeo-Christian tradition.

Transquil and serene, it is difficult to imagine that Feran was a cathedral city in the Middle Ages. You can stock up on supplies in the village shops

Wadi Natrun: (Day trip from Cairo) At one time there were many monasteries in this remote desert region. Today only a few monasteries remain. One can visit: St. Makarious, Dair al-Baramus, Deir Anba Bishoi and Deir as-Suryam. They are closed during fasts and festivities. Bring your own lunch and a gift for the monks (soap, tea, sugar, etc.).

Modern

Mausoleum of the Aga Khan: (2 hours) The Aga Khan III, the head of the Ismailia sect of Islam, is buried on a hill above Aswan which has a spectacular view overlooking the city and the river.

Kitchener's Island: (2 hours) Given to Lord Kitchener by the Egyptian people when he was Consul General of Egypt, the island is a botanical paradise begun by Kitchener. Today there are plants and trees from all over the world.

The High Dam and the Lake: (2 hours). Two miles wide and 364 feet (110 meters) high, the High Dam was completed in 1971 as a co-operative effort between the Soviet Union and Egypt. Built to solve Egypt's electricity and agricultural problems, the dam has, in the past few years, proven its value: drought in Ethiopia and Sudan has not effected Egypt.

Market at Daraw: (Day trip from Aswan) Open daily, but Sundays and Tuesdays find this native market in full swing. Vegetables, handicrafts and camel market where Sudanese and Rashida herdsmen trek in from the desert to trade. This is not a place for the squeamish and the traveler should be properly attired and should ask permission before attempting to snap a few photographs, particularly of the locals, for his or her family album back home.

Ismailia: (Day trip from Cairo) A little over an hour's journey from Cairo over a four-lane highway is the stratgic canal city of Ismailia. Things to see here includes the: **DeLesseps Museum, Ismailia City Musem** and of course the most exciting of all, would be the ocean-going vessel passing through the Suez Canal.

For scenic beauty and the feeling of being a desert explorer, take the loop road that links the four oases of Kharga, Dakhla, Farafrah and Bahriyyah. Long stretches of uninterrupted desert, clear sky and small villages with friendly people lure the traveler, filling him with a sense of adventure. The oases are best visited in the winter when a walk to a nearby sand dune can be enjoyed.

Kharga Oasis: (1 day) The **Temple of Hibis,** begun by Darius I and the Christian **Cemetery of Al-Bagawat,** dating from the seventh century, greet the traveler at the outskirts of Kharga City. There are hundreds of interesting sites scattered throughout the depression; but the biggest thrill is getting there. On the way one finds the **Valley of the Melons,** where huge circular boulders, seemingly flung from some mighty hand, are scattered on the ground. At the Kharga escarpment, the road descends downward like a serpent into the depression below, leaving an impressive image of natural beauty. There is a hotel and government rest house at Kharga City.

Between Kharga and Dakhla: (1 day) The quietness begins to impress itself upon you as you head toward Dakhla. The most arresting sight of the entire journey is a valley of hills that resemble the great pyramids on the Giza plateau. One must pause to look at them. The early settlers of the Nile valley passed this way and these hills could have inspired them to build the pyramids.

Dakhla Oasis: (2 days) This oasis is the largest in the western desert and has several towns. Set amid a palm grove is **Qasr,** the largest. It has wonderful gardens, a fortified fortress and a mosque dating from the Ayyubid era. A climb to the top of the minerat, though a bit precarious, gives an excellent view of the countryside, including the pink and white escarpment. There is a government resthouse.

Between Dakhla and Farafrah: (1 day) The longest and loneliest stretch of road linking Dakhla, in the south, to Farafrah in the north. The **dunes** beg to be climbed. Near the end of the journey, at **Bir Abu Mungar,** there is a check-point and the road appears to double back before it ascends the escarpment. Once atop it's time to pause. The view in either direction is spectacular. The long valley beyond has a variety of desert features including a wonderful chain of sand dunes. Try to arrive in the late afternoon.

Farafrah Oasis: (1-2 days) This is the largest depresssion and the smallest oasis. No one really knows its importance during pharaonic times, but it is mentioned in papyri and there are a few burial sites. Wonderful features lure the traveler there today: **Qasr**, the fortress, built in the Middle Ages is still inhabited and a walk through the covered streets brings the traveler into intimate contact with the people. Women have the greatest chance of being invited in for a cup of tea. **The Gardens** of Farafrah are cool and pleasant, under trees that are laden with fruit in season. The traveler must pay a visit to the *Umda*, and as part of desert hospitality, will be offered a cup of tea in his garden. (With the oasis becoming a tourist spot, this hospitality has become quite a burden: bring tea or sugar as a gift.) **The Springs** are a delightful place to swim. Bring something modest for bathing. There is a government resthouse there.

Bahriyya: There are five pharaonic tombs at **al-Bawiti**, the capital of Bahriyyah oasis. They are beneath the houses on the ridge called **Qarat al-Subi**. The village of **Manddisha** offers the traveler a true picture of oasis life, including the harsh reality of destruction caused by a sand dune. Part of the village is being swallowed up as year by year the ridge of dunes continue their march. There is a government resthouse at al-Bawiti.

Siwah Oasis: Permission to visit Siwah is obtained at **Mersa Metruh.** You will need your passport and an up-to-date visa. The Intelligence office is closed on Friday. The procedure will take two to three hours. When you arrive at Siwah you must register with the police. There is a new hotel (if you decide to stay there, they will register for you).

The **Temple of the Oracle** at Aghurmi was the destination of ancient travelers who wished to consult the oracle. Perhaps the most famous visitor was Alexander the Great who came here in the fourth Century B.C. The temple is located atop a huge rock (as are most things in this oasis) and is accessible via the northwestern corner. There are still things to see in the temple complex, but the rock is in danger of collapsing and one must be very careful while

touring. **The Temple of Umm Ubaydah:** lies on the plain below the rock of Aghurmi, admidst a grove of palm trees. Hundreds of **rock-cut tombs** dot the escarpment at Siwah. The most important are the **Tombs of Jabal al Mawta**, but none are as spectacular as tombs in the Nile valley.

Fortress of Siwah: The people of Siwah built a fortified village atop one of the hills of the oasis to protect themselves against desert invaders. For centuries all the inhabitants of the oasis lived within its gate. Today such defenses are no longer necessary and the fortress is falling to ruin.

THE EASTERN DESERT

Hurghada (Gharda'a): Once a fishing village, Hurgha is the main resort town on the Red Sea Coast. Several resort hotels offer all beach facilities including sailing, windsurfing, snorkeling and scuba diving. One can hire fishing boats by the day. There is good camping on the many islands in the area.

THE SINAI

Although many tourist villages are now under development, basic needs are not available in most areas. Check before hand and be sure to bring food, water, shade and toilet paper.

El Arish: Three thousand years ago authorities cut off the noses of prisoners and banished them to the wilds of El Arish. Later the Romans built a road across northern Sinai linking Africa to Asia and El Arish served as their major port. In modern times when the British built a railroad linking Egypt to Palestine, El Arish served as a major station. Today we can still travel over the **Via Maris** and still see portions of the **Allenby Railroad**. The city itself is disappointing. The inhabitants exist on fishing, date farming and trade. Unfortunately, the once beautiful beaches have been ruined by concrete block houses, but there is a local suq every Friday for good Bedouin finds. All facilities are available.

Rafah is a border town 5 miles (4 km) east of El Arish. The most interesting thing about it is the Bedouin suq, where admid produce and camels, Bedouin jewelry and dresses can be found. The suq day is Thursday. Be early. It begins at dawn and dwindles by noon. Bring your own food and water unless you are willing to eat and drink from the stalls at the site.

Hammam Fara'un (Pharaoh's Baths): Below Suez, on the western shore of Sinai (signs mark the way) are the hot springs of **Farion.** Seven in number, they are rich in minerals and the Bedouin have been trekking to them for centuries. Still in their natural state, the hot water flows into the Gulf of Suez creating steam when it hits the cool water of the gulf. It is worth seeing now, before it is turned into a health resort. Presently there are no facilities.

Turquoise Mines of Maraghab: Following a desert track 15 miles (25 km) into the Sinai hills from Abu Zunaymah one finds the main turquoise mines of the ancient Egyptians. Worked as early as the first Dynasty, there were many reliefs and stelae on the site. Unfortunately, the British, in an attempt to re-open the mines in 1901, destroyed much of it. However, a few inscriptions remain and the mine shafts are still visible. There are no facilities here.

You are advised to request for a Bedouin guide at **Abu Zunaymah** before you proceed to explore the area.

Serabit al-Khadim: The temple area, dedicated to Hathor and accompanied by many commemorative stelae of the Middle and New Kingdoms, covers approximately an acre. In it was found the bust of Queen Tiy of the Old Kingdom (now in the Egyptian Antiquities Museum in Cairo). Over 400 inscriptions are found in this area. Some, praising Hathor or giving instructions about the turquoise mines on the site, and others, hieroglyphic, and unquestionably Egyptian. More important, however, are the graffitti of the workers. Among them are unknown scripts called **protosinaitic**. They form the link between hieroglyphics and the Phoenecian alphabet from which our own alphabet is derived. No facilities. Ask for a Bedouin guide at Abu Zunaymah.

Granite Quarries:.Almost every temple in Egypt has some granite taken from the great quarries at Aswan. At one of these quarries, a half hewn obelisk can be seen. Not suprising that it was found to be flawed, and was thus left trapped in the rock or elseit would be sculptured to perfection to adorn some anciet temple.

Alexandria in summer is the most crowded resort in Egypt. Within the city limits are 10 beaches. West of the city are the beaches of **Agami** and **Hanoville,** while to the east are the beaches of **Mamourah** and **Montaz.** Several new tourist villages are under development between Hanoville and Alamayn.

Often overlooked by tourists, however, are the leisure time activities available in the country which offers fine beaches on the Mediterranean, good fishing in the Red Sea and, some say, the finest diving in the world. There are quite a few to choose from and listed below are a sampling of them.

Ras-al-Sidr: (one-day trip from Cairo). A sandy beach area south of the tunnel with no shade, food or fresh water, but excellent Red Sea shells. Crowded on Friday and holidays.

Sharm el Shaykh: At the tip of Sinai, it is the most developed resort area in Sinai. There are both hotel and camping facilities. It is a good base for day trips elsewhere.

Ras Mohammad: Thirty-one miles (50 km) south-west of Sharm el Shaykh, **Ras Mohammad** is a coral peninsula thrusting its head into the Red Sea. It is a nature reserve and one of the most outstanding snorkeling and diving areas in the world. At the Shark's Observatory a coral ridge falls over 262 feet (80 meters) into the open sea and the wary diver can float along its edge (under a meter/three feet deep at high tide) and look out into an underwater paradise. Although a haven for large fish, especially sharks, there has been no reported shark attack in the Red Sea for 25 years. There are no facilities there.

It can be visited for a day, but a permit is required for overnight camping. Permits are obtainable at El Tur, on the west coast of Sinai. Bring your passport.

Trian Island stands as a guardian over the entrance to the Gulf of Aqaba. There are dangerous reefs and currents in the sea. Shipwrecks dot the shoreline testifying to the degree of navigational difficulty between the reefs. No facilities.

Dahab which means "gold," is a resort village on the east coast of Sinai with a hotel, snorkeling and dive facilities.

Nuweib: The ferry to Aqaba leaves daily from the port. Camel treks lasting four to five days into the Sinai mountains led by a local Bedouin are available. Ask at the gas station or the Bedouin village nearby. Hotel and camping facilities available.

Fiord: There are many fine beaches on the Aqaba coast, the **Fiord** being the most secluded. You can drive your car down the cliff and camp on the flat beach. There is a restaurant under renovation on the cliff overlooking the alcove, which may or may not be open. Currently there are no facilities.

Gazirat Fara'un: The island is crowned with a castle built by Salah il Din to protect the overland route of the Hajj, the annual pilgrimage to Mecca, There is excellent swimming, snorkeling and diving in the bay.

NILE CRUISES

Tour Groups from all over the world have programs for Egypt ranging from five to thirty days. Most specialize in Nile valley tours, including excursions by boat. Recently the other wonders of Egypt have become available to the traveler. Trips to the oases, *felucca* journeys on the Nile, dive tours to the Red Sea and trekking tours in Sinai are all available.

There no less than 60 tourist boats sailing the Nile waters. Apart from restaurant cruises, there are five-day/four-night Nile cruises between Luxor and Aswan. In June, the Nileboats are brought to Cairo for repair. In September, they return to Luxor. Cheap fares are available for travel along the river during these times.

Feluccas journeys on the Nileare a bit primitivebut wonderful. For four-day trips, between Luxor and Aswan consult Wonder Travel, 6 Bustan St., Cairo or any boatman in Luxor and Aswan. Avearge price is about L.E. 150. For additional cruises consult a local travel agent.

There is also a wide range of cruises to choose from and depending on the operators, these tours are classified in terms of price and quality under a star rating system.

Five-Star Cruises
Mena House: *Shaherazade, Shaherayar.* Mena House, Oberoi, Pyramids Road, Giza. Tel: 855544.

Hilton: *Isis, Osiris*, Nile Hilton, Kornish el Nil, Cairo, Tel: 750666; Tlx: 92222UN.

Sheraton: *Ani, Aton, Hotp, Tut*, Sheraton International Hotel Company, 48B Giza St., Orman Building, Giza. Tel: 987200/ 988607; Tlx: 93355UN. International bookings, Tel: 800-334-8484.

Four-Star Cruises
Pyramids: *Queen Cleopatra, Queen Nefertiti, El Karnak.* Pyramids Tours Company, 1 Talaat Harb Square, Cairo. Tel: 758655; Tlx: 92575PYRAM UN.

Three-Star Cruises
Eastmar: *Memphis, Nefertari.* Eastmar Tours, 13 Kasr el Nil, Cairo. Tel: 75216; Tlx: 93743ESMR UN.

CULTURE PLUS

MUSEUMS

ALEXANDRIA

Greco-Roman Museum: Sh. Musé. behind Alexandria Municipality (Mohafsa). Open from 9 a.m. to 4 p.m. Friday closed from 11.30 a.m. to 1.30 p.m. The Greco-Roman Museum, founded in 1891, contains Hellenistic artifacts including a collection of Tanagra statuettes, frescoes and mosaics.

Mahmoud Said Museum, 6 Mahmoud Fasha Said St., Gianaclis. Open from 9 a.m. to 4 p.m. There is an entrance fee. It honors Egypt's greatest painter.

Marine Life Institute and Aquarium, near Qaitbay Fort. Open from 9 a.m. to 1.30 p.m. A collection of marine life from the seas around Egypt.

Natural History Museum, Open from 9 a.m. to 5 p.m.

Museum of Fine Arts (Musee des Beaux Arts), Sh. Menasce, Moharram Bey. Open from 9 a.m. to 2 p.m. and from 5 p.m. to 8 p.m. Closed on Monday.

Royal Jewelry Museum, Sh. Ahmed Yehya Pasha, Zizinia. Open from 9 a.m. to 4 p.m., closed Friday from 11 a.m. to 1.30 p.m. An interesting collection of items, mostly personal, belonging to members of the Muhammad Ali dynasty, housed in the former home of Princes Fatma Al Zahraa, daughter of Prince Ali Haidar, grand-daughter of Prince Rushdi, great-grand-daughter of Prince Mustafa Bahgat Fadil, and great-great-grand-daughter of Ibrahim Pasha.

Qaitbay Fort, Naval Museum, Eastern Harbor. Open from 9 a.m. to 1.30 p.m. The museum features whale skeletons, model ships and boats, from ancient to modern times. Across from it is the **Aquarium**.

Agricultural Museum, next to the Ministry of Agriculture in Dokki, Tel: 700063/702079/702933. Daily from 9 a.m. to 4 p.m., Friday from 9 a.m. to 11.30 p.m. and from 1 p.m. to 4 p.m.

Bayt Sennari, 17 Haret Monge, Tel: 938565. An old Islamic house which is now an Art Center. Open from 9 a.m. to 2 p.m., except Fridays.

Bayt Sihaymi, Darb al-Asfar, Gamaliyyah (off the Qsabah near the Al Hakim mosque). A typical old-fashioned Cairene townhouse (see pages 160 - 161), it houses a small collection of export-ware, Chinese procelain made speciafically for the Arab market. The Darb al Affar is the only street where over-hanging lattice-work windows have been restored.

Center For Art and Life, Manisteirli Palace, Roda Island, next to the Nilometer, Tel: 986931. Exhibits of Pharaonic art, ceramics, batik, painting, photography, handicrafts, glass, pottery and textiles. Open from 9 a.m. to 2.30 p.m. except Friday.

Coptic Museum, Old Cairo, Tel: 841766. Collection of objects from the Christian era including the Coptic textiles. Open daily from 9 a.m. to 4 p.m., Friday from 9 a.m. to 11 a.m. and from 1 p.m. to 4 p.m. In summer the hours are from 8 a.m. to 1 p.m.

Cotton Museum, beside the Agricultural Museum.

Egyptian Antiquities Museum, Midan El Tahrir, Tel: 754310. The finest collection of Pharaonic antiquities in the world. Open daily from 8 a.m. to 4 p.m., Friday from 9 a.m. to 11.15 a.m. and then from 1.30 p.m. to 4 p.m.

Entomological Society Museum, 14 Sharia Ramses. It houses a collection of birds resident and migrant in Egypt.as well as an insect collection. Visiting hours are from 9 a.m. to 1 p.m. daily except Sunday-and from 6 p.m. to 9 p.m. on Saturday, Monday and Wednesday.

Ethnological Museum, 109 Sharia Kasr El Aini, in the Geographic Institute. Display of crafts and costumes. Open daily from 9 a.m. to 1 p.m. except Friday and Wednesday open from 9.30 a.m. to 6 p.m.

Gawharah Palace Museum (Qasr el Gawharah) at the Citadel Tel: 926187. Furniture, Turkish paintings, clocks, glass, and 19th-century costumes. Special features include King Farouk's wedding throne and Khedive Ismail's bedroom furniture moved here from the Abdin Palace. Hours 9 a.m. to 5 p.m. E 25p, FLE2 (included as part of Citadel visit). See page 153.

Gayer Anderson House, adjoining Ibn Tulan Mosque, Tel: 847822. Two 16th- and 18th-century Islamic houses restored by Major Gayer-Anderson. Open daily from 9 a.m. to 3.30 p.m., Friday from 9 a.m. to 11 a.m. and from 1.30 p.m. to 3.30 p.m. (See page 149).

Gezira Museum in the Planetarium building at Gazirah. Exhibition Grounds, entrance on Sharia Tahrir at the Galaa Bridge, Tel: 806982. The museum houses paintings, sculptures and art objects that once belonged to the royal family. The collection includes glass, metalwork; pottery from Persia, Greece, Egypt and Asia Minor; Persian carpets, and paintings and sculpture from the French, English, Italian and Flemish schools including works by Rubens, Renoir, Rodin and others. In the same building is the **National Museum for Civilization** (Museum of Egyptian Civilization), Tel: 340-5198. This small museum contains paintings and models depicting the history of Egypt from prehistory to the present period. 9 a.m. to 3 p.m. daily, closed Friday. E 50p, FLE1.

Higher Institute of Folklore, 18 Borsa El Qadimah, Tel: 752460. Interesting collection of costumes, crafts and music from the different oases. Open daily from 9 a.m. to 2 p.m. except Friday.

Islamic Art Museum, Midan Ahmed Maher, Tel: 903930. Excellent collection of Islamic objects. Open daily from 9 a.m. to 4 p.m. Fridays from 9 a.m. to 11 a.m. and from 1.30 p.m. to 4 p.m. Entrance fee L.E. 2.00. The entrance ticket may also be used for visiting the Gayer Anderson House (see above).

Mahmoud Khalil Collection, Amr Ibrahim Palace, opposite Gezira Sporting Club, 1 Sharia El Sheikh Marsafy, Zamalek. Paintings, sculpture and other works, chiefly 19th-century European. Open daily from 9 a.m. to 2 p.m. and from 5 p.m. to 8 p.m. except Friday (see pages 170-171).

Manial Palace Museum, Roda Island, Tel: 843592. Palace and gardens, a private mosque and a small Hunting Museum with a collection of birds and animals. Exquisite furnishings. Open daily from 9 a.m. to 2 p.m.

Military Museum. The Citadel, Tel: 920955. A record of the military history of Egypt, with displays including swords, cannons, rifles, equipment and uniforms. Open daily from 9 a.m. to 2 p.m., except Tuesday.

Mukhtar Museum, Gezira, just before Al Galaa Bridge, Tel: 805198. Built by the late Ramses Wissa Wasse, it houses the works of Mahmoud Mukhtar, one of Egypt's leading sculptors. It opens at 9 a.m. till 5 p.m.

Musaferkhana Palace, behind El Hussein Mosque, Darb El Tablawi, Gamalia, Tel: 920472. Palace built by Mahmoud Moharram in 1779, later the birthplace of the Khedive Ismail. Restored by the Ministry of Culture, it now serves as a center for artists. Open daily from 8 a.m. to 2 p.m. If you wish to see the artists' work it is best to call for an appointment. It is closed on Friday

Museum of Hygiene and Medicine, Maydan Sakakini. Established in 1927 by King Fuad under the guidance of the Dresden Museum of Hygiene, it contains displays of human anatomy, physiology and pathology and is housed in the fantastic Sakakini Palace, built in 1898 by a family of Syrian financiers. The building alone is worth a visit. The hours are 9 a.m. to 2 p.m., daily but it is closed Friday.

Museum of Modern Art, 18 Sharia Ismail Abul Fetouh, off Midan El Sad Aali, Dokki, Tel: 815369. Permanent exhibits of Egyptian painters and sculptors. Open daily from 9 a.m. to 1.30 p.m.; Friday from 9 a.m. to 11.30 a.m.

National Art Development Institute of Mashrabeya, 47 Suleiman Gohar, Tel: 711604. 40 craftsmen are reviving the Islamic arts of wood and marble inlay, mashrabeya and metalwood. The best buys (made to order) in Egypt.

Nagi Museum. Below the Pyramids. Works and memorabilia of Mohammed Nagi (1888-1956), Alexandrian neo-Impressionist, pioneer of modern Egyptian painting. Closed Friday.

Natural History Museum Giza Zoo Sharia Giza Gl, Tel: 726314/233. This small museum contains an excellent display of birds, reptiles and mammals from all over the world. Fee 20p.

Ornithology Museum, in the Cairo Zoo, Tel: 896758. A small collection of birds.

Palace of Arts (Akhnaton Gallery), across from the Marriott Hotel, corner of 1 Sharia El Maahad El Swissry and 155 Sharia July 26, Zamalek. This former home of Aisha Fahmy now houses temporary exhibits of works of major artists. Open daily from 9 a.m. to 1 p.m. and from 5 p.m. to 8 p.m., Friday from 9 a.m. to 11 a.m. and from 5 p.m. to 8 p.m.

Post Office Museum, Midan El Ataba, Post Office Building, second floor, Tel: 910011. A collection of memorial stamps. Open daily from 9 a.m. to 1 p.m.

Shawqi Museum 6 Ahmed Shawki off Murad Giza, Tel: 729479. The home of the poet has been renovated to house memorabilia. Ahmed Shawki (1868-1932) composed lyrics which have been sung by such famous Egyptian singers as Abdel Wahab and Umm Kalthum. Hours 9 a.m. to 3 p.m., E 50p, FLE1.

The Geological Museum is situated at the beginning of the Corniche going toward Maadi with entrance on Atar al Nabi, Misr al Qadimah (Old Cairo), Tel: 982608/2580. Recently moved from its home on Sharia Sheikh Rihan to this temporary location, the museum is part of the Geological Survey of Egypt. Specimens on display include vertebrates, like the Fayoum Animal from the Eocene Period; invertebrates, rocks and minerals, including moon rocks, meteorites and gemstones; fossil skeletons, building stones and old Stone Age implements. 9 a.m. to 2 p.m. closed Friday. Visitors will have to pay an entrance fee.

The Mustafa Kamil Tomb and Museum below the Citadel, Midan Salah al Din, Tel: 919943. The great nationalit's tomb, in highly polished marble, is just inside the entrance. Additional rooms contain correspondence, photographs, clothing and library.

The Railway Museum east end of the main station at Midan Ramsis Tel: 763793. Established in 1933, this museum contains early steam engines, railway coaches, the Khedive Ismail's private train, and models of trains and stations throughout Egypt. 9 a.m. to 2 p.m. 9 a.m. to 11 a.m. on Friday, closed Monday and holidays. E 50p, FLE1.

The Royal Carriage Museum 82 26th July, Bulak Tel: 774437. With all the renovations that have occurred recently, it is hoped that this exceptional museum is high on the list of priorities for conservation Housed in the original building used by the Khedives as the Royal Stables and Carriage House, the museum now shares its space with a factory and a car park. The visitor must pass through these areas to get to the museum, which is well worth the effort. There are two floors, the first devoted to the carriages, the second to costumes and trappings. There are 78 royal carriages representing 22 different types of vehicles. Most were presented to the rulers of Egypt as gifts. One of the most impressive is a berlin given to the Khedive Ismail by Napoleon III and the Empress Eugenie in celebration of the opening of the Suez Canal. There are 7 displays and 20 cupboards on the second floor containing metals, saddles, uniforms, livery, trappings and oil paintings. There is also a rare collection of engineering drawings illustrating the construction of the carriages. Excellent catalog in Arabic with details on types and uses of carriages, descriptions of livery and trappings. 9 a.m. to 3.30 p.m. daily. E 10p, F25p. A second Carriage Museum with carriages borrowed from this collection exists at the Citadel.

The Saad Zaghloul Museum (or Beit al Umma, House of the Nation), 2 Saad Zaghloul, at the metro stop of the same name, Tel: 354-5399. This, the former residence of the Egyptian statesman, the main inspiration for the 1919 Revolution. It is directly across the street from his Neo-Pharoanic tomb. 9 a.m. to 3 p.m. closed Friday, E50p, FLE1.

The Solar Boat Museum on the southern side of Khufu's Pyramid, Tel: 857928. This museum houses the oldest known boat in the world (4,500 years old). Discovered in 1,200 pieces in a pit now under the museum, the 43m boat has been restored and maintained in controlled temperature and humidity conditions. 9 a.m. to 2.30 p.m. LE6.

The Wax Museum Ain Helwan Station, Helwan. This museum is very small and in a shabby condition with inferior wax models depicting events in Egyptian history. 9 a.m. to 5 p.m., closed Friday. E25p, FLE1.

Additional museums include: **Airport Museum** Cairo International Airport Tel: 291-4277, open 24 hours; **Helwan Palace Museum** Tel: 340-5198, currently closed to the public; **Mohammed Ali Palace and Museum** Corniche al Nil Shubra, currently closed to the public.

CAIRO OPERA HOUSE

The New Cairo Opera House (National Cultural and Educational Centre) is a state-of-the-art facility built and equipped by the Japanese,. It was opened at the Gazirah Exhibition Grounds in 1988, a belated replacement for the much-loved old one at Azbakiyyah burned in 1971 (see pages 168 and 170), where there were recitals and symphonic concerts, as well as an annual opera season during which both local and foreign companies performed. The new Opera House likewise provides not only avenue for visiting artists, but also a home for government-supported bodies such as the Cairo Symphony Orchestra, the Cairo Ballet, and the Cairo Opera Company.

The **Cairo Symphony Orchestra**, staffed by both Egyptian and foreign musicians, is said to have known better days.

The **Cairo Ballet** is the product of the National Ballet Institute, which was founded with Soviet help in 1960 and run for 12 years in accord with the high standards evolved by Russian tradition. Until 1972, when all the Soviet advisors were expelled by order of President Sadat, students at the Institute were thus Russian-trained. Gradutaes entered the corps de ballet, which performed at the old Opera House. The repertoire included Don Quichotte, The Fountain of Bakhchiserai and Chopiniana - and the best of themwent on for further training and performing experience with the Bolshoi in Moscow. Standards have declined, however, in recent years, despite popular enthusiasm, and public performances in Egypt are rarer than private ones in Saudi Arabia where it has become fashionable to hire the Cairo Ballet to add pomp and grandeur to wedding celebrations.

The **Cairo Opera Company,** which first performed in Arabic in 1961, currently consists of members of the Cairo Symphony Orchestra and several individual singers of a high professional quality.

THEATRES

Local and guest artists and directors perform year-round at the **National Theatre** in Azbakiyyah, the **Gomhouriya Theatre** near Abdin, the **Balloon Theatre** in Agouza, and the new **Opera House** on Gazirah. Performances are advertised.

Cairo Puppet Theatre: Performances are held in Azbakiyyah Gardens Thursday through Saturday at 6.30 p.m. and Friday and Sunday at 11 a.m. Dialogue is in Arabic, but the gestures and meanings of the local and visiting performers are not too difficult to follow.

Pocket and **Pioneer Theatre:** The Pocket Theatre, also called the Zaki Tolaimat Theater, located at Midan Attaba, is the avant-garde theater of Egypt. In Arabic, some performances are translations of foreign plays, while Arabic plays usually have controversial themes. The **Pioneer Theatre** is also *avant-garde* and features new talent.

AUC Theatre Company: Productions are in English, French and Arabic and are held from September to May in two theaters (Wallace and Howard), both on the campus of the American University in Cairo.

Sayed Darwish Theatres is located on Sharia Gamal el Din el Afghani in Cairo and in the old opera house in Alexandria. This theater is used by the ballet, opera company, student performers of the conservatory and the Academy of Arts. It is a showcase for performers of traditional Arabic music and composers working to develop new music with classical themes. There are Classical Arabic Music concerts every Thursday at 9.30 a.m.

City of Arts: Located on Pyramid Road, this complex houses the **National Conservatory of Music, National Ballet, Dramatic Arts Institute, Folk Art Institute** and **Cinegraphic Institute**.

National Folk Dance Troupes: The **National Folk Dance Troupe** was organized to preserve the folk heritage of Egypt. Performances are at the Balloon Theatre. The Reda Folklore Troupe winters in Cairo from October to March, also at the Balloon Theatre, and in Alexandria through the summer. The Aswan Nubian Folk Troupe performs nightly, except Friday, at the

Aswan Cultural Center, Aswan,

Egyptian National Circus: Founded in 1906, the Circus has three troupes: two traveling shows and one permanently in Cairo. (Alexandria in July and August). In 1960, it went through a renaissance with training by Soviet experts. It is now a one-ring extravaganza complete with band, acrobats, pantomime artists and animals. The big top is located south of the Balloon Theatre in Agouza. Performances start at 9 p.m. and usually end around 11.30 p.m.

NIGHTLIFE

NIGHT CLUBS

MOVIES

Cinema: Egyptian cinema, marketing 40-50 films a year, produces most of the films for the Arab World and has been called the "Hollywood of the East." The first cinema studio in Cairo, **Studio Misr**, built by Talaat Harb, is located on the Saqqarah Road. Like most other studios, it is owned by the government. **Studio Al Ahram** and **Studio Nahas** are two other leading studios in Egypt. They are also located near the Pyramids. **Studio Galal**, in Abbassiya, has been leased by the government to Youssef Shahin, Egypt's foremost film director.

Every major hotel has a disco, a gambling casino or a nightclub. The nightclubs feature western and eastern entertainment with, of course, belly dancers.

ALEXANDRIA

Au Privé Nightclub, 14 Ave., El-Horreya. Tel: 380-82/290-75.
Santa Lucia, 40 Safia Zaghloul St., Tel: 203-32.

CAIRO

Aladin, Cairo Sheraton Hotel, Tel: 730-333.
Ali Baba, Shepheard's Hotel, Tel: 553-800.
Arizona, Pyramid Road, Tel: 850-204.
Auberge De Pyramids, Pyramid Road, Tel: 852-548.
Casino Pariziana, 102 Pyramid St., Giza, Tel: 853-91
Churchill (Baron Hotel). Off Oruba, Heliopolis. Tel: 292-2468/291-5757 ext 2014.
Club 36, Roof of Ramses Hilton, Tel: 744-400.
Granada City, Midan Opera, Tel: 439-804.**Jackie's**, Nile Hilton. Tahrir Square Cairo. Tel: 74-0777.
Jet Set, Marriott Hotel. Saraya El Gezira St., Zamalek. Tel: 340-6728/340-8888.
Le Baron, Sheraton Heliopolis. Oruba St., Heliopolis. Tel: 66-7700/66-5500.
Le Papillion, Mövenpick Heliopolis. Airport. Tel: 66-4977.
Mena House, Pyramids Road, Tel: 855-444.
Meridien Hotel, Garden City, Tel: 845-

444.

Nile Hilton Hotel, Corniche El Nile, Tel: 740-777.**Pub 13 Disco**, Sweet Hotel. Rd 13 Maadi. Tel: 350-4544.

Raja Hotel, Sh. Mohied-Din Abu 'l' Ezz, Dokki. Tel: 700-096.

Rasputin, Green Pyramids Hotel. Helmiat Alahram St., Off Pyramids Rd. Tel: 85-6778/85-6887.

Régine's, Gezira Sheraton. Gezira. Tel: 341-1336/341-1555.

Rosen, El Nil Hotel. Garden City. Tel: 354-2800.

Saddle Disco, Mena House Oberoi Hotel. Pyramids Rd Giza. Tel: 85-5444/85-5523.

Sahara House, Pyramid Area, T el: 970-126.

Shalemar, Cairo/Alex Road Pyramid Area, Tel: 850-234.

Sheraton Hotel, Heliopolis, Tel: 665-500.

Sinbad, Sonesta Hotel. Al Tayaran St., Nasr City. Tel: 60-9444.

Sultana's Semiramis International Hotel, Corniche el Nil. Tel: 355-7171.

Tamango, Atlas Zamalek Hotel. 10 Gameat El Dowal Al Arabia, Mohandessin. Tel: 346-4175.

Tamerina, Siag Pyramids Hotel, Tel: 850-874.

Two Seasons Supper Club, Ramses Hilton Hotel, 1115 Corniche El Nil Cairo, Tel: 744-400.

Vendome, 287 Pyramid St., Giza, Tel: 854-138

Why Not, Belair Hotel. Mokattam Hills. Tel: 91-0000/91-6177.

SHOPPING

WHAT TO BUY

Best buys in **Alexandria** are **leather goods** (shoes, handbags) and *brocante*, the detritus of the city's cosmopolitan community, which left behind masses of the sort of junk that has almost disappeared elsewhere. Leather goods can be bought in shops in or near Sh. Nebi Danyal. For junk, Alexandrians sift through goods displayed or stored in the district known as the **Attarine**. Mass-produced Art Nouveau or Art Deco items are in good supply and lovers of Kitsch will not be disappointed. Among the miscellaneous bric-a-brac, treasures are sometimes found.

Cairo has always been a great consumer of luxury goods, which were being brought from as far away as Spain and China at a time when Europe was still in its Dark Ages. Dotted around the historic zone are the remains of **wakalat**, the caravanserais of merchants, which also served as warehouses and shopping centers. For a description of Cairo's remaining markets and bazaars, see pages 176-179. Most tourists are quickly introduced to **Khan al Khalili**, formerly a bazaar for Turkish importations—glass and carpets—but now an emporium for such locally-made goods as may be of particular interest to foreigners. Better bargains may be found in the Coppersmiths' Bazaar (see page 159) or in the **Tentmakers' Bazaar** (pages 156, 178), though it is said that treasures still occasionally surface in the Khan. And even Cairenes buy much of their jewelry there. Cairenes do a great deal more shopping, however, in public-sector department stores and in private-sector galleries and boutiques.

Shopping areas in **Luxor** include the arcades by the **Winter Palace** and the main suq street, **Sharia el Birka. Alabaster** workshops abound and it is the best to buy there. There are two types for purchase, hand-made with a dull finish and machine made with a matt polish.

In **Aswan**, the market is **Sharia Abtal el Tahrir**. Browsing through the mixture of spices, semi-precious stones, and animal artifacts, you will feel you have left the Arab World behind and plunged into Africa.

Baskets: Every region in Egypt has its own distinct type of basket. Best places to buy are in the village suqs. The **Badrisheen suq**, near Saqqarah, is held every Wednesday morning. The merchandise is meant for the villagers in the area, but the treasure hunter will find wonderful folk art items. In **Fayyum**, baskets are on sale by the waterwheel in the main square of Fayyum city. In Aswan, the typical flat plate-like baskets are getting harder and harder to find, but are still available. In Farafrah Oasis young girls will come running with baskets the minute they see you approaching. But the best buys of all are the wonderful wedding baskets from **Siwah**. If you are lucky enough to go there, just stand in the main square of Siwah City and say "basket." They'll bring them to you.

Ready-made clothes: Egypt boasts some excellent couturier-designers, almost all of whose work is carried out on commissions from abroad and is therefore not normally displayed. Other designers have created lines of ready-made clothes, however, that compete successfully with such international labels as Benetton and are available in all boutiques.

Gallebiyyas: For sleeping, lounging, or informal wear there is nothing like an Egyptian gallibeyyah. They are found in all suqs and in all sizes and designs. They can be bought off the rack or made to order in one day. Plain or highly elaborate in cotton, fine silk, brocade or synthetic fabric.

Bedouin Dresses: Women from different Bedouin tribes wear different style dresses, but all are handmade and most have a great deal of embroidery on them. The most beautiful are those from **Siwah**. Northern Sinai dresses are cross-stitched in reds, orange and yellows, or blues and pinks. They can be bargained for in the villages on the way to El Arish, the Khan il Khalili, Luxor Bazaar, or at Kerdassa.

Bedouin Jewelry: Again the styles vary, but they are always in silver or base white metal and usually quite large. Earrings, rings, bracelets and necklaces are mostly with heavy designs and are quite weighty to put on.

Bedouin rugs, made on small looms vary in design from tribe to tribe. The most popular ones are red and white stripped from the Northern Coast; the most difficult to find are the green and orange diamond patterns from the Sinai region.

Kirdassah is a village of weavers that once served the caravan routes to the western desert. You can watch rugs and fabrics being loomed. Big operators have usurped the main street, but one can still find excellent buys with a little effort.

Harraniya is an exciting place to visit. **Harraniya** tapestries were once woven by children. Now the second generation is learning the trade. One can visit the village on the Saqqarah Road, but buying is only at Senouhi's. Many imitation shops have opened, so be sure you are at Harraniyya. The village is constructed of mud brick vaults and domes.

Carpets and Tapestries: Egypt is a producer of both flat-woven (kelim) and hand-knotted carpets. Though not very inspired in their designs—adaptations of Persian patterns that have simply been assigned to a weaver for production—the hand-knotted carpets are serviceable and reasonably priced. Flat-woven carpets are also hand-made and many of them are considered as folk art.

Brass and Copper: In the **Coppersmiths' Bazaar** (see page 177) are artisans who have been handling down their skills from generation to generation. Best buys are brass trays inlaid with copper, silver; incised with Arabic calligraphy and Islamic designs. Also to be considered are plates, candlesticks, gongs, lamps, mugs, and nameplates, coffee-pots and cooking pots.

Glass: Muski glass in turquoise, brown, blue, pink or green is available in a variety of objects including Christmas ornaments. The imperfections, cracks and bubbles make each piece unique but very fragile.

Jewelry: Silver is fairly inexpensive and the designs are Pharaonic, Islamic and modern. For a good selection try **Saads** in the Khan. where beautiful plates with Islamic designs.are also available.

Gold: Chains are imported, but the bobbles that hang from them are crafted here in the form of **Scarabs, kartouches, eyes-of Horus, hand of Fatma** or **Arabic calligraphy**. For unusual jewelry, try **Al Ain** and **Senouhi**.

Papyrus: A few decades ago papyrus was virtually extinct in Egypt. Revived by Dr. Raghab of the Raghab Papyrus Institute (Alexandria, Cairo, Luxor, Aswan) there are now shops all over Egypt selling hand painted papyrus sheets from miniature size to large folio. Surest buys are at Dr. Raghab's, where a visitor is given a tour of the factory where they are made.

Pottery: A wide variety of turned pots serve the people of the Nile valley. The **zir**, in a variety of sizes, is to purify and cool water. The **ula** is a smaller version. Both are available in village bazaars. There are potters in Asyut, who throw large-mouthed round pots in a variety of sizes; in Ballas there are the elongated small-lipped pots often depicted as traditionally Egyptian; in Siwah, short fat wide-lipped pots with red designs, and, the most unusual you will ever see, in Farafrah, pots with elongated bullet shaped sides with a small lip in the center. But the best, and most functional, are the wonderful pots found in Luxor that come in a variety of shapes and sizes and can be used for cooking. The costs are in piasters. Twice a year (early December in Cairo and mid-May in Alexandria) the potters of Garagos, a village in Upper Egypt 17 miles (28 km) north of Luxor (any taxi driver will take you for about LE20) exhibit and sell their wares.

Fine pottery of a much higher quality—and price—is made by a number of artisans, the most notable of whom have kilns along the Saqqarah Road, in the village of Shabramant, and in the Fayyum.

Fakes: Be very wary of genuine antiquities. Some may in fact be old, forged 100 years ago for a tourist just like yourself, others crafted by workmen at Luxor. These men are highly skilled, and if you like an object, but it for its workmanship, but pay a quarter or less of the original asking price.

Book Stores: English language bookstores can be found in all major hotels. For rare books, try The Orientalist on Kasr il Nil Street, Cairo. Second hand books, in Arabic and English, can be found at the stalls in Opera Square, Cairo. The best English language bookshop in Egypt is the recently expanded **American University in Cairo Press Campus Shop** on the main campus of the university,

Alexandria Book Stores

Al-Ahram, 10 Fouad, (Avenue el-Horreva), Tel: 805-000.
Al-Maaref, 44 Saad Zaghloul, next to Brazilian Coffee, Tel: 333-63.
Dar El-Maaref, 42 Saad Zaghloul, Tel: 235-88.

Cairo Book Stores

Al Ahram Bookstore, 165 Mohamed Farid Sherif St., Tel: 924-499.
Eagles Book Shop, 87 Rd. 9 Maadi, Tel: 505-450.
El Arab Bookshop, (Oriental Books—Agent of the Library of Congress in the Middle East), 28 Faggalah St., Tel: 908-025.
Every Man's Bookshop, 12 Baghdad St., Heliopolis.
Lehnert & Landrock Bookshop, 44 Sherif Pasha St., Cairo, Tel: 755-324.
Les Livres de France, Kasr El Nil St., (Immobilia Bldg.), Cairo, Tel: 755-12.
Mangozzi Bookshop, 19 Sharia 26 July, Cairo, Tel: 750-955.
Nile Christian Bookshop, 8 Sharia Alfi, Cairo, Tel: 741-028.
The American University in Cairo Bookshop,
Zamalek Bookstore, 19 Shagaret El Dor Zamalek, Tel: 419-197.

SHOPS

The following is a listing of some of the bigger shops in Alexandria and Cairo.

ALEXANDRIA

El-Ostaz, 28 Rue de France, Manshia, near Souk el-kheet, Tel: 801-179.
Gopaldas, 52 Saad Zaghloul, Tel: 807-516.
Khan il-Khalili Bazaar, 32 Rue Fouad, Avenue el-Horreya, Tel: 823-06.
Miguo Khandjian, (Silver Jewelry), 5

Eglise Debbane, Tel: 806-057.

Mohamed El-Abd, 12 Souk Akadin, Manshia, off gold market, Tel: 800-288/ 809-814.

Petraki Bazaar, 32 Saad Zaghloul, Tel: 807-06.

Sacrabee, 16 Talaat Harb St., Tel: 806-086.

CAIRO

Abas Hegazi, (Galabayes), Tel: 924-730/ 939-352.

.AKhan Karoun, 150 El Nil St.,Tel: 802-928.

Al Ain Gallery, 73 Houssein St., Mohan-dassin.

Amir Agha Amir Zada, (Precious Stones), Tel: 905-474.

Andree Fahmy, (Exclusive pharaonic designs of jewelry), by appointment only, tel: 842-441

Arouani, Ibrahim, (Brass & Copper), Tel: 900-793.

Atlas, (Craftans & Galabeyyas), Tel: 906-139.

Bakr El Soudani, Mohamed, (Leather Goods), Tel: 934-306.

Dr Raghab Papyrus Institute, 3 El Nil Giza, Tel: 730-476.

El Ghaffar, Mohmoud Abd, (Scarves & Leather Goods), 73 Gawhar El Kayeed, Tel: 902-769.

El Lahlah, (Carpets), Tel: 900-173.

Hamdi, (Copper & Brass), Tel: 915-910.

Hassan & Aly Abdelaal, (Mother of Pearl & Inlaid Works), Tel: 903-361.

Khan Il Khalili Bazaar

Lamai Abdel Malek, (Ivory), Tel: 906-168.

M Ahmed Awad, (Copper & Brass), Tel: 919-430.

Mahmoud Aly El Sadfgy, (Ivory & Mother of Pearl), Tel: 904-844/904-976.

Mohamed A Mostafa, (Silver), Tel: 908-201.

Margaret's (Western cotton dresses), Zamalek.**Mohamed Said Hassan**, (Leather & Tent Works), Tel: 912-593.

Moustafa Soliman, (Tent Maker), 8 Wekalet El-Makwa, Tel: 901-864.

Morgana, Rd 9, Maadi.

Saad, (Silver), 10 Shwlkar Bldg., Khan il Khalili, Tel: 921-401; Ramses Hilton Hotel, Tel: 777-444.

Sayed Abd El Raouf, (Mousky Glass), Tel: 915-910.

Senouhiis, 54 Abdel Kahalek Sarwat, 5th Fl.

Sheahiras, 12 Abi Emama, 6th Fl., near Cairo Sheraton, Tel: 988-182.

The lists are by no means exhaustive and there are many good bargains to be enjoyed if the visitor is adventurous enough to look for them.

SPORTS

Gliding can be found at Embaba Airfield every Thursday and Friday. The **Egyptian Gliding Institute** provides four training gliders with double seats and four solo training gliders for advanced or professional pilots. The **Egyptian Aviation Society** has two double-seat motor gliders. Both groups offer lessons. A plane and pilot can be rented by the hour. Trips over the pyramids and the Nile are standard fare. It is forbidden to glide over the city. With special permission, long distance gliding can be arranged. For civilian airports, permisssion procedures take one day, but for military airports the wait is 15 days. The authorities at Ambaba have all the details.

Golf: There are only two nine-hole golf courses in Cairo, one at the **Gezira Club** in Zamalek and the other at the **Mena House Oberoi** in Giza, (with the pyramids as a backdrop). Equipment can be rented

Tennis: Tennis courts are available in most major hotels throughout the country and in sporting clubs (*see* below).

Riding: There are a number of stables near the pyramids, and the trails take you through agricultural land or the desert. The best time for riding is at sunrise or sunset. Long-distance trips to Saqqarah can be arranged. Stables in the Pyramids area include: **MG, KM, SA, AA**, and **FF**. They also provide riding lessons,

Shooting: Egypt is a major flight-path for migratory species and hunts for waterfront can be arranged through the **Shooting Club** in Dokki. The Egyptian environment is already endangered however, and matters have not been helped in recent years by parties of "sportsmen" from the Gulf and Southern Europe who have been allowed to use automatic weapons to carry out mass killings. In 1988, for example, one hunt by a small group of Maltese, in whose own country such shooting is banned, resulted in the deaths of 10,000 birds, including sparrows, many kinds of raptors, storks, herons and other species not normally considered game. Arab huntsmen have meanwhile not only reduced the resident falcon population by offering inflated prices for captured birds, but have also attacked endangered species of both birds and mammals, using weaponry that included machine guns. Egyptian standards of sportsmanship by contrast, are high and appropriate legislation do exist, though the Egyptian Wildlife Association has stated that it is rarely enforced, even in the Sinai.

Fishing: Sport fishing is available along the Nile on the Red Sea, and on the Mediterranean, as well as in the lakes along the northern coast, in the Fayyum and above Aswan. Protected areas, where it is forbidden to fish with lines, spears, nets or explosives, include the Gulf of Aqaba from Taba to Ras Mehammed. The Egyptian Wildlife Association urges persons seeing violations to report them to the nearest police station. The non-competitive fisherman can make arrangements year-round to fish at Hurghada and Marsa Allam on the Red Sea. For those who wish to compete, the Egyptian Game Fishing Federation sponsors four tournaments a year. In February and July international tournaments are held at Hurghada. In April and November tournaments are held at Sharm al Sheikh. **The Shooting Club** has premises at Marsa Allam on the Red Sea and can arrange expeditions for members. Equipment available from **Mohammed Amin** 2 Sabri Abu Alam Tel: 762007.

Rowing: There are 10 rowing clubs in Cairo, and almost all are located on the east bank of the Nile between Giza and Embaba. The largest is the **Arab Contractor's Rowing Club** and the oldest is the **Armed Forces Rowing Club**. Rowing competitions start in November and run through April. They are held every Friday. Schedules can be obtained from any rowing club. Lessons are available from the **Egyptian Rowing Club**, formerly the Royal Rowing Club, at 11 Sh. Al Nil, near Cairo Sheraton, Tel: 731639.

Scuba Diving and Snorkeling: The **Cairo Diver's Club** provides aqua diving instructions and certificates (PADI). Monthly diving trips are arranged. Meetings are held on the first Monday of the month at, Arusa Room, Nile Hilton, 7.30 p.m. **Diving and Internaitonal Ventures of Egypt** also gives lessons. Accredited PADI, NAWI, CEMAS. Included in the lessons are transport to a good dive area, boat, and two dives. Accepts groups of six or more.

Diving areas in the Red Sea: There are no facilities at present at **Ain Sukhnai;** however, for people in Cairo it is the closest point on the Red Sea where there are ridge reefs and sandy beaches.

Hurghada: There are many dive shops in Hurghadhah. Just ask. There is a good mix of sea-life in the coral reefs off the shore and excellent diving around the many off-shore islands. The local fishermen know all the reefs and are a wealth of information.

Safaga: Diving activities are to be found at the Safaga Hotel Dive Center. Experienced divers only. They provide rental of tanks and weight belts. Good area for hammerhead sharks

Sharm al Shaykh: Three are dive shops and dive boats. Free camping is also available. Close to Ras Mohammad and Dahab. Around Sharm are such dive spots as **Ras Umm Sid** (dolphin and turtles). **The Tower** (barracuda), **Nei'ma Bay** (turtles) and the **Near, Middle** and **Far Gardens**, which look like Japanese gardens.

Ras Nasrani is served by the dive shops at Sharm. Rays have been seen here.

Islands of Trian and **Sanafie** are also served by Sharm where boats can be rented by divers. There are currents and dangerous reefs around the islands. It is not a place for the novice.

Dahab: One dive shop. Best features are the Canyon and Blue Hole.

Nuweiba: One dive shop. Excellent area for beginners.

Ras Mohammad is a national park. The scenery, both above and below water level, is superb. Regular trips are arranged from Sharm al Shaykh. Ras Mohammad has rocky bottom, sandy bottom and reef dives. It has several good areas from which to begin including the **Shark's Observatory**. Novices and those fearful of the sea can wade to the edge of the shelf and look over. At low tide the water is less than waist high. What awaits is a 240-feet (80-meter) deep coral shelf and an open sea beyond. Two divers claim to have seen a herd of over 70 hammerhead sharks in the area.

Sailing: See "Yacht Clubs" below.

Swimming: Every hotel with a swimming pool which offers a yearly membership or day fees for non-guests which often includes lunch.

Swimming Sporting club pools are available to members. Hotel pools may be used on a daily basis for a fee which often includes lunch. Some hotels offer yearly memberships for all sporting facilities.

SPECTATOR

Horse Racing: Races take place on Saturday and Sunday from mid-November through May at the Gazirah Sporting Club track and at the **Heliopolis Hippodrome** in Heliopolis. Races begin at 1.30 p.m. Parimutuel betting

Arabian stud farms. The Arabian horse is known throughout the world for its beauty, stamina and intelligence. The characteristics of the Arabian include a compact body and a small head with wide eyes, nostrils and forehead, small ears and a wide jawbone. The body is noted for its straight back and legs and high set tail.

Among many stud farms in Egypt are four major ones. The biggest with 300 horses is the government-owned **Egyptian Agricultural Organization, EAO**. This farm has only pure-bred bloodlines and is the home of the most influential Arabian stallion of this century, **Nazeer**. Every important stud farm in the world has some of his offspring. The three other major stud farms are all privately owned: **El Badeia**, owned by Nasr and Hassan Marei, tel: 3400166/535297; **Hamdan** owned by Ahmed Hamza, Tel: 537167; and **Shams el Asil** owned by Wegdan Barbary. These farms may be visited, but by appointment only.

In Alexandria, the **Yacht Club of Alexandria** is next to Fort Qait Bey. There is also the **Alexandria Sporting Club**. Sporting Station Avenue el-Horreya, Tel: 597629.

In Cairo, there is the **Cairo Yacht Club**, 3 Sharia el Nil, Giza, Tel: 348-9415 and the **Maadi Yacht Club**, Corniche el Nil.,Both have mooring facilities for motorboats, sailboats and yachts. Regattas are held on winter weekends. Lessons are available.

British Golfing Society. Meets regularly the last Saturday of every month at 10 a.m. at the Mena House golf course for competitions. Restriction to British passport holders not strictly enforced. Newcomers may play as guests. Nominal fee for membership. Contact Andy Matthew, Tel: 353-2342/352-0495.

British Sub Aqua Club 21 Lebanon Mohandessin Tel: 346-1105/09/10/23. Primarily a diving club, this organization also offers monthly meetings every third Monday at 8 p.m., slide shows, underwater videos, trips and equipment for hire.

Cairo Rugby Club 2 Road 161, Maadi. Weekly training Wednesday at 5 p.m. at Victory College, Maadi. Social hours Wednesday and Friday evening at club house. Facilities include dancing, pool, softball and soccer. Tel: 353-0301/350-3340/346-7962.

Cairo Sporting Club. In front of Gezirah Sheraton, Giza. Tel: 340-1204.

Cairo Yacht Club. El Nil, Giza. Tel: 348-9415.

Egyptian Rowing Club. 11 El Nil, Giza. Tel: 348-9639.

Egyptian School for Scuba Diving (Ehab Tomoum). 13 Mona, Dokki. Tel: 348-6498.

El Gezirah Sheraton Health Club (Pool/Health Club). El Gezirah Island. Tel: 341-1336.

Gezira Sporting Club (All facilities, temporary membership). Saray El Gezira, Zamalek. Tel: 340-6000.

Helio Lido Sports Club. Galaa St., Heliopolis.

Heliopolis Racing Club (Horse Rentals/Lessons). Near Hyatt El Salam Hotel, Heliopolis. Tel: 245-4090.

Heliopolis Sheraton Sports Club (Swim/Tennis/Jog). Oruba St., Heliopolis, Tel: 66-6500.

Heliopolis Sporting Club. 17 Merghany St., Heliopolis. Tel: 67-0631.

Hyatt El Salam Health Club (Swim/Health Club). 61 Abdel Hamid Badawai St., Heliopolis. Tel: 245-5155.

Indji Solh Dance Center (Dance/Aerobics/Taekwondo). 4 Omar Ibn Abd El Aziz St., Mohandessin. Tel: 349-7213.

Maadi Sporting Club. Damascus St., Maadi. Tel: 350-5504.

Marriott Health Club (Tennis/Swim/Health Club). Saray El Gezi ra St., Zamalek. Tel: 340-8888 (ask for Health).

Mena House Oberoi Sports Club (Golf, Tennis, Swimming). Pyramids Road Giza.. Tel: 85-7999.

Meridien Sports Club (Swimming/Health Club). Corniche El Nil, Garden City. Tel: 84-5444.

National Sporting Club (Home of the Ahli Football Team). Near Cairo Tower, Zamalek, Tel: 340-2112.

Nile Hilton Sports Club (Swim/Tennis/Health Club). Corniche El Nil, Cairo, Tel: 74-0777.

SheriNile Health Club (Health Club/Beauty Trtmts). 3 Essam El Daly, Giza. Tel: 349-6225. Ramses Hilton Cairo. Tel: 77-7113. Meridian, Heliopolis. Tel: 290-6672.

Shooting Club. El Sayed, Dokki. Tel: 70-4353.

Tawfikeya Sports Club. Mahrousa, Mohandessin. Tel: 346-1930.

The Cairo Diver's Club: First Monday of the month at Intercontinental Hotel 7.30 a.m. to 9.30 p.m. Aqua Diving instructions and certificates (PADI). Diving trips. Open to divers and non-divers.

The Cairo Hash House Harriers. Weekly Friday afternoon runs at Pyramids, in the desert and other locations followed by picnics and social hours. Tel: 712674.

Valentines Fitness Centre (Dance/Exercise/Wt Rm). 70 Merghany, Heliopolis. Tel: 291-4756.

Zamalek Sporting Club. Mohandessin. Tel: 347-6677.

PHOTOGRAPHY

Egypt is a photographer's paradise and it has often been called "the greatest outdoor museum in the world." Add to that the variety of the people and the diversity of the natural beauty and there is a picture to be taken every minute. So plan to bring a lot of film, then double the quantity. The best film speeds for Egypt are low (under 100), but your fast films (ASA 400, ASA 1000) will do well for spectacular night shots like the moon over the Nile or the Sound and Light at the Pyramids or Karnak. (Don't use flash. You'll only annoy those around you and get a picture of the railing in front of you.)

Restrictions. In historic areas all natural light subjects are permissible, but photography is not allowed in most tombs, museums, military zones, bridges and security areas. There are a variety of rules governing different monuments. Signs are usually posted in restricted areas. Heed them. In some areas you are permitted to take photographs if you pay a fee. At present the fees are LE 25 for still cameras, LE 50 for videos and movies. These restrictions are stricly enforced.

Exceptions. People with a genuine project can apply for a special **antiquities pass** from the Egyptian Antiquities Organization. The procedure may take some time, and passes are not given out freely; but, if you must get one, it is well worth the effort. Fees must still be paid at monuments, but with the blessings of the Egyptian Antiquities Organization comes the expertise of a guide and a host of guards who are very helpful.

Sneak Shots. There is no reason to sneak a shot at King Tut's tomb. Buy a postcard or a professional slide. Visitors should be aware of the problems facing the authorities and should put in their bit towards not aggravating the situation. The rising water table and the hundreds of bodies that enter the tombs daily are creating humidity problems.

The tombs, paintings are also flaking off. The heat from flash bulbs would only worsen the problem. Without the flash the frame will probably be wasted anyway, and you may risk having the guard confiscate your film

Photographing people also requires a bit of common sense and consideration. You are one of many tourists the Egyptian people see everyday. They are constantly having cameras pushed in their faces, so be courteous and ask. If they don't want their picture taken, don't take it. If they want to be paid, bargain first, then take the photo (no more than 50 piasters). If you don't want to pay, don't take the picture. You will find plenty of good shots elsewhere.

LANGUAGE

ARAB WORDS IN ENGLISH

From Albatross to Zero: Silks and spices were not the only products that traveled along the medieval caravan routes—words traveled too. For example, the word **zero**, and the concept attached to it, started in India, passed through the Arab world and moved on to Europe and the United States. In fact, the road leads as far as San Francisco Bay where the island of **Alcatraz** was named by the Spanish from a word they got from their Arab conquerors.

Look into the sky on a starry night and search out **Altair, Aldebran, Algol, Deneb** or **Rigel**? The Arabs named those stars. Then, they added the words **zenith** and **nadir** and the sky became a celestial road map that enabled the Arabs to become the greatest navigators of the medieval world. After that Arabic words really started to travel. As sailors the Arabs gave us the terms **admiral, magazine, arsenal, bark, cable, monsoon, albacore** and even the Ancient Mariner's **albatross.** As traders, the Arabs introduced the words **gauze, satin, mohair, muslin, damask, cotton, sash,** and **sequins.** The Arabs put tariffs on their goods and wrote checks to pay for goods such as **saffron, tamarind,** and **caraway.** And there's more. The Arabs were the original **alchemists** and they gave us **alcohol, alkali, alizarin, elixir,** and **alembic** while their mathematical genius gave us words like **algebra, cipher,** and **average.**

The Arab road went everywhere. In music we have the **lute** and the **tambour.** And in farming **alfalfa, artichoke, kafir,** and **hashish.** And in art and architecture **alcove, adobe** (ultimately from the Coptic) and of course that exotic word, **arabesque.**

VOCABULARY

Airport	*ma Taar*
Boat	*markeb*
Bridge	*kubri*
Car	*'arabiyya*
Embassy	*sefara*
Hospital	*mostashfa*
Hotel	*lokanda, funduq*
Post Office	*bosta*
Restaurant	*ma T am*
Square	*midaan*
Street	*shaari'*
And/or	*wal/walla*
Yes/no	*aywalla' or la'a*
Please/thank you	*minfa Dlak/shukran*
Big/little	*kibeer/Sughayyar*
Good/bad	*kuwayyis/mish kuwayyis*
High/low	*'aali/waaTi*
Possible	*mumkin/*
impossible	*mish mumkin*
Here/there	*henal/henaak*
Hot/cold	*sukhn/baarid*
Many/little	*kitiir/olayyel*
Up/down	*fo'/taHt*
More/no more	*kaman/kefaaya*
Again/enough	*kaman/kefaaya*
Breakfast	*feTaat/ifTaar*
Lunch	*ghada*
Dinner	*'asha*
Today	*enneharda*
Tomorrow	*bokrah*
Yesterday	*embareH*
After tomorrow	*ba'd bokrah*
Morning	*el SobH*
Noon	*el Dohr*
Afternoon	*ba'd el Dohr*
At night	*bellayl*
Next week	*el esbou'iggaya*
Next time	*el marra iggaya*
Last time	*el marra illi fatit*
After a while	*ba'd shwayya*
I/you/he/she/ they/we	*anal/ental/howwal/ heyya/hommal eHna*

NUMBERS

1	*WAH-hid*
2	*It-nane*
3	*Ta-LAH-TAH*
4	*Ar-bah-AH*
5	*KHAM-sah*
6	*SIT-tah*

7	Seb-ah
8	Taman-yah
9	TISS-a'ah
10	Ah-sha-rah
11	EH-DA-shahr
12	IT-NAH-shahr
13	Ta-lat-ta-shahr
14	Ar-ba'TA-shahr
15	Kha-mas-TA-shahr
16	Sit-TA-shahr
17	Saba-TA-shahr
18	Ta-man-TA-shahr
19	Tissa'ta-shahr
20	Ish-reen
30	Ta-la-teen
40	Ar-ba-EEN
50	Kham-SEEN
60	Sit-TEEN
70	Sab-EEN
80	Ta-ma-NEEN
90	Tiss-EEN
100	May-yeh

MONEY

1/2 piasters	ta-REE-fa
1 piasters	ERCG (or) saagh
1 1/2 piasters	ta-la-tah ta-REE-fa
2 piasters	noos a-frank
2 1/2 piasters	kham-sah ta-REE-fa
4 piasters	frank
5 piasters	kham-sag saagh (or)
shillin	
10 piasters	Ash-a-rah saagh (or)
bareez-a (or)	noos re-AL
20 piasters	re-AL
25 piasters	kham-sah wa aishreen
saagh (or)	roba' guinea
50 piasters	khamseen ERSH (or)
noos guinea	
75 piasters	kham-sah wa seb-EEn
ERSH (or)guinea	ella-roba
Money	feloos
Change/no change	fakka/mafiish fakka
The bill	el hesaab
This/that	di/da
How much?	bekaam?
How much is this?	di bekaam?
How much do you want (male asking)	'aayis kaam?
How much do you want (female asking)	'ayza kaam?
All/half	kul/nuS
Pound/half pound	genayh/nus genays

TIME

What time is it?	Kam es-sa-ah?
It is 1.00.	Es-sa-ah wah-dah.
It is 2.30.	Es-sa-ah it-nane wa noos.
It is 3.15.	Es-sa-ah ta-LAH-ta wa roba.
It is 4.20.	Es-sa-ah ar-bah-AH wa tilt.
It is 4.40.	Es-sa-ah KHAM-sah ella tilt.
It is 5.45.	Es-sa-ah sit-tah ella roba.

DAYS OF THE WEEK

Sunday/Monday/ Tuesday	el Had/el etnayn/el talaat
Wednesday/ Thursday	el arba' el Khamiis
Friday/Saturday	el gom! aa/el sabt

MONTHS OF YEAR

January/February/ March	yanayer/febrayer/maris
April/May/ July/August/	abriil/mayo/yonyo
Seeptember	yoyo/aghostosl/sebtembe
October/November/ December	octobar/november/disember

COMMON EXPRESSIONS

Welcome	AH-lann wa SAH-lann
Good morning	Sab-BAH el-Khair
Good evening	Ma-Saa el-Khair
Good night (until I seeyou again)	Tiss-BAH ala-Khair
Goodbye (to one leaving)	Ma-ah es-LA-mah
My name is..	Iss-me...
What is your name?	I SS-mak aih? (m) /ISS mik aih? (f)
How are you?	I z-ZAY-ak? (m)/ Iz-ZAY-ik? (f)
(The reply) I am well thanksbe to God	KWI-yes (m)/Kwi-ESS-ah (f) il-Hamdu liLAH

SPICES

Aniseed	Yansoon
Bay Leaf	Waraq lawra
Caraway	Carawiya

English	Arabic
Cardamon	*Hab han*
Chard	*Salq*
Cinnamon	*'irfa*
Cloves	*Qoronfel*
Coriander	*Cozbara*
Corncockle or Black	
Cumin	*Habet el baraka*
Cumin	*Cammoon*
Dill	*Shabat*
Ginger	*Ganzabeel*
Mistic	*Mistika*
Mixed Spice	*Boharat*
Mint	*Na'na'*
Nutmeg	*Goztet teeb*
Oregano	*Za'tar*
Parsley	*Ba'dooness*
Pepper	*Filfil*
Pepper (Hot Cayenne	
or Chilli)	*Shatta*
Safflower	*Osfor*
Sesame	*Simsim*
Sumac	*Summa'*
Greens	*Khodra*

FURTHER READING

MODERN HISTORY

Abdel-Malek, Anouar. *Egypt: Military Society*. New York: Vintage Books, 1968.

Amherst, Mary, R.M. *A Sketch of Egyptian History from the Earliest Times to the Present Day*. London: Methuen & Co., 1904.

Blunt, Wilfred Scawen. *Secret History of the English Occupation of Egypt*. New York: Howard Fertig, 1967.

Crabbs, Jack D. *The Writing of History in Nineenth-Century Egypt*. Detroit: Wayne State University Press, 1984.

Cromer, Evelyn Baring. *Modern Egypt*. Vols. I and II. London: MacMillan, 1908.

Cromer, Evelyn Bariong. *Modern Egypt*. New York: Praeger, 1967.

Crouchley, A.E. *The Economic Development of Modern Egypt*. London: Longmans Green, 1938.

Goldschmidt, Arthur, Jr. *A Concise History of the Middle East*. Second Edition. Cairo: THe American University in Cairo Press, 1983.

Heikal, Mohamad. *The Road to Ramadan*, London: William Collins Sons, 1975.

Hunter, F. Robert. *Egypt under the Khedives, 1805-1879*. Pittsburgh: University of Pittsburgh Press, 1984.

Issawi, Charles Philip. *Egypt at Mid-Century: An Economic Survey*, Oxford University Press, 1954.

Issawi, Charles Philip. *An Economic History of the Middle East and North Africa*, London: Methuen and Company.

Issawi, Charles Philps. *Egypt: An Economic and Social Analysis*. London: Oxford University Press, 1947.

Issawi, Charles Philip. *Egypt in Revolution, An Economic Analysis*, London: Oxford University Press, 1963.

Jarvis, H. Wood. *Pharaoh to Farouk.* London: John Murray, 1955.

Keay, Seymour. *Spoiling the Egyptians.* London: Kegan Paul, Trench and Co., 1882.

Little, Tom. *Egypt.* London: Ernest Benn Ltd, 1958.

Lloyd, Lord. *Egypt Since Cromer*, Vols. I and II. New York: AMS Press, 1970.

Mansfield, Peter. *The British in Egypt.* New York: Holt, Rinehart and Winston, 1971.

Marlowe, John. *A History of Modern Egypt and Anglo-Egyptian Relations, 1800-1953.* New York: Praeger, 1954.

Marsot, Afaf L. *A. Egypt and Cromer,*, New York: Praeger, 1970.

Marsot, Afaf L.A. *Egypt in the Reign of Muhammed Ali.* Cambridge: Cambridge University Press, 1984.

McBride, Barrie S. *Farouk of Egypt.* New York: A S. Barnes, 1967.

Mitchell, Richard P. *The Society of the Muslim Brothers.* London: Oxford University Press, 1969.

Naguib, Mohammed. *Egypt's Destiny.* Garden City, New York: Doubleday, 1955.

St John, Robert, *The Boss.* New, McGraw Hill, 1960.

Sabry, M. *L'Empire Egyptian sous Mohamed-Ali et la question d'Orient (1811-1849).* Paris: Librarie Orientaliste Paul Geuthner, 1930.

Schölch, Alexander. *Egypt for the Egyptians: The socio-political crisis in Egypt 1878-82.* St. Anthony's Middle East Monographs no. 14. London: Ithaca Press, 1981.

Vatikiotis, P.J. *The Egyptian Army in Politics.* Bloomington, Indiana: Indiana University Press, 1961.

The History of Egypt. Baltimore: Johns Hopkins University Press, 1980.

Waterbury, John. *The Egypt of Nasser and Sadat: The Political Economy of Two Regimes.* Princeton: Princeton University Press, 1982.

Waterbury, John. *Egypt: Burdens of the Past, Options for the Future.* Bloomington, Indiana: American Universities Field Staff, 1978.

Waterfield, Gordon. *Egypt.* London: Thames and Hudson, 1967.

Wheelock, Keith. *Nasser's New Egypt.* New York: Praeger, 1960.

PHARAONIC HISTORY

Adams, William Y. *Nubia, Corridor to Africa.* Allen Lane, London, 1977.

Breasted, James. *A History of Egypt.* London: Hodder & Stoughton, 1950.

Gardiner, Sir Alan. *Egypt of the Pharaohs.* Oxford University Press, 1961.

COPTIC HISTORY

Badaway, Alexander. *Coptic Art and Archaeology.* Cambridge, Massachusetts:., 1978.

History of Eastern Christianity. Rev. ed. 1980.

Butler, Alfred J. *The Ancient Coptic Churches of Egypt.* 2 vols. Clarendon Press, Oxford, 1884. New ed. 1970.

Kamil, Jill. *Coptic Egypt.* American University in Cairo Press, Cairo, Egypt, 1986.

Meinardus, Otto. *Monks and Monasteries of the Eastern Desert.* The American University in Cairo Press, 1961.

Christian Egypt, Ancient and Modern. 2nd ed. The American University in Cairo Press, 1977.

Christian Egypt Faith and Life. French Institute of Oriental Archaelogy, Cairo, 1970.

CAIRO

Abu Lughod, Janet. *Cairo 1001 Years of the City Victorious.* Princeton: Princeton University Press, 1971.

Antoniou, Jim et al. *The Conservation of the Old City of Cairo.* London: UNESCO, 1980.

Baedeker, Karl. *Egypt and the Sudan: Handbook for Travellers.* Leipzig Karl Baedker, 1914.

Baines, John, and Malek, Jaromir. *Atlas of Ancient Egypt.* Oxford: Plaidon, 1980.

Baud, Marcelle. *Egypte.* Paris: Librarie

Hachette, 1950.

Behrens-Abouseif, Doris. *Azbakiyya and Its Environs from Azbak to Ismail, 1476-1876*. Cairo: IFAO 1985.

Behrens-Abouseif, Doris. *The Minarets of Cairo*. Cairo: The American University in Cairo Press, 1985.

Budge, Wallace. *The Nile: Notes for Travellers in Egypt*. Ninth Edition. London and Cairo: Thomas Cook and Sons, 1905.

Bulletin Architectural Information. Supplement no. 89, November, 1984. Paris and Singapore: Institut Francais d'Architecture and *Mimar*, 1984.

Le Caire. Autrement, hors, serie no. 12, fevrier 1985, Paris: *Autre ment*, 1985.

Carman, Barry, and McPherson, John, eds. *The Man Who Loved Egypt: Bimbashi McPherson*. London: BBC, 1985.

Colloque International sur l'Histoire du Caire. Cairo: Ministry of Culture of the U.A.R., 1969.

Creswell, K.A.C. *The Muslim Architecture of Egypt*. Two vols. Oxford: Clarendon Press, 1952-1960.

Devonshire, R.R., Mrs. *Quatre-vingt mosquées et autres monuments musulmans du Cairo: Guide des visiteurs*. Cairo: Societe Royale de Geographie d'Egypte, 1924.

Edwards, I.E.S. *The Pyramids of Egypt*. London: Ebury Press and Michael Joseph, 1972.

Fargeon Maurice. *Les juifs en Egypte depuis les origines jusqu'a ce jour*. Cairo: Maurice Sananes, 1938.

Habachi, Labib. *The Obelisks of Egypt, Skyscrapers of the Past*. Cairo: The American University in Cairo Press, 1984.

Kamil, Jill. *Sakkara*. London: Longman, 1978.

Keating, R. *Nubian Rescue*. Hawthorn Books, New York, 1975.

Kessler, Christel. *The Carved Stone Domes of Cairo*. Cairo and London: The American University in Cairo Press and AARP.

KHS-Burmester, O.H.E. *A Guide to the Ancient Coptic Churches of Cairo*. Cairo: Société d'Archéologie Copte, 1955.

Lane, Edward William. *The Manners and Customs of the Modern Egyptians*. London: Dent, 1908.

Lauer, Jean-Philippe. *Le Probléme des pyramides d'Egypte*. Paris: Payot, 1948.

Murnane, William J. *The Penguin Guide to Ancient Egypt*. Harmonsworth: Penguin, 1983.

Parker, Richard B., and Sabin, Robin. *Islamic Monuments in Cairo: A Practical Guide*. Third Edition revised and enlarged by Caroline Williams. Cairo: American University Cairo Press 1985,

Petrie, Flinders, Bevan, Edwyn, Milne, J.E., and Lane-Poole, Stanley. *A History of Egypt*. Six vols. London: Methuen, 1894-1901.

Revault, Jacques, and Maury, Bernard. *Palais et Maisons du Caire du XIVe au XVIIIe siécle*. Four vols. Cairo: IFAC, 1975-1983.

Serjeant R.B. ed. *The Islamic City*. Paris: UNESCO, 1980.

Seton-Williams, Veronica, and Stocks, Peter. *Egypt*. London: Ernest Benn, 1983.

Simaika, Marcus H., Pasha. *Guide Sommaire du Musée Copte et des principales églises du Cairo*. Cairo: Musee Copte, 1937.

Sladen, Douglas. *Oriental Cairo, the City of the "Arabian Nights."* London: Hurst and Blackett, 1911.

The Sphinx Jubilee Number. Cairo: The Sphinx, 1946.

USEFUL ADDRESSES

TOURIST INFORMATION OFFICES

Cairo: Main Office, 5, Adli St., Tel: 923657; Pyramids Office, Pyramids Area, Tel: 850259; Cairo Airport Office, Main Terminal, Tel: 667475. The emergency phone no. is126.

Alexandria: Main Office. Plaza Saad-Zaghlul, Tel: 807985; Railway Station, Tel: 25985; Port Office, Tel: 800100.

Port Said: Palestine St., Tel: 3100.

Suez: Palace of Culture, Tel: 2381.

Luxor: Tourist Bazaar, Tel: 2215.

Aswan: Tourist Bazaar, Tel: 3297.

EMBASSIES & CONSULATES

ALEXANDRIA

Austria, 8 Debbana Church St., Tel: 80-7500/46953.

Belgium, 15 Saad Zaghloul, Tel: 809121.

China, 6 Badawi, Rassafa, Moharram Bey.

Cyprus, 236 Canal De Suez, Tel: 806508.

Denmark, 15 Salah Salem St., (Sherif), Tel: 4929863.

Finland, 2 Avenue el-Horreya, Tel: 807295.

France, 2 Orabi Square, Tel: 800606.

Germany, 5 Rue Mina, Roushdy, Tel: 45475/45443.

Greece, 63 Alexander the Great St., Tel: 4938454.

Italy, Saad Zaghloul Square, Tel: 4927292.

Japan, 41 Moustafa Abu Heif, Tel: 49966.

Lebanon, 6 Dr. Ibrahim Abdel Sayed St., Tel: 4924167.

Netherlands, 35 Salah Moustapha, Tel: 204557.

Norway, 32 Tahrir Square, Tel: 4928133.

Panama, 1 El-Falaki St., Tel: 805610.

Peru, 2 Avenue el-Horreya St., Tel: 806171)

Rumania, 81 RUS El-Shahid Salah Moustapha, Tel: 807670.

Saudi Arabia, 7 Ibrahim Al-Sayid St., Tel: 809589.

Spain, 101, Avenue el-Horreya, Tel: 4928346.

Sudan, 95, 26th of July St. (El-Corniche), Tel: 804258.

Sweden, 57, 26th July St. (El-Corniche), Tel: 804202.

United Kingdom, 3 Rue Mina, Roushdy, Tel: 47166.

United States of America, 110, Avenue el-Horreya, Tel: 492560/801911.

CAIRO

Afghanistan (Embassy of India), 59 El Orouba, Heliopolis, Tel: 66-6653/66-4104.

Albania, 29 Ismail Mohamed, Zamalek, Tel: 341-5651.

Algeria, 14 Brazil, Zamalek, Tel: 340-2466

Angola, 12 Midan El Nasr, Dokki, Tel: 70-7602/70-8683.

Apostolic Internuncio (Vatican), 5 Mohamed Mazhar, Zamalek, Tel: 65-1152/65-1250.

Argentina, 8 El Saleh Ayoub, Apt. 2, Zamalek, Tel: 340-1501/340-5234/341-7765

Australia, Corniche El Nil, 77-7498, Cairo Plaza 5th Fl., Boulac, Tel: 77-7900/77-7273/77-7994.

Austria, El Nil St., Corner Wissa Wassef 5th Fl., Giza, Tel: 73-7640/73-7658/73-7602. Commercial - 6A Ismail Moh. St., Zamalek, Tel: 341-1150.

Bahrain, 8 Gamayet El Nisr, Mohandessin, Tel: 70-5413/70-6202.

Bangladesh, 40 Syria, Dokki, Tel: 349-0646.

Belgium, 20 Kamel El Shinnawi, Garden City, Tel: 354-7494/354-7495/354-7496.

Bolivia, 19 Gamal El Din Abu El Mahasen, Garden City, Tel: 354-6878.

Bourkino Fasso, 40 El Thawra St., Madinet El Zobbat, Dokki, Tel: 70-9754.

Brazil, 1125 Corniche El Nil, Maspero, Tel: 75-6938/77-3013.

Bulgaria, 141 Tahrir, Dokki, Tel: 341-3025/341-6077.

Burma, 24 Mohamed Mazhar, Zamalek, Tel: 340-4175/341-6793/341-2644.

Burundi, 13 El Israa Medinet, Mohandessin, Tel: 346-2173/347-9940.

Cameroon, 42 Babel, Dokki, Tel: 70-4622/70-4954/70-4843.

Canada, 6 Mohamed Fahmy El Sayed, Garden City, Tel: 354-3110/354-3119.

Central Africa, 13 Shehab, Mohandessin, Tel: 71-3291/71-3152.

Chad, 31 Adnan Omar Sidki, Dokki, Tel: 70-3232/70-4726.

Chile, 5 Shagaret El Dorr, Zamalek, Tel: 340-8446/340-8711.

China, 14 Bahgat Aly, Zamalek, Tel: 341-7691.

Colombia, 20A Gamal El Din Abou El Mahasin, Garden City, Tel: 355-9226/354-6152/354-3402.

Cuba, 9 Hassan Ahmed Rashed, Dokki, Tel: 348-1703/348-1704.

Cyprus, 23 Ismail Mohamed, Zamalek, Tel: 341-1288/341-0327.

Czechoslovakia, 4 Dokki, Dokki, Tel: 348-5531/348-5469/348-6550.

Denmark, 12 Hassan Sabri, Zamalek, Tel: 340-2502/340-7411/340-8673.

Djibouti, 157 Sudan, Mohandessin, Tel: 349-0611/349-0515.

Ecuador, 8 Abdel Rahman Fahmy, Garden City, Tel: 354-6372/354-6113.

El Salvador, 20 El Sad El Aali, Dokki, Tel: 70-0834.

Ethiopia, 59 Iran, Dokki, Tel: 70-5133/70-5372.

European Economic Community (EC Delegation), 6 Ibn Zanki, Zamalek, Tel: 340-8388.

Finland, 10 El Kamel Mohamed, Zamalek, Tel: 341-3722/341-1487/340-2801.

France, 29 El Nil (Nassa)/Giza (Murad) Avenue, Giza, Tel: 72-8275/72-8649/72-8497.

Consulate: 5 Sh. Al Fadi, off Talaat Harb, Tel: 393-4316.

Gaboh, 17 Maka El Mokarama, Dokki, Tel: 70-9699/348-1395.

Germany (Democratic Republic), 13 Hussein Wassef, Dokki, Tel: 348-4500/348-4525/348-4544.

Germany (Federal Republic), 8A Hassan Sabri, Zamalek, Tel: 341-0015/340-6017/340-3687.

Ghana, 24 El Batal Ahmed Abdel Aziz, Dokki, Tel: 70-4275/70-4154/70-4395.

Great Britain, 7 Ahmed Ragheb St., Garden City, Tel: 354-0850/354-0852.

Greece, 18 Aisha El Taymouria St., Garden City, Tel: 355-0443/355-1074/355-5915.

Guatemala, 29 Dr Mohamed Mandour St., Nasr City, Tel: 60-8094/60-0371.

Guinea, 46 Mohamed Mazhar St., Zamalek, Tel: 341-0201/340-8109.

Holland 18 Hassan Sabri St., Zamalek, Tel: 340-8744/340-6434/340-6872. 92028 **Nedam Un**

Hungary, 36 Mohammed Mazhar, Zamalek, Tel: 346-2215/346-5091/346-2240.

India, 5 Aziz Abaza, Zamalek, Tel: 341-3051/341-0052/340-6053.

Indonesia, 13 Aisha El Taymouria, Garden City, Tel: 354-7200/354-7209/354-7356.

Iran, 12 Rifa'a, Dokki, Tel: 84-7447/98-7288/98-7199.

Iraq, 9 Mohamed Mazhar, Zamalek, Tel: 340-9815/340-2633/340-794.

Ireland, 3 Abu El Feda Tower, Gabalaya, Zamalek, Tel: 340-8264/340-8547/341-4653.

Israel, 6 Ibn Malek, Giza, Tel: 72-6000/72-8264/72-9329.

Italy, 15 Abdel Rahman Fahmy, Garden City, Tel: 354-3195/354-0658/354-0657.

Ivory Coast, 39 El Kods El Sherif, Mohandessin, Tel: 69-9009/340-4902.

Japan, 14 Ibrahim Naguib, Cairo Center Bldg 3rd. Fl. Garden City, Tel: 354-4518/355-3962-3-4/354-928.

Jordan, 6 El Gohainy, Dokki, Tel: 348-5566/348-6169/348-7543.

Kampuchea, 2 El Tahawia, Giza, Tel: 73-1436/73-1634.

Kenya, 20 Bolous Hanna Dokki, Tel: 70-4455/70-4546.

Korea (Democratic - North), 6 Saleh Ayoub, Zamalek, Tel: 65-0970/69-8219/65-1615.

Korea (South), 6 El Hisn, Giza, Tel: 84-6637/84-7101/84-2564.

Kuwait, 12 Nabil El Wakkad, Dokki, Tel: 70-1673/70-1724.

Lebanon, 5 Ahmed Nessim, Giza, Tel: 72-8315/72-8266/72-8454.

Liberia, 11 El Brazil, Zamalek, Tel: 341-9864/341-9865/341-9866

Libya, 7 El Saleh Ayoub, Zamalek, Tel: 80-5863/80-5864.

Malaysia, 7 Wadi El Nil, Mohandessin, Tel: 346-0988/346-0958.

Mali, 3 Kawsar St, Madinet El Attiba, Dokki, Tel: 70-1641/70-1895.

Mauritania, 31 Souria St, Dokki, Tel: 349-0671/349-1048

Mauritius, 72 Abdel Moneim Riad, Tel: 347-0929/346-7642/346-4659.

Mexico, 5 Dar El Shifa, Garden City, Tel: 354-8622/354-3931.

Mongolia, 3 El Nasr Square, Dokki, Tel: 346-0670.

Morocco, 10 El Saleh Ayoub, Zamalek, Tel: 340-9677/340-9849/341-4718.

Nepal, 9 Tiba Madinet, El Kodah, Dokki, Tel: 70-4447/70-4541.

Netherlands, 18 Hassan Sabri, Zamalek, Tel: 340-8744/340-6872/340-6434.

Niger, 101 Pyramids Ave, Sh. Al-Ahram, Giza, Tel: 85-6617/85-6607.

Nigeria, 13 El Gabalaya, Zamalek, Tel: 69-8042/69-8311/69-8573.

Norway, 24 Hassan Assem, Zamalek, Tel: 340-8046/340-3340/341-3955.

Oman, 30 Montazah, Zamalek, Tel: 340-7811/341-9073/340-2942.

Pakistan, 8 El Saluli, Dokki, Tel: 348-7806/348-7677/348-7900.

Panama, 97A El Mirghani, Apt. 9, Heliopolis, Tel: 66-2547/66-6163.

Peru, 11 Brazil, Zamalek, Tel: 341-1754/340-1971.

Philippines, 5 Ebn El Walid, Dokki, Tel: 348-0398/348-0396.

Poland, 5 Aziz Osman, Zamalek, Tel: 340-5416/340-5907.

Portugal, 15A El Mansour Mohamed, Zamalek, Tel: 340-5583/340-5907.

Qatar, 10 El Themar, Mohandessin, Tel: 70-4537/70-4559.

Romania, 6 El Kamel Mohamed, Zamalek, Tel: 341-0107/340-9546.

Rwanda, 9 Ibrahim Osman, Mohandessin, Tel: 346-1039/346-0946/346-0896.

Saudi Arabia, 2 Ahmed Nessim, Giza, Tel: 72-8012/72-6037.

Senegal, 46 Abdel Moneim Riad, Mohandessin, Tel: 346-1039/346-0946/346-0896.

Sierra Leone, 6 Hindawi, Midan Finney, Dokki, Tel: 70-0699/70-8364.

Singapore, 40 Babel, Dokki, Tel: 70-4645/70-3772.

Somalia, 38 Abdel Moeim Riad, Mohandessin, Tel: 70-4038/70-4577.

Spain, 9 Hod El Laban, Garden City, Tel: 354-7069/354-7359/354-7648.

Lanka, 8 Yehia Ibrahim, Zamalek, Tel: 341-7138/340-4966/340-0047.

Sudan, 3 El Ibrahimi, Garden City, Tel: 354-5043/354-5044/354-9661.

Sweden, 13 Mohamed Mazhar, Zamalek, Tel: 340-5377.

Switzerland, 10 Abdel Khalek Sarwat, Tel: 75-8133/77-0545/75-8284.

Tanzania, 9 Abdel Hamid Lotfi, Dokki, Tel: 70-4286/70-4155.

Thailand, 2 El Malek El Afdal, Zamalek, Tel: 341-0094/340-8356.

Tunisia, 26 El Gezira, Zamalek, Tel: 341-8962/340-4940.

Turkey, 25 El Falaki St Bab El Louk, Tel: 354-8364/354-3736.

Uganda, 9 El Missaha Square, Dokki, Tel: 98-0329/98-1945.

Union of Soviet Socialist Republics (USSR), 95 El Giza, Giza, Tel: 348-9353/348-9354/348-9355.

United Arab Emirates, 4 Ibn Sina, Giza, Tel: 72-9107/72/9226/72-9955.

United States of America, Sh. Amrika Latiniyya, Garden City, Tel: 355-7371.

Uruguay, 6 Lutfallah, Zamalek, Tel: 340-3589/341-5137.

Venezuela, 15A El Mansour Mohamed, Zamalek, Tel: 341-3517/341-4332.

Vietnam, 47 Ahmed Heshmat, Zamalek, Tel: 340-2401.

Yemen, 28 Amin El Rafee, Dokki, Tel: 98-3796/98-3035.

Yugoslavia, 10 Ibn Zanki, Zamalek, Tel: 340-9876.

Zaire, 5 El Mansour Mohamed, Zamalek, Tel: 341-1069/340-3662/341-7954.

Zambia, 22 El Nakhil, Dokki, Tel: 70-9620/70-9667.

CULTURAL RESOURCE CENTERS

ALEXANDRIA

Austrian Cultural Center, 8 Debbana St., Tel: 807500.

French Cultural Center, 30 Sharia Nebi Daniel, Tel: 4922503.

Goethe Institute, 10 Sharia Ptolemees, Tel: 809870.

Cavafy Library and Museum, Greek Consulates, 63 Sharia Alexander the Great, Tel: 38454

Greek Center for Language Instruction, 9 Sinadino St., Soter.

Italian Cultural Center, 52 Avenue el-Horreya, Tel: 34924.

Spanish Cultural Center, 101 Avenue el-Horreya, Tel: 28346.

Union of Soviet Socialist Republics Cultural Center, 5 Sharia Ptolemees, Tel: 800649/22840.

The British Council, 9 Sharia Ptolemees, Tel: 35288.

The American Cultural Center, 3 Rue Pharana, Tel: 21009/ 44305.

CAIRO

All Saints' Cathedral Library, Michel Lutfallah, Zamalek, Tel: 341-8391.

American Cultural Center, 7 Ahmen Rahed, Garden City, Tel: 354-9601.

American Research Center in Egypt, 2 Midan Qasr El Doubarah, (Simín Bolíver) Garden City, Tel: 355-3052/354-8239.

American University in Cairo Main Library, Sh. Muhammad Mahmud, Tel: 354-2964 ext. 6901/6914.

American University in Cairo - Center for Arabic Studies Library (Creswell Collection), Sh. Shaykh Rihan, Tel: 354-2964 extension 5060.

Austrian Archaeological Center, 8A Ismail Mohamed, Apt. 62 Zamalek, Tel: 340-6871. Open to recognized scholars only, 8.30 a.m. to 2.30 p.m. except Sunday.

Austrian Cultural Center, 103 Corniche El Nil Apt. 7, Garden City, Tel: 354-7436/ 354-4063.

British Council, 192 El Nil, Agouza, Tel: 346-4759/347-6118.

Canadian Institute, 32 Road 103 Maadi, Tel: 350-7214. Open 9 a.m. to 4 p.m. Saturday to Thursday.

Chicago House, Sharia al Nil, Luxor, Tel: 82525.

Christian Science Society Reading Room, 3 Midan Mustafa Kamel 2nd Fl., Cairo, Tel: 350-6194/351-7850/351-6102.

Egypt Exploration Society c/o The British Council, 192 al Nil, Agouza, Tel: 345-3281/84.

Egyptian Center for Int'l Cultural Cooperation, 11 Shagaret El Dor, Zamalek, Tel: 341-5419.

French Cultural Center (see FAO), 1 El Huquq El Farnaiya, Hounira, Cairo, Tel: 355-3725. 27 Sabri Abou Alam, Heliopolis, Tel: 66-3241. 37 El Youssef, Mounira, Cairo, Tel: 77-4922/75-4316.

German Archaeological Institute, 22 Gezira al Wusta (entrance on 31 Abd al Feda), Zamalek. Tel: 340-1460/2321. Open Monday to Thursday 8 a.m. to 1p.m.

Goethe Institute (Language Department), 6 El Sherifein, Cairo, Tel: 393-1169/393-1088.

Goethe Institute (Library), 5 Abdel Salam Aref Bustan, Cairo, tel: 77-9479/75-9877.

Greek Cultural Center, 14 Emad El Din, Cairo, Tel: 75-3962/75-3833.

Institut Francais d'Archaeologle Orientale (IFAO), 37 Sheikh Ali Youssef, off Qasr Aini, Tel: 354-8245. Founded in 1880. Open 9 a.m. to 1 p.m. daily except Saturday and Sunday. Mounira adjacent to French Cultural Center. Library open Monday to Thursday from 2 p.m. to 6 p.m. Access available to scholars and students upon approval of director.

Italian Institute of Culture and Italian Institute of Archaeology, 3 Sheikh al Marsafi, Zamalek, Tel: 340-8791. Library hours 10 a.m. to 1.30 p.m. daily except Saturday and Sunday.

Israeli Academic Center in Cairo, 92 El Nil St., Apt 33, Dokki/Giza, Tel: 349-6232.

Japanese Cultural Center, 10 Ibrahim Naguib St., Garden City, Tel: 354-4518/ 355-1477/355-3963.

Korean Cultural Center/Commercial Section, 56 Gameat El Dowal El Arabia Cairo, Tel: 349-7690/71-5543.

Netherlands Institute of Archaeology and Arabic Studies, 1 Dr. Mahmoud Azmi, Zamalek, Tel: 340-0076 Hours 9 a.m. to 2 p.m. Monday to Friday.

Polish Center of Mediterranean Archaeology, 14 Baron Empain, Heliopolis. House Sunday to Thursday 9 a.m. to 1 p.m.

Soviet Center, 127 Tahrir St , Giza.

Swiss Institute of Archaeology and Architectural Studies, 11-13 Aziz Abaza (Maahad el Swissri), Zamalek, Tel: 340-9359 Exclusively for Swiss archaeologists. No access. No requests.

AIRLINES

Aeroflot, 8 Kasr El Nil, Cairo, Tel: 75-3386/74-3132.

Air Algerie, Aviatrans, G.S.A. Iberia, El Nasr Bldg, El Nil St., Guiza, Tel: 72-9618/72-7243/75-0688. Airport, Tel: 66-6688 Ext. 4279. Tlx: 93889 MENAT UN.

Air Djibouti, 16 Adly St., Cairo, Tel: 391-2345/391-8874..
Tlx: 92827 BOVO UN.

Air France, 2 Talaat Harb Square, Cairo, Tel: 74-3300/3516/3479/3624/66-1028.

Air India, 1 Talaat Harb Square, Cairo, Tel: 75-4864/75-4873. Airport, Tel: 66-6500/69-2700.

Alia Royal Jordanian Airlines, 6 Qasr al Nil, Tel: 750-905/750-875. Zamalek Club Gate, Mohandessin, Tel: 344-3114/346-7540.

Alitalia, Nile Hilton Hotel, Cairo, Tel: 74-0984/3488/75-3449. Airport, Tel: 66-5143. Sales, Tel: 76-3103. Admin. Tel: 76-7109.

Arab Wings (c/o Aviatrans), El Nasr Bldg El Nil St., Gixa, Tel: 72-9618/72-7243.

Austrian Airlines, 13 Talaat Harb Square, Cairo, Tel: 74-2755/75-2699/74-0228.

Belgian Airlines (Sabena), Mariette St Tahrir Square, Cairo, Tel: 77-7125/75-1194/74-3984.

Brazilian Airlines (Varig), 37 Abdel Khalek Sarwat St., Cairo, Tel: 91-3318.

British Airways, 1 Abdel Salam Aref, Bustan, Tahrir Square, Cairo, Sales, Tel: 76-2852/77-2746, Reservations, Tel: 77-7045/75-9977/77-2981. Airport, Tel: 67-1741/67-3038. Management, Tel: 76-2723/Accounts 77-2865. Cargo, Tel: 66-2963. Maadi Office Helwan Agri Rd., Tel: 350-2264/350-2265.

Bulgarian Airlines, 17 Kasr El Nil, Cairo,

Tel: 75-1211/75-1152.

Cathay Pacific, 26 Mahmoud Bassiouni St., Cairo, Tel: 75-8939/76-1769/76-0071.

Cyprus Airways, 16 Adly St., Cairo, Tel: 391-2345/391-8874. 18 Ismail Mohamed St., Zamalek, Tel: 340-4716. 25 Ibrahim St., Heliopolis, Tel: 259-1945/259-1311. Tlx:.21826 IML UN/92827 BOVO UN. 2 Mostafa Kamel Maadi, Tel: 350-1240.

Czecholovak Airlines (CSA), 9 Talaat Harb St., Cairo, Tel: 75-0416/75-0395.

Djibouti Air, 16 Adly St., Cairo, Tel: 92-0669/92-0090/93-3950. 2 Mostafa Kamel St., Maadi, Tel: 350-1160/350-1240/350-1241. 18 Ismail Mohamed St., Zamalek, Tel: 340-4716.

Egyptair, 16 Adly St., Cairo, Tel: 92-0999/92-2444. Nile Hilton Hotel, Cairo, Tel: 75-9806/75-9703. Cairo Sheraton Hotel, Cairo, Tel: 98-5408/84-9460. Heliopolis, Tel: 66-8552. Zamalek, Tel: 341-2027/340-8991/340-4501. Airport, Tel: 45-4049/45-4400.

El Al Airlines, 5 El Makrizi St., Zamalek, Tel: 341-1429/341-1620/345-9795.

Emirates Airlines, Tel: 340-1102/340-6416.

Ethiopian Airlines, Nile Hilton Hotel, Cairo, Tel: 74-0603/74-0911/74-0852.

Finnair, 15 Tahrir Square, Cairo, Tel: 76-9571.

Gulf Air, 26 Mahmoud Bassiouni St., Cairo, Tel: 75-0852/75-8391/75-3349.

Hungarian Airlines (MALEV), 12 Talaat Harb St., Cairo, Tel: 74-4959/75-3111.

Iberia c/o Emeco Travel Maadi, Tel: 351-6967/350-2818. 15 Tahrir Square, Cairo, Tel: 74-9955/74-9716. c/o Happy Home, Heliopolis, Tel: 66-4441. Tlx:93889 MENAT UN.

Int Air Cargo, 22 Taha Hussein St., Zamalek, Tel: 341-6550.

Interflug, 1 Adly St., Cairo, Tel: 93-3828.

Iraq Airways, 22 Kasr El Nil St., Cairo, Tel: 75-4200/75-4149.

Japan Airlines (JAL), Nile Hilton Hotel, Cairo, Tel: 77-9845/74-0621/74-0809. Airport, Tel: 66-9859/66-0843.

KLM Royal Dutch Airlines, 11 Kasr El Nil, Cairo, Tel: 74-7747/74-0999/74-0650. Airport (1st) & Freight (2nd), Tel: 66-2226/66-2256.

Kenya Airways, Nile Hilton Hotel Commercial Center, Tel: 76-2494/77-6771 Ext. 465. Tlx: 92222 UN.

Kuwait Airways, 4 Talaat Harb St., Cairo, Tel: 75-9866/75-7482.

Libyan Arab Airlines, 37 Kasr El Nil St., Cairo, Tel: 75-3727/74-4595/74-4683. Airport, Tel: 66-4774.

Lufthansa German Airlines, 6 Sheikh El Marsafi St., Zamalek, Tel: 342-0471/342-0693 Reserv. 9 Talaat Harb St., Cairo, Tel: 393-0366. Airport Terminal, Tel: 66-6975. Cargo, Tel: 66-0907.
Tlx: 93203 CAILH UN.

Middle East Airlines, 12 Kasr El Nil St., Cairo, Tel: 75-0984/74-3100/74-3151. Airport, Tel: 66-3670/66-4057. Freight, Tel: 66-5396.

Nile Delta Air Service, 1 Talaat Harb Square, Cairo, Tel: 74-6197.

Olympic Airways, 23 Kasr El Nil St., Cairo, Tel: 75-1277/75-1318. Airport, Tel: 66-4503.

Pakistan Intl Airways (PIA), 22 Kasr El Nil St., Cairo, Tel: 74-4055/4213/4134/75-1604. Airport, Tel: 67-4154.

Pan American (Pan Am), c/o Emeco Travel, 2 Talaat Harb, Cairo, Tel: 74-7007/74-7399/74-7325). c/o Emeco Travel, Maadi, Tel: 350-2818/351-6967. 93698 EMECO UN.

Philipine Airways, 17 Ismail Mohamed St., Zamalek, Tel: 341-9409/340-1948.

Polish Airlines (LOT), 1 Kasr El Nil St., Cairo, Tel: 75-7403/74-7312.

Royal Air Maroc, 9 Talaat Harb St., Cairo, Tel: 77-9574/74-0378/75-0561.

Sabena. See Belgian Airlines.

Saudi Arabian Airlines, 5 Kasr El Nil St., Cairo, Tel: 74-1353/1200/77-9999/7088. Airport, Tel: 66-4627.

Scandinavian Airlines (SAS), 2 Champollion St., Cairo, Tel: 75-3889/3955/3546/3627.

Singapore Airlines, Nile Hilton Hotel, Cairo, Tel: 76-2702/76-2492.

Somalia Airlines, 14 Champollion St., Cairo, Tel: 74-1770/74-3537.

Sudan Airways, 1 Abdel Salam Aref (Bustan), Tahrir Square, Tel: 75-7245/74-7299/75-9790. Airport, Tel: 66-0049.

Swissair (c/o Bon Voyage), 2 Mostafa Kamel St., Maadi, Tel: 350-1240/350-1241. Downtown, Tel: 74-1522/75-7955. Airport, Tel: 69-7966.

Thai Airways Internaitonal, 16 Adly St., Cairo, Tel: 391-2345/391-8874. 2 Mostafa Kamel St., Maadi, Tel: 350-1240/350-1241.

18 Ismail Moh. Zamalek/25 Ibrahim Hel. Tel: 340-4716//259-1945.

Trans World Airlines (TWA), 1 Kasr El Nil St., Cairo, Tel: 74-9900/75-7256/7364/7242. Airport, Tel: 66-9203/66-9615/66-9522.

Tunis Air, 14 Talaat Harb St., Cairo, Tel: 76-9726/75-3476. Airport, Tel: 66-6500.

Turkish Airlines, 25 Mahmud Bassiouni, Tel: 758939.

United Airlines, 42 Abdel Khalek Sarwat, Cairo, Tel: 390-5090/391-1950/390-8099. 2 Mostafa Kamel St., Maadi. 18 Ismail Moh. Zamalek/25 Ibrahim Hel. Tel: 340-4716/259-1311.

Varig. See Brazilian Airlines.

Yemen Air, 17 Mahmoud Bassiouni St., Cairo, Tel: 74-0711/74-3313.

Yugoslav Airlines (JAT), El Sherifein St., Cairo, Tel: 74-2166/74-2054.

BUSINESS ORGANIZATIONS

American Chamber of Commerce in Egypt, Suite 1541, Marriott Hotel.Tel: 340-8888 ext 514.

Cairo Chamber of Commerce, Tel: 354-8491.

Egypt-US Business Council, El Nil Tower, 21 Sh. Gizah, Gizah.

Egyptian Businessmen's Association. Tel: 737-285.

European Economic Community Delegation. 4 Sh. Gazirah, Zamalek. Tel: 340-8388.

Federation of Egyptian Chambers of Commerce, Tel: 987-103.

Federation of Egyptian Industries, Tel: 748-945.

French Chamber of Commerce, 4 Maydan Falaki, Bab al Luq, Tel: 354-2897/354-2898/354-8491.

German Agency for Technical Cooperation. German Embassy, 8 Sh. Hasan Sabri, Zamalek, Tel: 341-2445.

German-Arab Chamber of Commerce, 3 Sh. Sherif Pasha, Tel: 769-327/741-754.

Greek-Arab Chamber of Commerce, 10 Sh. Soliman al Halabi, Tel: 741-190.

International Executive Service Corps. Nile Hilton Center, Tel: 776-771 ext 22/23.

Italian-Arab Chamber of Commerce, 33 Sh. Abdel Khalak Tharwat, Tel: 760-275.

Japanese Chamber of Commerce, 31 26th of July St. Tel: 740-942/740-659.

Netherlands Development Corporation. 13 Sh. Gizah, Gizah. Tel: 723-054.

Rotary International. Cairo Main: Tuesday 2 p.m., Nile Hilton; **Cairo North:** Wednesdays 2 p.m., Nile Hilton; **Cairo South:** Sundays 8 p.m., Maadi Yacht Club; **Cairo West:** Mondays 2 p.m., Meridien Hotel; **Zamalek:** Mondays 8.30p.m., Nile Hilton; **Heliopolis:** Mondays 2.30 p.m. Heliopolis Sheraton; **Gizah:** Wednesdays 2.15 p.m., Sheraton Gizah; **Gizah Pyramids:** Mondays 2.30 p.m., Sheraton Gizah.

INTERNATIONAL BANKS

There are over 80 banks in Cairo. The following is representative list of international banks, Egyptian and foreign:

American Express Bank Limited 4 Ibn Zanki St., Zamalek, Tel:341-0236/341-2287

Bank Saderat Iran 28 Sherif St., Cairo. Tel: 393-1147, Tlx: 92611 UN

Bank of America 106 Kasr El Aini St., Garden City. Tel: 357-7333/354-7788, Tlx: 92425/93804

Bank of Credit & Commerce (Misr SAE) 106 Kasr El Aini St., Garden City. Tel: 77-5327/355-7328

Bankers Trust Co (BTCO) 17 Kasr El Nil , 3rd Fl., Cairo P.O. Box 308, Moh. Farid. Tel: 392-3427/392-3898 Tlx: 93514/93826 BTCAI UN

Banque de Caire et de Paris 14 El Saray El Kobra St., Garden City Tel: 355-0396/354-4194

Cairo Barclays Internaitonal Bank SAE 12 Midan El Sheikh Youssef Garden City, P.O. Box 2335 Tel: 354-2195/354-9415/354-9422, Tlx: 92343/93734 CABAR UN

Chemical Bank 14 Talaat Harb St., Cairo P.O. Box 2171, Cairo. Tel: 76-2357/74-0707/74-0652, Tlx: 92066/93423 CHEMBK UN

Citibank, NA 4 Ahmed Pasha St., Garden City P.O. Box 188 Cairo. Tel: 355-1873-7/

354-7246, Tlx: 92162/92832 CITAR UN

Commercial International Bank (formerly Chase National) 12 El Birgas St., Garden City, Tel: 354-5263/355-0686/354-5265

21-23 Giza St., Nile Tower Giza Tel: 72-6132/3/4/5/6/7, 12 El Saleh Ayoub St., Zamlek, Tel: 340-2667/68/69

P.O. Box 2430, Cairo Tlx: 20201 CNBCA UN/92394 CNBCA UN, 16 Hoda Sharawi St., Cairo, Tel: 75-6467/75-6139/75-568467 Rd. 9 Maadi

Tel: 351-7872/7831-7949, 24 El Mirghani St., Heliopolis Tel: 258-4847/258-5708

Commerzbank AG Representative Office 2 Aly Labib Gabr (Behler), Cairo, Tel: 392-3203/393-1661 Tlx: 92194 CBK UN

Crédir Lyoorais Abu Feda Bldg., 3 Abul El Feda, Zamalek, Tel: 340-3712/43/61

Credit Suisse 6 Okba St., (Off Tahrir St.,) Dokki 22 Taha Husein St., Zamalek, Tel: 341-3195/65-1752, Tlx: 93655 PRES UN

Deutsche Bank AG Representative Office 23 Kasr El Nil St., Cairo Tel: 76-2341/74-1373, Tlx: 92306 DUECAI UN

Development Industrial Bank 10 Galaa St., Cairo, Tel: 77-5966/77-9188/77-9247

Dresdner Bank AG 33 Qasr El Nil St., 7th Fl., Left Wing, P.O. Box 2386 Cairo,. Tel: 393-3941, Tlx: 92603 DRESAG UN

Egyptian American Bank (EAB) 4 Hassan Sabri St., Zamalek P.O. Box 1825 Cairo. Tel:341-6150/6157/6158/4532, Tlx: 92683 EGANBK UN

Hong Kong Egyptian Bank (SAE) Abu El Feda Bldg., 3 Abu El Feda, Zamalek, Tel: 340-9186/9286/8938/4849, Tlx: 20471 HKEB UN

Lloyds Bank Internaitonal 44 Mohamed Mazhar St., Zamalek, P.O. Box 97, Tel: 340-6508/341-8366/340-6437, Tlx: 92344/22400 LLOYD UN

Manufacturers Hanover Trust Co 3 Ahmed Nessim St., Giza P.O. Box 1962 , Tel: 98-8266/72-6703/84-1434, Tlx: 92297/92660 MHTCO UN

Misr America International Bank (MAIB) 8 Ibrahim Naguib St., Garden City P.O. Box 1003 Garden City. Tel: 355-7071/2445/2247/4359-63

National Bank of Egypt Head Office, 24 Sherif St., Cairo. Tel: 74-4143/75-9143/74-4175, 39 Abdel Khalek Sarwat St., Cairo,. Tel: 74-4143/74-4248/74-4175

Nile Bank 35 Ramses St., Cairo Tel: 74-

1417/9187/3674/76-4435, 87 Rd. 9 Maadi Tel: 350-4480/5740/5940 19 El Hegaz St., 20 Ibrahim St., Heliopolis. Tel: 258-2241/ 258-0859 P.O. Box 2741, Tlx: 22344/ 93368/20785 BANIL UN

State Bank of India 15 Kamel El Shinawy St., Apt. 6 1st Fl., Garden City. Tel: 354-2522/354-3504, Tlx: 93068

Swiss Bank Corporation 3 Ahmed Nessim St., Giza, Tel: 72-7005/72-9384, Tlx: 92469 SECET UN

ART/PHOTO CREDITS

INDEX

A

B

C

G

H

I

O

N

P

Q

S

R